ICSA PROFESSIONAL DEVELOPMENT CORPORATE LAW 2003–4

MICHAEL GRIFFITHS

Published by ICSA Publishing Ltd
16 Park Crescent
London W1B 1AH

Typeset by Fakenham Photosetting Ltd, Fakenham, Norfolk

Printed and bound in Great Britain by The Basingstoke Press Limited

British Library Cataloguing in Publication Data

A catalogue record for this book is available from the British Library.

ISBN 186072-217-2

Contents

Introduction

The ICSA Professional Development Series is designed especially for students on professional and post-qualification courses who need study material with a strong practical and business-oriented approach.

The series is also suitable for professionals who want to develop their expertise and skills through self study.

Each title in the series is a self contained unit, covering the essentials of accountins and finance, law, strategy, administration and governance. Topic coverage is in a format designed to aid understanding, as shown on the next page in the How to Use guide.

Corporate Law

This guide is a practical account of the law governing the operation of companies in the UK. Coverage is comprehensive – ranging from company formation right through to insolvency and dissolution – and is supported by a full range of case law examples.

Written in a clear, non-legalistic style, the guide includes full coverage of key concepts such as the corporate veil, *ultra vires* and shareholder remedies and core topics such as incorporation, shares and share dealing, and directors' duties.

How to use this guide

Contents

Each guide is divided into three main sections:

- preliminary material
- the text itself, divided into Parts and Chapters
- additional information for guidance and reference

The preliminary section includes quick reference aids such as an extended contents list, lists of Acronyms, Abbreviations or Legal Cases.

Each **Part** opens with a list of the chapters to follow and an overview of what will be covered.

Every **Chapter** opens with a list of the topics covered and the learning outcomes specific to that chapter. This should help you break the material down into manageable sections for study.

Features

The guide is enhanced by a range of illustrative and self-testing features to assist understanding. Each feature is presented in a standard format, so that you will become familiar with how you can use them in your study.

The guide also includes a number of tables, figures and checklists and, where relevant, sample documents and forms.

Each chapter ends with a brief summary to recap the material which has been covered.

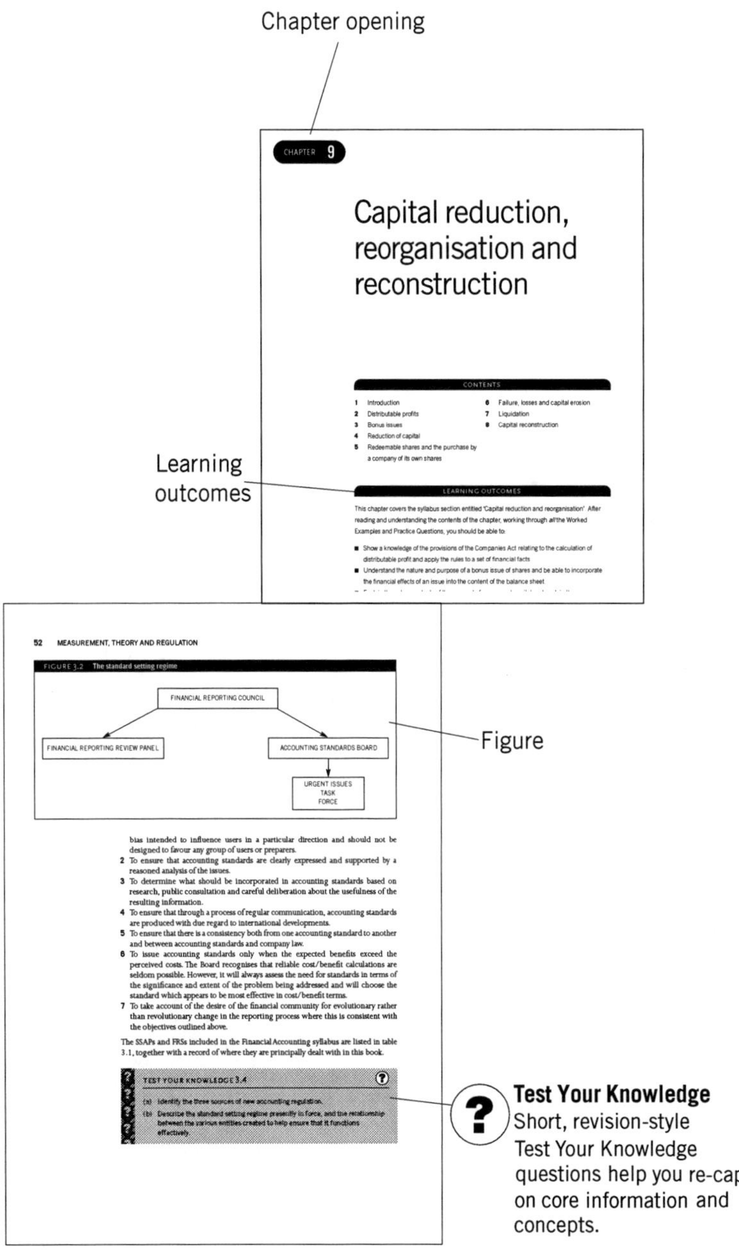

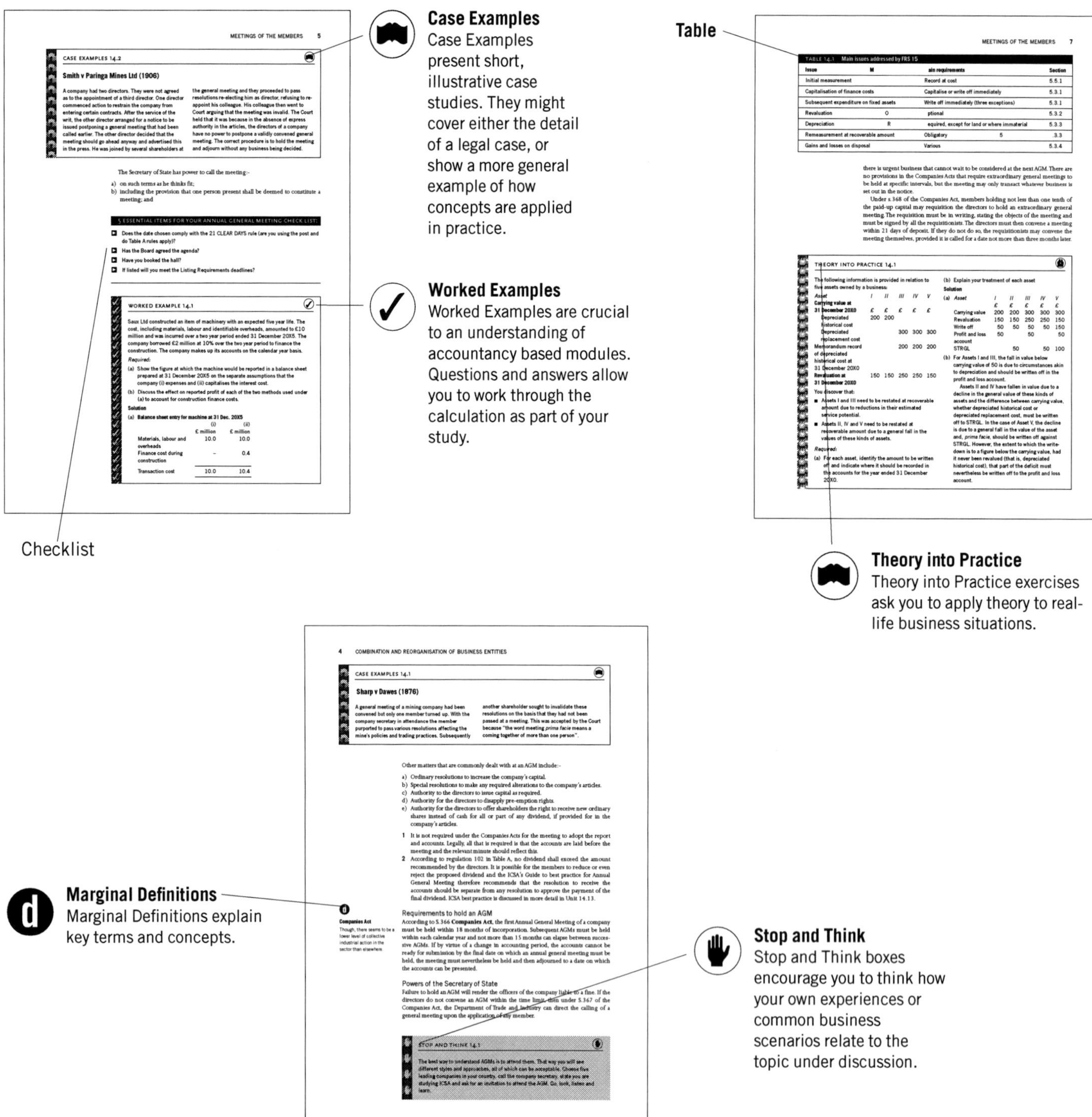

Reference Material

The guide ends with a range of additional guidance and reference.

Where relevant guides will include an **Appendices** section comprising additional reference material specific to that subject.

Other reference material includes a **Glossary** of key terms, a **Directory** of further reading, web-based resources and useful organisations, and a comprehensive **Index**.

The Institute of Chartered Secretaries and Administrators (ICSA)

About ICSA

The Institute of Chartered Secretaries and Administrators (ICSA) is a Chartered professional body which offers a wide range of qualifications for those working or wishing to work in legal, financial and senior administrative roles in the corporate, not-for-profit and public sectors. Established in 1891, ICSA has a long history of meeting the need for qualified company secretaries, share registrars and other senior professionals. ICSA now has 44,000 members and 28,000 students in over 70 countries.

The ICSA International Qualifying Scheme

The ICSA International Qualifying Scheme is a professional qualification that enables candidates to become a Chartered Secretary, a Member of the Institute, and use the designatory letters ACIS (Associate) and FCIS (Fellow) after their name. It is the only qualification specifically designed to train candidates for the company secretarial role.

The International Qualifying Scheme is a post-graduate qualification, designed to be gained through self study. As part of their registration fee, candidates on Parts 1 and 2 of the Professional Programme (final eight modules) receive dedicated study texts and access to online support to allow to them study and pass the examinations.

The programme includes modules in law, management, accounting, Corporate Secretaryship and Corporate Governance.

Further information is available from www.icsa.org.uk, email info@icsa.co.uk

ICSA Self Standing and Professional Awards

ICSA also runs a series of Self-Standing Awards, Certificate and Diploma programmes and post-qualification courses specially designed to meet sector needs. These stand-alone qualifications have been developed for candidates interested in shorter courses related to their specific occupational areas.

For further information is available from www.icsa.org.uk, email shortcourses@icsa.co.uk

ICSA Seminars

The official seminar and conference company of the ICSA provides seminars and in house training for company secretaries, directors and their professional advisors. A full listing is available at www.icsa.org.uk. E-mail: seminars@icsa.co.uk/telephone:020 7612 7031.

The ICSA Professional Development Series

Titles in the ICSA-endorsed Professional Development Series are designed to support professionals studying on a range of professional and post-qualification courses or who wish to keep themselves informed and up to date about key business topics.

Books in the series are available from ICSA Publishing. For further details, visit www.icsapublishing.co.uk or call 020 7612 7020.

List of Statutes

List of Statutory Instruments

List of Cases

Acronyms and Abbreviations

AA	Articles of Association
AC	Appeal Cases
AIN	Alternative Investment Market
All ER	All England Law Reports
BCC	British Company Cases
BILC	British International Law Cases
CA	Companies Act
CH	Company House
CDDA	Company Directors (Disqualification) Act
CHD	Chancery Division
CJA	Criminal Justice Act
CPD	Common Pleas
DTI	Department of Trade and Industry
ExD	Exchequer
EWCA	Court of Appeal
FSA	Financial Services Authority
GLC	Greater London Council
HL	House of Lords
IA	Insolvency Act
KB	King's Bench
LR	Law Reports
PAYE	Pay as You Earn
QB	Queen's Bench
RIE	Recognised Investment Exchange
Plc	Public Limited Company
WLR	Weekly Law Reports

part **one**

Company Structure and Incorporation

LIST OF CHAPTERS

Overview

In this first part we shall be looking at company structure and incorporation. A company is a legal entity recognised by the law as having an existence of its own. In the case of a company, incorporation is achieved by registration with the Registrar of Companies. We shall examine how registration takes place and the role in this process of the promoters, the people who have taken the business decision to form the company. For registration to occur, certain documents must be sent to the Registrar. These are examined in Chapter 1. The people who form a company are known as the promoters. Their relationship with the company and with third parties is examined in Chapter 2. Of the documents that they have to send to the registrar to obtain incorporation, the most important is the Memorandum of Association. Every company must have a unique Memorandum, which is in effect the external constitution of the company, setting out, among other things, its name, the purpose for which it is being formed and its authorised share capital. The internal rules of the company are contained in the Articles of Association. It is not necessary for a company to have its own Articles. There is a model set known as Table A and most companies adopt this with some modifications. Sometimes these public documents are supplemented by a further private document, a shareholder agreement. This is non-statutory and is simply a contract made between the members of the company. These documents are examined in Chapter 3.

CHAPTER 1

Incorporation and the corporate veil

CONTENTS

LEARNING OUTCOMES

This chapter covers the nature of a company, the meaning of incorporation and the instances where the courts will look behind the corporate veil. After reading and understanding the contents of the chapter and studying the case examples, you should be able to:

- Understand the different types of trading organisation in the United Kingdom.
- Explain the difference between a company limited by shares and a company limited by guarantee.
- Explain the difference between unlimited and limited companies.
- Explain the difference between public and private companies.
- Understand why sometimes business entities trade as groups of companies.
- Define a subsidiary company.
- Understand the meaning and effects of incorporation.
- Identify the principal circumstances where the courts will lift the corporate veil.

1 The reasons for the existence of companies

Historically, merchants and businessmen always used to trade either on their own account or in partnerships if they wished to spread their risk. There were no difficulties with this while their businesses were profitable, but when their businesses failed, they could be made bankrupt and, in some countries, sent to prison or otherwise vilified until their debts were paid. This meant that only very bold or wealthy entrepreneurs would set up in business, and overall it served as a disincentive. It became apparent to politicians and economists that a country where few people felt inclined to set up businesses would ultimately become economically impoverished, as there would be fewer opportunities for wealth creation, employment and taxation.

What was needed was a method of separating the entrepreneur from his business, so that although the entrepreneur's business might collapse, on the whole he did not personally become bankrupt unless he had behaved fraudulently. The method that was devised was the creation of a new legal entity, the corporation, which had a legal existence of its own, separate from those who owned the corporation, and from those who managed it.

Early corporations (also increasingly known by an alternative name, 'companies') owed their existence to special Acts of Parliament or Royal Charters, but eventually in the mid-nineteenth century the current system of registration of companies as we now know it was devised. Companies are registered on a central register, given a special legal existence, and have to comply with various complex rules of which the most important is the public disclosure of the details of the companies' accounts, ownership, management and constitution. In return for such disclosure, the owners of certain companies are given 'limited liability', which means that even if the companies became insolvent, the owners are not necessarily liable for their companies' debts.

As anticipated, such insulation from the companies' debts does indeed encourage entrepreneurs, wealth creation and employment, and the idea of the limited liability company has proved one of the most successful business ideas ever, being adopted world-wide.

At the same time, however, limited liability has its drawback:

- Instead of the entrepreneur bearing all the risk of the company's insolvency, the company's creditors bear the risk collectively.
- Because an entrepreneur bears little risk himself, he may be tempted to act fraudulently towards the company's creditors or even his fellow investors.

In response, a body of company law has gradually been built up which, at least in theory, is designed to encourage entrepreneurs, to protect the concept of limited liability and to prevent people from taking unfair advantage of the benefits that limited liability affords. So the law encourages business but also polices it to minimise the opportunities for fraud and self-serving behaviour.

This is the law that we shall be studying in the course of this text. Corporate law is about the incorporation and management of companies and the arrangements that need to be put in place if a company gets itself into difficulties. The main body of company law in the UK is to be found in the Companies Act 1985 (CA 1985), supported by other relevant legislation like the Insolvency Act 1986 or the Company Directors Disqualification Act 1986. Students also need to be aware of the impact the European Union is having on UK company law.

1.1 Types of trading entity

Although there is only one body of company law, mostly to be found in the Companies Act 1985 and the Insolvency Act 1986, there are several different types of company in the UK.

The main types of trading entity in the UK are as follows.

sole trader

An individual who is in business on his own account i.e. he is not in partnership on his nor does he trade through a corporate body.

Sole traders

Some trading is done by **sole traders**, a person trading alone. The sole trader runs the business, carries all the responsibilities and is entitled to all of the profits. A sole trader is not obliged to disclose his accounts to anyone apart from the Inland Revenue and the Customs and Excise, but he does have the benefit of the complete control of his

partnership
The relation which subsists between persons carrying on a business in common with a view of profit.

Registrar of Companies
The person at Companies House to whom documents are sent to form a company and to whom the necessary returns are made during the lifetime of a company.

limited company
A company the liability of whose members is limited and formed either by Act of Parliament or by registration under the Companies Act.

limited partnership
A partnership having limited partners i.e. sleeping partners whose liability in the event of the partnership's insolvency is limited to the amount that such partner has agreed to contribute.

limited liability partnership
A body corporate the liability of whose members is limited and formed by registration under the Limited Partnerships Act 2000.

business. However, if he is ill, or is a poor businessman, he runs the risk of being made bankrupt and losing most of his possessions. Being a sole trader is relatively uncomplicated and consequently is cheap and convenient for many small businesses.

Partnerships

As being a sole trader is a very exposed position to be in, sole traders with a common business commonly band together to form partnerships. A **partnership** is defined in the Partnership Act 1890 as 'the relation which subsists between persons carrying on a business in common with a view of profit'. With a partnership the members (partners) share any profits, but, by the same token, are also liable for any losses. There is no need for a partnership to be registered with anyone such as the **Registrar of Companies**. Indeed, there is no need even for a written agreement between the partners. A partnership can arise merely by two or more people agreeing to trade together in the hope of making a profit. Although there is slightly more regulation of a partnership than a sole trader, a partnership is still relatively unregulated.

Limited companies

By contrast, **limited companies** are extensively regulated, and must be registered with the Registrar of Companies. However, the owners (members) of a limited company have limited liability and are not generally personally liable for the company's debts, as will be seen in greater detail later.

Limited partnerships

A **limited partnership** is a partnership, regulated under the Limited Partnership Act 1907. It has two types of members: general partners and limited partners. It is run by the general partners, who have unlimited liability for its debts. The limited partners are merely passive investors in the business. Their liability is limited to the amount of capital that they agree to invest in the business. However, if they take any part in the management of the business they lose the benefit of their limited liability altogether and become liable with the general partners for all the debts of the business. A limited partnership has to be registered with the Registrar of Companies (Limited Partnership Act 1907 s. 14), who maintains a special register for limited companies. Limited Partnerships are not incorporated.

Limited liability partnerships

Limited liability partnerships became available from April 2001, made possible by the Limited Partnerships Act 2000. The title of the Act is misleading because limited liability partnerships are not partnerships at all, and are more like limited companies than partnerships. Even more confusingly, the owners of a limited liability partnership are not called 'partners' as might have been expected, but 'members'. As with a company, the liability of the members is limited. Limited liability partnerships must be registered with the Registrar of Companies, and are subject to many of the same rules and regulations, particularly as regards insolvency, as a limited liability company. Limited liability partnerships are already proving very popular and many partnerships in the professions, such as lawyers and accountants, are taking advantage of the new legislation in order to incorporate themselves as limited liability partnerships.

The reason why limited liability partnerships were introduced into English commercial law is very simple. In a conventional partnership each partner bears an absolute liability for any contractual or tortious liability incurred by his fellow partners through the work of the partnership. Thus if a member of a partnership of accountants were through his negligence to cause serious loss to a client, that client could sue the firm and, if the award were sufficiently large, this could result in the winding up of the partnership and the bankruptcy of all the partners. Over recent decades there has been a significant increase in the number of successful negligence claims against firms of accountants and solicitors. Partnerships, or the business equivalent of our partnerships, can incorporate as limited liability businesses in places such as Jersey, Guernsey and the Isle of Man. Some large firms of accountants were threatening to do this.

It would result in the income tax on the partners' profits would be paid in the place if incorporation of the business rather than to the English Exchequer. This would mean the loss of considerable tax revenue. It was to keep the ultimate taxation to be paid on behalf of the business entity in-shore that limited liability partnerships were created. The members of a limited liability partnership have to pay income tax on the profits just as if they were conventional partners. But here the similarity between the two types of business entity ends. The limited liability partnership, in spite of its name, is not a partnership at all. It is a body corporate formed by registration with the Registrar of Companies. Its members are not partners but simply members. They do not have unlimited liability. On a winding up of a limited liability partnership they have simply to ensure that they have paid up that amount of capital that they have agreed to put into the business.

This Corporate Law text is concerned primarily with limited companies. These are formed by registration with the Registrar of Companies. Once registered, a company is a separate legal entity in its own right – see section 4 below for more details.

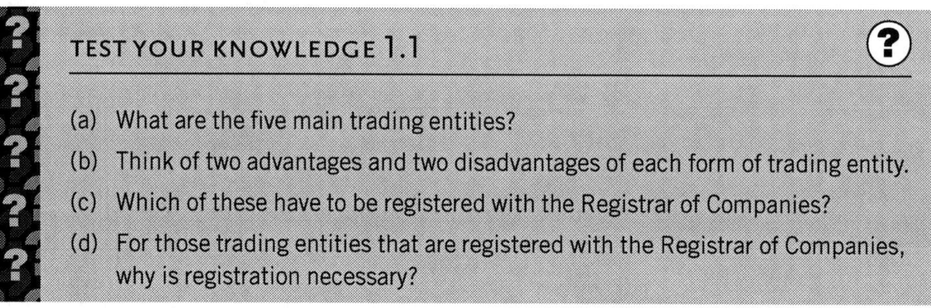
TEST YOUR KNOWLEDGE 1.1

(a) What are the five main trading entities?
(b) Think of two advantages and two disadvantages of each form of trading entity.
(c) Which of these have to be registered with the Registrar of Companies?
(d) For those trading entities that are registered with the Registrar of Companies, why is registration necessary?

2 Registered companies

The Joint Stock Companies Act 1844 allowed, for the first time in English law, the ordinary businessman to form a company by registration. This is today done under the Companies Act 1985 (CA 1985). Certain documentation and the appropriate fees are sent to the Registrar of Companies, and in return he issues a certificate of incorporation which may be considered the birth certificate of the company (CA 1985 ss. 10, 12 and 13). Chapters 2 and 3 look in more detail at the necessary procedures and documentation associated with registration.

2.1 Companies limited by shares and by guarantee

Registered limited companies may be divided into two categories:

1 those limited by shares; and
2 those limited by guarantee.

member
A shareholder in a company limited by shares or a guarantor in a company limited by guarantee.

Memorandum (of Association)
The key constitutional document of a company setting out, amongst other things, its name, objects and capital.

Company limited by shares

In a company limited by shares the liability of its **members** is limited. They have to pay what they have agreed to pay for their shares but no more (CA 1985 s. 1(2)(a)). Their liability is limited as stated in the company's **Memorandum** (one of the main documents in its constitution – see Chapters 2 and 3 for more details). If the members' shares are fully paid for when the members acquire the shares from the company, the members will never have anything further to pay, irrespective of how insolvent the company is. Sometimes shares are issued partly paid. In this case the member is liable to pay what remains unpaid on his shares if the company is wound up.

liquidation

The winding up of a company; the process whereby the existence of a company is brought to an end.

Thus, where a member holds shares which he has completely paid for, he has no fear that, on **liquidation**, he will be held personally liable for the debts of the firm.

THEORY INTO PRACTICE 1.1

A Ltd has an issued share capital consisting of 10,000 ordinary shares of £1.00 nominal value each. The shares were only 25p paid when they were issued.

Required

If the company were to be wound up on the grounds of its insolvency, how much could the liquidator demand from each shareholder per share owned by the shareholder?

Answer

Each shareholder would have to pay 75p per share that he owned, making a total of £7,500 available to the creditors of the company.

Company limited by guarantee

A company limited by guarantee has the liability of its members limited by its Memorandum to such amount as the members may have agreed to contribute to the assets of the company in the events of its being wound up (CA 1985 s. 1 (2)(b)).They are used usually for charitable or non-profit-making organisations.They may also be used for trade associations or for management purposes – for example, for a block of flats where the individual owners of the flats become members of a company limited by guarantee so as to achieve continuity of ownership of the common parts and the provision of services on a non-profit-making basis.

The sort of company which is usually limited by guarantee is one where capital is provided by fees paid in advance, such as a private school, and where, because funds are provided in advance, there is no need for members to provide the working capital. As has been said, the liability of the members in the event of an insolvent winding up is limited to that amount which they have guaranteed. Usually, this is fixed at some very low level such as £10.The remainder of the Memorandum is very similar to that of a company limited by shares, and in particular there will be a clear statement that the liability of the members is limited. Since 22 December 1980, companies limited by guarantee must be formed without a share capital. Before this date a company limited by guarantee could be formed with a share capital. If this happened, the Memorandum had to state, not only the amount guaranteed by the members, but also its nominal capital and the nominal value of the shares into which it was divided. Such companies may still exist but no new ones can be incorporated today. A company limited by guarantee cannot be a public company.

Charitable companies

By the Charities Act 1993 s. 97 a charitable company is one formed and registered under the Companies Act 1985 or to which the provisions of that Act apply as they apply to such a company. Essentially, the Memorandum or Articles must prohibit any distribution of profits to the members of the charity and ensure also that, if the company were to be wound up, no surplus assets would be returned to its members. By s. 68(1), if a company is a charity and its name does not include the word 'charity' or 'charitable', then the fact that it is a charitable company must be clearly stated on all business letters, notices, official publications, bills of exchange including cheques, conveyances purporting to be executed by the company, invoices, receipts and letters of credit.

2.2 Limited and unlimited companies

Another division of companies is into limited and unlimited companies.

As has just been seen, limited companies are companies whose members' liability is limited either by shares or by guarantee. In other words, the members of such companies know from the outset of their association with the company what their liability might be.

liquidator
The person who undertakes the liquidation of a company.

Unlimited companies, as the name implies, are companies where there is no limit on the liability of their members (CA 1985 s. 1(2)(c)). In the event of an unlimited company being wound up, and where its liabilities exceed its assets (in other words, where it is insolvent), the **liquidator** will go to the members asking for a contribution pro rata (i.e. in proportion to the number of shares they hold) to make good the deficit. This liability arises only when the company is wound up, and the creditors of the company have no right to sue the members direct: the members' contributions may be sought by the liquidator only.

Advantages of unlimited companies

- Subject to certain provisions, such companies generally enjoy the privilege of not having to deliver annual accounts to the Registrar of Companies (CA 1985 s. 254). This allows them to maintain a level of secrecy unavailable to limited companies, which must file annual accounts (CA 1985, s 242(1)). This privilege is not enjoyed by an unlimited company that is a subsidiary of a limited company, nor by a banking or insurance company (CA 1985 s. 254(2), (3)).
- Unlimited companies can buy back the shares of their members without the need to go through the formalities that are required when this is done by a limited company (see Chapter 5).

public limited company
A company the name of which ends with the letters plc (or the names represented by those letters in full), the Memorandum of which states that it is a public company, the share capital of which has a nominal value of at least £50,000 and which is registered as a public company.

2.3 Public and private companies

Yet another division is into public and private companies. A **public company** has to satisfy four criteria, which are designed to put potential investors and creditors on notice that the company has a minimum level of capital and could potentially, at some stage, offer its shares to the public:

1. Its Memorandum must state that it is to be a public company (CA 1985 s. 1(3)).
2. Its name must end with the words 'public limited company' (CA 1985 s. 25(1)).
3. The nominal value of its issued share capital must be at least £50,000 (CA 1985 ss. 11 and 118).
4. It must be registered as a public company (CA 1985 s. 1(b)).

private company
Any company that is not a public company.

listed company
A company the shares of which are listed on a recognised stock exchange.

Any company not a public company is a **private company** (CA 1985 s. 1(3)). A point on which there is sometimes confusion is how to refer to companies such as Marks and Spencer plc or GKN plc. Often they are spoken of colloquially as public companies with the intention that the word should indicate that their shares are traded on a recognised investment exchange (RIE), of which the best known is the London Stock Exchange. The use of the word 'public' can be misleading in this context. Such companies might be more accurately described as 'market' or 'quoted', or '**listed**' if listed on the Official List of the London Stock Exchange. Any company whose shares are publicly traded must be a public limited company ('plc'), but not all plcs have their shares publicly traded. Indeed, most plcs do not have market quotations. Chapter 6 looks at shares and the process of share dealing in more detail.

In summary, registered companies can be divided as follows:

Public:	Market/quoted or listed
	Off market
Private:	All off market

holding company
A company having subsidiary companies.

2.4 Groups of companies: holding and subsidiary companies

Companies sometimes operate in groups, with one company, known as the **holding company**, holding shares in other companies, known as subsidiary companies. This may be a difficult concept: the key is to appreciate that membership of a company is not limited to human beings; companies can also be members of companies. There is a variety of reasons for this:

1. Where a business enterprise wants to carry on a variety of diverse activities, it is sometimes administratively convenient to do so through separate subsidiary companies, each of which substantially manages its own affairs.
2. It also is a means by which a company can limit its exposure to risk. For example, a company may wish to embark on some development that is financially risky. If it does this through a subsidiary it can liquidate the subsidiary in the event of the development becoming unprofitable.

subsidiary company
A company which is controlled by another company, known as its parent or subsidiary company, which usually holds the majority of its voting shares.

A company is said to be a **subsidiary** of another company if the holding company:

1. holds a majority of the voting rights in the subsidiary;
2. is a member of the subsidiary and has the right to appoint or remove a majority of the board of directors;
3. is a member of the subsidiary and controls alone, through a shareholders' agreement, a majority of the voting rights in the subsidiary; or
4. is a subsidiary of a company which is itself a subsidiary of that other company (CA 1985 s. 736(1)).

For accounting purposes only there is effectively another definition of 'subsidiary'. In this case, a parent undertaking (a term that encompasses companies, partnerships, limited partnerships and limited liability partnerships) is defined as an undertaking:

1. holding a majority of the voting rights in another undertaking,
2. being a member of another undertaking and has the right to appoint or remove a majority of its board of directors,
3. having a right to exercise a dominant influence over another undertaking
4. by virtue of provisions contained in the undertaking's Memorandum or Articles, or
5. by virtue of a control contract; or
6. being a member of another undertaking and controlling alone, pursuant to an agreement with other shareholders or members, a majority of the voting rights in the undertaking (CA s. 258(2)).

The reason for this further definition is that an undertaking with many subsidiary or related undertakings is required to consolidate its accounts in order to give a true indication of its overall solvency and profitability, without which an undertaking might be able to hide some of its liabilities. This provision deters 'off-balance sheet accounting' as was seen in the Enron scandal in the USA, which would not have been possible in the UK because of the above rules.

FIGURE 1.1 **Types of Business Organisation**

	Plc	Ltd	Unlimited	Guarantee	LLP	Unincorporated
Profit	Yes	Yes	Yes		Yes	Yes
Not for profit				Yes		Yes
Liability of members limited	Yes	Yes		Yes	Yes	
Liability of members unlimited			Yes			Yes
Financial information confidential			Yes			Yes
Financial information public	Yes	Yes		Yes	Yes	
Profits of the business assessed for tax on owners					Yes	Yes
Profits of the business assessed for tax on the trading vehicle	Yes	Yes	Yes	Yes		
Shares offered for subscriptions to the public	Yes					
Shares offered to a defined restricted membership		Yes	Yes	Yes	Yes	Yes

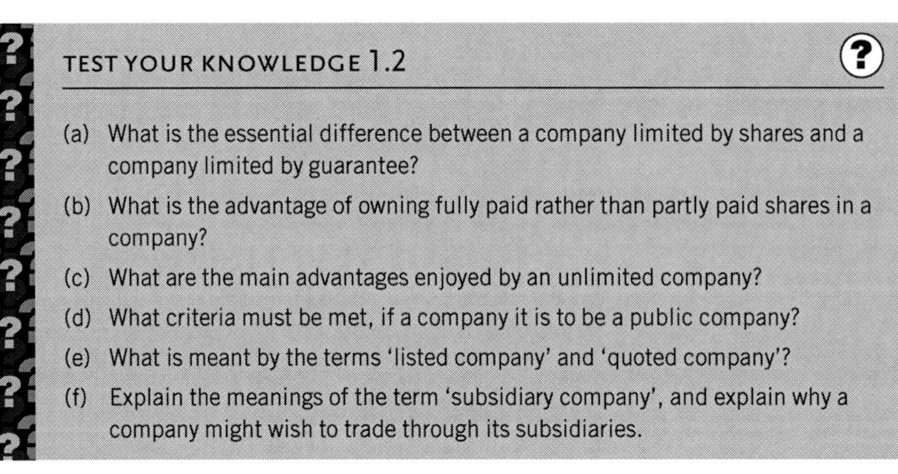

TEST YOUR KNOWLEDGE 1.2

(a) What is the essential difference between a company limited by shares and a company limited by guarantee?
(b) What is the advantage of owning fully paid rather than partly paid shares in a company?
(c) What are the main advantages enjoyed by an unlimited company?
(d) What criteria must be met, if a company it is to be a public company?
(e) What is meant by the terms 'listed company' and 'quoted company'?
(f) Explain the meanings of the term 'subsidiary company', and explain why a company might wish to trade through its subsidiaries.

3 The effects of incorporation

Incorporation gives the company a proper legal status. The company can use its registered name and is given a number from which it can be identified. From the date of incorporation the company can trade in its own name and the directors may manage its affairs. There are two main consequences of incorporation.

3.1 Perpetual succession

Once formed, a corporation will continue until such time as it is wound up. The fact that a member, even one holding 90 per cent of the shares in the company, dies has no effect on the legal existence of the company.

3.2 Limited liability

floating charge

A charge secured on a class of assets, present and future. The class is likely to change in the ordinary course of business from time to time. It is anticipated that the company will be free to deal with those assets subject to the charge until such time as the company ceases to carry on business in the usual way.

general meeting

A meeting of the members of a company.

common seal

The seal of a company; a device used for making an impressed mark upon a document so as to authenticate it.

Once incorporated, a limited company's members enjoy limited liability, i.e. as long as they have paid for their shares they will be under no further personal liability in the event of the winding up of the company.

Other consequences include the following:

- The company may sue and be sued in its own name.
- The company may own property; its assets belong to the company itself and not to its members.
- The company enjoys greater flexibility in the raising of capital. In particular it can raise capital by means of a **floating charge**, which is a type of security for a loan and which is only available to registered companies and limited liability partnerships. Floating charge forms a major area of company law and will be discussed in substantial detail in Chapter 7.
- Ownership and management may be separated. While with small private companies this may not be the reality, in that the directors are often also the major shareholders of the company, it is certainly not usually the case with public companies having a London Stock Exchange listing. The company may be said to have two main organs of power: the members in a **general meeting** and the board of directors. Much of the study of company law is concerned with examining the division of power between members and directors and the system of checks and balances which operate on the relationship.
- Once a company is formed, it is subject to the rules of company law: all fees prescribed by the law must be paid, all filing requirements must be satisfied, those accounts prescribed by law must be kept, and corporation tax must be paid if profits are made.
- The company will/may have a **common seal**, which it uses in the execution of deeds. Share certificates issued by the company usually bear the impression of this seal if the company has one, failing which they are simply signed by either two directors or one director and the secretary (CA 1985 s. 186).

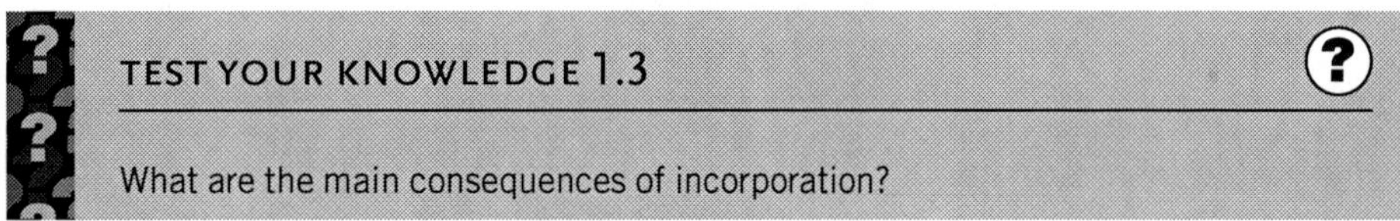

TEST YOUR KNOWLEDGE 1.3

What are the main consequences of incorporation?

4 The concept of corporate personality: the corporate veil

As indicated above, the distinct feature of the registered company is that it has its own legal existence, separate from those who own it, those who manage it and those who are employed by it. This concept is fundamental to English law, and is often referred to as 'the corporate veil'. It holds true even when those who own the company are also its managers or its employees. The separate and distinct legal personality of the limited liability company was first clearly established in English law in the case of *Salomon v A Salomon & Co. Ltd* [1897] AC 22.

CASE EXAMPLE 1.1

***Salomon* v *A Salomon & Co. Ltd* [1897] AC 22**

Salomon had for over 30 years carried on a boot and shoe manufacturing business in Whitechapel, London, as sole trader. He decided to form the business into a limited company and so he registered a limited company in which he and six members of his family held the shares. He then sold his business to the company for something under £40,000. This was paid for by the company issuing shares and paying cash to the value of £30,000 to Salomon and his family and a secured debenture of £10,000 to Salomon himself. This meant that, as shares can be paid for in kind instead of cash, an asset was transferred to the company at a total value of £40,000 – namely, the business that Salomon had been carrying on as a sole trader.

The company fell on hard times: there was a trade recession, accompanied by strikes. In the hope of tiding the company over, Salomon transferred his secured debenture to an outsider, a Mr Broderip, so as to raise cash to lend to the company as an unsecured creditor. In spite of all Salomon's efforts, the company went into liquidation. There were assets worth about £6,000; unsecured trade creditors were owed £7,000; Mr Broderip claimed the £10,000 owing to him under the debenture. In the circumstances, who was entitled to the £6,000 assets: the unsecured creditors, or the debenture holder, Mr Broderip?

It was held by the House of Lords that Mr Broderip could claim the £6,000. The unsecured creditors argued that the debenture, which was, of course, initially in favour of Salomon, was in fact a debt owing by Salomon to himself – which in law is not possible. This argument was rejected by the House of Lords. It was held that the company was a separate legal entity, completely distinct from its members, and as such could owe money to its members. Accordingly, the debenture in favour of Salomon was valid and so, when Salomon transferred the debenture to Mr Broderip he, too, was entitled to the priority originally afforded to Salomon by the security contained in the debenture.

The significance of the *Salomon* decision cannot be overstated. It is the foundation stone of English company law. A company is a separate legal entity from its members, allowing members to have a contract with the company. For example, a majority shareholder who is a director of the company in which he holds these shares can have a contract of employment with that company. Therefore, if he were to sell the shares he would be able to enforce any rights he enjoys under his contract of employment against the company. Similarly, if the company owes money to a supplier of goods to it, that creditor has to pursue his claim to be paid against the company. He cannot enforce it against a director who ordered the goods from him on behalf of the company.

An excellent example of a director and dominant shareholder against the company is to be found in the Privy Council case of *Lee* v *Lee's Air Farming*.

CASE EXAMPLE 1.2

***Lee* v *Lee's Air Farming Ltd* [1961] AC 12**

Lee was a New Zealander in the business of aerial crop-spraying. He had formed a small company to run the business. The share capital was 3,000 shares of £1.00 each; Lee held 2,999 of these himself. He was the sole governing director, and the company's chief pilot and had a contract of service with the company. Under the New Zealand Workers' Compensation Act 1922, where a worker died in the course of his employment, his widow was entitled to compensation. Under that Act a worker was defined as 'any person who has entered into or works under a contract of service with an employer'. Lee died in a flying accident while working on his company's business, and the question arose as to whether his widow was entitled to compensation. This hinged upon whether he was a worker under the terms of the Act. The argument put forward against Mrs Lee's claim was that her deceased husband could not possibly have been employed by the company since he effectively was the company. This contention was upheld by the New Zealand Court of Appeal, but the Privy Council held that Lee was indeed a worker within the definition under the Act. The company was in law a person completely distinct from him and so could enter into a contract of service with him.

5 Lifting the corporate veil

The principle established in *Salomon v A Salomon & Co. Ltd* that a company upon incorporation becomes a separate legal person, completely distinct from its members is illustrated by the following example: a third party makes a contract with a company. If something goes wrong with the contract, the third party will sue the company. The third party cannot take proceedings directly against a director or a shareholder of the company. In other words, he cannot lift the corporate veil.

Nevertheless, the concept of the corporate veil is not so sacrosanct that it is not subject to some exceptions. There is no coherent pattern created by those cases where the court has been prepared to go behind the corporate veil. While all instances can be described as being founded upon policy considerations, it is probably best to consider them under a series of headings:

1. where the company is a sham or a party to a fraud;
2. groups of companies;
3. enemy ownership or unlawful purpose;
4. provisions under company law;
5. where a company is regarded as an agent of another company.

These will now be considered in some detail.

5.1 Where the company is a sham or a party to a fraud

The court will lift the corporate veil where the company is a sham formed for some fraudulent purpose or so that the proprietors of the company can exploit rules of law in an improper manner. A good example occurred in *Re Bugle Press Ltd*.

CASE EXAMPLE 1.3

***Re Bugle Press Ltd* [1961] Ch 270**

Under what is now CA 1985 s. 428, if a bidder acquires 90 per cent of the shares in the company during a takeover, the bidder can insist that any minority shareholder with 10 per cent or less than 10 per cent of the company's share capital must sell those shares to him at the contract rate. In this case, Jackson, Shaw and Treby were shareholders in Bugle Press Ltd. Jackson and Shaw each held 4,500 £1 shares and Treby held 1,000 shares, thus making a total share capital of £10,000. Jackson and Shaw wanted to buy Treby out, but he was unwilling to sell. Accordingly, Jackson and Shaw formed a company having a share capital of £100, Jackson and Shaw (Holdings) Ltd, in which they each held half the shares. They then caused Jackson and Shaw (Holdings) Ltd to make an offer to purchase all the shares in Bugle Press Ltd at £10 per share. Jackson and Shaw accepted the offer (which was hardly surprising) but Treby rejected it on the ground that the price was too low. Thereupon Jackson and Shaw (Holdings) Ltd sought to invoke what is now CA 1985 s. 428 to force Treby to sell out at £10 per share.

It was held by the Court of Appeal that Treby could not be forced to sell. The new company was clearly a sham formed to get Treby out of the business.

A similar decision was reached in *Jones v Lipman*.

CASE EXAMPLE 1.4

***Jones* v *Lipman* [1962] 1 WLR 832**

Lipman entered into a contract to sell land to Jones. He then changed his mind and formed a company to which he subsequently conveyed the land. The strategy behind this was to prevent Jones from obtaining an order for specific performance forcing Lipman to convey the land to him. In the circumstances, had the company been bona fide and owned by third parties such a conveyance could not have been set aside. However, Russell J held that the company was a sham formed for the sole purpose of defeating Jones's claim to the land and, as such, the corporate veil should be lifted. Specific performance was accordingly ordered against Lipman and his company. The contract with Jones had to be honoured.

Another instance of the court's being prepared to lift the corporate veil arose in *Gilford Motor Co.* v *Horne.*

CASE EXAMPLE 1.5

***Gilford Motor Co.* v *Horne* [1933] Ch 935**

E. B. Horne had been employed by Gilford Motor Co. as its managing director. By his contract of service he had covenanted not to solicit customers of the company after leaving its employment. When his employment came to an end, he started business on his own account. In an effort to get around the restrictive covenant, he traded through a company, J M Horne & Co. Ltd, in which his wife and an employee were the directors and shareholders. Horne himself had no tangible interest in the company.

The Court of Appeal held that the corporate veil should be lifted to disclose that the company was a mere sham. Accordingly an injunction was granted against both Horne and his company to prevent their breaching the restrictive covenant with Horne's former employer.

However, the courts will not lift the corporate veil lightly under this category. For example, the Court of Appeal refused to do so in *Adams* v *Cape Industries plc.*

CASE EXAMPLE 1.6

***Adams* v *Cape Industries plc* [1991] Ch 433**

Cape Industries plc was the parent of a South African subsidiary. As a result of a successful claim brought against the subsidiary for negligence, the South African company went into insolvent liquidation. It was held that there could be no lifting of the corporate veil to allow the South African litigants to recover against the English parent company.

The case is of the greatest significance because it represents the most detailed examination of the concept of the veil of incorporation by the English courts. The judgement is exceedingly long and comprehensive. It was stated that while the layman might find the distinction between the situation where a company trades directly in a foreign country and the situation where it trades in a foreign country through a subsidiary, whose activities it has power to control, a very slender one, there is question in law that a company by operating through a group comprising of a number of subsidiary companies is entitled to organise the group's affairs in such a way as to minimise its exposure to the risk of liability. In other words, the courts will not go behind the corporate veil just because it seems convenient to do so or simply to achieve a fair and just result to a problem situation.

This reasoning was followed recently by the Court of Appeal in *Ord* v *Belhaven Pubs Ltd.*

CASE EXAMPLE 1.7

***Ord* v *Belhaven Pubs Ltd* [1998] 2 BCLC 447**

A company ('B Ltd') was in the business of acquiring, renovating and letting out public houses. On one such occasion, the plaintiff tenant (Ord) who took over the lease of a renovated public house claimed that B Ltd had made various misrepresentations to him. However, by the time those misrepresentations came to light, B Ltd had been removed from the register (dissolved) and its former shareholders were now trading through a new company, the defendant, Belhaven Pubs Ltd. The question arose whether the plaintiff could sue the new company. It was held that this could not be done. If the plaintiff had a complaint against B Ltd he should bring his action against B Ltd. To do this he should first bring proceedings to restore B Ltd to the register. Then he would have B Ltd in existence again so he would be able to sue the company. If it turned out that B Ltd's assets had been improperly removed from B Ltd to the defendant, B Ltd could be wound up and the liquidator could have the assets returned to B Ltd. But in the meantime, in the absence of any proven impropriety on the part of the defendant, the plaintiff had no claim against the defendant.

In *Ord* v *Belhaven Pubs Ltd* the Court of Appeal referred to its own previous decision in *Adams* v *Cape Industries plc*. Essentially, the rule of law is that if you have a complaint with a company you must sue the company. The company alone is liable for its wrongs. The court will not lift the corporate veil merely because justice demands.

Even more recently a similar approach has been followed by the Court of Appeal in *Trustor AB* v *Smallbone*.

CASE EXAMPLE 1.8

***Trustor AB* v *Smallbone* [2001] 3 All ER 987**

Trustor was a Swedish company. A director misappropriated a considerable amount of money which he paid to another company that he controlled. Some of this money was then paid by that company to the dishonest director and members of his family. The Swedish company wanted to recover this money and the question arose whether the veil could be lifted on the company controlled by the dishonest director. The court allowed the veil to be lifted. The company was clearly a sham and there was no innocent third party involved in it. However, the court expressly rejected an argument put forward by counsel for the Swedish company that the veil can be lifted whenever justice requires. The court refused to accept this, citing as authority *Adams* v *Cape Industries*.

Sometimes the existence of the corporate veil will result in injustice. This is unfortunate. But the veil cannot be lifted just because justice would be best served by so doing.

An example of the court refusing to lift the veil merely because justice demands is to be found in *Yukong Line Ltd* v *Rendsburg Investments Corporation*.

CASE EXAMPLE 1.9

***Yukong Line Ltd* v *Rendsburg Investments Corporation* [1998] 294**

A **charterparty** was signed by R on behalf of the defendant company. The defendant failed to carry out the terms of its charterparty properly and the victim of this breach (the plaintiff) obtained an **injunction** to prevent the assets of the defendant being deliberately removed by R in order to make it a pointless exercise extracting damages from the defendant company. It was then discovered that the defendant company's assets had indeed been transferred to another company under the control of R. The court refused to make either R or the second company liable for the breach. The court said that the proper remedy was to put the defendant into liquidation and for the liquidator then to recover the missing sums from R and his company; but in the absence of clear proof of impropriety R could not be held liable.

charterparty

A contract for the hire of a ship.

injunction

An order of the court preventing the doing of a specified thing.

It is difficult, if not impossible, to rationalise all these cases. However, if they are looked at in chronological sequence, it would seem that the corporate veil as established in *Salomon* v *A Salomon & Co Ltd* is becoming increasingly sacrosanct so that it is harder than ever today to persuade the court to look behind it, even when apparently there are quite good reasons for doing so. The courts appear, at the present, to be anxious to protect the concept of the corporate veil, conscious, no doubt, that any significant change from that position might have major deleterious commercial consequences for the country.

Personal liability of directors

However, while the courts seem reluctant to go behind the corporate veil without good legal reason, it is essential to appreciate that, increasingly, the law is imposing personal liabilities upon directors as well as making the companies themselves liable for breaches of various criminal statutes. Numerous pieces of legislation such as the Health and Safety at Work etc. Act 1974 and the Environmental Protection Act 1990 impose liability not only upon companies but also upon their directors personally. This needs always to be borne in mind when advising directors. Two recent cases have raised a rather interesting question as to when a director can be made personally liable for a tort committed by his company. The first is *Williams* v *Natural Life Health Foods* [1998] 2 All ER 577.

CASE EXAMPLE 1.10

Williams* v *Natural Life Health Foods Limited.

A health food shop in Salisbury advertised for potential franchisees. A brochure was sent to Mr Williams, a potential franchisee, together with detailed financial projections regarding the future profitability of a franchised outlet in Rugby. The franchise was duly entered into. There had in fact been misrepresentations made but by the time they came to light the franchisor company had been wound up. The question that the court had to determine was whether the franchisee could sue the controlling director of the company who had been responsible for the misrepresentations.

It was held that no liability arose. The misrepresentations had been made on behalf of the company and the company was vicariously liable for them. The misrepresentations were in the nature of a contractual wrong and the remedy had to run between the contracting parties. The court added that a director of a limited company will only be personally liable for loss suffered as a result of negligent advice if he has assumed personal responsibility for advice given. Thus if the advice had been given face to face to the victim then a remedy may have run in negligence. However, in the absence of negligence there was no personal liability upon the director.

However, a director cannot hide behind the vicarious liability of his company where he has been fraudulent.

In *Standard Chartered Bank* v *Pakistan National Corporation* (No. 2) [2003] 1 All ER 173 a director knowingly and deliberately made a false statement in order to obtain payment on a letter of credit. The House of Lords held that the director could escape personal liability for deceit on the ground that what he did had been done on behalf of and for the benefit of his company. Although an agent might assume responsibility on behalf of another person without incurring personal liability in respect of negligent misrepresentation (as had been the case in Williams), the same reasoning could not be applied in the case of fraud. Where he has committed a fraud, the director may be sued for his own tort rather than for his company's tort.

5.2 Groups of companies

There was a time when the courts looked at a group of companies as a single economic unit. In a sense, this was inevitable given the way in which legislation regarding the company accounts had moved towards accounting for groups as a single entity. The lifting of the corporate veil in the context can be illustrated by the case of *DHN Food Distributors* v *London Borough of Tower Hamlets*.

CASE EXAMPLE 1.11

***DHN Food Distributors Ltd* v *London Borough of Tower Hamlets* [1976] 3 All ER 462**

DHN ran a wholesale grocery business from premises which were owned by a wholly owned subsidiary company, Bronze. Bronze and DHN had exactly the same directors. Bronze was not a trading company and its only assets were the premises from which DHN traded. DHN occupied the premises as a licensee. The local authority, Tower Hamlets, compulsorily acquired the premises. Because of this, DHN had to cease trading. If DHN had been a mere licensee, the local authority would have been obliged only to pay compensation based upon the site value. On the other hand, if DHN could have been shown to have had an interest in the land over and above that of a mere licensee, substantial compensation for disturbance would have been payable.

It was held by the Court of Appeal that the group of companies should in the circumstances of this case be treated as a single trading unit. Accordingly, substantial compensation should be paid. Shaw LJ said that too legalistic a view should not be adopted. The exact facts of the case should be considered: 'The respective roles which the companies filled had to be borne in mind . . . No abuse is precluded by disregarding the bonds which bundled DHN and Bronze together in a close and, as far as Bronze was concerned, indissoluble relationship'.

This case has come under pressure from subsequent judgements. While it has not been expressly over-ruled, it was distinguished in the Scottish case of *Woolfson* v *Strathclyde Regional Council*.

CASE EXAMPLE 1.12

***Woolfson* v *Strathclyde Regional Council* 1986 SLT 415**

This case, like the DHN one, concerned whether a parent and a subsidiary company should be regarded as a single entity for the purposes of receiving compensation following compulsory purchase of its land. The House of Lords distinguished the DHN case on its facts but questioned whether it was appropriate in such circumstances to go behind the corporate veil. It was expressly stated that the veil should only be lifted where the company is a sham designed to hide the real situation that exists. The House of Lords was unwilling to treat Woolfson's group of companies as a single economic entity and made clear that they were unpersuaded by the decision in the DHN case.

It might be thought that the unwillingness of the courts to lift the corporate veil may well result in injustice, and indeed this is the case and is recognised as such by at least some of the judges. In *Re Southard & Co. Ltd* [1979] 1 WLR 1198 Templeman LJ said:

> 'English company law possesses some curious features which may generate curious features. A parent company may spawn a number of subsidiary companies, all controlled directly or indirectly by the shareholders of the parent company. If one of the subsidiary companies ... turns out to be the runt of the litter and declines into insolvency to the dismay of its creditors, the parent company and other subsidiary companies may prosper to the joy of the shareholders without any liability for the debts of the insolvent subsidiary.'

5.3 Enemy ownership or unlawful purpose

The courts are prepared to lift the corporate veil to reveal that the company is enemy-owned in wartime. This is illustrated by *Daimler Co. Ltd* v *Continental Tyre and Rubber Co. (Great Britain) Ltd*.

CASE EXAMPLE 1.13

***Daimler Co. Ltd* v *Continental Tyre and Rubber Co. (Great Britain) Ltd* [1916] 2 AC 307**

All but one of the shares in the Continental Tyre Co. were owned by persons resident in Germany. All its directors were resident in Germany. The question arose whether such a company had sufficient standing at a time when England and Germany were at war to bring proceedings in the English courts for recovery of a debt.

It was held by the House of Lords that the corporate veil should be lifted to reveal the true nature of the company and expose the fact that it was German owned and controlled – notwithstanding the fact that, as it was incorporated in England, the company could not bring proceedings in the English courts. Lord Parker of Waddington thought that an English company could, in the circumstances of this case, assume an enemy character. 'This will be the case if its agents or the persons in de facto control of its affairs, whether authorised or not, are resident in an enemy country. Or, wherever residents are adhering to the enemy or taking instructions from or acting under the control of enemies.' He went on to say that a company registered in the UK, but carrying on business in a neutral country through agents, properly authorised or not, and resident here or in the neutral country, is **prima facie** to be regarded as a friend, but may, through its agents or persons in **de facto** control of its affairs, acquire an enemy character.

prima facie
On the face of it; at first sight.

de facto
In reality.

The courts will also lift the corporate veil to reveal an unlawful purpose. On one occasion, the court lifted the veil to show that a company had been formed for the purpose of prostitution. In proceedings brought by the Attorney-General, the court ordered that the company be struck off the register (*R* v *Registrar of Companies, ex parte Attorney-General* [1991] BCLC 476).

5.4 Provisions under company law

There are a number of instances where particular provisions of the Companies Acts can be used to lift the corporate veil. Some of the more important of these are as follows.

CA 1985 s. 24: membership below two

If a public company carries on business without having at least two members and does so for more than six months, a person who, for the whole part or any part of the period that it is in business after those six months, is a member of the company and knows that he is the only member, becomes liable (jointly and severally with the company) for the payment of the debts of the company contracted during the period or, as the case may be, that part of it. This does not apply to private companies; these can operate with a single member.

CA 1985 s. 229: group accounts

If, at the end of its financial year, a company has subsidiaries, the directors must, as well as preparing individual accounts for that year, also prepare group accounts. These are accounts or statements which deal with the state of affairs and profit or loss of the company and the subsidiaries.

CA 1985 s. 349: personal liability where company name not used

'If an officer of a company, or a person on its behalf, signs or authorises to be signed on behalf of the company any bill of exchange, promissory note, endorsement, cheque or order for money or goods in which the company's name is not mentioned . . . in full', he commits a criminal offence. He also becomes personally liable to the holder of the bill, etc. for the amount of it, unless it is duly paid by the company. This is illustrated by *Hendon* v *Adelman*.

CASE EXAMPLE 1.14

***Hendon* v *Adelman* (1973) 117 SJ 631**

The directors of L & R Agencies Ltd signed a cheque on behalf of the company 'L R Agencies Ltd.' The ampersand (&) was missing from the company's name. The company's bank failed to honour the cheque. It was held that the directors were personally liable.

A fairly recent decision concerning s. 349 is *Jenice Ltd* v *Dan* [1994] BCC 43.

CASE EXAMPLE 1.15

***Jenice Ltd* v *Dan* [1994] BCC 43**

The name of the company was 'Primekeen Limited'. Its cheques were printed with the name 'Primkeen Limited (with the letter 'e' omitted). Some such cheques bounced. The court had to consider whether the person who had signed the cheques could be made personally liable for the sums due. The judge found that he was not liable.

THEORY INTO PRACTICE 1.2

Many commentators have suggested that this decision is in fact wrong. At the end of his judgement the judge said: 'Putting the matter in its simplest possible terms . . . the question is: In the circumstances of this particular case, has the company Primekeen had its name mentioned in legible characters on these cheques? And in my judgement it has, despite a spelling or typographical error.' Where did the judge go wrong?

Answer

He seemingly did not bother with the Act. The Act clearly says: 'if the company's name is not mentioned . . . in full'. If a letter is missing, the name is not there 'in full'. The judge chose instead to ignore the Act. What he described as 'the simplest possible terms' is not in the Act at all. He made it up. There is nothing in the provision about whether a reader can tell from the face of the cheque what the company is. The question is: Does the name appear in full? And it did not. It's a salutary lesson. Even a judge can get the answer wrong if he doesn't read the statutory provision he is trying to apply.

misfeasance

Misconduct or breach of duty. The remedy brought by a liquidator against directors and other officers of a company whom he thinks may have been in breach of their duty towards the company.

Insolvency Act 1986 s. 212: **misfeasance**

If, in the course of a winding up, it appears that an officer has been in breach of a fiduciary or other duty in relation to the company, the liquidator or any creditor may ask the court to examine that person's conduct and to order that compensation should be paid. The issue of misfeasance will be dealt with more fully in Chapter 11.

Insolvency Act 1986 s. 213: fraudulent trading

If, in the course of the winding up of a company, it appears that any business of the company has been carried on with intent to defraud creditors of the company or creditors of any other person, or for any other fraudulent purpose, the liquidator may apply to the court for a declaration that any persons who were knowingly parties to the carrying on of the business in such manner should be liable to contribute as the court thinks proper to the assets of the company. The issue of fraudulent trading will be dealt with more fully in Chapter 11.

Insolvency Act 1986 s. 214: wrongful trading

If, in the course of a winding up of a company, it appears that the company has gone into insolvent liquidation and at some time before the commencement of the winding up a director knew or ought to have concluded that there was no reasonable prospect that the company would avoid going into insolvent liquidation, the liquidator may apply to the court for a declaration that the director should be liable to contribute as the court thinks proper to the assets of the company. The director has a defence in such proceedings if he can show that he took every step with a view to minimising the potential loss to the company's creditors that he ought to have taken assuming him to have known that there was no reasonable prospect that the company would avoid going into insolvent liquidation. Wrongful trading will be more fully dealt with in Chapter 11.5.

TEST YOUR KNOWLEDGE 1.4 

(a) In the case of *Salomon* v *Salomon & Co. Ltd* why was Salomon able to make a valid contract of loan with his company?

(b) What are the main instances when the courts will lift the corporate veil?

(c) What is the effect of lifting the corporate veil?

(d) Why are the courts apparently reluctant to lift the corporate veil except in certain well-defined statutory circumstances?

Company Directors Disqualification Act 1986 s. 15 – Disqualified directors

If a person who is disqualified as a director or who has given an undertaking not to act as a director takes part in the management of a company without the consent of the court, he becomes personally liable for debts of the company. The liability is described as being joint and several with the company. This means that the creditor can sue either the company or him personally of both together. Interestingly, the company does not necessarily have to be insolvent for this to happen. Disqualification has the effect of being a sort of forward looking lifting of the corporate veil in the event of the disqualification being breached. The issue of disqualification of directors will be dealt with more fully in Chapter 8.

5.5 **Agency**

Where a legal agency situation exists between two separate person, the principal and his agent, the principal generally is liable for anything that the agent does with the scope of the agency. Whether in a given situation an agency exists is a question of fact that the court must determine from the precise circumstances of the case.

One instance where it was found to exist was in *Firestone Tyre & Rubber Co Ltd v Lewellin* [1957] 1 All ER 561.

CASE EXAMPLE 1.16

Firestone Tyre & Rubber Ltd v Lewellin

An English company manufactured tyres within England and then used them to satisfy orders made by customers of an American wholly owned subsidiary. The House of Lords found that the business was in reality the business was that of the parent company carried out by and through its agent, the American subsidiary. For this reason corporation tax could be assessed in England on the profits made from the sale of the tyres in America. The agency was inferred by the court from the nature of the trading arrangements between the parent and its subsidiary.

The Impact of the European Union

The EU is having a substantial impact on company law. The importance of EU law on business was graphically described by Lord Denning MR in *HP Bulmer Limited v J Bollinger SA* [1974] Ch 401, where he described it as '*an incoming tide. It flows into the estuaries and up the rivers. It cannot be held back*'.

The most common form of EC legislation in the area of company law is the Directive. This is addressed by the Community to the member states and requires them to enact its provisions by way of domestic legislation. Increasingly, however, new rules are being made by way of Regulations coming from the Council of Ministers or the Commission. These are self-executing and apply directly to all member states.

CHAPTER SUMMARY

- In this chapter, we have seen that companies may be categorised as unlimited or limited by shares or by guarantee; as public or private; or as members of a group. The definitive category is that of public companies.
- Once a company has come into existence it acquires a personality separate from that of its members. At that stage, it can do most things that an individual can do.
- Furthermore, its members, being separate from the company, may have the advantage of limited liability. That is, their liability for the company's debts is limited to the amount, if any, unpaid on their shares.
- This separation of the corporate personality from its members is known as the corporate veil. The corporate veil may cause difficulties or may be used as a vehicle for fraud. The courts are, therefore, prepared to go behind the veil in certain circumstances and to look at the reality of the company's ownership. This is known as 'lifting the veil'.
- There is no general principle which can be applied to cases where the courts are prepared to lift the corporate veil. The occasions where the veil has been lifted often are policy decisions, although many of them are based on the courts' reluctance to allow the corporate veil to be used to cause harm to people outside the company, to company members or even to the company itself.

CHAPTER 2

Promoters, pre-incorporation contracts and company registration

CONTENTS

LEARNING OUTCOMES

This chapter covers the role of and legal rules governing promoters of companies. After reading and understanding the contents of the chapter and studying the case examples you should be able to:

- Understand where promoters fit in with the process of company formation.
- Explain the duties that the law imposes upon promoters.
- Understand how promoters may be remunerated.
- Understand the nature and effect of pre-incorporation contracts.
- List and explain the documents that have to be sent to the Registrar in order to incorporate a company.
- Explain the procedure for the various types of re-registration.
- Understand the reasons for re-registration.

Introduction

In Chapter 1, we saw that, to form a company, certain documents and fees have to be sent to the Registrar of Companies. The people who undertake this task are known as the promoters of the company. They ensure that the company has the necessary share and loan capital that is needed for the business and will acquire whatever assets are needed to enable the company to start trading as soon as the necessary formalities are completed. You will remember that the company comes into existence and acquires a separate legal personality only after it has been incorporated. The promoters, however, have to act for the company before this stage is reached. They have to act as agents before they have a principal. Although technically a company cannot enter into a contract before the company has been incorporated (because the company has no legal existence), promoters occasionally set up what are known as pre-incorporation contracts. Such contracts may cause difficulties for promoters and may result in them being made personally liable on those pre-incorporation contracts.

Companies, once formed, sometimes need to change from being one type of company to another. This is known as re-registration. The procedure and reasons for re-registration are explained at the end of this chapter.

d

promoter

A person who undertakes to form a company and who takes the necessary steps to achieve that end.

1 Definition of promoters

There is no general comprehensive statutory or judicial definition of a **promoter**. The word used to be used in the now repealed s. 67 of the Companies Act 1985 but only in relation to liability for false statements in the prospectus. There was no definition as such. The section provided merely that 'a promoter who was a party to the preparation of the prospectus or any portion of it containing the untrue statement is liable to compensate any person who suffers loss thereby'. The courts, too, have not given a precise meaning to the word promoter, although they have given general guidelines. For example, in *Twycross v Grant* (1877) 2 CPD 469, Cockburn CJ defined a promoter as '*one who undertakes to form a company with reference to a given project and to set it going, and who takes the necessary steps to accomplish that purpose*'.

Another judge, Bowen J, speaking in the case of *Whaley Bridge Calico Printing Co. v Green* (1880) 5 QBD 109, stated that the word promoter was one of business not law, covering those business operations which are necessary to bring a company into existence (e.g. finding directors and shareholders, acquiring assets, complying with the registration formalities, etc).

These are cases from over a century ago, when promoters would undertake to bring the newly formed companies to the stock market and arrange to offer the company's shares to the public. In those unregulated days it was easy to do this. Under current regulations, before a company may offer its securities to the public, it must comply with the following requirements:

- the Financial Services Act 1986;
- the Public Offer of Securities Regulations 1995;
- the Financial Services and Markets Act 2000; and above all
- the Listing Rules.

This means that the role of promoters is nowadays minimal, their role, as far as offering securities to the public is concerned, being fulfilled by stockbrokers and specialist banks. However, it is still necessary to retain the law relating to promoters in order to maintain standards of probity and transparency amongst those involved in offering securities to the public. A promoter, therefore, is a person who is involved in the setting-up of a company and is only involved to a limited extent thereafter. The promoter's functions usually end when the board of directors is appointed.

2 Duties of the promoter

As indicated above, the duties imposed on the promoter were formulated during the latter years of the nineteenth century and the early years of the twentieth century. This was because some promoters promoted companies more for their own benefit than for the company's or the shareholders' benefit, and abused their position by, for example, selling their own property at a highly inflated price to the companies they were promoting. To counteract this, promoters were required to exercise a fiduciary duty towards their companies much as in the same manner as directors (see Chapter 9). Not only must promoters explain and account for any profit that they may be making from the promotion, they must also get such profit approved either by an independent board of directors or, if this is not possible, by the members.

2.1 Promoter's fiduciary duty

The promoter must make full disclosure of any benefits he receives from the company and is accountable for any secret profit he may make out of the promotion. The promoter, however, is not a trustee. He may make a profit out of the promotion provided he discloses his interest and the company consents to his keeping the profit, as illustrated in the case of *Erlanger* v *New Sombrero Phosphate Co.* (1878) 3 App Cas 1218.

CASE EXAMPLE 2.1

***Erlanger* v *New Sombrero Phosphate Co.* (1878) 3 App Cas 1218**

Erlanger and his friends formed a syndicate to buy the lease of an island stated to be full of phosphate which could be used for making fertiliser. They acquired the lease for £55,000. They then formed a company, to which they sold the lease of the island for £110,000 (an enormous sum in those days). They then invited members of the public to subscribe for shares in the company. Although Erlanger and his friends did disclose the sale of the lease to the directors of the company, of those directors two were abroad at the time of the disclosure, one was the Lord Mayor of London and thus too busy to give the matter much attention, a fourth was the paid agent of the Erlanger and his friends and a fifth was 'a mere instrument of the vendors'. It was held, therefore, that there had not been sufficient disclosure and that Erlanger, as promoter, was not entitled to keep the profit he had made.

As an alternative to disclosure to an independent board, it is just as effective if the promoter discloses his interest to all members of the company. For example, disclosure may be made in a prospectus issued by the company, for when they apply for shares being issued under the prospectus, the shareholders are, by their conduct, consenting to the promoter retaining his profit. Disclosure by a promoter to himself in his capacity as director, however, will not be sufficient (*Gluckstein* v *Barnes* [1900] AC 240; see below).

Most of the cases concerning secret profit arise when a promoter sells his own property to the company at an inflated value. Such a profit may also be made, for example, where the promoter obtains a commission from the vendor of the property. However the profit is made, if it is not fully disclosed to the company, the company may claim a full account from the promoter, as again, for example, in the case of *Gluckstein* v *Barnes*.

d

mortgage debenture

A secured loan evidenced in writing and giving the lender a priority over other creditors of a company.

CASE EXAMPLE 2.2

***Gluckstein* v *Barnes* [1900] AC 240**

In this case a syndicate was formed to buy Olympia, the exhibition site in London, from a company which was being wound up. The syndicate, comprising G and three others, intended to buy Olympia and then to resell it, either to a company formed for the purpose of buying it or to another purchaser. In the event of a company being formed, the syndicate members were to be its promoters and first directors.

A company to buy Olympia was formed. It was called the Olympia Company Ltd and, in its prospectus, the promoters stated that they had personally bought Olympia for £140,000 and were selling it to the company for £180,000. The prospectus also mentioned 'interim investments' but gave no further details about these.

These 'interim investments' in fact, were certain **mortgage debentures** in the company that had owned Olympia and which the promoters had bought at less than face value. These debentures were now redeemed at face value out of the proceeds raised by the sale of Olympia to the promoters. This transaction made a further £20,000 profit for the members of the syndicate.

It was held that the £20,000 was a secret profit which was recoverable by the company. The fact that the promoters had disclosed the profit to themselves as directors was irrelevant. The mention in the prospectus of 'interim investments' was not sufficient disclosure.

The action was brought against G and he had to account for the full amount with a right-to-claim contribution from his co-promoters.

TEST YOUR KNOWLEDGE 2.1 

(a) What do promoters do?

(b) Even though promoters are little in existence nowadays, what rules apply to them and why are those rules still necessary?

Restrictions on promoters of public companies

Under CA 1985 s. 104, for two years from the date of issue of the certificate entitling it to commence business, a public company may not acquire non-cash assets from subscribers to the Memorandum (see Chapter 3 for details) who hold an aggregate value equal to at least one-tenth of the nominal value of the issued share capital unless certain requirements are satisfied. Although the promoters of a public company do not have to subscribe to the Memorandum, it is very probable that they will do so. They will therefore be restricted from selling non-cash assets to the company unless there is compliance with s. 104.

The requirements that must be satisfied before such a sale can take place are:

1 The asset must have been valued by an independent accountant who states that the value of the consideration to be received by the company is not less than the value of the consideration to be given by the company.
2 The valuation report must have been circulated to members along with notice of a meeting to consider the matter.
3 By **ordinary resolution** the company must approve the terms and acquisition of the asset.
4 A copy of the resolution and report must be filed with the Registrar within 15 days of the passing of the resolution (CA 1985 s. 109).

ordinary resolution

A resolution passed by a simple majority of the members in a general meeting.

Failure to comply with the above requirements means that:

1 If the agreement has not yet been put into effect, it is void (CA 1985 s. 105(2)).
2 If cash has been paid for the asset, the company may recover the payment (CA 1985 s. 105(1)).
3 If all or part of the payment for the non-cash asset takes the form of an issue of shares, the subscriber must pay in cash the difference in value of the asset and the value of the shares. He must also pay interest on this amount (CA 1985 s. 105(3)(b)). The interest rate is 5 per cent per annum but this may be varied by statutory instrument (CA 1985 s. 107).

Similar rules apply (a) to promoters who are also subscribers to the Memorandum of a private company and (b) to promoters who sell their own assets to that company, and when (c) that company is re-registered as a public company within two years of the sale of those assets (CA 1985 s. 104(3)).

These rules do not apply where the asset is acquired in the ordinary course of the company's business. The provisions are designed to protect investors who subscribe to a public company formed to buy property from its founding members.

Remedies for breach of duty

The above rules describe the penalties arising when a promoter who is a subscriber to the Memorandum sells assets of his to the company. Sometimes, however, a promoter is not a subscriber to the Memorandum or otherwise caught by CA 1985 s. 104 but is still making a secret profit, perhaps by selling his own property to the company at an over-valuation without disclosing this fact. The company may then bring an action against the defaulting promoter. Remedies available against a promoter who has improperly sold his property to the company depend on whether he acquired the property *before* or *after* the time he began to act as promoter.

Property purchased by promoter *before* the promotion

In this case, the company may:

1 Rescind the contract, thereby recovering the purchase price and returning the property to the promoter (NB The right to rescind must be available, so the remedy will not be available if a third party has obtained an interest in the property). Or,
2 Keep the property and sue the promoter for damages for any loss suffered (e.g. the difference between the purchase price paid by the company and the market value of the property).

Property purchased by promoter *after* the start of the promotion

In this case the company may:

1 Rescind the contract (as above). Or,
2 Regard the promoter as agent of the company in his purchase of the property and recover the profit made.

TEST YOUR KNOWLEDGE 2.2 

How may a promoter legitimately make a profit from what he is doing in the promotion of a company?

3 Remuneration of promoters

Before the company is incorporated, it has no legal existence and thus cannot enter a valid contract. A promoter, therefore, has no legal right to claim his expenses or his fees for setting up the company, as shown in *Re National Motor Mail-Coach Co. Ltd, Clinton's Claim* [1908] 2 Ch 228.

CASE EXAMPLE 2.3 

***Re National Motor Mail-Coach Co. Ltd, Clinton's Claim* [1908] 2 Ch 228**

In this case one company promoted another company to acquire a mail contracting business. The promoting company incurred expenses in promotion fees. Both the promoting and promoted companies were subsequently wound up and the liquidator of the former proved in the winding up of the latter for the promotion fees.

It was held that the liquidator's claim should fail. Since the company being promoted was not in existence when the payments were made it could therefore not have requested that such liability be incurred.

CASE EXAMPLE 2.4 

***Re English and Colonial Produce Co. Ltd* [1906] 2 Ch 435**

Here, at the request of the future directors of a company he was asked to form, a solicitor prepared all company documentation and paid the registration fees. The Court of Appeal held that he could not recover his costs from the company. The fact that the company had had the benefit of his services did not impose any equitable obligation on it to pay for them.

A promoter may, however, have provision made in the Articles to empower the directors to pay the promotion expenses. Although this does not bind the company and may not be enforced by the promoter as part of the contract in the Articles (*Re English and Colonial Produce Co Ltd*), since the promoter or his nominee will probably be amongst the first directors it is likely that such payment will be made. A promise made by a company after incorporation to pay for services performed prior to its formation applies because, in English law past consideration cannot be used to support a contractual promise. To ensure payment, however, the promoter should make a contract with the company by way of a deed after its incorporation because deeds can be enforced without the need for a plaintiff to show that he has given consideration.

4 Pre-incorporation contracts

Pre-incorporation contracts are contracts made apparently for the benefit of a company even though the company has not in fact been incorporated. The usual reason for pre-incorporation contracts is that the promoters of the company are so keen for the company to be party to some commercially advantageous contract that they try to have the company enter the contract even though the company does not yet exist. However, by virtue of CA 1985 s. 36C, a promoter incurs personal liability on a contract he makes on the company's behalf before it is incorporated. The provision states 'A contract which purports to be made by or on behalf of a company at the time when the company has not been formed has effect, subject to any agreement to the contrary, as one made by the person purporting to act for the company or as agent for it, and he is personally liable on the contract accordingly'. This liability arises whether the promoter contracts as agent or not, as is seen in the case of *Phonogram Ltd v Lane*.

CASE EXAMPLE 2.5

***Phonogram Ltd* v *Lane* [1981] QB 938**

In this case it was proposed to form a company, Fragile Management Ltd, to run a pop group. Phonogram Ltd had agreed to advance £6,000 to the pop group who signed 'for and on behalf of Fragile Management Ltd' an agreement whereby the £6,000 was to be repaid to Phonogram in the event of a contract between the two companies not being completed within the month. Fragile Management Ltd was never formed and the group did not perform under its management. The £6,000, however, was not repaid.

The Court of Appeal held that, under what is now CA 1985 s. 36(C), Lane, by claiming to act and contract on behalf of Fragile Management Ltd at a time when the company had not been formed, was making himself personally liable on the contract. The fact that he signed 'for and on behalf of' the company made no difference to his liability. These words were not sufficient to constitute 'an agreement to the contrary' for the purposes of s. 36(4). To constitute such an agreement, the words would have to comprise an express exclusion of personal liability. Thus, a promoter may be personally liable on pre-incorporation contracts. As the company does not exist when the contract is made, it cannot ratify (i.e. adopt) it. Thus, as was seen in *Re National Motor Mail-Coach Co. Ltd* (1908) (see Case Example 2.3), a company may receive the benefits of pre-incorporation contracts without thereby incurring any liability to pay.

An example of the enforcement of a pre-incorporation contract by a promoter arose in the case of *Braymist Limited v Wise Finance Company Limited* [2002] 2 All ER 333.

CASE EXAMPLE 2.6

***Braymist Limited* v *Wise Finance Company Limited* [2002] 2 All ER 333**

Solicitors acting for Braymist Limited signed an agreement for the sale of some land to a purchaser company. Unknown to the purchaser, Braymist Limited was in the process of being incorporated when the contract was signed. The purchaser failed to complete. Braymist Limited and its solicitors sued to enforce the contract against the purchaser relying upon s. 36C. The Court of Appeal held that not only did the statutory provision entitle a party who had entered into a contract with an unformed company to enforce that contract against the person purporting to act for or as agent of the unformed company; it also entitled such a person or agent to enforce the contract against the other party. For this reason the solicitors could enforce the agreement against the purchaser. They should be treated as having signed the agreement on their own behalf and could enforce in that capacity.

4.1 When will a company be bound by a pre-incorporation contract?

After incorporation, the company may make a new contract with the third party with whom the promoter has been dealing. Although this does not of itself release the promoter from liability, he may protect himself by putting a clause in the pre-incorporation contract that his personal liability will end if the company, once incorporated, enters into a similar contract with the third party.

The company may make such a contract either expressly or by implication by its conduct. To be sufficient to create a contract in these circumstances, however, the company's conduct must unequivocally refer to the alleged agreement and will, even then, only amount to an offer, which will be converted into a contract if the third party accepts it. This is illustrated in Case Example 2.7.

CASE EXAMPLE 2.7

***Natal Land and Colonization Co.* v *Pauline Colliery and Development Syndicate* [1904] AC 120**

Under a pre-incorporation contract, P Co. agreed to take an option on a lease of land provided it was coal bearing. Once it had been incorporated, the company entered the land and, finding coal, asked for a lease. In the meantime, the original landowner had transferred her interest in the property to N Co. N Co. refused to grant the lease to P Co. P Co. sued.

It was held that P Co. should fail. By entering the land and looking for coal, P Co. was not unequivocally showing its intention to take the lease. Even if the action had shown such an intention, however, it would have amounted merely to an offer and there was no evidence of acceptance by either the original landowner or N Co.

The company, therefore, must clearly and unequivocally show an intention to enter a new contract. Thus, if it acts under the mistaken belief that it is bound by the pre-incorporation agreement, the company will not be taken to be making an offer. If, however, once it has been incorporated, the company freely acts on the pre-incorporation contract, this may be taken as an offer.

In the case of *Howard* v *Patent Ivory Manufacturing Co.* (1888) 38 Ch D 156 the directors renegotiated the terms of a pre-incorporation contract. This was held to amount to an offer to enter a fresh agreement which, when accepted, constituted a binding contract between the company and the third party.

4.2 How may a promoter protect himself from personal liability for pre-incorporation contracts?

Although a promoter will not be liable if, for example, the company makes a fresh contract with the third party, this may be felt to be too uncertain to give the promoter the protection he wants. He may avoid personal liability therefore by:

1 Making the agreement with the third party 'subject to contract'. This means that there is no contract, and therefore no liability on the promoter, until the company, after incorporation, enters the contract with the third party.
2 Making the contract himself and then, once the company has been incorporated, assigning the benefits of the contract to it and, in return, persuading it and the third party to enter into a contract of novation, whereby the liabilities will also be transferred.
3 Taking out an option on property he intends to acquire for the company when the company is incorporated and if it wishes to take the property, the promoter will exercise the option and then transfer the property to the company. If the company decides against the property, the promoter will not exercise the option.
4 Expressly providing in the pre-incorporation contract that he is not personally

liable on it, thus utilising the exclusion allowed in CA 1985 s. 36C. This facility is, however, very rarely used in practice.

5 Purchasing a company that has already been formed by someone else (an off-the-shelf company). There are many businesses that specialise in setting up temporarily non-trading companies which remain dormant until they are sold to someone wishing to acquire a company in a hurry and with which he can trade. The advantage of acquiring such a company is that it can be acquired for the person who formed it very quickly. For example, in London one can be acquired within less than a couple of hours of the order being placed by the purchaser. Normally there will be changes needed to the Memorandum and Articles of the company. For example, the company will have been formed in the name given to it by its promoter. The purchaser may well want to give it another name. Such companies afford a complete protection to a person setting up a new business so long as any contract he makes is made through the off-the-shelf company.

TEST YOUR KNOWLEDGE 2.3

(a) What is a pre-incorporation contract and why are they sometimes made?
(b) Why is a company unable to enter into a pre-incorporation contract?
(c) What are the five ways in which a promoter may avoid personal liability on a pre-incorporation contract?

4.3 When does s. 36C not apply?

Section 36C can only assist in the enforcement of a contract made on behalf of a company that has not yet been formed. It does not apply to a contract purportedly made on behalf of a company that has been struck off. This was the decision of the Court of Appeal in *Cotronic (UK) Limited v Dezonie* [1991] BCC 200.

CASE EXAMPLE 2.8

***Cotronic (UK) Limited* v *Dezonie* [1991] BCC 200**

The plaintiff was claiming a payment for work and materials supplied by him to the defendant company. The plaintiff company had been dissolved in 1981 and its proprietor was acting in breach of CA 1985 s. 34 by trading under the name of a company which was not duly incorporated. It was held that s.36C could not assist a company that did not exist.

It has also been held that the provision cannot assist a company that has been formed but was not properly named in the contract. This was the decision of the Court of Appeal in *Badgerhill Properties Limited v Cottrell* [1991] BCC 463.

CASE EXAMPLE 2.9

***Badgerhill Properties Limited* v *Cottrell* [1991] BCC 463**

The Plaintiff company was claiming payment for work and materials supplied to the Defendant. Estimates for the work had been provided by the Plaintiff on stationery headed with the trading name 'The Plumbing Centre'. The name 'Badgerhill Property Limited' appeared at the foot. This misdescription was a printer's error.

It was held that so far as the estimates were concerned, their contents clearly established that the Defendant was contracting with the Plumbing Centre. All evidence showed that the Company was trading as the Plumbing Centre. The contracts did not purport to be made by Badgerhill Property Limited within the meaning of s. 36.

registration

The process whereby a company comes into existence. Documents are sent to the Registrar of Companies and in return he sends out a certificate of incorporation.

5 Company registration

5.1 To apply for registration

The following documents must be sent to the Registrar of Companies in order to obtain registration of the company:

1 Memorandum of Association (see Chapter 3).

2 Articles of Association (see Chapter 3).

3 A statutory declaration made by a solicitor involved in the formation of the company, or by a person named as a director or secretary of the company, that all the requirements of the Companies Act with regard to registration have been complied with (s.12). This document is known as Form 12 (because it corresponds with CA 1985 s. 12).

4 Form 10 (corresponding with CA 1985 s. 10), setting out the address of the registered office and a statement of directors and secretaries, giving full information, including any directorships held either currently or within the previous five years. This statement must be signed by or on behalf of the subscribers of the Memorandum and each director and the secretary must sign to indicate their consent to act as such. The people named in the statement are, on incorporation, deemed to have been appointed as the first directors or secretaries of the company.

5 A fee of £20.

certificate of incorporation

The document that brings a company into existence. The 'birth certificate' of a company.

It is now possible for registered agents to submit these forms and documents electronically to the Registrar by company formation agents that have registered in this regard with the Registrar of Companies (in practice almost all company formation agents), in which case Form 12 is not required and the Memorandum and Articles of Association are not witnessed. If the forms and documents are in order and the necessary fees are paid, the Registrar must issue a **Certificate of Incorporation**. This is conclusive proof of the existence of the company (CA s. 13(3)). It should be added that Company House is now offering electronic corporation with a 24-hour turnround rate. The result of this has been that the larger company registration agents have moved away from having shelf companies.

TEST YOUR KNOWLEDGE 2.4 

What documents are needed to incorporate a company?

ICSA PUBLISHING

10

Please complete in typescript, or in bold black capitals.

CHFP087

Notes on completion appear on final page

First directors and secretary and intended situation of registered office

Company Name in full

Proposed Registered Office

(PO Box numbers only, are not acceptable)

Post town

County / Region

Postcode

If the memorandum is delivered by an agent for the subscriber(s) of the memorandum mark the box opposite and give the agent's name and address.

Agent's Name

Address

Post town

County / Region

Postcode

Number of continuation sheets attached

You do not have to give any contact information in the box opposite but if you do, it will help Companies House to contact you if there is a query on the form. The contact information that you give will be visible to searchers of the public record.

Tel

DX number DX exchange

Companies House receipt date barcode

Form April 2002

When you have completed and signed the form please send it to the Registrar of Companies at:

Companies House, Crown Way, Cardiff, CF14 3UZ **DX 33050 Cardiff**
for companies registered in England and Wales
or
Companies House, 37 Castle Terrace, Edinburgh, EH1 2EB
for companies registered in Scotland **DX 235 Edinburgh**

Company Secretary (see notes 1-5)

CHFP087

NAME *Style / Title | *Honours etc

* Voluntary details

Forename(s)

Surname

Previous forename(s)

Previous surname(s)

† Tick this box if the address shown is a service address for the beneficiary of a Confidentiality Order granted under section 723B of the Companies Act 1985 otherwise, give your usual residential address. In the case of a corporation or Scottish firm, give the registered or principal office address

Address †

Post town

County / Region | Postcode

Country

I consent to act as secretary of the company named on page 1

Consent signature | **Date**

Directors (see notes 1-5)

Please list directors in alphabetical order

NAME *Style / Title | *Honours etc

Forename(s)

Surname

Previous forename(s)

Previous surname(s)

† Tick this box if the address shown is a service address for the beneficiary of a Confidentiality Order granted under section 723B of the Companies Act 1985 otherwise, give your usual residential address. In the case of a corporation or Scottish firm, give the registered or principal office address

Address †

Post town

County / Region | Postcode

Country

Day Month Year

Date of birth | **Nationality**

Business occupation

Other directorships

I consent to act as director of the company named on page 1

Consent signature | **Date**

Directors (see notes 1-5)

Please list directors in alphabetical order

CHFP087 **NAME**

*Style / Title: ______ *Honours etc: ______

Forename(s): ______

Surname: ______

Previous forename(s): ______

Previous surname(s): ______

† Tick this box if the address shown is a service address for the beneficiary of a Confidentiality Order granted under section 723B of the Companies Act 1985 otherwise, give your usual residential address. In the case of a corporation or Scottish firm, give the registered or principal office address.

Address † ______

Post town: ______

County / Region: ______ Postcode: ______

Country: ______

Date of birth Day Month Year ______ **Nationality** ______

Business occupation ______

Other directorships ______

I consent to act as director of the company named on page 1

Consent signature ______ **Date** ______

This section must be signed by

Either

an agent on behalf of all subscribers — **Signed** ______ **Date** ______

***Or* the subscribers** — **Signed** ______ **Date** ______

(*i.e those who signed as members on the memorandum of association.)* — **Signed** ______ **Date** ______

Signed ______ **Date** ______

Signed ______ **Date** ______

Signed ______ **Date** ______

Signed ______ **Date** ______

Notes

1. Show for an individual the full forename(s) NOT INITIALS and surname together with any previous forename(s) or surname(s).

   If the director or secretary is a corporation or Scottish firm show the corporate or firm name on the surname line.

   Give previous forename(s) or surname(s) except that:

   - for a married woman, the name by which she was known before marriage need not be given.

   - names not used since the age of 18 or for at least 20 years need not be given.

   A peer, or an individual known by a title, may state the title instead of or in addition to the forename(s) and surname and need not give the name by which that person was known before he or she adopted the title or succeeded to it.

   Address:

   Give the usual residential address.

   In the case of a corporation or Scottish firm give the registered or principal office.

   Subscribers:

   The form must be signed personally either by the subscriber(s) or by a person or persons authorised to sign on behalf of the subscriber(s).

2. Directors known by another description:

   - A director includes any person who occupies that position even if called by a different name, for example, governor, member of council.

3. Directors' details:

   - Show for each individual director the director's date of birth, business occupation and nationality.
     The date of birth must be given for every individual director.

4. Other directorships:

   - Give the name of every company of which the person concerned is a director or has been a director at any time in the past 5 years. You may exclude a company which either **is** or at **all times during the past 5 years,** when the person was a director, **was**:

   - dormant,

   - a parent company which wholly owned the company making the return,

   - a wholly owned subsidiary of the company making the return, or

   - another wholly owned subsidiary of the same parent company.

   If there is insufficient space on the form for other directorships you may use a separate sheet of paper, which should include the company's number and the full name of the director.

5. Use Form 10 continuation sheets or photocopies of page 2 to provide details of joint secretaries or additional directors.

5.2 Trading as a public company

A public limited company must have a minimum issued share capital of £50,000. As such, the letters plc (the common abbreviation for 'private limited company') at the end of a company's name are a mark of some financial respectability. There is no minimum capital requirement for a private company. Therefore, the word 'limited' at the end of a company's name must be taken as a warning to its creditors that they should be careful in their dealings with it. Because of the financial respectability implied by the letters plc a public company may not commence trading before it has obtained a certificate from the Registrar to allow it to do so. Such a certificate – known as an **s. 117 trading certificate** – is required by CA 1985 s. 117 before a public company can start trading or exercising its borrowing powers. Such a certificate is not required for a private company.

section 117 trading certificate

The certificate that has to be obtained by a public company before it can lawfully trade or borrow.

If a public company starts trading without a s. 117 trading certificate, the company and any officer in default will be liable to be fined and, if the certificate has not been obtained within a year of registration, the Secretary of State may present a petition for the winding up of the company (IA s. 122(1)(b)). Trading without the certificate, however, does not affect the right of creditors to sue the company. However, if, within 21 days of a demand being made, the company fails to fulfil its obligation to obtain a trading certificate, the company's directors are jointly and severally liable to indemnify the creditors (CA 1985 s. 117(8)).

A s. 117 trading certificate will be granted by the Registrar when the company has filed a statutory declaration in the required form (117), signed by a director or secretary of the company (or the electronic equivalent) and stating:

1 that the company's allotted share capital has a nominal value which is not less than the authorised minimum, i.e. £50,000 (see Chapter 1);
2 the amount which has been paid up on the company's allotted share capital at the time of the application;
3 the amount of the company's preliminary expenses, and the recipient or likely recipient of any such expenses;
4 what benefit the promoter has received or is to be given and the consideration he has supplied in return.

The Registrar must further be satisfied that the nominal value of the company's allotted share capital is not less than the authorised minimum of £50,000 and that the company has received not less than 25 per cent of the nominal value of each issued share together with the whole of any premium on such shares. There will be no account taken of any share allotted in pursuance of an employees' share scheme unless it is paid up to at least 25 per cent of its nominal value and the whole of any premium on the share is fully paid.

In practice, very few plcs are formed as such. Nearly all plcs start life as private companies which are then re-registered as plcs. This obviates the need for an s. 117 trading certificate, the statutory requirements for being a plc being fulfilled by other means to be described shortly.

TEST YOUR KNOWLEDGE 2.5 

(a) Which documents have to be sent to the Registrar to form a company?

(b) What has to be done to form a public company that can trade?

117

Application by a public company for certificate to commence business

Please complete in typescript, or in bold black capitals.

CHFP087

Company Number [ ]

Company Name in full [ ]

applies for a certificate that it is entitled to do business and exercise borrowing powers, and, for that purpose,

I, [ ]

of [ ]

❶ Please delete as appropriate.

❶ [a director][the secretary] of the above company do solemnly and sincerely declare that:-

1. the aggregate nominal value of the company's allotted share capital is not less than £50,000
2. the aggregate amount paid up on the allotted share capital of the company at the time of this application is £
3. the ❶ [estimated] amount of the preliminary expenses of the company is £

❷ Please insert the name(s) of person(s) by whom expenses paid or payable.

❷ [ ]

Please give the name, address, telephone number and, if available, a DX number and Exchange of the person Companies House should contact if there is any query.

Tel

DX number DX exchange

Companies House receipt date barcode

Form revised July 1998

When you have completed and signed the form please send it to the Registrar of Companies at:

Companies House, Crown Way, Cardiff, CF14 3UZ **DX 33050 Cardiff**
for companies registered in England and Wales
or
Companies House, 37 Castle Terrace, Edinburgh, EH1 2EB
for companies registered in Scotland **DX 235 Edinburgh**

❶[4a. no amount or benefit has been paid or given or is intended to be paid or given to any of the promoters of the company]

❶[4b. the amount or benefit paid or given or intended to be paid or given to any promoter of the company is:]

❶ Please delete as appropriate.

Promoter No 1;

The amount paid or intended to be paid	£
Any benefit given or intended to be given	
The consideration for such payment or benefit	

Promoter No 2;

The amount paid or intended to be paid	£
Any benefit given or intended to be given	
The consideration for such payment or benefit	

Promoter No 3;

The amount paid or intended to be paid	£
Any benefit given or intended to be given	
The consideration for such payment or benefit	

And I make this solemn Declaration conscientiously believing the same to be true and by virtue of the Statutory Declarations Act 1835.

Declarant's signature

Declared at

Day Month Year

on

❸Please print name. before me ❸

Signed **Date**

A Commissioner for Oaths or Notary Public or Justice of the Peace or Solicitor

6 Re-Registration

Companies may wish to change their form from time to time. It is permissible to change from a private to a public company, a limited to an unlimited company, an unlimited to a limited company and a public to a private company. It is not possible to change from a private company limited by shares to a private company limited by guarantee, though a public company could become a company limited by guarantee (CA 1988 s. 53(3)). A guarantee company may change to being an unlimited company (CA 1985 s. 49(1)).

6.1 Changing a private company to a plc

The most common change is from a private company to a public company. The main reasons for so doing arise out of the greater apparent respectability of a plc, as evidenced by the minimum capital requirement of £50,000 and the more onerous accounting and disclosure rules required of plcs relative to private companies. Furthermore, if a company's directors ever wish to offer their company's shares to the public, at some stage the company will have to become a plc as a transitional stage before a flotation of the company's shares on a recognised investment exchange.

The procedure is complicated but is designed to ensure that the company genuinely has the required minimum issued and authorised capital of £50,000. This does not necessarily mean that the company has £50,000 in its share capital account: s. 45(2)(b) requires that each share must be paid up to the extent of at least one quarter of its nominal value plus any premium payable on it. This means that in practice a plc must initially have assets of at least £12,500 but could call upon its members to pay the outstanding balance on each share if necessary.

The procedure, to be found at CA 1985 s. 43, is as follows:

1 The members pass a special resolution that the company should be re-registered as a plc.
2 They may also need to pass an ordinary resolution increasing the authorised share capital to at least £50,000 if the company's authorised share capital is less than that figure.
3 The company's Memorandum and Articles are amended to make them conform to the Companies Acts requirements for public companies (including the company's name becoming 'plc' or 'public limited company' rather than 'limited').
4 The directors complete an application in the required form and send it to the Registrar of Companies together with the above documentation.
5 The company's auditors must provide the **Registrar of Companies** with a statement confirming that in their opinion the company's net assets, as indicated on a balance sheet prepared not more than seven months before the application for re-registration, are not less than the aggregate of the company's called-up share capital and undistributable reserves.
6 The directors must provide a copy of the relevant balance sheet referred to by the auditors, and the relevant balance sheet must bear an unqualified report by the auditors confirming that the balance sheet was properly prepared in accordance with the provisions of the Companies Acts.
7 The directors must also provide a valuation report if shares have been allotted in the period between the balance sheet date and the application date and those shares were allotted either wholly or partly for non-cash consideration; in which event that consideration must be valued in accordance with the provisions of CA 1985 s. 108 (see Chapter 5) unless the consideration was in the form of shares, or a class of shares, in another company. If the consideration was in the form of work or services, the work or services must already have been performed, while if the consideration is for an undertaking to be carried for the company, that under-

Registrar of Companies
The person at Companies House to whom documents are sent to form a company and to whom the necessary returns are made during the lifetime of a company.

taking must contractually be stated to be performed within five years of the resolution in (1) above.

8 The directors must also provide a statutory declaration in the required form confirming that the special resolution was properly passed and that between the balance sheet date and the application for re-registration there has been no deterioration in the net asset position of the company such that the net assets are less than the aggregate of the called-up share capital and the undistributable reserves.
9 The directors must also ensure that each share is paid up to the extent of one quarter.

Assuming that all these documents and forms are in order, the Registrar will issue a certificate of re-registration which is conclusive evidence of re-registration as a plc.

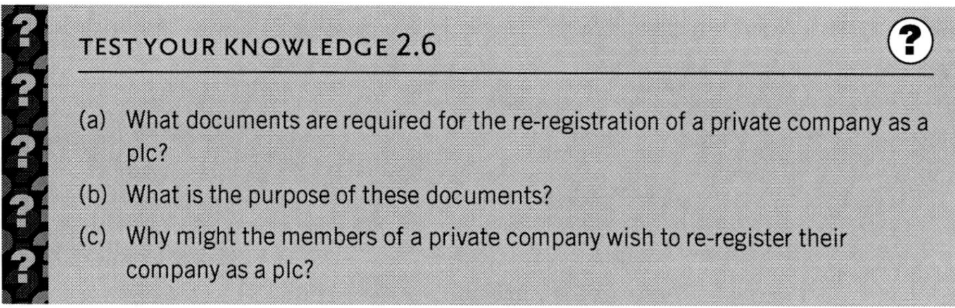

TEST YOUR KNOWLEDGE 2.6

(a) What documents are required for the re-registration of a private company as a plc?

(b) What is the purpose of these documents?

(c) Why might the members of a private company wish to re-register their company as a plc?

6.2 Changing a limited company to an unlimited company

The advantages of being an unlimited company are that:

1 there is no requirement to publish the company's accounts, subject to certain exceptions (CA 1985 s. 254);
2 the company may buy back or redeem its own shares without following the normal procedure required for limited companies as outlined in CA 1985 ss. 159–81.

However, the members of an insolvent unlimited company may be made responsible for its debts without limit which is why all the members of the company must consent to the re-registration of the company as unlimited.

To enable re-registration to take place, (under CA 1985 s. 49):

- The Memorandum and Articles of the company must be suitably amended to show the new unlimited status.
- There must be a resolution signed by all members consenting to the re-registration.
- The directors must sign a statutory declaration confirming that all the members have signed the resolution.

These documents may be sent to the Registrar in paper form or electronically. Assuming all the documentation is correct, a certificate of re-registration will in due course be issued (CA 1985 s. 50).

6.3 Re-registration of an unlimited company as a private limited company (limited either by shares of by guarantee)

This is likely to occur when the members wish to obtain the benefit of limited liability even at the price of having to disclose their accounts. Under CA 1985 s. 51, the members must pass a special resolution approving the change, and the Memorandum and Articles of Association must be suitably modified. The revised Memorandum and Articles, together with the required form, should be sent to the Registrar and in due course a certificate of re-registration will be issued.

6.4 Re-registration of a public company as a private company

This might take place where the members no longer wish to abide by the more onerous disclosure and other requirements applicable to public companies.

Under CA 1985 ss. 53–5:

- The members must pass a special resolution to re-register the company as private.
- The Memorandum and Articles must be suitably changed so that there are no longer references to being a plc.
- The requisite forms must be sent to the Registrar of Companies.

Unusually, the legislation allows objections to the re-registration by minority shareholders holding 5 per cent of the company's issued share capital, or of any class thereof, or by not less than 50 of the company's members, if they believe the resolution for re-registration should be cancelled. No objector may, however, have previously voted in favour of re-registration. The objectors must apply to the court within 28 days of the resolution, and the court may order as it sees fit in response to the objectors' application, commonly requiring the company or the majority shareholders to acquire the objectors' shares at a fair price. A reason for objection might be the loss of opportunity by the objectors to sell their shares on a recognised investment exchange. Assuming there are no objectors, or their concerns are satisfied, in due course the Registrar of Companies will issue a certificate of re-registration.

CHAPTER SUMMARY

- In this chapter, we have looked at the position and role of promoters. A promoter is a person who takes the necessary steps to form a company and to exercise control over the company's affairs until the formation is complete.
- Promoters may be in a position to defraud the company they are establishing by making a secret profit out of their work.
- To prevent this, the law imposes a fiduciary duty on promoters generally, and also limits the rights of promoters of public companies to sell their own property to the company for two years after the formation. If the promoter improperly sells his own property to the company, the law gives the company rights either to rescind the contract or to keep the property and obtain compensation from the promoter.
- A difficulty faced by promoters is that, if they enter contracts on the company's behalf, they will be personally liable on these contracts. This liability will exist even if the company makes a new contract with the third party with whom the promoter has been dealing.
- We have seen, however, that a promoter may protect himself from personal liability by the way in which he makes the original contract.
- We looked at the documents which have to be sent to the Registrar of Companies in order to obtain registration of the company. Once these documents have been filed and the fees paid, the Registrar will issue a certificate of incorporation. At this point, private companies may start trading.
- Public companies, however, cannot trade or exercise their borrowing powers until they have obtained a s. 117 certificate. As we have seen, such a certificate can be granted only if the Registrar is satisfied that the company complies with certain requirements.
- Companies may change their status, from private to public, from limited to unlimited, from unlimited to limited and from public to private. There are restrictions on changing a company's status more than once. In every case the appropriate resolution (unanimous or special as the case may be) must be passed and the Memorandum and Articles amended accordingly.

CHAPTER 3

The Memorandum and Articles of Association

CONTENTS

LEARNING OUTCOMES

This chapter covers the Memorandum and Articles of Association. After reading and understanding the contents of the chapter and studying the case examples, you should understand:

- The nature of the Memorandum and Articles of Association.
- The clauses to be found in the Memorandum.
- The rules governing company names.
- The function of the registered office of the company.
- The significance of the objects clause.
- The nature of the limited liability clause.
- The statutory contract.
- The nature of the Articles of Association and the significance of Table A.
- How the Articles of Association can be altered.

Introduction

At the end of the last chapter we saw that in order for a company to be incorporated certain documents have to be sent by the promoters to the Registrar of Companies. In this chapter we look in more detail at two of those documents:

The Memorandum of Association; and

The Articles of Association.

Between them these documents contain the constitution of the company. Broadly speaking, the Memorandum governs the company's relations with the outside world and the Articles its internal affairs and dealings.

1 The Memorandum of Association

1.1 Purpose and contents

The purpose of the Memorandum is to enable any investors, creditors and other interested parties to ascertain the company's name, its objects, its share capital and whether the liability of its members is limited.

By CA 1985 s. 2 the Memorandum of every company must state:

1. The name of the company.
2. Whether the registered office is to be situated in England and Wales or in Scotland.
3. The objects of the company.
4. Whether the liability of the members is limited.
5. In the case of a company limited by shares, the amount of share capital and the statement that such capital is divided into shares of a stated amount.

The Memorandum of a public company must, by CA 1985 s. 1(3), also state that the company is a public company.

In addition to this, other clauses may deal with any matter which could otherwise be provided for in the company's Articles of Association. For example, charitable companies sometimes have a provision in the Memorandum stating that if the purposes for which the charitable company was set up no longer exist, the assets of the company should be transferred to a similar company and for a similar charitable purpose.

subscription clause

The clause at the end of the Memorandum which is signed by the subscribers and will result in their becoming the first members of the company.

The Memorandum ends with a **subscription clause**. By CA 1985 s. 2(6) this must be signed by each subscriber in the presence of at least one witness who must attest the signature. The subscribers become the first members of the company upon incorporation (CA 1985 s. 22(1)). This provision ensures that no company is formed without members.

A sample Memorandum is included as an appendix to this volume.

TEST YOUR KNOWLEDGE 3.1 

What information must be included in a company's Memorandum of Association?

2 The company's name

The first clause of the Memorandum contains the name of the company. There are a number of rules which govern the choice of a company's name:

1. By CA 1985 s. 25 the name of a limited company must end with either the word 'limited' or the words 'public limited company', as the case may be. If the company's registered office is situated in Wales, then it has the right to choose the Welsh equivalents, 'cyfyngedig' or 'cwmni cyfyngedig cyhoeddus', respectively.
2. By CA 1985 s. 26 the name must not be the same as one appearing on the Registrar's index of names. This is an index which the Registrar of Companies is obliged to keep under CA 1985 s. 7. It contains the names of all companies registered under the Act, all overseas companies registered as trading here, all limited partnerships registered under the Limited Partnerships Act 1907, all limited liability partnerships registered under the Limited Liability Partnerships Act 2000 and all societies registered under the Industrial and Provident Societies Act 1965.
3. By s. 26 the name must not be one which, in the opinion of the Secretary of State, constitutes a criminal offence. For example, it is a criminal offence for a company to use a name which suggests that it carries on a banking activity unless it is authorised under the Financial Services and Markets Act 2000.
4. By s. 26 a company cannot be formed with a name that, in the opinion of the Secretary of State, is offensive.

FIGURE 3.1 Restricted company names

It is not necessary for students to be familiar with all of the restricted words, but a flavour of the rules can be obtained from the following examples:

Abortion or pregnancy termination – Consent needed from the Department of Health
Contact lens – Consent needed from theGeneral Optical Council
Dental, dentistry – Consent needed from General Dental Council
King, Queen, Royal, Royale, Prince, Princess, Windsor – Consent needed from the Home Secretary
Nurse, nursing – Consent needed from United Kingdom Central Council for Nursing, Midwifery and Health Visiting
Polytechnic, special school – Consent needed from Department for Education and Employment
University – Consent needed from the Privy Council

passing off

A tort whereby a business wrongly adopts a name similar to that of a similar business in such a way as to cash in on its reputation and so expropriate its goodwill.

tort

A civil wrong such as negligence, defamation, trespass or passing off.

5. By s. 26 a company in addition may not be registered with a name which suggests a connection between the company and Her Majesty's Government or a connection with any local authority unless the Secretary of State permits. Moreover, under the Company and Business Names Regulations 1981 (SI 1981/1685) there are certain words which require the consent either of the Secretary of State or of some other official body. Details of these words and the persons from whom consent should be obtained are listed in Companies House Guidance Booklet *GBF 3 Business Names*, which can be downloaded free of charge from the Companies House website (see Directory).
6. The name must not pass off that of another business. **Passing off** is a **tort** which occurs when a person or business uses a name which is so like that of an existing business as to be likely to cause confusion in the minds of potential customers and a possible divergence of trade away from the plaintiff's business.

CASE EXAMPLE 3.1

***Ewing* v *Buttercup Margarine Co. Limited* [1917] 2 Ch D 1**

The plaintiff traded under the business name of The Buttercup Dairy Co. The Buttercup Margarine Co Limited was registered and the plaintiff brought an action against him for passing off. An injunction was granted prohibiting the defendant using the name Buttercup since the names of the two businesses were so similar that the public might think there was a connection between them.

It might be noted that the courts are rather more lenient when considering words which are in common use and which form part of the name of a company (see Case Example 3.2).

CASE EXAMPLE 3.2

***Aerators Limited* v *Tollitt* [1902] 2 Ch 319**

Tollitt formed a company called Automatic Aerators Patents Limited. The plaintiff company, Aerators Limited, was concerned by the use of the words 'aerators' in Tollit's company's name. The plaintiff company feared that it would lose customers to Tollitt's company because of the similarity of the two companies' names. However, the plaintiffs failed to obtain an injunction restraining Tollitt from using the word 'aerators' in his company's name. As Farwell J said: '*If the name is simply a word in ordinary use representing a machine or an article of commerce, the probability of deception is out of all proportion less than it would be in the case of an invented or fancy word.*'

The courts will not generally prevent a person from using his own name in his own business, provided there is no dishonest intent (as in *Wright, Layman and Unmey Ltd* v *Wright* (1949) 66 RPC 149, CA, where Wright who had worked for the plaintiff company was allowed to set up a business in his own name) but the court will not extent that latitude to nicknames (*Biba Group Ltd* v *Biba Boutique* [1990] RPC 413, where the clothing designer whose nickname was 'Biba' and who had sold her business was forbidden from using her nickname in a new shop she was setting up).

2.1 Change of name

A company may change its name at any time by special resolution passed in general meeting. The new name must, of course, not contravene any of the rules which have to be observed by the company in regard to its choice of name on incorporation. When the name is changed the company must send to the Registrar a copy of the special resolution and also of the amended Memorandum of Association. There is a £10 fee payable. The Registrar must enter the new name on the register in place of the altered name and issue to the company a revised certificate of incorporation.

Even though the change of name takes effect from the date on the revised certificate of incorporation, legal proceedings which have already been commenced by or against the company in the old name may be continued in the new name. Moreover, the change of name has no effect on the liabilities of the company.

2.2 Compulsory change of name

There are four instances when a company must change its name:

1 By s. 28, if a company is registered by a name which is either the same as one already appearing on the index or which is too similar to a name on the index, the Secretary of State may, within 12 months either of the incorporation of the company or the adoption of the name, order the company in writing to change its name.

2 Also by s. 28, if it appears to the Secretary of State that a company has given misleading information for the purpose of being registered with a particular name or has given undertakings or assurances which have not been fulfilled, he may, within five years, order the company in writing to change its name.

ordinary resolution

A resolution passed by a simple majority of the members in a general meeting.

3 By s. 32, the Department of Trade and Industry may order a company to change its name if it is so misleading in its indication of the company's activities as to be likely to cause harm to the public as seen in Case Example 3.3.

In each of the above instances there is no indication of what sort of resolution is necessary to bring about the change. It is generally thought that an **ordinary resolution** will be sufficient.

CASE EXAMPLE 3.3

Re Association of Certified Public Accountants of Britain **[1997] BCC 736**

A company registered using this name. The case had been directed by the Secretary of State to change its name on the ground that it was so misleading as to be likely to cause harm to the public. The company appealed against the order to change its name. The court, however, held that the order was well founded since the name was likely to cause harm to the public because people expect a certain level of probity and expertise from qualified accountants and the term 'Certified Public Accountant' was misleading having regard to the fact that members of the body might not necessarily be up to this high standard.

4 When the court issues an injunction against a company prohibiting the use of a name on the ground of passing off, the company must either cease trading altogether or change its name. In this case the change must be by special resolution using the procedure in s. 28 as described above.

2.3 Business names

Any business, whether a sole trader, a partnership or a corporate body, may trade under a name other than its own name. Such a name is known as its business name. It is the name under which a business trades. For example, ABC (Restaurants) Ltd runs a business, the Flamenco Restaurant. 'The Flamenco Restaurant' is the business name. 'ABC (Restaurants) Ltd' is the company name. It was stated above that there are certain names and words for which the approval of the Secretary of State or some other person or body must be obtained. By s. 2 of the Business Names Act 1985 these rules apply also to business names.

Section 4 of that Act states that any company using a business name must set out its company name, in legible characters, on all:

- business letters;
- orders for goods and services;
- invoices and receipts;
- written demands for the payment of business debts;

together with an address in Great Britain at which service of any document relating to the business will be effective. In addition, the company must display a notice containing this information in a prominent position at any premises at which it carries on business and/or to which customers or suppliers have access. Any person with whom business is being or may be conducted has a right to ask the company to supply him with this information in writing.

If these rules are not observed then s. 5 of the Business Names Act provides a civil remedy. If a company in default of the rules brings legal proceedings to enforce a contract, the action will be dismissed if the other party can show that by reason of the breach of the Act either:

1 he has been unable to pursue some claim against the company under that contract; or
2 he has suffered some financial loss under the contract,

unless the court thinks that, in all the circumstances, it is just and equitable to permit proceedings to continue. The other party may, of course, sue the company in default.

2.4 Publication of the company's name

Before considering these rules, it should perhaps be made clear what is meant by 'publication'. It is easy to assume that it is only used in connection with matters such as bringing out a book or a newspaper. It, in fact, has a far wider meaning than this. It means literally 'to make public'. Thus, what we are dealing with here is making public the company's name.

As already mentioned, every company must have its name painted or affixed on all business premises and also clearly stated on all business documents and negotiable instruments. In the event of default, both the company and its officers are liable to be fined. Also, by s. 349 any officer of the company who signs a negotiable instrument, such as a cheque, which does not bear the name of the company in full may be made personally liable on that instrument if it is not paid by the company (see also Chapter 1, section 5.4).

2.5 Power to omit the word 'Limited'

There are very few instances where companies may omit the word 'limited' from their names. By s. 30 a company may omit the word 'limited' from its name only if the following criteria are satisfied:

1 It must be a private company limited by guarantee.
2 Its objects must be the promotion of commerce, art, science, education, religion, charity or any profession.
3 Its Memorandum or Articles must require its profits and any other income to be applied in the promotion of its objects.
4 These documents must also prohibit the payment of any dividends to its members.
5 These documents must also require that, if the company is wound up, all its assets will be transferred to some other body having similar objects or to a charity.

If a company wishes to omit the word limited from its name, then a statutory declaration that it satisfies these criteria may be made either by the person forming the company or by a person stated to be the director or secretary of the company. The declaration must be filed with the Registrar. The Registrar has the power both to accept such a declaration as sufficient evidence that the required criteria are satisfied, and to refuse to register a company with a name that omits the word 'limited' unless such a declaration has been received by him.

Such a company cannot change its Memorandum or Articles to take it outside these criteria. Moreover, if it appears to the Secretary of State that the company has infringed any of these provisions, he may order the company to change its name so as to include the word 'limited'.

2.6 Public company names

The Memorandum of a public company must contain a statement that it is a public company. This will be the second clause in the Memorandum of a public company.

TEST YOUR KNOWLEDGE 3.2

(a) What statutory rules determine the choice of company name?
(b) What is 'passing off'? What happened in the two leading cases?
(c) What are the provisions outlined by The Business Names Act, s. 4?
(d) On what grounds may the Secretary of State compel a company to change its name?
(e) List the requirements of CA s. 30 for a company to be permitted to omit the word 'limited' from its name.

3 The registered office

domicile

The place where a man or a company has his or its fixed or permanent home.

The second clause in the Memorandum of a private company and the third in that of a public company will be a statement of the *country* in which the registered office is situated. This is not the address of the registered office, but a statement, for example, in the case of an English company, that the registered office is situated in England and Wales. This establishes the **domicile** of the company: that is, where the company is incorporated and registered. This determines the law which applies to the company. Thus, a company incorporated in England is subject to English law. A company can have only one domicile and this clause cannot be changed.

Domicile should be distinguished from residence. Residence is usually where the company's central place of management is. It can, however, carry on business in any number of countries and will be subject to taxes locally.

registered office

The address of the office of a company to which formal notices and legal documents should be addressed and sent.

3.1 The importance of the registered office

By s. 287, a company must have a **registered office**. By s. 10, the intended address of the registered office must be notified to the Registrar before incorporation of the company (see Chapter 2 for more details). Although a company cannot change its domicile, there is no reason why it should not change the address of its registered office within the country of incorporation. By s. 287 any change of registered office must be notified to the Registrar within 14 days by the submission of form 287. Consent of the members is not needed for the change. The directors can do it as part of the day-to-day running of the company.

By s. 351 the registered office address must be stated on all business letters and order form of the company.

The purpose of the registered office is twofold:

1 It is a place on which formal documents can be served on the company. Obviously, if a writ is to be served on an individual, it is normally given to him personally. Since a company is an artificial person it cannot receive writs by personal service in this way. Hence the need for a registered office.
2 The registered office is also an address where certain essential records must be kept. These are:
   (a) register of members (s. 353),
   (b) register of interests in shares (s. 211),
   (c) register of directors and secretaries (s. 288),
   (d) register of directors' interests in shares and debentures (Schedule 13 Part IV),
   (e) **register of charges** (s. 407),
   (f) copies of instruments creating charges (s. 406),
   (g) register of debenture holders (s. 190), and
   (h) minute books of general meetings (s. 383).

register of charges

The statutory register that has to be maintained by every company to contain details of all charges over the company or its property.

There is provision for some of these registers, particularly the register of members and register of debenture holders, to be kept at another location where the business

287

Change in situation or address of Registered Office

Please complete in typescript, or in bold black capitals.
CHFP087

Company Number

Company Name in full

New situation of registered office

NOTE:

The change in the situation of the registered office does not take effect until the Registrar has registered this notice.

For 14 days beginning with the date that a change of registered office is registered, a person may validly serve any document on the company at its previous registered office.

PO Box numbers only are not acceptable.

Address

Post town

County / Region | Postcode

Signed | **Date**

† Please delete as appropriate.

† a director / secretary / administrator / administrative receiver / liquidator / receiver manager / receiver

Please give the name, address, telephone number and, if available, a DX number and Exchange of the person Companies House should contact if there is any query.

Tel

DX number | DX exchange

Companies House receipt date barcode

Form revised June 1998

When you have completed and signed the form please send it to the Registrar of Companies at:
Companies House, Crown Way, Cardiff, CF14 3UZ **DX 33050 Cardiff**
for companies registered in England and Wales
or
Companies House, 37 Castle Terrace, Edinburgh, EH1 2EB
for companies registered in Scotland **DX 235 Edinburgh**

of maintaining them takes place. This is known as a transfer office and Companies House must be notified when this occurs.

3.2 Statutory books

register of members
The record that a company must keep of its members.

There are certain registers, records and documents, collectively known as the 'statutory books', which a company must maintain by law. These are:

1. **register of members** (s. 352);
2. register of charges (s. 407);
3. register of interests in shares (s. 211);
4. register of directors and secretaries (s. 288);
5. register of directors' interests in shares and debentures (s. 325);
6. directors' service contracts (s. 318);
7. minute books of general meetings and directors' meetings (s. 382); and
8. accounting records including details of receipts and expenditure, assets and liabilities and stock (s. 211).

All these must be made available for inspection by members, with the exception of the directors' minute book and the company's accounting records. The reason for the exception is that these latter two documents must by their nature remain confidential. If members had access to board minutes then a director of X plc, a competitor of Y plc, would only have to buy a few shares in Y plc to obtain access to confidential information concerning the company.

TEST YOUR KNOWLEDGE 3.3 

(a) What is meant by a company's domicile? How does this differ from its registered address?

(b) List the essential registers, records and documents which are generally kept at a company's registered office.

4 The objects clause

This clause sets out what the company may do; it defines the specific purpose for which the company was formed. It is traditionally said to be a protection for the members and creditors of a company by restricting the purposes for which the company's funds can be used, though that function is of much reduced importance nowadays. Since the Companies Act 1989, a company's objects may simply state that it is a general commercial company. This leaves the directors free to take the company into any area of business which they see as potentially profitable.

Where a company does not state that it is a general commercial company, a company's objects clause will state what the company may do in both general and detailed terms. When this is so, the directors must ensure that all activities of the company fall within those objects; otherwise a member may obtain an injunction to prevent an *ultra vires* act under CA s. 35(2); and in principle the company should then cease to carry out the forbidden activity (subject to certain safeguards for third parties). The *ultra vires* rule is explained in greater detail in Chapter 4.

By CA 1985 s. 4, a company may change its objects for any reason by special resolution. When such a resolution is passed the directors must wait for 21 days during which the holders of 15 per cent of the shares of the company may object. When such an objection is raised the matter must go to court for it to sanction the alteration. In so doing the court may make any order it thinks fit to meet the objection. In the 15 days following the 21-day period, so long as no objection is raised, the directors must file with the Registrar of Companies a copy of the amended Memorandum and of the special resolution.

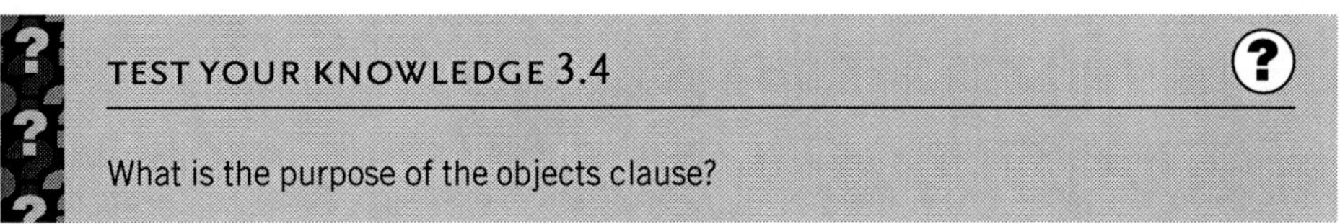

TEST YOUR KNOWLEDGE 3.4

What is the purpose of the objects clause?

5 The limited liability clause

The fourth clause in the Memorandum of a private company and the fifth in the case of a public company is a statement that the liability of members is limited if such is the case. In a company limited by shares, the liability of members is limited to any amounts unpaid on their shares. Partly paid shares are very rare today. If the company is limited by guarantee, the liability of the members is limited to the amount which they agreed to pay upon the winding up of the company.

It is possible for a limited company to re-register as unlimited and an unlimited company to re-register as limited. However, such re-registration is a one-way process. Once a limited company has re-registered as unlimited or an unlimited company has re-registered as limited the procedure cannot be reversed. By s.16, the liability of a member can never be increased without his consent in writing. The process of re-registration has already been detailed in Chapter 2.

6 The Articles of Association

6.1 The nature and purpose of the Articles

Articles (of Association)
The internal regulations of a company sent to the Registrar on incorporation.

Whereas the Memorandum of Association deals with matters such as the name, objects and capital of the company, all of which can be said to govern the external relations of the company, the **Articles of Association** are essentially concerned with its internal management. The Articles, and to a lesser extent the Memorandum, encapsulate the rights of the members.

6.2 Table A

Whereas every company must have its own separate Memorandum of Association, if only because the names of all companies are different, there is a considerable degree of common ground in the rules governing the internal running of almost all companies. For this reason, Parliament has provided a model set of Articles known as Table A (to be found in the Companies (Tables A to F) Regulations SI 1985/805 as amended by the Companies Act 1985 (Electronic Communications) Order 2000) which apply to all companies except where a company has its own special Articles. Table A contains considerable detail, running to over 100 articles, on matters such as the shares of the company, its meetings, directors, secretary and dividends, and many other miscellaneous matters.

Whenever there is a consolidation of company law, Parliament introduces a new Table A. A particularly troublesome matter in practice is that there are often significant differences from one Table A to another and it is the Table A which was in force at the time of the incorporation of a company which applies to it. For example, during the twentieth century there were new Table As in 1908, 1929, 1948 and 1985. Thus, a company incorporated in 1954 is subject to the 1948 Table A, a company incorporated in 1935 is subject to the 1929 Table A, and so on. The 1985 Table A applies to companies incorporated on or after 1 July 1985.

It is possible for a company to adopt Table A in total. Section 7 of CA 1985 provides

FIGURE 3.2 Using Table A in practice

A simple illustration should explain how Table A applies to companies and how it may be disapplied. Articles 50 and 88 of the 1985 Table A provide that the chairman of the board of directors has a second or casting vote in board meetings and general meetings. Thus if a company has two shareholders, each of whom have 50 per cent of the shares, and they vote on a resolution, one for and one against, whichever of them is chairman has a second vote and so may carry the resolution.

This may well not be acceptable to the person who is not chairman and so the company may well have its own special Article which states that Articles 50 and 88 of Table A in so far as they relate to a chairman's casting vote do not apply to the company. Thus, there is no casting vote and neither member can dominate the other in meetings.

that a company limited by shares may register Articles whereas an unlimited company or a company limited by guarantee must do so. Since we are predominantly concerned in this syllabus with limited companies, Table A is of the greatest significance. By s. 8(2) Table A applies to all such companies unless specifically excluded or modified by the company's own Articles. For the purposes of the Corporate Law syllabus you are expected to be familiar with the key provisions of the 1985 Table A.

6.3 Statutory rules concerning Articles

By CA 1985 s. 7(3), any special Article which a company files with the Registrar must be:

1 printed;
2 in numbered paragraphs; and
3 signed by the subscribers to the Memorandum in the presence of a witness.

7 The statutory contract

section 14 contract

The statutory contract that states that the Memorandum and Articles, once registered, constitute a contract between the company and its members and between the members themselves.

By CA 1985 s. 14, the Memorandum and Articles, once registered, bind the company and the members as though signed and sealed by each member and as though they contained covenants by the members to observe their provisions. This is known as the **s. 14 contract**. As such, the Memorandum and Articles constitute a contract between the company and its members and between the members themselves and can be enforced by a member against the company, by the company against a member and by a member against a member.

As described above, the Articles contain many provisions which affect the company and its members. For example, they may contain the following provisions:

1 Each member shall have one vote for every share which he holds.
2 If any member wishes to sell his shares, the other members shall take them from him pro rata at a valuation determined by the auditor.

Not all members buy their shares directly from the company, as outlined in Figure 3.3.

FIGURE 3.3 **The statutory contract between company and member**

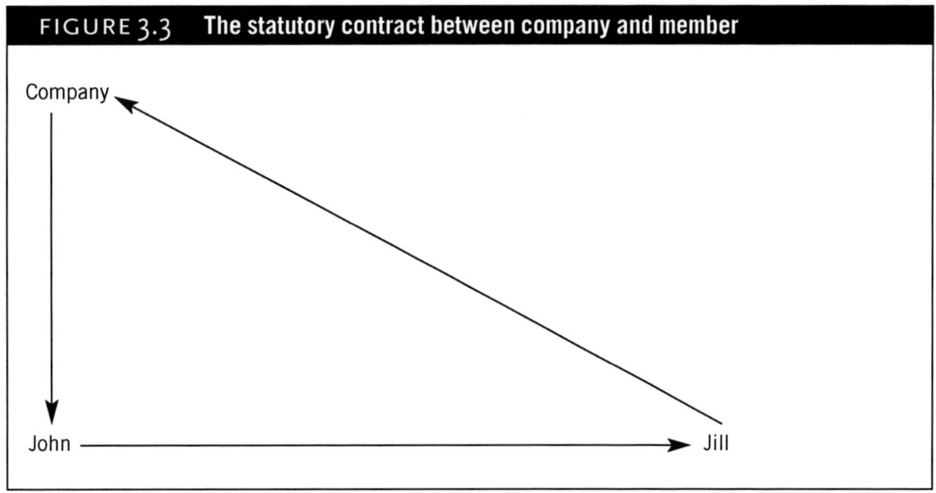

John bought his shares by way of an issue by the company. After a while, he sold his shares to Jill. Since John bought his shares from the company, there is a contractual relationship between him and the company. There is, however, no common law contractual relationship between Jill and the company. The effect of the statutory contract is that Jill and the company are treated as being in a contractual relationship. This allows Jill to enforce a provision of the Articles, such as how her votes can be exercised.

Similarly, members of a company are not in a contractual relationship together, as outlined in Figure 3.4.

Both Peter and Paul have bought shares from the company, and so they are both in a common law contractual relationship with the company. However, there is no common law contractual relationship between Peter and Paul. The effect of the statutory contract in this example is that, if Peter wishes to leave the company, and the Articles apply, he can force Paul to buy his shares.

FIGURE 3.4 **The statutory contract between members**

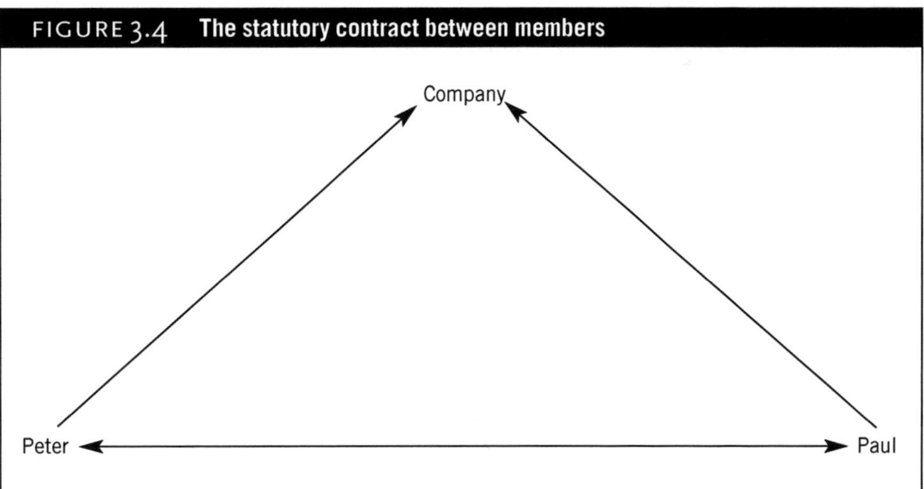

The wording of s. 14 is not very satisfactory and the courts have made rather hard work of interpreting it. However, the generally accepted effect of this statutory contract can be expressed in the following propositions:

1 The members are contractually bound to the company in so far as the Articles give them obligations in their capacity as members, as seen in Case Example 3.4.

CASE EXAMPLE 3.4 

***Hickman* v *Kent or Romney Marsh Sheep-Breeders' Association* [1915] 1 Ch 881**

A company's Articles of Association stated that any dispute between the Association and its members should go to arbitration. A member tried to take proceedings against the company in court. It was held that the Articles constituted a contract between the company and the member and the member in question therefore had to submit to arbitration. His legal proceedings had to be discontinued.

2 The company is similarly bound to the members in their capacity as members (see Case Example 3.5).

CASE EXAMPLE 3.5 

***Salmon* v *Quin & Axtens Ltd* [1909] 1 Ch 311**

The Articles provided that although the general management of the company was under the control of the directors, no resolution could be passed by the directors for acquiring or letting premises without the express consent of Salmon, the managing director. A resolution was passed by the directors for acquiring or letting premises in circumstances where Salmon expressly dissented. It was held that Salmon could obtain an injunction to restrain the company from acting in breach of this Article.

3 The Articles constitute a contract between the members in their capacity as members (see Case Example 3.6).

CASE EXAMPLE 3.6 

***Rayfield* v *Hands* [1960] Ch 1**

An Article of the company provided every member who intends to transfer shares shall inform the directors, who will take the said shares equally between them at a fair value. A member informed the directors that he wished to transfer his shares, but they refused to buy them from him. It was held that the Article created an obligation upon the directors as members to take the shares and the member wishing to leave the company could force the directors to acquire them.

However, the company is only bound to the members in their capacity as members (see Case Example 3.7).

CASE EXAMPLE 3.7 

***Eley* v *Positive Life Assurance Co. Ltd* [1876] 1 Ex D 20**

An Article of the company stated that Eley should be the solicitor to the company for life. He bought shares in the company. Subsequently, the company disposed of his services. Eley sued for breach of contract. It was held that his action must fail since the Article in question gave rights to him in a capacity other than as a member of the company. In other words, they gave him the right as legal adviser. The court said that the s. 14 contract only gave rights to members in their capacity as members.

There has been much academic writing about this decision over recent years. The wording of s.14 leaves a lot to be desired, and statutory revision is urgently needed. The section itself states that, once registered, the Memorandum and Articles constitute a contract between the company and its members and contain no exceptions to this rule. However, the general interpretation is that only membership rights can be enforced by the use of the section. Thus, an entitlement to receive a dividend or vote in general meeting can be enforced in this way where such a right is contained in the Articles. However, a right such as that enjoyed by Eley, that he should be solicitor to the company for life, could not be enforced since it was not a general membership right.

However, it is possible for a separate service contract expressly to incorporate the provisions of a company's Articles as seen in Case Example 3.8.

CASE EXAMPLE 3.8

***Re New British Iron Co. Ltd ex parte Beckwith* [1898] 1 Ch 324**

An Article stated that the directors should be paid £1,000 p.a. remuneration. The directors were members of the company. When they were not paid they sued the company for breach of contract and it was held that the Article was evidence of the terms of that contract.

Nowadays, it would be unusual for directors to rely on the Articles protect the rights due to them under their service contracts. Generally, directors have properly drawn up service contracts detailing their rights and obligations to the company.

Problems arise occasionally where Articles fail to refer to some matter which should have been clarified.

CASE EXAMPLE 3.9

***Bratton Seymour Service Co. Ltd* v *Oxborough* [1992] BCLC 693**

The Articles of a company set up to manage a block of flats omitted to state that the members were required to contribute towards the charge for certain amenity areas and the swimming pool. Although it was clear that this was an oversight, it was held that the Memorandum and Articles form a distinctive type of contract in that the members' rights with regard to the company are encapsulated within the Memorandum and Articles – which are on public record and available for all creditors to inspect – and it is not possible to introduce extrinsic evidence as to what the original founders of the company meant to have included in the Articles, or for the courts to rewrite the Articles. The only way to make the members pay for the amenities and swimming pool (at least in terms of company law) was to alter the Articles by means of a special resolution.

The issue of what rights members may expect to have arisen also in Case Example 3.10.

CASE EXAMPLE 3.10

***Re Astec (BSR) plc* [1998] 2 BCLC 556**

Minority shareholders in a company registered in Hong Kong but listed on the London Stock Exchange retained shares in their company in the expectation that the majority shareholders would abide by the Listing Rules and buy the minority shareholders out. Contrary to their expectations, the majority shareholders did not do so, and so the minority petitioned the court under Companies Act 1985 s. 459 for relief (see Chapter 10). It was held that although the minority's expectation was understandable, being bought out in terms of the Listing Rules was nevertheless not a requirement that was specified in the company's Articles. The minority members had entered the company in the knowledge of the effect of the Hong Kong equivalent of Companies Act 1985 s.14 and could not expect to have any further rights than those given to them under the Memorandum and Articles, notwithstanding that the company was not adhering to the Listing Rules.

This case therefore reinforces the supremacy of the s. 14 'mutual covenants' and the view that the Memorandum and Articles state the rights of the parties thereto.

8 Shareholders' agreements

Sometimes the members of a company will determine to regulate the relationship between them by means of a shareholders agreement. This is a contract entered into sometimes between just the members themselves and sometimes between the members and the company. Such a document is a contract and its provisions can be enforced by any party to the contract against another. Shareholder agreements were considered in *Russell v Northern Bank Development Corporation Limited*.

CASE EXAMPLE 3.11

***Russell* v *Northern Bank Development Corporation Limited* [1992] 3 All ER 161**

The company had been formed with twenty £1 shares. Four individuals held 20 shares; the remaining 120 were held by the Bank. There was a shareholders agreement between all the members whereby there should be no increase in the share capital unless every member agreed. Some of the members wanted to amend this, arguing that any provision in the Articles of Association of a company purporting to restricted the statutory power to alter those Articles was invalid and that therefore an agreement outside the Articles imposing such a fetter should likewise be invalid. It was held by the House of Lords that the provision in the shareholders agreement did not constitute any unlawful or invalid fetter on the company's statutory power to increase its share capital. It was merely a personal agreement outside the Articles between the shareholders who had executed it as to how they would exercise their voting rights in relation to any further issue of shares.

9 Alteration of the Articles

special resolution

A resolution passed by a three-quarters vote of those members present and voting or voting by proxy.

d

general meeting

A meeting of the members of a company.

By CA 1985 s. 9, a company may alter its Articles at any time by **special resolution** in **general meeting**. When this is done, copies of the resolution and the amended Articles must be filed with the Registrar.

Although a company is free to alter its Articles, this freedom is subject to a number of rules:

1 Of the two documents, the Memorandum and Articles of Association, the Memorandum is the superior document. If there is any conflict between provisions in the Memorandum or Articles, the Memorandum prevails. Thus the alteration must be subject to the Memorandum.
2 The alteration must be lawful. In other words it must not conflict either with the provisions of the Act or with any other rule of law (s. 9).
3 When members object to an alteration of the objects under CA 1985 s. 5, or when the court deals with an unfair prejudice application under s. 459 (see Chapter 8), it is open to the court to alter the company's Articles and to prohibit any further alteration of that amended Article without the consent of the court. When such an order is made, any alteration must be with the consent of the court.
4 By s. 16, an alteration cannot increase the liability of any member without his consent in writing.
5 If the alteration is of class rights, it is subject to the right of dissentients to object under s. 127 (see Chapter 5).
6 Any alteration must be bona fide for the benefit of the company as a whole. It must not be a potential fraud on minority shareholders. This is explored in the cases outlined in Case Example 3.12.

CASE EXAMPLE 3.12

***Brown* v *Abrasive Wheel Co.* [1919] 2 Ch 90**

A proposed alteration of the Articles would have permitted the directors to expropriate the shares of any member. It was held that such alteration was unlawful as being a potential fraud on members.

On the other hand:

***Sidebottom* v *Kershaw, Leese & Co. Limited* [1920] 1 Ch 154**

A proposed alteration of the Articles would permit the directors to expropriate the shares of any member who carried on a competing business it was held that such an alteration was valid as being genuinely for the protection of the company.

Another case where this was considered was:

***Allen* v *Gold Reefs of West Africa Ltd* [1900] 1 Ch 656**

Articles gave the company a lien on partly paid shares in respect of all debts and liabilities owing to the company by the members. A member died with unpaid calls due on his shares. The Articles of the company were altered so as to give the company a lien on fully paid shares.

It was held that the alteration was valid. The fact that the member concerned was actually the only member of the company with fully paid shares gave rise to some suspicion as to whether the alteration was bona fide, but on balance it was felt that the alteration was for the benefit of the company.

It is for the shareholders rather than for the court to say whether an alteration is for the benefit of the company, unless this is so apparent that no reasonable man could consider it otherwise, as in Case Example 3.13.

CASE EXAMPLE 3.13

Shuttleworth v Cox Bros & Co. (Maidenhead) Ltd [1927] 2 KB 9

Articles provided that Shuttleworth and some other persons should be permanent directors of the company, unless they were disqualified from office by the occurrence of one of several specified events. None of these events occurred but on no less than 22 occasions in a period of a year Shuttleworth failed to account for the company's money which he had received. An alteration was made to the Articles to disqualify a director from office if the other directors, in writing, requested that director's resignation. A request for Shuttleworth's resignation was made pursuant to the Article.

It was held that the alteration was bona fide for the benefit of the company. Clearly, the members as a whole felt that it was so beneficial that the court would not interfere with the allegation.

An alteration is not necessarily not for the benefit of the company even if those members voting for the alteration have a personal interest in the outcome of the resolution, as in Case Example 3.14.

CASE EXAMPLE 3.14

***Greenhalgh* v *Arderne Cinemas Ltd* (1951)**

Articles of a private company provided that shares could not be transferred to a non-member as long as any other member of the company was prepared to buy them at a fair value. The holder of the majority of the shares in the company wished to transfer his shares to a non-member, and so the Articles were altered to allow shares to be transferred to any person so long as an ordinary resolution of the members was passed approving the transfer. It was held that such alteration was valid notwithstanding the loss by the minority of their rights of pre-emption.

TEST YOUR KNOWLEDGE 3.5

(a) What is Table A and what is its function?

(b) What rules restrict a company's freedom to alter its Articles of Association?

10 Future reforms

ultra vires
Literally 'beyond its powers'. The expression is usually used to refer to a transaction entered into by a company that is beyond its powers. Sometimes it is also used to refer to a transaction beyond the powers of the directors.

There is taking place, at the time of writing, a far-reaching review of company law and it is likely that if its recommendations are implemented the traditional Memorandum and Articles will be replaced by a company constitution containing the key provisions of the Memorandum and Articles. In the process it is envisaged that the objects clause and the **ultra vires** rule (see Chapter 4) may well be dispensed with. However, the existing rules may be retained to some extent for charitable companies.

CHAPTER SUMMARY

- This chapter deals with the contents of the Memorandum and Articles of Association. These documents represent the constitution of the company.
- The Memorandum gives such information as is necessary for anyone considering dealing with, or investing in, the company.
- The Memorandum, therefore, deals with matters such as the company's name, its registered office and the purposes for which it was formed. The restrictions imposed by the law on the information contained in the Memorandum are designed in part to protect those members of the public who deal with the company.
- The Articles govern the company's internal workings and the way in which it conducts its business.
- Delegated legislation made under the Companies Act 1985 provides a model set of Articles (Table A) which companies may adopt if they choose.
- Although a company may alter its Articles it cannot escape liability for breach of contract by doing so. If, however, the alteration results in the company being in breach, the person so affected may have a right of action against the company
- The Memorandum and Articles once registered constitute a contract between the company and its members and between the members themselves.

Note: We shall be referring to the Memorandum and, especially, to the Articles throughout the rest of the book.

part **two**

Company Transactions, Shares and Debentures

LIST OF CHAPTERS

Overview

In Part 2 we examine company transactions, shares and debentures. First, we look at how a company can make a contract and matters that arise on the contract. Then, we move on to look at the capital of a company. Every company requires capital and this capital can be provided either by way of shares or debentures (loan capital). We shall look at the rules governing the issue of shares, their transfer and transmission. Next, we consider at how in certain circumstances companies can acquire their own shares. Finally, we look at loan capital and the remedies of the providers of loan capital when a company defaults.

CHAPTER 4

A company's contracts

CONTENTS

LEARNING OUTCOMES

This chapter covers the way in which companies make contracts and limitations upon the authority to make contracts that might be imposed by the Memorandum and Articles of the company. After reading and understanding the contents of the chapter and studying the case examples, you should be able to:

- Understand the nature and purpose of the objects clause and the *ultra vires* rule.
- Understand why directors usually can make whatever contracts they wish on behalf of their companies.
- Explain why the law was in need of revision in the late 1980s.
- Explain the changes that were result of of this.
- Understand the limitations that might be imposed on the powers of directors.
- Know how a company can execute a document.

1 Introduction: the objects clause and the *ultra vires* rule

As we have seen, a company is a body corporate, an artificial legal person. Being an artificial legal person it cannot make contracts itself. It can only act through agents. These agents are usually the directors, and the actions of the directors are constrained partly by company law generally and partly by the Memorandum and Articles of Association.

1.1 The objects clause

Historically, the directors have always been expected to ensure that the company only carried out acts that were encompassed within the terms of the objects clause. In a once celebrated case, *Re German Date Coffee Co.* (1882) 20 CH D 169, a small number of members were able to have their company wound up on the grounds that the company had not precisely followed the wording of the objects clause – even though the company was solvent and most of the other members had no objection to the company's deviation from the objects clause. Consequently, a great deal of attention has to be paid to the wording of the objects clause.

CA 1985 s. 2 states that the Memorandum must set out the objects of the company. Lord Wrenbury, in *Cotman v Brougham* [1918] AC 514, said:

> 'When the Act says that the Memorandum must "state the objects" the meaning is that it must specify the objects, that it must delimit and identify the objects in such plain and unambiguous manner that the reader can identify the field of industry in which the corporate activities are to be confined.'

1.2 The *ultra vires* rule

In the very early days of company law the objects clause would be short and very much to the point, stating as pithily as possible precisely what the company was there to do. A contract entered into which is beyond the powers of the company is referred to as an *ultra vires* contract. This means literally 'beyond its powers'.

constructive notice

Deemed knowledge. A person dealing with a company traditionally is assumed to know of matters registered at Companies House. Thus, for example, a person taking security from a company is taken to be aware of any charges registered in the name of the company.

Under common law an *ultra vires* contract was a total nullity and could not be enforced by anyone, neither by the company nor by a third party. The justification for the harshness of this rule was the doctrine of **constructive notice**. Because the Memorandum and Articles of Association were public documents, anyone dealing with the company was presumed to be aware of their contents. Should he not have checked the documents before dealing with the company, he had only himself to blame if he could not enforce the contract. This could, of course, be very unfair to creditors, who might not have had the opportunity to inspect the company's objects clause.

Throughout the formative period of company law, these twin doctrines of *ultra vires* and constructive notice dominated its development. This was the case even though they were clearly out of line with commercial reality. It was, of course, ridiculous that an ordinary person dealing with a company should be taken to have read – and understood – its objects clause. In addition, to get round the twin effects of the *ultra vires* rule and the constructive notice rule, company lawyers had resorted to very long and complicated objects clauses permitting a company to carry out almost any act it wished – as most directors, perfectly reasonably, wanted, and in the process rather defeating the point of the rules. Reform was needed. Accordingly, it went to a company law specialist for his suggestions as to what should be done to clarify and simplify the law, and so the inroads made into the *ultra vires* doctrine do not reflect the position as it is now.

2 Reform

2.1 The Prentice Report

In 1985 the DTI asked Dr Prentice of Oxford University to report on the legal and commercial implications of the abolition of the *ultra vires* rule. In his report, he recommended that a company should have the capacity to carry on any activity whatever. He also recommended the abolition of the doctrine of constructive notice not only in respect of the contents of its Memorandum and Articles, but also of other matters such as special resolutions registered with the Registrar of Companies. The reforms in regard to the objects clause and the *ultra vires* rule were implemented by the Companies Act 1989. Constructive notice has still to be abolished.

2.2 The Companies Act 1989

Provisions introduced into the Companies Act 1985 by the Companies Act 1989 draw a distinction between defects in the capacity of the company and limitations on the authority of directors. Section 35(1) now provides that the validity of an act done by a company shall not be called into question on the ground of lack of capacity by reason of anything in the company's Memorandum. This means that a third party dealing with a company can generally assume that the company has the capacity to enter into the transaction that is being made. In other words, for all practical purposes it abolishes the *ultra vires* doctrine so far as third parties are concerned.

Ultra vires and members

By s. 35(2) a member may bring proceedings to restrain the doing of an act which, but for s. 35(1), would be beyond the capacity of the company, though such proceedings will not be permitted if the company is already under a legal obligation to proceed with the *ultra vires* transaction. In practice, this means that a member who discovered that his company was contemplating entering into a contract that was *ultra vires* the company's objects clause could obtain an injunction to prevent the contract taking place. However, if the contract had already been signed and was in the process of being carried out, to obtain an injunction to prevent the company from taking part in the contract would be unfair on the other party to the contract, and would also possibly render the company liable for breach of contract. So s. 35(2) provides that it is not possible to obtain an injunction once the contract is in place and the other party is expecting the company to fulfil its part of the bargain. This provision is necessary because of the so-called rule in *Foss* v *Harbottle* (1843) 67 ER 189 (considered in Chapter 10 below) which determines that when a wrong is done to a company the only person who can sue for a remedy is the company itself, either as a result of a decision to seek a remedy taken by the board or, if they fail to do so, by the members in general meeting. Section 35(2) provides an exception to this rule. A single member can sue to restrain an *ultra vires* act.

Ultra vires and directors

By s. 35(3) it is still the duty of the directors to observe any limitations on their powers flowing from the company's Memorandum. Any action by the directors which but for s. 35(1) would be beyond the capacity of the company may be ratified by the company only by special resolution of the members. This means that even though the directors have made the company enter into a contract which is not permitted by the objects clause, the members could nevertheless, by passing a special resolution, override the objects clause and permit the company to enter into the contract. Presumably (though the Act does not make this clear), in this situation the company could, by going to court, overturn any injunction obtained by a member objecting to the breach of the objects clause. Such a resolution to ratify an *ultra vires* transaction does not of itself relieve the directors or any other person from any personal liability. Such relief would have to be agreed separately by special resolution. The reason for this is that a prime duty falling upon the directors of a company is that they should be fully conversant with and understand the constitutional documents of their company. If, because they fail to observe the provisions of these constitutional documents, the company suffers loss, the company may bring proceedings against the directors for an indemnity for that loss. It should be noted that the provision applies not only to the directors but also to 'other persons'. It is assumed that these words have been added so as to include officers or employees of the company who participated with the directors in the *ultra vires* act.

TEST YOUR KNOWLEDGE 4.1 

(a) If a member of a company discovered that the company was about to enter an ultra vires contract which, in terms of its objects clause, it should not be entering, what may the member do about it?

(b) If the company is already in the middle of an ultra vires contract when the member discovers that the contract is already in place, what can the member do about it?

(c) If the members collectively discovered that the company was about to enter into an ultra vires contract, what could they do to render the contract acceptable?

(d) What should they further do to ensure that the directors were not liable to the company for making the company enter into the ultra vires contract?

3 Limitations on the authority of directors

A company's Articles may sometimes contain provisions which limit the power of directors.

The directors' authority may be further restricted by the objects clause. This restriction is preserved by s. 35(3) (see above). Until modifications were brought about in this area of law, the usual agency principle under which a third party could rely on the **ostensible authority** of an agent was substantially modified by the doctrine of constructive notice. The doctrine of constructive notice was itself modified by the rule in *Royal British Bank v Turquand* (1856) 6 El & Bl 327. In essence this rule provided that a third party dealing with the company could assume that any internal procedural rule had been complied with so long as there was no way in which he could have checked that this would be the case. For example, suppose the Articles were to provide that loans above a certain amount had to be approved by an ordinary resolution of the members. Since there was no way in which a third party would have access to such a resolution (since ordinary resolutions do not generally have to be filed with the Registrar) he could assume that the required resolution had indeed been passed. It would, of course, be otherwise if the required resolution were a special one, since all special resolutions have to be filed and so a third party would have been taken to have constructive notice of it.

d

ostensible authority

Apparent or seeming authority. The authority that one can assume a person purporting to act as an agent has.

CASE EXAMPLE 4.1 

***Royal British Bank* v *Turquand* (1856) 6 E&B 327**

Directors of a company were permitted to issue bonds, but only if they obtained prior authorisation from the members of the company. A bond was issued to the bank without such authorisation. The court had to decide whether the bond was valid. It was held that it was indeed valid and enforceable since the bank had no right to inspect the resolution of the members. Accordingly the Bank was entitled to assume that the resolution authorising the borrowing had been duly passed.

Although the rule in *Royal British Bank v Turquand* still has some limited applicability (for example, if a company followed the decision of an inquorate board) to most intents and purposes CA s. 35A provides the current law.

Section 35A deals with the related matters of lack of authority and constructive notice. 35A(1) provides that: 'In favour of a person dealing with a company in good faith, the power of the board of directors to bind the company, or to authorise others to do so, shall be deemed to be free of any limitations under the company's constitution.' It will be noted here that the provision is not restricted to transactions decided upon by the directors. In other words, it recognises that often corporate transactions will be entered into by officers of the company appointed by and acting under the authority of the board.

Under s. 35A(1) the third party must also be acting in good faith. The Act states that he is not in bad faith merely because he knows the transaction is *ultra vires*. Therefore, bad faith probably means that the third party must be a party to a fraud involving the company if he is not to be allowed to enforce the transaction.

The position changes if the third party is a director of the company. If a director were to make an *ultra vires* contract with his own company, he would be taken to know of the fact that the contract was *ultra vires* and therefore would not be allowed to enforce it against the company (CA 1985 s. 322A).

The application of s. 35A(1) was recently considered in the case of *Smith* v *Henniker-Major* [2002] BCC 768.

CASE EXAMPLE 4.2

***Smith* v *Henniker-Major* [2002] BCC 768**

A member of a two-man board purported to assign to himself a right of action against a solicitor who had allegedly been in breach of duty to the company. The purported assignment took place at a board meeting attended by the solicitor alone. Thus the board meeting was inquorate and so any decisions it purported to make were, on the face of it, void. The question which the Court of Appeal had to determine was whether the assignment was protected by s. 35A(1) and thus valid.

It was held that s. 35(A) did not save the transaction. The position of the director here was exceptional. He was not simply a director having some involvement in a corporate decision. He was the chairman of the company and, as such, it was his duty to know its constitution. Part of his duty was to ensure the correct application of that constitution. He had attempted to turn himself into a one-man board. He had made a mistake, and an honest mistake at that. Yet s. 35(1) did not save the transaction.

Section 35B states that: 'A party to a transaction with a company is not bound to enquire as to whether it is permitted by the company's Memorandum or as to any limitation on the powers of the board of directors to bind the company or authorise others to do so.' This adds very little to what is contained in ss. 35 and 35A. At the time of its being introduced the government intended revising the rules governing the registration of charges and the doctrine of constructive notice. The significance of s. 35B will lie with its interrelationship with the provisions that will be necessary to bring about these changes if and when they are introduced. However, since the provisions have not been implemented, there is no need to consider s. 35B further here.

WORKED EXAMPLE 4.1

A board of directors enter into two transactions with a third party. The first is *ultra vires* the company. The second is within the company's powers but beyond the scope of the authority of the board of directors under its Articles. The third party is refusing to honour either of the transactions. How do you advise the directors?

Answer

The company cannot simply enforce either of the transactions. The board should be aware of the internal illegality of each of them. The transaction that is *ultra vires* the company can be enforced only following its ratification by the members by special resolution under s.35(3). The second can be enforced only after ratification by ordinary resolution. It will be observed that s.35A contains no reference to ratification, and so ratification of a matter simply beyond the powers of the board is done by the common law method, namely by an ordinary resolution of the members.

By s. 735 these provisions are only of application to companies registered under company legislation. Thus the *ultra vires* doctrine still applies to:

- Companies incorporated by Act of Parliament;
- Building societies;

- Industrial and provident societies.

It is also retained with some modification in the case of charitable companies. However, in most other respects, the *ultra vires* doctrine is of limited significance.

Implied authority of employees to bind their companies

Sometimes the courts look at acts done by an individual director or officer of the company and hold the company to be bound by these acts by reason, not that he had actual authority, but rather that the board effectively put him in such a position that he could hold himself out as the agent of the company and further that it acquiesced in his so doing.

CASE EXAMPLE 4.3

***Hely-Hutchinson* v *Brayhead Ltd* [1967] 3 All ER 98**

The chairman of the company acted as its *de facto* managing director even though he had never been formally appointed as such. He purported to give a guarantee on behalf of the company. The question arose as to whether the company was bound to honour this guarantee. It was held by the Court of Appeal that the company was bound. While the director had no actual authority ensuing from his position as chairman, he had authority from the board to act as the company's chief executive, and the guarantee was just such a transaction that fell within the authority that would normally be expected to be enjoyed by a person in that position.

Sometimes the courts approach this by referring to the apparent authority of the officer concerned.

CASE EXAMPLE 4.4

***Freeman and Lockyer* v *Buckhurst Park Properties (Mangal) Ltd* [1964] 1 All ER 630**

The board of a property development company allowed one of its number to act as though he were the company's managing director. He employed architects on behalf of the company. The court had to consider whether the company was bound by this contract. It was held that it was bound. Even though the director concerned had never been appointed as managing director, his actions were within his apparent authority. This authority derived from the knowledge of the board that he was purporting to act as the agent of the company and its acquiescence in his so acting.

A similar approach might be adopted where the agent of the company is a senior employee rather than a director.

CASE EXAMPLE 4.5

***Pharmed Medicare Private Limited* v *Univar Limited* [2002] EWCA Civ 1569**

Through an employee (not a director) Univar ordered from Pharmed a medical preparation to be supplied at eight metric tonnes per month over a ten-month period at a price of $18 per kilo. Subsequently, the price of the product fell in the UK to $16 per kilo with the result that Univar would be making a considerable loss on what they had agreed to buy in.

The employee had previously ordered medical preparations from Pharmed, albeit of smaller amounts than under the present contract, and these transactions had been properly performed by both sides. Univar tried to get out of liability by claiming that the lack of internal authority of the employee to make contracts of this magnitude was sufficient to negate his contractual authority.

Longmore LJ said: '*For my part I cannot see why any grounds for suspicion should have existed. Previous transactions had been honoured. No one in Univar had made any suggestion that [the employee's] authority was, in any way, limited. There was no reason to think that Univar would not want to acquire or be unable to distribute eight metric tonnes per month, if the price was right. No complaint was, in fact, made about the transaction until Univar realised the price had not risen as far as they had expected.*'

Accordingly, Univar was bound by the contract.

The Court of Appeal had decided this case on the basis of the ostensible authority of the employee. No reference was made to CA s. 35A. It is suggested that the case could probably just as easily have been decided under this provision which provides 'in favour of a person dealing with a company in good faith, the power of the board of directors to bind the company, authorise others to do so, shall be deemed to be free of any limitation under the company's constitution', as could the Freeman and Lockyer and Hely-Hutchinson cases had they not have been decided before s.35A was enacted.

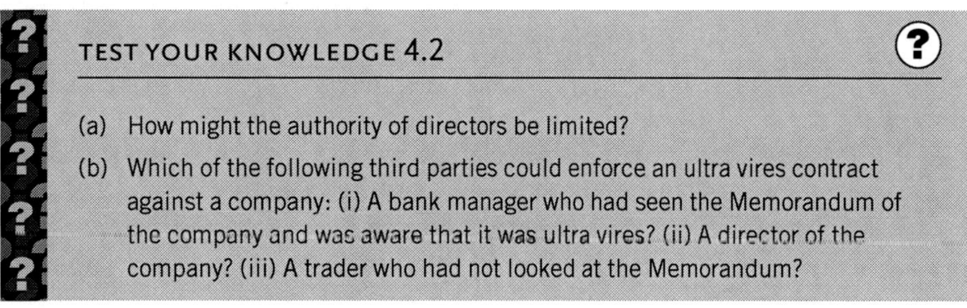

TEST YOUR KNOWLEDGE 4.2

(a) How might the authority of directors be limited?

(b) Which of the following third parties could enforce an ultra vires contract against a company: (i) A bank manager who had seen the Memorandum of the company and was aware that it was ultra vires? (ii) A director of the company? (iii) A trader who had not looked at the Memorandum?

4 Drafting the objects clause

4.1 The traditional approach

In theory the objects clause should be a fairly short statement of a company's purpose. However, it is perhaps logical that directors should wish to feel free to move their companies into any area of potentially profitable commercial activity. For this reason, objects clauses generally grew to be extensive and extremely comprehensive documents.

There are three techniques needed when drafting a traditional objects clause to ensure that the directors can do almost anything they wish:

1 The objects clause would be drawn extremely widely, with verbs being included to describe evry conceivable type of corporate activity.
2 The *Cotman* v *Brougham* clause (so named after the case of that name, reported at [1918] AC 514 where the efficacy of such a clause was first recognised) saying that each object should be read as being an object in its own right and that no object should be regarded as subsidiary or auxiliary to any other entry in the objects clause.
3 The *Bell Houses Ltd* v *CityWall Properties Ltd* clause (again so named after the case where its usefulness was first recognised, reported at [1996] 2 All ER 674) stating that the directors could carry on any trade or business which in their subjective view could be advantageously carried by the company in connection with or ancillary to any of the businesses specified in the objects clause.

Dr Prentice made the point in his report that instead of spending something in the region of twenty pages (as used to be the case) saying that in essence the company could do anything, the company might just as well in a couple of lines in its objects clause state that the company could do anything.

For this reason, a new s. 3A was introduced into the 1985 Act. This allows the Memorandum of a company to provide that it is a 'general commercial company', which permits the company 'to carry on any trade or business whatsoever'. Accordingly, the company then has power to do 'all such things as are incidental or conducive to the carrying on of any such trade or business by it'. Clearly, the intention here is to discourage the voluminous objects clauses which had prevailed.

However, the new provision is not without its problems:

- Does the reference to carrying on a trade or business imply that at the end of the day a profit must be intended to be made on behalf of the company? If so, problems could arise if the directors were to wish to make gratuitous donations, for example, for charitable or political purposes or to give guarantees.

- Also, could the reference to carrying on a trade or business preclude the selling off of part of a business?

For this reason, objects clauses taking advantage of the general commercial company format sometimes read:

> 'The company is a general commercial company but, without prejudice to the generality of the foregoing, it is hereby declared that . . .'

and then a further range of general powers is added. However, it is increasingly the case that companies are renouncing long objects clauses in favour of shorter ones, as was intended by the legislation. Certainly, since the implementation of s. 3A, there have been no significant reported cases on the *ultra vires* rules, and the reforms are beginning to have the desired effect.

The 'general commercial company' form of objects is therefore very seldom found without other provisions following.

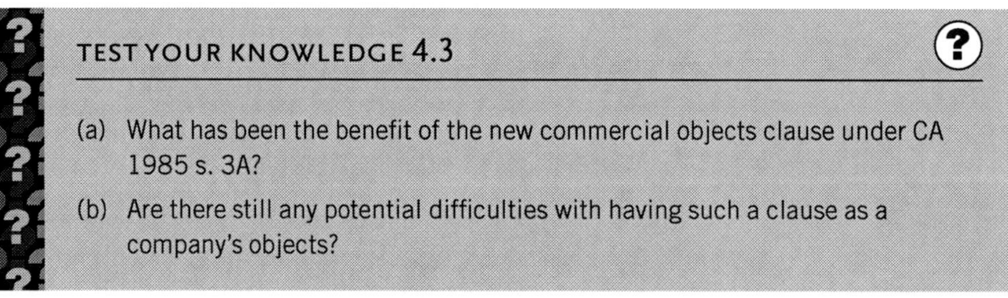

TEST YOUR KNOWLEDGE 4.3

(a) What has been the benefit of the new commercial objects clause under CA 1985 s. 3A?

(b) Are there still any potential difficulties with having such a clause as a company's objects?

common seal

The seal of a company; a device used for making an impressed mark upon a document so as to authenticate it.

5 Execution of documents by companies

A company may execute a document by affixing its **common seal** in the manner prescribed by its Articles of Association. Usually two directors, or the director and the company secretary, sign their names alongside the place where the impressed mark made by the seal on the stationery appears. They do not necessarily have to be present at the time the seal is affixed.

At one time all companies had to have a seal, but that requirement went in 1989. CA s. 36A now provides that a document signed by two directors or by a director and the secretary and expressed to be executed by the company shall be treated as given under seal. When execution is done in this way, the document concerned is treated as though the company has a seal which has been impressed upon the document. To protect third parties, a document that purports to be executed by the company and which is signed by a director and the secretary or by two directors of the company is deemed to have been duly executed by the company under seal. In other words, there is no need for third parties to investigate whether any persons purporting to sign documents in these capacities have been properly appointed.

The above procedure is generally required for formal legal documents, especially deeds, but may, if wished, be used for any legal document issued by the company. However, if the company is simply wanting to make a contract which does not have to be a deed, it is sufficient that this is simply done by a director or someone else having proper authority. Very few contracts have actually to be put into writing. If writing is needed, the signature of a director or other authorised person is sufficient formality.

TEST YOUR KNOWLEDGE 4.4 

State two ways in which a company can authenticate a legal document.

CHAPTER SUMMARY

- In this chapter we have looked at the manner in which a company makes its contracts and the limitations that may exist on its power to do so.
- A company acts *ultra vires* when it acts beyond the powers contained in its Memorandum.
- Today, the fact that a third party has entered into an *ultra vires* contract with a company does not generally preclude him from enforcing that contract against the company.
- However, the company is taken to know that it has acted unlawfully and so cannot simply enforce the contract, it has first to have the members pass a special resolution in general meeting to ratify the contract.
- A person dealing with a company can assume that the person with whom he is dealing has the authority to act as he is.
- Documents can be executed by the company impressing its seal upon the paper or stating that the document is executed by the company. In either case the signatures either of two directors or of a director and the secretary must be inserted on the document.

CHAPTER 5

Shares and share capital

CONTENTS

LEARNING OUTCOMES

This chapter covers the legal rules governing shares issued by a company. After reading and understanding the contents of the chapter and studying the case examples, you should be able to:

- Appreciate the ways in which a company can raise capital and the difference between share and loan capital.
- Understand how shares in both public and private companies are issued and paid for.
- Understand the way in which shares may be issued at a premium and the legal treatment of share premium account.
- Understand what the directors of a public company should do when the company suffers a serious loss of capital.
- Appreciate the various ways in which the capital of a company can be reduced.
- Understand reduction of capital.
- Understand the redemption of shares.
- Understand how a company might buy its own shares.
- Understand the register of members and the register of substantial share interests.

Introduction

debenture
The written evidence of a debt owing by a company; the document which creates or evidences a debt. Usually, though by no means always, a debenture is secured. This gives the creditor holding the debenture a priority over the unsecured creditors

class right
A right attaching to a class of share, usually in regard to a right to receive a dividend, the right to receive a return of capital on a winding up or the right to vote in general meeting.

In this chapter we look at the meaning of capital. Put at its simplest, this is the assets, expressed in monetary terms, with which the company operates. It can take two forms: share capital and loan capital. Share capital is the money provided by the members for the operation of the company. Loan capital is money borrowed for the purpose of operating the business, whether borrowed from a bank or other lending institutions or from individual **debenture holders**. We then move on to look at the different classes of shares which exist and the rights enjoyed by share holders, known as **class rights**. The holders of shares are **members** of the company. As such they have those rights that are given to them by the Memorandum and Articles. These rights may relate to the payment of dividends, the return of capital on a winding up and the entitlement to vote at a general meeting. The word 'debenture' means a written memorandum of a loan, a document which creates or evidences a debt. Debenture holders are lenders to the company. They are not members. They are owed money by the company and so are creditors. Debentures are covered in more detail in Chapter 7.

THEORY INTO PRACTICE 5.1

A company with existing shareholders wishes to raise further funds, and the existing shareholders are unwilling to invest further funds into the company. Further funds could be raised by the issue of shares to new shareholders or by the issue of debentures. What are the advantages and disadvantages from the point of view of the company and the provider of the funds in each case?

Answer

With shares, the existing shareholders will have their stake in the company watered down. The company will have an increased number of owners and if the same level of profits is maintained despite the injection of capital, shareholders will receive lower dividends. Advantageously for the company, the new investor cannot expect to receive dividends on his investment unless profits are made. However, if in the long run the investment is a good one and the company makes profits, the investor may ultimately obtain capital appreciation from his shares as well as dividends, thus providing a double benefit to him.

member
A shareholder in a company limited by shares or a guarantor in a company limited by guarantee.

With debentures the existing owners of the company do not have their stake in the company watered down; this is because debenture holders do not own the company and are merely creditors of the company. However, irrespective of the level of profits, interest must be paid on debentures otherwise the debenture holders have various remedies available to them. For example, if the debenture is secured a receiver may be appointed over the company's affairs. In addition, debenture holders receive their interest before shareholders receive their dividends, so that in some respects a debenture is a more reliable, if less exciting, investment.

capital
The money or money's worth through which a company finances its business.

1 The meaning of capital

At its very simplest, **capital** can be defined as the assets, expressed in monetary terms, with which a company operates. It takes a number of different forms.

authorised or nominal capital
The face value of the shares of a company which the company is permitted to issue by its Memorandum of Association.

1.1 Types of capital

Authorised capital

Authorised capital, expressed in terms of the total nominal value, is the amount of share capital which the company is authorised to issue. It is set out in the Memorandum of Association (see Chapter 3). The amount of the company's authorised capital depends on the business requirements of the company and, in the early days, the ability of the promoters to provide funds.

Issued capital

Issued capital is that part of the company's authorised capital which has actually been issued to the members. A company is under no obligation to issue all its authorised capital and frequently there is a difference between the level of authorised capital and the level of issued capital. The nominal value of the issued share capital of a public limited company must be at least £50,000 (CA 1985, ss. 11 and 118).

paid-up capital
That amount of a company's issued share capital that has been paid by its members.

Paid-up capital

Paid-up capital is that part of the issued capital of a company which has been paid up by the members. For example, a company may issue 1,000 shares of £1 nominal value of which 25p has been paid. The paid-up-capital of the company is therefore £250. The members still owe the company 75p for each share which they hold.

uncalled capital
The amount of a company's issued share capital that remains to be paid by its members.

Uncalled capital

Uncalled capital is the amount of capital which has been issued to the members but not yet paid for. It used to be a mark of respectability in companies that they had large amounts of uncalled capital. The rationale of this was that if the company were to go into liquidation, the liquidator would call in the uncalled capital and the creditors could be sure that this amount at least would be available for the payment of the company's debts. However, the experiences of many investors in the recession of the 1920s, when often they were called upon to make such payments after their companies had gone into liquidation, resulted in uncalled capital becoming unfashionable. Today, shares are almost always fully paid up on issue or within a relatively short time after issue.

Reserve capital

When a company has uncalled capital, it may by special resolution resolve that all or part of that uncalled capital will only be called up in the event and for the purpose of the company being wound up. When it does this, that part of the capital which was the subject of the resolution can only be called up in the event of the company going into liquidation (s. 120).

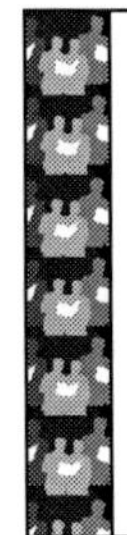

THEORY INTO PRACTICE 5.2 

Why do you think that reserve capital is very rarely encountered in practice?

Answer

Because it can only be called up by a liquidator. In other words, as far as the shareholders are concerned, it is simply throwing good money after bad when a liquidation occurs.

Reference to capital on a company's stationery

Very occasionally a company will refer to the amount of its share capital on its stationery. When it does so the reference must be to its paid-up share capital (s. 351(2)).

TEST YOUR KNOWLEDGE 5.1 

(a) What is the difference between authorised and issued capital?
(b) Define uncalled capital.

2 Payment for shares

2.1 The general rule

allottee

A person to whom shares have been allotted by a company; a shareholder.

By s. 99(1), shares allotted by a company and any premium on them may be paid up in money or money's worth. In other words, when a company **allots shares** either to an existing member or to someone who is becoming a member for the first time (allottee), those shares must be paid for either in cash or by the transfer of an asset to the company. Money's worth includes goodwill and know-how.

For example, if two people are starting a business and each has £500 to put into the business, they could each take 500 £1 shares. They might also put into the business their cars in exchange for further shares. Suppose that each has a car worth £4,500 then, together with the money which they are putting in, the total assets of the company would be £10,000 and the share capital 10,000 shares of £1 each. The share capital is shown on the liability side of the balance sheet, the cash and cars on the assets side.

It is sometimes difficult to see how goodwill can be regarded as a payment for shares. However, think of the case of *Salomon v Salomon & Co. Ltd* (see Chapter 1). In this case a shoe manufacturer sold his business which he had built up as a sole trader to a limited liability company of which he was the dominant shareholder. The entire undertaking of the business, including the goodwill, was what he put in to the limited liability company in return for the shares which he took in it.

CASE EXAMPLE 5.1

Examine the following balance sheet:

Ordinary shares £20,000	Cash	£2,000
	Property	£18,000

In this example, the shares have been partly paid up by cash and partly by the transfer of property to the company. The shares are shown on the balance sheet as a liability since it is something that the liquidator must seek to repay on a liquidation. However, in practice, it is the locked-in shareholders interest to which the creditors can look for the payment of debts owing to them. As such, the law dictates that the company must seek to do what it can to maintain its capital. For example, dividends must be paid out of profits rather than from capital.

In the absence of fraud, the courts will not enquire into the value that the directors of a private company put on any non-cash asset being taken into the company in return for shares. This is illustrated by Case Example 5.2.

CASE EXAMPLE 5.2

***Re Wragg Ltd* [1897] 1 Ch 796**

Goodwill, stock in trade and other property belonging to a business was sold to a company and was partly paid for in shares. The value was shown in the company's books at a figure significantly less than that placed on it in the contract of sale. The company subsequently went into liquidation and the liquidator brought misfeasance proceedings against the directors. It was held that provided they had acted honestly the directors were not liable; the agreement that they had made on behalf of the company for it to acquire the assets could not be reopened. As there was no suggestion that the directors had acted dishonestly the adequacy of the consideration could not be questioned.

2.2 Special rules governing the allotment of shares by public companies

A number of special rules apply only to public companies:

allottee

A person to whom shares have been allotted by a company; a shareholder.

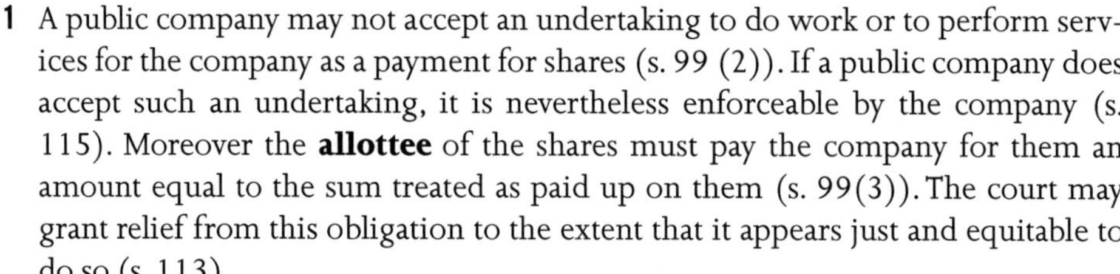

1 A public company may not accept an undertaking to do work or to perform services for the company as a payment for shares (s. 99 (2)). If a public company does accept such an undertaking, it is nevertheless enforceable by the company (s. 115). Moreover the **allottee** of the shares must pay the company for them an amount equal to the sum treated as paid up on them (s. 99(3)). The court may grant relief from this obligation to the extent that it appears just and equitable to do so (s. 113).

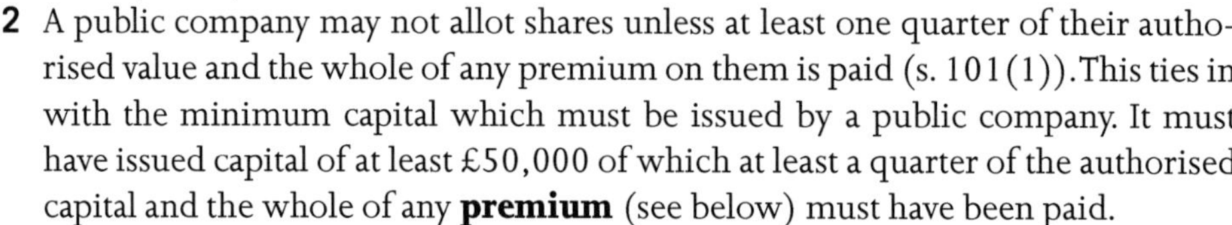

2 A public company may not allot shares unless at least one quarter of their authorised value and the whole of any premium on them is paid (s. 101(1)). This ties in with the minimum capital which must be issued by a public company. It must have issued capital of at least £50,000 of which at least a quarter of the authorised capital and the whole of any **premium** (see below) must have been paid.

premium

The amount paid for a share by an allottee over and above the nominal value of that share.

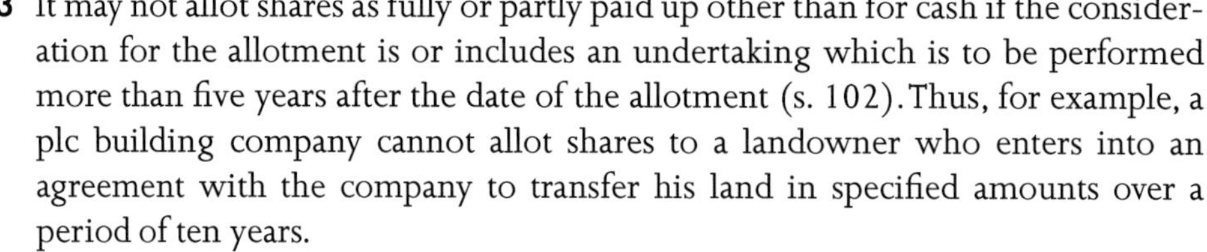

3 It may not allot shares as fully or partly paid up other than for cash if the consideration for the allotment is or includes an undertaking which is to be performed more than five years after the date of the allotment (s. 102). Thus, for example, a plc building company cannot allot shares to a landowner who enters into an agreement with the company to transfer his land in specified amounts over a period of ten years.

4 It may not allot shares as fully or partly paid otherwise than for cash unless the consideration for the allotment has been independently valued (s. 103). This means that, to take the above example of a landowner transferring land to the company in return for shares, before the land is transferred it must be valued.
   - A report on the valuation must be made to the company within the six months immediately prior to the allotment of the shares, a copy sent to Companies House and a copy of the report must also be sent to the proposed allottee of the shares (s. 103(1)).
   - The valuation must be done by an independent person, who must be a person qualified to be appointed or to continue to be an auditor of the company (s. 108(1)). This does not mean that the valuer must necessarily be the auditor of the company, though he must be a qualified auditor. The Companies Act permits the independent person appointed to make the valuation to delegate the actual task of carrying out the valuation to a person who appears to him to have the requisite knowledge and experience to value the consideration. Such a person must not be an officer or servant of the company (s. 108(2)). The underlying rationale of this section seems to be that a professionally qualified auditor must take charge of the valuation process though he need not himself actually carry out the valuation.

   The requirement for non-cash assets to be valued does not apply to the allotment of shares by a company in connection with a proposed merger with another company (s. 103(5)).

In the event of shares being allotted in contravention of any of these provisions, the allottee becomes liable to pay the company the amount which should have been paid in respect of the share or the amount which is treated as paid on the share. This is subject to the overriding right of the court to grant relief from this obligation if and to the extent that it appears just and equitable to do so (s. 113(2)). Thus, for example, suppose a plc building company allots shares to the value of £1 million in respect of land transferred to the company in circumstances where no valuation was made of the land. There is a prima facie liability on the allottee of the shares to pay to the company the £1 million allowed in respect of the land. He also has to pay interest on this money at the appropriate rate from the time of allotment of the shares (s. 105(31)). The 'appropriate rate' means 5 per cent per annum or such other rate as may be specified by the Secretary of State by statutory instrument (s. 107). If, however, on enquiry the land is found to be worth at least the £1 million allowed for it, the court would doubtless exonerate the allottee from his obligation to make the payment since the company will have received an appropriate level of consideration for the shares.

stock watering

The issue of shares by a company in return for the transfer to the company of assets worth significantly less than the value placed upon them in the contract.

asset value

The underlying value of a share expressed in terms of the assets that it represents. It is calculated by taking the net value of all the assets of the company and dividing this figure by the number of shares that the company has issued.

The reason for all the above rules is to prevent 'dilution' of equity or '**stock watering**'. This means the allotment of shares by a company in return for the transfer to the company of assets worth significantly less than the value placed upon them in the contract or in return for services or undertakings that may never be carried out or are worth less than suggested. The real value of shares is underpinned by their **asset value**. If further shares are allotted by a company in return for overvalued assets, the underlying asset value of the shares held in the company prior to that allotment will be reduced. Thus, the rule protects the existing shareholders in the company and to some extent should reassure creditors.

2.3 Allotment of shares at a premium

Sometimes a company will allot shares for a sum greater than their nominal value. This is known as allotting shares at a premium. Case Example 5.3 illustrates why companies may wish to allot shares at a premium.

CASE EXAMPLE 5.3

A and B commence business with a share capital of £1,000. Each has 500 £1 shares. The nominal value of the shares is £1. On the day the company commences trading there is £1,000 in the bank and thus the underlying asset value per share is also £1. After trading for one year, the company has made a further £1,000 profit. Thus, there is £2,000 in the bank. Accordingly, the underlying asset value per share is £2. Suppose that at this point C were to join the company. He is prepared to invest £1,000. If C were to be allowed 1,000 shares in the company of £1 nominal value, there would then be 2,000 shares and an asset base of £3,000 (i.e. the initial £1,000 put in by A and B 1 £1,000 profits 1 £1,000 from C). Thus, upon C joining in this way the underlying asset value per share held by A and B has dropped dramatically. To avoid this C would be allowed to join the company by taking 500 shares at a price of £2, i.e. £1 nominal value and £1 premium. The share capital of the company would go up to £1,500 and the asset base to £3,000. A and B would maintain the asset value of their shares at £2 per share. In other words, whenever a successful company allots shares to an outsider, those shares must be allotted at a premium if the existing shareholders are to maintain the value of their holdings within the company.

If a company issues shares at a premium, whether such issue is for cash or for consideration other than cash, a sum equal to the value of the premiums must be transferred in the accounts of the company to 'the share premium account'.

This is very substantially treated as share capital and all the provisions of the Act which relate to the reduction of a company's share capital apply as if the share premium account were part of the paid-up share capital of the company (s. 130(3)).

To this general principle there are five exceptions. The share premium account may be used to:

1 Pay up unissued shares which are allotted to members as fully paid bonus shares. What this means is that the funds in the share premium account are converted into further shares in the company and are then issued to the members in proportion to their existing holdings. This reduces the size of the share premium account but increases the number of shares in the company. Since normally it is very difficult to take funds from the share premium account without a reduction of capital, it is also a way of releasing capital to the members since the members may be able to sell their newly obtained shares.

2 Write off the company's preliminary expenses.
3 Write off the expenses of or the commission paid or discount allowed on any issue of shares or debentures of the company.
4 Provide for the premium payable on the redemption of debentures of the company (s. 130(2)).
5 Pay off any premium on the redemption or purchase by companies of their own shares (s. 171).

Shares may be allotted not only for cash but also for a consideration other than for cash. This applies whether or not the shares are issued at a premium. To return to our example of a company allotting shares in return for land being transferred to it, suppose that the company is allotting shares to the nominal value of £1 million in return for land valued at £1,200,000. The additional £200,000 is a premium on the shares and has to be shown as such in the accounts of the company. This also applies where a company acquires shares in another company as a result of a takeover, in circumstances where the value of the shares acquired is greater than the value of the shares which are allotted. Once again the difference has to be placed in the share premium account.

Historically, the result of this was that profits in the books of the company which was acquired in the takeover become frozen in the share premium account of the company which effected the takeover. As such they could not be used for the payment of dividends, since dividends cannot be paid out of capital (s. 263). As this rule was a significant barrier to takeover activity, the law was changed and the current position is to be found in ss. 131–3. If the issuing company acquires 90 per cent or more of the shares in another company by way of a share exchange, there is no need to transfer to the share premium account any excess value received over and above the nominal value of the shares being issued (s. 131). Similar relief is given in the case of group reconstructions. If a wholly owned subsidiary company acquires a shareholding in another subsidiary company in return for an issue of shares, then again any excess value received over and above the nominal value of the shares issued need not be transferred to a share premium account (s. 132).

2.4 Issue of shares at a discount

A company may not allot shares at a discount (s. 100(1)). This means that a company may not issue shares at a nominal value of, say £1.00, but only ask the members to pay 60p for each share while undertaking never to call upon the members for the outstanding 40p per share. If shares are allotted in contravention of this, the allottee must pay the company an amount equal to the amount of the discount together with interest at the appropriate rate (s. 100(2)). The appropriate rate is 5 per cent. As allotment of shares would also lead to accounting difficulties, in that the share capital would not be correct, it would be highly unusual to find any company attempting to issue shares at a discount save in the following exception:

flotation

The offer of shares or debentures to the public.

- By s. 97 a company may pay a commission of up to 10 per cent of the price payable for shares being offered in a **flotation** to an **underwriter** who agrees to take up the shares himself if the public generally does not take them up (a subscriber who does this is said to be underwriting the flotation, since he takes the risk that the flotation may not be successful).

underwriter

A person who agrees to take up a flotation if they are not applied for by the public.

In such a case, in the extremely unlikely event of the company's issuing the shares at their authorised value, the shares would be issued at a discount since the company itself would not be receiving their face value. Usually, however, shares are floated at a considerable premium to their nominal value for the reasons given above in regard to share premium account, and so there is no risk of their being issued at a discount on the nominal value.

Where shares in a private company are issued in return for an overvalued non-cash consideration (as in *Re Wragg Ltd* (Case Example 5.2, above)), there is an effective issue at a discount. Although this may seem to contradict the rule against the issue of shares at a discount, the asset will be shown in the balance sheet at its originally agreed cost. If the transaction was an undervalue, this may open the directors to an obligation to compensate the company.

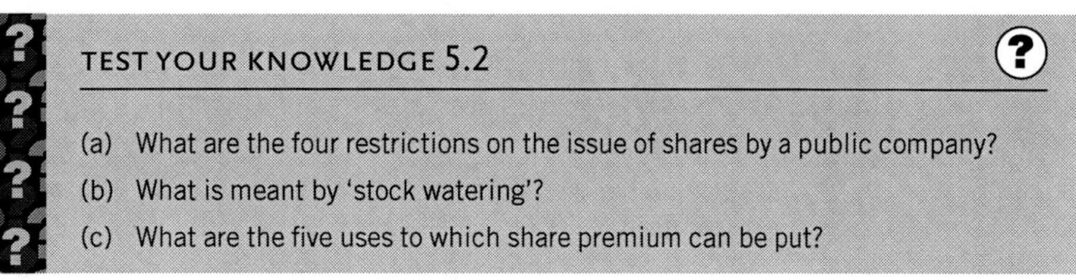

TEST YOUR KNOWLEDGE 5.2

(a) What are the four restrictions on the issue of shares by a public company?
(b) What is meant by 'stock watering'?
(c) What are the five uses to which share premium can be put?

3 Alteration of share capital

A company limited by shares may, if so authorised by its Articles, alter the conditions of the authorised capital clause in its Memorandum of Association (s. 121(1)). This is done by an ordinary resolution (Table A, Article 32). If a company has Articles which do not provide for such an alteration, but wishes to make one, then it must first change its Articles under s. 9 to incorporate such authorisation.

Section 121 allows for alteration of share capital on one of five grounds:

1 The company may increase its authorised share capital by new shares of such amount as it thinks expedient. This would occur where a company wishes to issue further shares but has insufficient unissued shares available to do so. This is by far the most common ground on which alteration is made.

2 It may consolidate and divide all or any of its share capital into shares of larger amount. Suppose a company has 25p shares and it is decided to consolidate these in to £1 shares. A shareholder having 400 25p shares would, after the alteration, have 100 £1 shares.

3 It may convert its shares in to stock or stock in to shares. How the capital of a company is provided is largely a matter of preference according to the country in which the company is formed. In the United States, for example, the capital of a company is usually provided in the form of stock rather than shares. In the UK it is usually provided by shares. A share is the smallest unit that a member can hold in a company. It is impossible to transfer half a share. It is, however, theoretically possible to transfer minuscule amounts of stock. For example, a company having a share capital of 1,000 shares of £1 nominal value has only 1,000 units (namely the shares) which are capable of being transferred. On the other hand a company having a capital of £1,000 worth of stock can, in theory at least, see that stock transferred in units of 1p. It is impossible in English company law for a company to issue stock directly. The only way in which a company may have stock is if it converts existing fully paid shares into stock under s. 121. The differences between shares and stock were considered in *Morrice v Aylmer* (1875) LR 7 HL 717.

   (a) Shares in a company cannot be bought and sold in units of less than a share. Stock can be split up into as many small fractions as the seller and buyers may wish.
   (b) Although shares need not necessarily, be paid up, stock must always be paid up.
   (c) The conversion of shares into stock does not alter the original voting rights. 1,000 £1 shares converted into stock only carry the voting rights attaching to the capital as shares.

4 It may subdivide its shares into shares of a smaller amount. In the nineteenth century shares of large denomination were fashionable. It was not uncommon to have shares of nominal value of, say, £1,000. Since a share is the smallest unit in a company which is capable of being transferred, the marketability of shares of high nominal value is restricted. For this reason it is desirable for a company having, say, a share capital of 10 shares of £ 1,000 to subdivide them into 10,000 shares of £1.

5 It may cancel shares which have not been issued. This is simply a tidying-up process where there is a significant difference between the authorised and the issued capital of a company and it is desired that the difference is eradicated. This is not a reduction of capital. It has no effect on the issued capital of the company (s. 121(5)).

When a company increases its share capital under s. 121, it must give notice of the increase to the Registrar of Companies within 15 days after the passing of the resolution (s. 123(1)). In the case of all other alterations under s. 121, notice of the alteration must be given to the Registrar within one month of the passing of the resolution (s. 122(1)). In either case, failure to give the required notice is a criminal offence and the company and every officer of it who is in default may be fined.

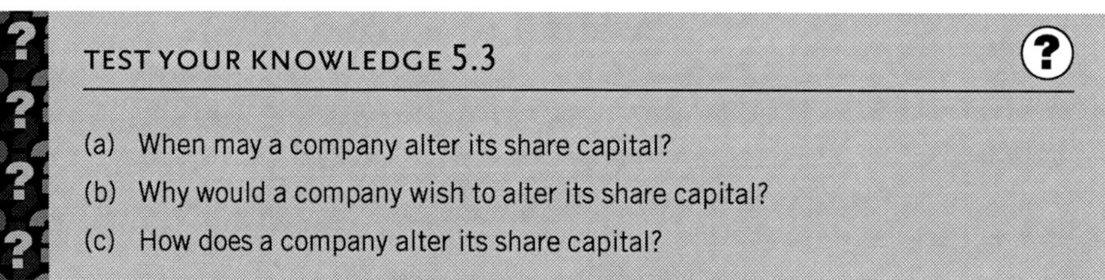

TEST YOUR KNOWLEDGE 5.3

(a) When may a company alter its share capital?
(b) Why would a company wish to alter its share capital?
(c) How does a company alter its share capital?

4 Company share issues: procedures

When issuing shares, the directors must ensure that the company has sufficient unissued shares authorised by the capital clause of the company's Memorandum. If this is not the case, they must have the members pass an ordinary resolution under CA 1985 s. 121 to increase the share capital.

They must also have the authority to issue shares by the company's Articles or by ordinary resolution of the members (s. 80). In either case, the authority must state the maximum number of shares which may be issued and the maximum period of time in which the issue may take place. In either case there is a maximum time limit of five years – either from the incorporation of the company if the authorisation is contained in the Articles, or from the passing of the resolution if the authorisation is given by ordinary resolution.

Alternatively, for private companies only, authority may be given by an elective resolution unanimously passed by the members under s. 80A, giving the directors general authority to issue shares at any time, although only up to the maximum number of shares which may be issued.

4.1 Pre-emption rights

pre-emption or preferential right

The right of an existing shareholder to acquire further shares in the company, the number of shares usually being in proportion to the number of shares at the time held by the shareholder.

As well as ensuring that they have this authority, the directors must also observe the constraints imposed upon them by CA 1985 s. 89. By this, any company, whether public or private, which is proposing to allot shares in return for cash, must offer them first to its existing shareholders before offering them to any other persons. This is known as a **pre-emption right** or a preferential right. Existing shareholders are given the opportunity to acquire any newly available shares before those shares are offered to any new shareholders. This means that the existing shareholders may, if they wish, maintain their voting power and share of control of the company. Shareholders are not obliged to exercise their right of pre-emption and may instead waive their pre-emption right.

Since on occasion the pre-emption rights may be inconvenient for the company, under s. 95 the company may, when giving authority under s. 80 for the issue of shares, either by its Articles or by special resolution, at the same time provide that the directors may disregard the pre-emption rights conferred by s. 89. When sending out notice of any general meeting of the company at which a resolution to disregard the pre-emption rights is to be approved, the directors must explain to the shareholders why the shareholders rights under s. 89 are to be disregarded. Alternatively, in the case of a private company only, it is possible to exclude the normal s. 89 pre-emption rights by a clause to that effect in the company's Memorandum or Articles of Association (CA 1985 s. 91).

ordinary share
A share entitling its owner to receive a dividend (if one is paid by the company) only after the payment of a set dividend to the holders of preference shares.

preference share
A share giving its holder preferential rights in respect of dividends and sometimes in respect of a return of capital on a winding up.

4.2 Disapplication of pre-emption rights

There are five sets of circumstances where pre-emption rights do not apply:

1. Pre-emption rights only apply to equity rights. These are shares having a right to participate in the surplus profits of the company. Thus pre-emption rights apply only to the holders of **ordinary shares** and not to the holders of **preference shares** (CA 1985 s. 94(5)(a)).
2. Where shares are being issued under an employee share scheme (CA 1985 s. 89(4), (5) and s. 94(4)(5)(a)). (These are extensively examined in the Company Secretarial Practice module.)
3. Under s. 91 where the Memorandum or Articles of a private company contain a provision expressly and clearly excluding the pre-emption rights.
4. Where the members pass a special resolution for the pre-emption rights not to apply (as specified above)(CA 1985 s. 95(1), (2)).
5. Where the shares to which the allotment relates are being paid up wholly or partly by non-cash consideration(CA 1985 s. 89(4)). This means that where shares are being allotted in exchange for assets being transferred to the company, pre-emption rights do not apply.

In addition, as stated above, members may choose to waive their pre-emption rights.

Where shares are allotted in contravention of the provisions regarding pre-emption rights, then by s. 92 the company and every officer of it who knowingly authorised or allowed the contravention are jointly and severally liable to compensate any person to whom an offer should have been made for any loss, damage, costs or expenses which that person has suffered by reason of the contravention, though any claim must be made within two years of the improper allotment.

4.3 Notification to the Registrar of Companies

By s. 88 a return of the allotment of shares must be notified by the company to the Registrar of Companies within one month of the allotment. This is done on form 88(2).

4.4 The issue of shares

Allotment is the process whereby a member receives an unconditional right to have his name entered into the register of members. The moment his name is entered into the register of members is technically the moment he becomes a member and the shares are said to be issued to him. By s. 22 membership of a company can be acquired in two ways.

1. The subscribers to the Memorandum become members upon incorporation of the company.
2. Any other person becomes a member when, pursuant to his agreement to become a member, his name is entered upon the register of members.

4.5 Restriction on public offers of shares by private companies

By s. 81 a private company commits an offence if it offers shares or debentures to the public. Thus, private companies are effectively denied access to the capital markets.

88(2)

Return of Allotment of Shares

Please complete in typescript, or in bold black capitals.

CHFP087

Company Number

Company name in full

Shares allotted (including bonus shares):

	From			To		
Date or period during which shares were allotted *(If shares were allotted on one date enter that date in the "from" box)*	*Day*	*Month*	*Year*	*Day*	*Month*	*Year*

Class of shares *(ordinary or preference etc)*			
Number allotted			
Nominal value of each share			
Amount (if any) paid or due on each share *(including any share premium)*			

List the names and addresses of the allottees and the number of shares allotted to each overleaf

If the allotted shares are fully or partly paid up otherwise than in cash please state:

% that each share is to be treated as paid up			

Consideration for which the shares were allotted
(This information must be supported by the duly stamped contract or by the duly stamped particulars on Form 88(3) if the contract is not in writing)

Companies House receipt date barcode

Form revised January 2000

When you have completed and signed the form send it to the Registrar of Companies at:

Companies House, Crown Way, Cardiff CF14 3UZ **DX 33050 Cardiff**
For companies registered in England and Wales

Companies House, 37 Castle Terrace, Edinburgh EH1 2EB **DX 235 Edinburgh**
For companies registered in Scotland

Names and addresses of the allottees *(List joint share allotments consecutively)*

Shareholder details	Shares and share class allotted	
Name	Class of shares allotted	Number allotted
Address		
UK Postcode		
Name	Class of shares allotted	Number allotted
Address		
UK Postcode		
Name	Class of shares allotted	Number allotted
Address		
UK Postcode		
Name	Class of shares allotted	Number allotted
Address		
UK Postcode		
Name	Class of shares allotted	Number allotted
Address		
UK Postcode		

Please enter the number of continuation sheets (if any) attached to this form

Signed ______________________ **Date** ______________

A director / secretary / administrator / administrative receiver / receiver manager / receiver *Please delete as appropriate*

Please give the name, address, telephone number and, if available, a DX number and Exchange of the person Companies House should contact if there is any query.

Tel
DX number DX exchange

G

COMPANIES FORM No. 88(3)

Particulars of a contract relating to shares allotted as fully or partly paid up otherwise than in cash

88(3)

CHFP087

Please do not write in this margin

Pursuant to section 88(3) of the Companies Act 1985

Please complete legibly, preferably in black type, or bold block lettering

Note: This form is only for use when the contract has not been reduced to writing

To the Registrar of Companies
(address overleaf)

For official use | Company number

Please do not write in the space below. For Inland Revenue use only

The particulars must be stamped with the same stamp duty as would have been payable if the contract had been reduced to writing. A reduced rate of ad valorem duty may be available if this form is properly certified at the appropriate amount

Name of company

* insert full name of company

*

gives the following particulars of a contract which has not been reduced to writing

1 The number of shares allotted as fully or partly paid up otherwise than in cash	
2 The nominal value of each such share	£
3a The amount of such nominal value to be considered as paid up on each share otherwise than in cash	£
b The value of each share allotted i.e. the nominal value and any premium	£
c The amount to be considered as paid up in respect of b	£
4 If the consideration for the allotment of such shares is services, or any consideration other than that mentioned below in 8, state the nature and amount of such consideration, and the number of shares allotted	

Presentor's name address and reference (if any) :

For official Use (02/00)

Capital Section	Post room

5 If the allotment is a bonus issue, state the amount of reserves capitalised in respect of this issue	£	

6 If the allotment is made in consideration of the release of a debt, e.g., a director's loan account, state the amount released	£	

7 If the allotment is made in connection with the conversion of loan stock, state the amount of stock converted in respect of this issue	£	

8 If the allotment is made in satisfaction or part satisfaction of the purchase price of property, give below:		
a brief description of property:		
b *full particulars of the manner in which the purchase price is to be satisfied*	£	p
Amount of consideration payable in cash or bills		
Amount of consideration payable in debentures, etc		
Amount of consideration payable in shares		
Liabilities of the vendor assumed by the purchaser:		
Amounts due on mortgages of freeholds and/or leaseholds including interest to date of sale		
Hire purchase etc debts in respect of goods acquired		
Other liabilities of the vendor, ...		
Any other consideration		

Please do not write in this margin

* Where such properties are sold subject to mortgage, the gross value should be shown

9 Give full particulars in the form of the following table, of the property which is the subject of the sale, showing in detail how the total purchase price is apportioned between the respective heads:

	£
Legal estates in freehold property and fixed plant and machinery and other fixtures thereon*	
Legal estates in leasehold property*	
Fixed plant and machinery on leasehold property (including tenants', trade and other fixtures)	
Equitable interests in freehold or leasehold property*	
Loose plant and machinery, stock-in-trade and other chattels (plant and machinery should not be included under this head unless it was in actual state of severance on the date of the sale)	
Goods, wares and merchandise subject to hire purchase or other agreements (written down value)	
Goodwill and benefit of contracts	
Patents, designs, trademarks, licences, copyrights, etc.	
Book and other debts	
Cash in hand and at bank on current account, bills, notes, etc	
Cash on deposit at bank or elsewhere	
Shares, debentures and other investments	
Other property	

‡ Insert Director, Secretary, Administrator, Administrative Receiver or Receiver (Scotland) as appropriate

Signed

Date

Designation‡

§ This certificate must be signed by the persons to whom the shares have been allotted, as well as by an officer of the company.

Certificate of value§

It is certified that the transaction effected by the contract does not form part of a larger transaction or series of transactions in respect of which the amount or value, or aggregate amount or value, of the consideration exceeds **£**

Signed

Date

1. Before this form is delivered to Companies House it must be "stamped" by an Inland Revenue Stamp Office to confirm that the appropriate amount of Stamp Duty has been paid. Inland Revenue Stamp Offices are located at:

Birmingham Stamp Office
5th Floor
Norfolk House
Smallbrook Queensway
Birmingham B5 4LA

DX: 15001 Birmingham 1
Tel: 0121 633 3313

Bristol Stamp Office
The Pithay
All Saints Street
Bristol
BS1 2NY

DX: 7899 Bristol 1
Tel: 0117 927 2022

Manchester Stamp Office
Alexandra House
Parsonage
Manchester
M60 9BT

DX: 14430 Manchester
Tel: 0161 476 1741

Newcastle Stamp Office
15th Floor, Cale Cross House
156 Pilgrim Street
Newcastle Upon Tyne
NE1 6TF

DX: 61021 Newcastle Upon Tyne
Tel: 0191 261 1199

Edinburgh Stamp Office
Mulberry House
16 Picardy Place
Edinburgh
EH1 3NF

DX: ED 303 Edinburgh 1
Tel: 0131 556 8998

London Stamp Office
(Personal callers only)
South West Wing
Bush House
Strand
London WC2B 4QN

Tel: 020 7 438 7252/7452

Worthing Stamp Office
(Postal applications only)
Ground Floor
East Block
Barrington Road
Worthing BN12 4SE

DX: 3799 Worthing 1
Tel: 01903 508962

Cheques for Stamp Duty must be made payable to "Inland Revenue - Stamp Duties" and crossed "Not Transferable".

NOTE. This form must be presented to an Inland Revenue Stamp Office for stamping together with the payment of duty within 30 days of the allotment of shares, otherwise Inland Revenue penalties may be incurred.

2. After this form has been "stamped" and returned to you by the Inland Revenue it must be sent to:

For companies registered in:

England or Wales:

The Registrar of Companies
Companies House
Crown Way
Cardiff CF14 3UZ

DX: 33050 Cardiff

Scotland:

The Registrar of Companies
Companies House
37 Castle Terrace
Edinburgh EH1
2EB

DX: 235 Edinburgh

TEST YOUR KNOWLEDGE 5.4 

What are the three statutory provisions that must be addressed when directors wish to increase the capital of the company?

5 Reduction of capital

maintenance of capital

The principle whereby it is ensured that the capital of a company should at all times be a fund available for the payment of its creditors.

The capital of a company is treated as being something which must be maintained, primarily for the benefit of the creditors of the company. The '**maintenance of capital**' principle, as it is known, postulates that the share capital and other undistributable reserves (such as share premium accounts and capital redemption reserves) exist as a fund from which to satisfy creditors should there be no other source such as retained profits. For this reason the capital is sometimes known as the 'creditors' buffer'. Although the principle is undermined by the fact that many small companies have capital of very small amounts such as £100, which is of little use to creditors, the principle still stands. It is for this reason that dividends cannot be paid out of capital and that a company's capital may not be reduced without proper safeguards for creditors. Furthermore, in general, a company may not purchase its own shares or give financial assistance for the acquisition of its own shares. However, there are a number of exceptions to the principle:

a) The company may reduce its share capital (s. 135).
b) The company may in appropriate circumstances, purchase or redeem its shares.
c) In other circumstances, a court may order that a company buys its own shares, for example:
   (i) under s. 459 on an allegation of unfair prejudice to minority members;
   (ii) under s. 5 on an objection to an alteration of the company's Articles;
   (iii) under s. 54 following an objection by a shareholder when a public company is re-registered as private.

   By s. 135, a company may reduce its share capital in any way provided three requirements are met:

1 It is done by special resolution.
2 Its Articles permit (Table A, Article 34).
3 The court confirms the reduction (s. 135(1)).

Although s. 135(1) refers to the company being able to make the reduction 'in any way', the Act clearly envisages the reduction being in one of the following three ways:

1 **The extinguishing or reducing of liability on any shares in respect of share capital not paid up** (CA 1985 s. 135(2)(a))
   This is extremely uncommon in practice. For it to apply the following situation would have to exist:
   (a) the company must have issued partly paid shares,
   (b) the company must have enough working capital without requiring the unpaid capital.

   Few companies are now in this position, partly because partly paid shares are rare nowadays, and partly because if a company has excess working capital it suggests that the company is poorly managed or is not taking advantage of new opportunities.

2 **The cancellation of any paid up share capital which is lost or unrepresented by available assets** (CA 1985 s. 135(2)(b))
   This is a relatively common occurrence which usually arises where the value of the company's assets have depreciated significantly or where the company has suffered substantial trading losses which would, particularly if the company is a plc, prevent it paying dividends. We shall see later that dividends are essentially

payments out of profits. The profits that are available for this purpose are stated in s. 262(3) to be the accumulated realised profits less the accumulated realised losses. The word 'accumulated' requires that all losses that have been made by the company must be carried forward in its accounts until they have been written off. Thus suppose a company had losses on its balance sheet as follows:

Shares	£20,000,000	Assets	£15,000,000
		Losses	£5,000,000
	£20,000,000		£20,000,000

This company would be unable to pay a dividend until it had cleared the losses from the balance sheet. A balance sheet carrying such losses would deter future investors and because of the requirement to make good accumulated losses it could be some years before dividends could be paid. If it were to write off some of share capital to represent the true asset position, the company might have reduced its capital but could instead start paying dividends again, once it made profits.

It could use s. 135 for this purpose. Following the procedures therein it could cancel one share in four. The balance sheet would then read as follows:

Shares	£15,000,000	Assets	£15,000,000

The members would have one quarter less shares than before the reduction but their proportionate stake in the company would, of course, be exactly the same. All that has happened is that by a cosmetic device the losses have been cleared from the balance sheet.

3 **The paying off of any paid up share capital which is in excess of the company's needs** (CA 1985 s. 135(2)(c))

This might occur in three situations:

(a) where the company can obtain finance more advantageously from another source;

(b) where the company has disposed of part or the whole of its undertaking;

(c) where the company simply wishes to reduce the scope of its business and has excess cash.

An example of the last situation would arise where a company has made very substantial profits and has large cash reserves. In such an instance it might wish to return some of this surplus capital to its members. It could do this using the procedures under s. 135. Since the relaxation of the rules relating to the purchase by a company of its own shares, this situation does not arise much nowadays.

Although the above three examples are the ones referred to in the Companies Act, there have been other occasions when reduction of capital has been permitted, such as cancelling a share premium account to use the released funds for the acquisition of goodwill from another company (*Re Ratners Group plc* [1988] BCLC 685).

Once the special resolution reducing the capital has been passed by the members in general meeting, the matter then goes to the court for confirmation. If the case involves either the extinction or reduction of liability on partly paid shares, or the payment to a shareholder of any paid-up share capital in excess of the company's needs, any creditor of the company is entitled to object to the reduction (CA 1985 s. 136(2)). The creditor may also object in any other case if the court so directs, but equally if steps have been taken, as noted below, to satisfy the creditor, the court may not entertain his objection. A creditor may not normally object if the reduction of capital involves the cancellation of any paid-up share capital which is unrepresented by shares. A creditor may only object if at the time of the court hearing the creditor (or such other date as agreed by the court) has a valid claim against the company. Before the court approves the confirmation of the reduction it will need to be assured that all the creditors who might object have been given the opportunity to do so, and the court may name a date by which creditors must enter their name on the list of creditors entitled to object. In order for the creditor to object, the creditor will need to be told about the proposed reduction of capital, usually by notice in a newspaper (CA 1985 s. 136(4)). Since this might attract unwelcome publicity, it is common for the company to pay the objecting creditor's debt first, thus obviating objection, or if the claim is disputed, to pay a sum into court or elsewhere which could be used to satisfy the debt should the debt be proved (CA 1985 s. 136(5)) and by this means the court can dispense with the need to obtain the consent of the objecting creditor to the proposed reduction.

It was said in *Westburn Sugar Refineries Ltd, Petitioners* [1951] AC 625 that the court should usually approve a reduction unless the proposed reduction is unfair having regard to the interests of:

1 the creditors;
2 the shareholders;
3 the public who may have dealings with the company.

When the court makes an order confirming the reduction it may, if it thinks proper to do so, make an order directing that the company shall for a specified period add to its name as its last words the words 'and reduced' (s. 137(2)), though in practice this very rarely happens.

The Company Law Review

The Company Law Review Steering Group has been examining the current procedure for reduction of capital which clearly needs reform. In particular it has recommended that the court procedure referred to above should be dispensed with, at least as far as private companies are concerned, and that the procedure should be simplified generally.

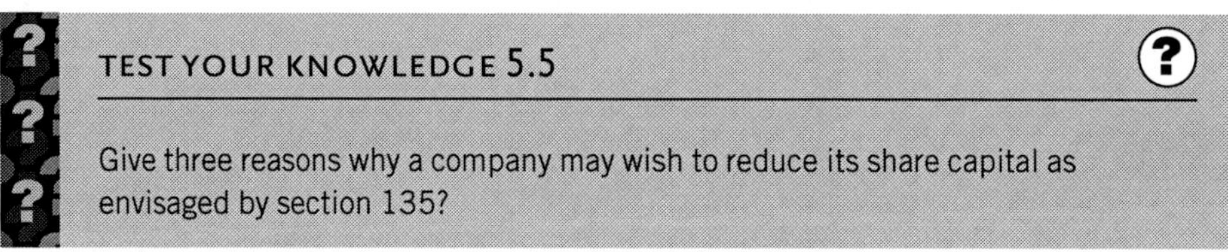

TEST YOUR KNOWLEDGE 5.5

Give three reasons why a company may wish to reduce its share capital as envisaged by section 135?

5.1 **Duty of directors of a public company on a serious loss of capital**

If the net assets of a public company fall in value to half or less than half of the amount of its called-up share capital, the directors must, within 28 days of becoming aware of this fact, call an extraordinary general meeting to be held within 56 days of so becoming aware (CA 1985 s. 142). The purpose of the meeting is to consider whether any and if so what steps should be taken to deal with the situation. Unfortunately, the legislation gives no indication of what else the company should do other than 'considering' what steps to take, but as a matter of practice, one option is to put the company into voluntary liquidation before the situation gets any worse.

6 Purchase by a company of its own shares

Formerly, companies were unable to acquire their own shares except in very restricted circumstances. This was because it was feared that unscrupulous directors could use company money to purchase the company's shares, thus driving up the price. When the price was high enough, the directors would then sell their own shares and disappear, leaving the remaining shareholders to discover that the company's assets had been squandered.

However, it is now recognised that there are sometimes good reasons for a company acquiring its own shares. These include the following:

1 The company can buy out a undesirable shareholder.

2 The members themselves may not be able to afford to buy a retiring shareholder's shares, but the company may be able to do so.
3 If the company has more reserves than it knows what to do with, it can effectively return the unwanted capital to the members by buying back their shares.
4 If the company continues to makes the same level of profit as before but with fewer shares, the **earnings per share** increase.
5 Buying back the shares may make it difficult for a takeover bidder to seize control of the company.

earnings per share

The proportion of the income of a company that can attributed to a single share.

For many years a company has been able to acquire its own shares in a variety of ways:

1 Acquisitions of shares in a reduction of capital made under s. 135 (see above).
2 The purchase of shares pursuant to a court order under s. 5 (alteration of objects clause (see Chapter 4)), s. 54 (litigated objection to resolution for public company to be re-registered as private (see Chapter 3)) or s. 459 (relief to members unfairly prejudiced (see Chapter 10)).
3 The forfeiture of shares, or the acceptance of shares surrendered in lieu, pursuant to the Articles, for failure to pay any sum due in respect of the shares (Table A, Regs. 12–22).

To these must now be added:

4 The redemption or purchase of shares in accordance with the provisions of Chapter VII of the Companies Act.

We have already looked at (1) in some detail, (2) takes place only following a court order, and (3) is now very rare. We shall shortly examine (4) in depth.

6.1 The issue of redeemable shares

redeemable shares

Shares which may be redeemed or acquired back from their holders by a company.

A **redeemable share** is one that is intended to be bought back by the company at some predetermined time. The main reason for companies to issue redeemable shares is to raise capital from venture capitalists. Persons such as merchant banks are encouraged to buy shares in a company. If the company does well, they will benefit a few years later by the company's redeeming their shares. Because of the good profits that the venture capitalist will make when a company is successful, he can afford a relatively high proportion of such investments not succeeding. By CA 1985 s. 159(1), a company limited by shares may, if authorised to do so by its Articles, issue shares which are either definitely to be redeemed or otherwise are liable to be redeemed at the option of the company or of the shareholder.

Other types of investor sometimes like redeemable shares because they can be reasonably confident that their shares will be bought back from them by the company – which may be useful if there is no other market for the shares, particularly in a small unquoted company. Companies welcome redeemable shares because it means that an investor with redeemable shares will invest for a while but will not remain with the company for ever: once there are sufficient distributable profits, the redeemable shares can be redeemed and control of the company can revert to those who controlled the company before the investor joined the company.

6.2 Redemption of redeemable shares

For redemption to take place the following conditions must be satisfied:

1 The redemption must be permitted by the Articles (s. 159(1)).
2 There must be shares issued by the company which are not redeemable (s. 159(2)).
3 The shares to be redeemed must be fully paid (s. 159(3)).
4 The shares must be redeemed either out of **distributable profits** of the company or out of the proceeds of a fresh issue of shares made for the purpose of the

distributable profits

Profits within the company that may be used for the payment of a dividend.

redemption (s. 160(1)(a)) (although it is permissible for a private company in limited circumstances to purchase its shares out of capital).

5 Any premium payable on redemption must be paid out of distributable profits (s. 160(1)(b)).

There is an exception to (5) above. If the redeemable shares were issued at a premium, any premium payable on the redemption may be paid out of the proceeds of a fresh issue of shares made for the purposes of the redemption. In this case the **premium** on redemption may come from the share premium account but the payment must not exceed whichever is the lesser of:

share premium account

An account into which all payments made for shares over and above their nominal value are credited.

1 The aggregate of the premiums received by the company on the original issue of shares redeemed; or
2 The current amount of the company's **share premium account**, including any sums standing to the balance of that account in respect of any premiums on the fresh issue of shares made for the purpose of the redemption (s. 160(2)).

The point of this provision is that it is possible to exhaust the share premium account to pay for the premium on the redemption of shares, but it is not possible to have a negative share premium account.

Any shares which are redeemed under this section must be treated as cancelled on redemption (CA 1985 s. 160(4)). This means that the amount of the company's issued share capital must be diminished by the nominal value of the shares being redeemed. However, the authorised share capital of the company remains undiminished and so shares may subsequently be issued at a later date without the authorised share capital of the company having to be amended under s. 121.

TEST YOUR KNOWLEDGE 5.6 

(a) Why would a company wish to issue redeemable shares?
(b) What rules apply to the issue of redeemable shares?
(c) From where would a plc obtain the funds to pay the nominal value of redeemable shares on redemption? Would the position be any different for a private company?
(d) From where would a plc obtain the funds to pay any premium on the redemption of redeemable shares? Would the position be any different for a private company?
(e) What happens to redeemed shares after redemption? Does this affect the company's authorised share capital?

6.3 Purchase of own shares: procedures

Under CA 1985 s. 162, a company limited by shares may, if authorised to do so by its Articles, purchase its own shares, even if when those shares were issued they were not considered as redeemable. A purchase may not be made under this provision if as a result of the purchase there would no longer be any member of the company holding shares other than redeemable shares.

In considering the purchase by a company of its own shares there are two distinct factors to be considered:

1 whether the purchase is a market or off-market purchase; and
2 where the necessary funding comes from.

recognised investment exchange

A place where shares in quoted companies may be dealt.

6.4 Market and off-market purchases

Section 163 distinguishes between market and off-market purchases. An off-market purchase is one where the shares are either:

1 purchased otherwise than on a **recognised investment exchange**; or

2 purchased on a recognised investment exchange but not subject to a marketing arrangement. A marketing arrangement includes both a full listing and membership of the Alternative Investment Market.

In effect this means that an off-market purchase is any purchase involving a private company (since no private companies may trade their shares on a recognised investment exchange) and any purchase by a company whose shares are normally traded on a recognised investment exchange but in this instance are the subject of a private deal between the company and the shareholder. Any purchase which is not an off-market purchase is by definition a market purchase.

Market purchase

When a market purchase is being made, the only authority required is an ordinary resolution of the members in general meeting (CA 1985 s. 166(1)). The authority may be general or limited to shares of a particular class. It may also be unconditional or alternatively made subject to conditions (CA 1985 s. 166(2)). The authority must nevertheless:

1 specify the maximum number of shares to be acquired (CA 1985 s. 166(3)(a));
2 determine both the maximum and minimum prices which may be paid for the shares (CA 1985 s. 166(3)(b)); and
3 state a date on which the authority is to expire (not more than 18 months from the passing of the ordinary resolution) (CA 1985 s. 166(4)), though this may be revoked, renewed or varied as necessary.

The reason that both a maximum and a minimum price are given is because the share price will vary as the company makes the purchases over a period of time: the company's purchases will be likely to increase the cost of the shares. By placing limits on the prices it prevents the company over-paying for the shares. Sometimes a formula for calculating the payable price is used instead (CA 1985 s. 166(5)).

A copy of the resolution giving the authority must be filed with the Registrar of Companies within 15 days notwithstanding that it is only an ordinary resolution (CA 1985 s. 166(7)).

It is not possible for a company to assign to a third party its rights to repurchase the shares in a market purchase (CA 1985 s. 167(1)), though the company may be released from the agreement to purchase the shares by a special resolution (CA 1985 s. 167(2)).

off-market purchase
The purchase back by a company of its shares when such shares are not dealt with on a market.

Off-market purchases

Before an **off-market purchase** can be authorised, there must be a contract (or a memorandum) for the purchase (see below), and a special resolution must be passed in advance (s. 164 (2)). In the case of a public company, the authority conferred by the resolution must state a date on which the authority is to expire, and in any event this date must not be later than 18 months after the passing of the resolution (CA 1985 s. 164(4)). Authority for an off-market purchase is not effective if the member whose shares are to be repurchased exercises his votes in respect of the shares to be repurchased and the resolution could not have been passed without those particular votes (CA 1985 s. 164(5)).

For an off-market purchase, whether the company is public or private, a copy of the contract of purchase or alternatively a written memorandum of its terms must be available for inspection by members of the company, both at the company's registered office for a period of not less than 15 days ending with the date of the meeting at which the resolution is passed and also at the meeting itself (CA 1985 s. 164(6)).

6.5 Disclosure of particulars of purchase

By s. 169(1), within the period of 28 days beginning with the date on which any shares purchased by the company are delivered to the company, the company must send to the Registrar of Companies for registration a return stating the number and nominal value of the shares purchased and the date on which they were delivered to the company. Additionally, where the company concerned is a public company, the return must also state:

1 the aggregate amount paid by the company for the shares (s. 169(2)(a)); and
2 the maximum and minimum prices paid in respect of shares of each class purchased (s. 169(2)(b)).

In addition to notification to the Registrar, the company concerned must also keep at its registered office either a copy of the purchase contract or a memorandum of its terms for a period of ten years (s. 169(4)), and copies of the document must be available for inspection without charge by any member and, in the case of a public company, not only by members but also by any other persons (s. 169(5)). A listed company has to notify the London Stock Exchange (Listing Rules Ch. 15) as well as the Registrar of Companies.

As with a market purchase, it is not possible to assign the rights to an off-market purchase (s. 167(1)), though the company may be released from its agreement by a special resolution (s. 167(2)).

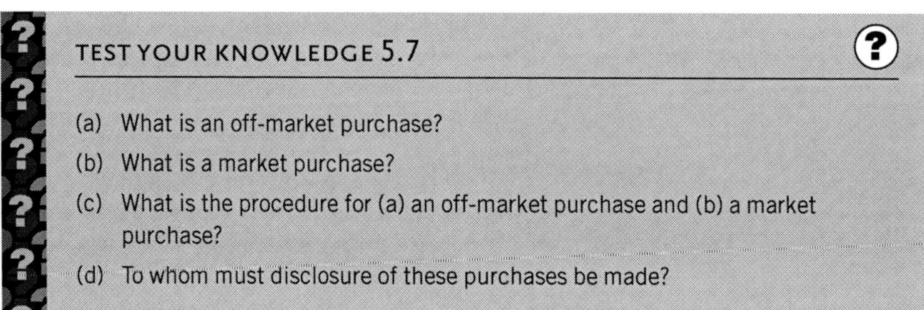

TEST YOUR KNOWLEDGE 5.7

(a) What is an off-market purchase?
(b) What is a market purchase?
(c) What is the procedure for (a) an off-market purchase and (b) a market purchase?
(d) To whom must disclosure of these purchases be made?

6.6 Sources of funds for purchase of own shares

Capital redemption reserve

capital redemption reserve
A reserve fund into which profits are allocated for the purpose of redeeming or buying back shares in the company.

Any company, whether public or private, may pay for its shares out of capital redemption reserve. When shares are redeemed or purchased wholly or partly out of the company's profits, the amount by which the company's issued share capital is diminished on cancellation of the shares redeemed or purchased must be transferred to a special reserve known as the **capital redemption reserve** (CA 1985 s. 170(1)).The idea behind the capital redemption reserve is that if shares were cancelled on the redemption or purchase of shares, the share capital would diminish, thus breaching the principle of capital maintenance. By creating a new capital fund, called the capital redemption reserve, into which funds equivalent to the nominal value of redeemed or purchased shares are placed, the company's capital position remains the same after the redemption or purchase as before – thus, at least in theory, protecting the creditors.

WORKED EXAMPLE 5.2

XYZ Ltd

Balance sheet as at 31 March 20X1

	£	£
Fixed assets		50,000
Current assets		
(excluding cash in bank)	22,500	
Creditors	(10,500)	
		12,000
Cash in bank		17,500
		79,500
Financed by		
40,000 ordinary £1.00 shares fully paid		40,000
15,000 redeemable £1.00 shares fully paid		15,000
Profit		24,500
		79,500

On 1 April 20X1 10,000 redeemable shares are redeemed at a premium of 10 per cent (i.e. £1,000 in total premiums). This is the new balance sheet.

	£	£
Fixed assets		50,000
Current assets		
(excluding cash in bank)	22,500)	
Creditors	(10,500)	
		12,000
Cash in bank		
(17,500 – 10,000 – 1000)		6,500
		68,500
Financed by		
20,000 ordinary £1.00 ordinary shares fully paid		40,000
5,000 redeemable £1.00 ordinary shares fully paid	5,000)	
Capital redemption reserve	10,000)	
Profit (24,500 – 10,000 – 1000)	13,500)	
	68,500)	

As can be seen, the capital redemption reserve has been created equal in value to the nominal value of the redeemed shares. The distributable profits have been reduced to pay for the redemption (which will no doubt reduce the company's ability to pay future dividends), and the company's reserves, in the form of cash in the bank, have also been reduced to reflect the payment for the redemption.

TEST YOUR KNOWLEDGE 5.8

(a) What is the point of the capital redemption reserve?

(b) What is placed in the capital redemption reserve?

If shares are redeemed wholly or partly out of the proceeds of a fresh issue of shares (with the balance coming from distributable profits) and the amount of those proceeds is less than the aggregate nominal value of the shares redeemed or purchased, the amount of the difference must be transferred to the capital redemption reserve.

The provisions of the Act with regard to the maintenance of the share capital of the company apply as if the capital redemption reserve were in fact paid-up share capital of the company (CA 1985 s. 170(4)) subject to the following exceptions:

1 The reserve may be used by the company to pay up unissued shares which are to be allotted to members of the company as fully paid bonus shares (CA 1985 s. 170(4)).
2 The reserve may be authorised by the court to be used for the redemption or purchase of shares out of capital (CA 1985 s. 171(5)).

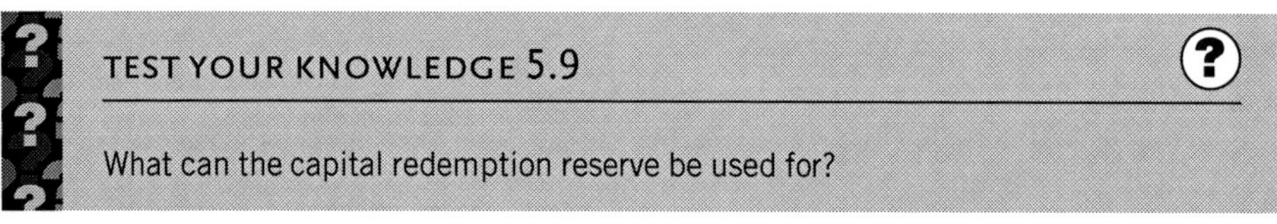

TEST YOUR KNOWLEDGE 5.9

What can the capital redemption reserve be used for?

Redemption or purchase by a private company of shares out of capital

By s. 171 a private company may, if authorised by its Articles, make a payment in respect of the redemption or purchase of its own shares other than out of distributable profits or the proceeds of a fresh issue of shares. This is to enable a payment on redemption to be made where there are insufficient other sources of funds. Since this involved the reduction of capital, the legislation requires strict adherence to the following rules in order to ensure that such reduction is undertaken carefully and with due consideration for the interests of creditors and the members whose shares are not being redeemed or purchased. The main reason why a purchase is made in this way is because a shareholder wishes to leave the company and take his capital with him. This could happen, for example, when a shareholder leaves a company because of retirement, or following a boardroom dispute.

The use of the terminology 'payment out of capital' is somewhat confusing in this context. For this purpose, a purchase is made out of capital if it is made other than out of distributable profits or from the proceeds of a fresh issue of shares (s. 171(1)) even if this is not absolutely the normal meaning of 'payment out of capital' (s. 171(2)). Under s. 171(3), the amount payable out of capital is known as the permissible capital payment. This is the amount (A), which, taken together with any available profits of the company (B) and the proceeds of any fresh issue of shares (C) made for the purposes of the redemption or purchase, is equal to the price of the redemption or purchase (D).

FIGURE 5.1 Payment over of capital

For example, suppose a company had to pay £100 to redeem its shares (D); if its available profits were £50 (B) and the proceeds of a fresh issue of shares were £30 (C), the permissible capital payment would be £20 (A).

If the permissible capital payment (in the above case, £20) is less than the nominal amount of the shares to be purchased (£100), the amount of the difference (£80) must be transferred to the company's capital redemption reserve (s. 171(4)). Normally (or in a plc), the sum of £100 (being the equivalent of the nominal value of the redeemed shares) would have been transferred to the capital redemption reserve on the redemption of the shares. In other words, because of the payment out of capital, the capital redemption reserve is not credited with as much as would otherwise be the case.

However, if the permissible capital payment is more than the nominal amount of the shares redeemed or purchased, then the difference in value may be from any capital redemption reserve, share premium account, fully paid share capital or any amount representing unrealised profits arising in a revaluation of fixed assets (i.e. a revaluation reserve) (s. 171(5)). So, for example, if a company had to redeem 100

£1.00 nominal value redeemable shares at a premium of 20p per share, making a total payment of £120 (D), and the company's distributable profits were £5 (B), and the proceeds of a fresh issue of shares were £10 (C), the permissible capital payment would be £105 (A). In this case, the permissible capital payment (£105) (A) is greater than the nominal value of the redeemed shares (£100) so £5 may come from any of the sources above (capital redemption reserve, share premium account, share capital or revaluation reserve). In practice this results in a reduction of capital.

TEST YOUR KNOWLEDGE 5.10 

(a) Why might a company wish to use capital to pay for the redemption of its shares?

(b) How is the permissible capital payment calculated?

Before a private company may redeem or purchase its own shares out of capital, the payment for the purchase or redemption must be approved by a special resolution of the members in a general meeting (s. 173(2)). The directors have also to make a statutory declaration specifying the amount of the permissible capital payment for the shares in question and stating that, having made a full enquiry into the affairs and prospects of the company, they are of the opinion that there are no grounds on which the company will be unable to pay its debts immediately following the purchase back and that, as regards its prospects for the year following the purchase back, it will be able to carry on business as a going concern and thus be able to pay its debts as they fall due throughout that year (s. 173(3)). In addition, there must be attached to the directors' statutory declaration a report addressed to the directors by the company's auditors stating that they have enquired into the company's state of affairs and have formed the opinion that they are not aware of anything to indicate that the opinion expressed by the directors in their declaration is unreasonable in all the circumstances (s. 173(5)).

The special resolution authorising the redemption or purchase out of capital must be passed on or within the week immediately following the date on which the directors made their statutory declaration and the payment must be made no earlier than five and no later than seven weeks after the date of the resolution (s. 174(1)).The resolution is ineffective unless both the statutory declaration and the auditors' report are available for inspection by the members at the meeting at which the resolution is passed(s. 174(4)). Moreover, the resolution is also ineffective if it would not have been passed had it not been for the vote of any member, who holds shares to which the resolution relates, exercising the voting rights attached to those shares (s. 174(2)).

Gazette
An official publication of the Department of Trade and Industry which comes out every business day and in which formal announcements concerning companies are made, such as when a winding-up order is made or when a winding-up resolution is passed.

Within a week following the passing of the resolution the company must publish in the **Gazette** a notice stating that the company has approved a payment out of capital for the purpose of acquiring its own shares, specifying the amount of the permissible capital payment and the date of the resolution, stating that the statutory declaration of the directors and the auditors' report are available for inspection at the company's registered office and stating that any creditor of the company may at any time within the five weeks immediately following the date of the resolution apply to the court for an order prohibiting the payment being made (s. 175(1)). Within a week following the date of the resolution the company must also publish a similar notice in a national newspaper circulating throughout England and Wales, or Scotland as the case may be, to give notice in writing to that effect to each of the company's creditors (s. 175(2), (3)). During this time the company must also deliver to the Registrar of Companies a copy of the statutory declaration of the directors' and of the auditors' report (s. 175(5)).

Under s. 176 any member of the company, other than one who consented to or voted in favour of the resolution, and any creditor of the company may within five weeks of the passing of the resolution apply to the court for the cancellation of the resolution. Upon such objection the court may confirm or cancel the resolution or it may adjourn the proceedings in order that an arrangement may be made to the satisfaction of the court for the purchase of the interests of the dissentient members or for the protection of the dissentient creditors (s. 177(1)). In particular, the court may provide for the purchase by the company of the shares of the dissentient members (s. 77(1)). It may also alter the Memorandum or Articles of the company in such a way that any further alteration of these altered provisions is only possible with the leave of the court (s. 177(3), (4)).

Liability of past members and directors in respect of redemption or purchase out of capital

By IA 1986 s. 76, where a company is being wound up and the winding up commenced within one year of the company making a payment out of capital for the redemption or purchase of its own shares, but the company has insufficient assets to meet its debts and the costs of the winding up, the court may order both any person from whom the shares were redeemed or purchased and also the directors who signed the statutory declaration (unless they can show that they had reasonable grounds for their opinion) to contribute towards the deficiency (IA 1986 s. 76(2)).

The liability of a person from whom any of the shares were redeemed or purchased is limited to the amount of payment which was made to him in respect of the shares. The directors are jointly and severally liable to this extent with the shareholder or former shareholder (IA 1986 s. 76(3)).

TEST YOUR KNOWLEDGE 5.11 

(a) What is the procedure for a payment out of capital?
(b) What is the purpose being making the procedure so complex?
(c) Once the payment out of capital has been made to a member, does his liability to the company cease?
(d) When might directors be liable to the company in connection with a redemption out of capital?

Financial assistance by a company for the purchase of its own shares

An extension of the general prohibition that a company cannot purchase its own shares can be found in the rule that a company may not give financial assistance for such a purchase. The general rule is contained in CA 1985 s. 151. It is not lawful for a company or any of its subsidiaries to give financial assistance, whether directly or indirectly, for the purpose of the acquisition of shares in itself, whether such assistance is given before or at the same time as the acquisition takes place. The reason for the prohibition is to prevent abuses occurring where, say, there is a takeover of a cash-rich company achieved by means of a bridging loan which is then repaid immediately following the takeover by the withdrawal of funds from the coffers of the cash-rich company.

The prohibition covers both direct assistance, as for example where a direct loan is given to the intending shareholder, and indirect assistance, as where a guarantee is given by the company in respect of a loan made by a third party.

To this general rule there is a number of exceptions:

1 Where the company's principal purpose in giving assistance is:
  (a) not to reduce or discharge any liability incurred by a person for the purpose of the acquisition of shares in the company or its holding company;
  (b) where the reduction or discharge of any such liability is just an incidental part of some larger purpose of the company;
  (c) the assistance is given in good faith and in the interests of the company. This

might appear to be rather a vague provision but it may be used to support a management buy-out where a subsidiary company provides financial assistance of some sort to its senior executives so that the executives can purchase shares held in it by its holding company.

2 Where the loan is made as part of the ordinary course of business. This would occur, for example, where the tending of money is part of the company's ordinary business and the loan is made in the ordinary way. Thus, a bank overdraft may be used by the borrower for the purpose of acquiring shares in the bank.
3 Employee share schemes. There is no prohibition against a company lending money to employees, including directors, to enable them to purchase shares in the company in accordance with an employee share scheme.
4 Loans to employees. A company may lend money to employees, other than directors, to enable them to purchase shares in the company for their own benefit.

Other exceptions

Section 153(3) lists a number of other exceptions where money may be provided by a company to a person who subsequently uses that money to purchase shares therein. These are:

1 a distribution of the company's assets by way of a lawful dividend or a distribution made in the course of a winding up of the company;
2 the allotment of bonus shares;
3 a reduction of capital confirmed by an order of the court under s. 137;
4 a redemption or purchase of shares made in accordance with Chapter VII of the Companies Act 1985;
5 anything done in pursuance of an order of the court under s. 425 (compromises and arrangements with creditors and members);
6 anything done under an arrangement made in pursuance of IA 1986 s. 110 (acceptance of shares by liquidator in winding up as a consideration for sale of property) ; or
7 anything done under an arrangement made between the company and its creditors which is binding on the creditors by virtue of IA 1986, Part I.

Contravention of the prohibition

If a company acts in contravention of the prohibition on the giving of financial assistance, it is liable to a fine and every officer of the company who is in default is liable to imprisonment or a fine or both. There is no provision in the Companies Act as to the effects of such illegality on the transaction itself. However, cases give some assistance. In *Selangor United Rubber Estates Ltd* v *Cradock* (No 3) [1967] 2 All ER 1255 it was held that any security given for the purpose of providing financial assistance is void. Similarly, in *Heald* v *O'Connor* [1971] 2 All ER 1105 it was held that any guarantee to support financial assistance was unenforceable. In *Wallersteiner* v *Moir* [1974] 3 All ER 217 Lord Denning stated that every director who is in breach of the prohibition is guilty of misfeasance and breach of trust and is thus liable to pay to the company any loss occasioned to it as a result of the default.

In the light of these cases it is well recognised that the criminalisation of the financial assistance and the fact that any transactions associated with the financial assistance will be void has unfortunate consequences for unwitting third parties caught up in the transaction. It is also unfortunate to penalise the company for something that the directors may have authorised but which the shareholders might not have known anything about. Consequently the Company Law Steering Group has been reviewing the current laws on financial assistance, and it is likely that the current rules on the prohibition of financial assistance will be removed entirely as far as private companies are concerned, and that the decision in *Brady* v *Brady* (see Case Example 5.4) will be reversed by new legislation.

Relaxation of these rules for private companies

Under CA 1985 s. 155, private companies are treated very much more favourably than public companies since they are exempted from the prohibitions described above on the giving of financial assistance so long as certain prescribed conditions are satisfied. These conditions are as follows:

1. The financial assistance may only be given so long as the company has net assets which are not thereby reduced or to the extent that, if they are reduced, the financial assistance is provided out of distributed profits (s. 155(2)).
2. Financial assistance may not be given by a company for the purpose of acquisition of shares in its holding company if the holding company is itself a public company or is otherwise a subsidiary of a public company (s. 155(3)).
3. Unless the company proposing to give the financial assistance is a wholly owned subsidiary the giving of assistance must be approved by special resolution of the company in a general meeting (s. 155(5)).
4. The directors of the company proposing to give the financial assistance and, where the shares acquired or to be acquired are shares in its holding company, the directors of that company and of any other company which is both the company's holding company and a subsidiary of that other holding company must, before the financial assistance is given, make a statutory declaration in the prescribed form as described below (s. 155(6)).
5. The statutory declaration must contain particulars of the financial assistance to be given and of the business of the company of which the persons making the statement are directors and must identify the person to whom the assistance is to be given (s. 156(1), (1A)).
6. The declaration must state that the directors have formed the opinion that, after the giving of the assistance, there will be no ground on which it could be found that the company was unable to pay its debts, and that if it were to go into liquidation in the 12 months following the giving of assistance, the company would be able to pay all its debts in full within 12 months of the commencement of that winding up (s. 156(2)).
7. The directors' statutory declaration must have annexed to it a report addressed to them by the company's auditors stating that the auditors have enquired into the state of affairs of the company and that they are not aware of anything to indicate that the opinion expressed by the directors is unreasonable in all the circumstances (s. 156(4)).
8. The statutory declaration and the auditors' report must be delivered to the Registrar of Companies either when a copy of the special resolution described above is filed with the Registrar in compliance with CA 1985 s. 380 or, where no such resolution has to be passed, within 15 days after the making of the declaration (s. 156(5)).
9. The financial assistance may not be given until four weeks after the passing of the special resolution unless every member of the company which passed the resolution who is entitled to vote at general meetings of the company voted in favour of the resolution (s. 158(2)).
10. During the 28 days following the passing of the resolution the holders of not less than 10 per cent in nominal value of the company's issued share capital or any class of it, may apply to the court for the cancellation of the resolution so long as no person who consented to or voted in favour of the resolution is included in this number. In the case of such an objection being made, the financial assistance may not be given until such time as the court permits (s. 157).
11. The financial assistance may not be given after eight weeks has elapsed from the making of the statutory declaration unless the court, on an application for the cancellation of the resolution, orders otherwise (s. 158(4)).

CASE EXAMPLE 5.4

Brady v Brady **[1989] AC 755**

A group of private companies ran two separate businesses each of which was controlled by one of two brothers. The two brothers fell out and deadlock resulted. The obvious solution to the problem was to divide the businesses between the brothers. However, one business was worth rather more than the other. To resolve this imbalance a complex series of transactions was proposed, one of which involved the creation of some loan stock which would then be paid off by the transfer of assets from the debtor company to the creditor company. These assets were then used to pay for the shares which the debtor company held in the creditor company. There was doubtless a breach of s. 151 in the way in which the transaction had been set up.

The House of Lords, in what some consider a very narrow interpretation of awkwardly drafted legislation, was of the opinion that the transaction could not be justified under the exception which allowed assistance where the financial assistance was part of some greater purpose of the company (though, contrary to the Court of Appeal, they did hold that the transaction has been undertaken in good faith). However, the House then went on to say that since the company was both private and solvent the assistance could be given under the relaxation of the rules for private companies described above. Accordingly, the assistance could lawfully be given so long as the brothers made the declaration of solvency, obtained the sanction of the auditors and generally followed the required procedures of the Act.

This decision, which hinged on the exact meaning of the words 'greater purpose', has caused difficulties, particularly for public companies wishing to provide legitimate financial assistance. Although the decision has been followed in a number of subsequent cases, the Company Law Review Steering Group recommended that it be overturned by legislation in favour of a clearer set of guidelines on what forms of financial assistance may be legitimate.

TEST YOUR KNOWLEDGE 5.12

(a) Why is financial assistance in principle prohibited?

(b) Why, equally, may financial assistance be useful and beneficial to all those involved?

(c) To what extent may plcs provide financial assistance?

(d) Private companies may provide financial assistance to its shareholders. What is the procedure for doing so?

A subsidiary may not normally hold shares in its holding company

In general, a company cannot be a member of its holding company. However, sometimes banks and other financial institutions will set up subsidiaries which can be used to hold their customers' assets. For example, if a person held shares in a bank, he might wish to borrow funds from the bank against the value of those shares. Since he could not very well transfer his shares to the bank in security of the loan, (since the bank would then, albeit temporarily own its shares) it is normal for the borrower to transfer his shares to a subsidiary of the bank which will hold the shares as security for the loan. If the borrower defaults, the subsidiary may sell the shares to recoup the loan. In this instance, the subsidiary is acting effectively as a trustee for the borrower (since the subsidiary will return the shares to the borrower on the repayment of the loan) and the beneficial interest in the shares is retained by the borrower. This and similar transactions are permitted under CA 1985 s. 23.

7 Classes of shares

A company is not obliged to issue all its shares with the same rights. Indeed, we have already seen in this chapter the possibility of a company issuing redeemable shares.

Sometimes, some shares will carry voting rights and others not. In such a case there would therefore be voting and non-voting shares. Sometimes, it will issue different classes of shares bearing different rights. Usually, when a company chooses to divide its shares it will have no more than two classes. These are usually referred to as 'ordinary' shares and 'preference' shares. There is no general rule as to what sort of rights attach to these classes of shares. Such class rights are determined by the company's Articles or by the terms of issue of the shares.

The power under which the company issues different classes of shares is usually contained in the company's Articles of Association. For example, Article 2 of Table A states:

> 'Subject to the provisions of the Act and without prejudice to any rights attached to any existing shares, any share may be issued with such rights or restrictions as the company may by ordinary resolution determine.'

A company may sometimes, though very rarely today, have a third class of share known as deferred shares. These are sometimes referred to as 'founders" shares or 'management' shares. They were not uncommon in the last century but they are rarely issued today and most that have been issued have been converted into ordinary shares. They were usually of a relatively small nominal value and had a right to receive a dividend only after a fixed amount of dividend had been paid on the ordinary shares of the company.

7.1 Class rights

The rights attaching to the various specific classes of shares depend on the terms on which they were created (i.e. the Articles) or the terms of issue. Well-drafted Articles will set out class rights in a clear and coherent manner. However, in practice sometimes the wording of special Articles conferring particular rights on various classes of shares are badly drafted and less than coherent. In practice, class rights are usually concerned with one or more of the following:

1. right to dividends;
2. right to return of capital;
3. right to participate in surplus assets on a winding up;
4. right to attend and vote at meetings.

Over the years various decisions of the courts have laid down the general rules applicable in the absence of any contrary provision in the Articles or in the terms of issue for determining the rights of a particular class of shares. The main rules are as follows:

1. All shares rank equally except in respect of any rights for which special provision is made. For example in *Birch v Cropper* (1889) 14 App Cas 525 it was held that dividends were payable to shareholders in proportion to the nominal amount of their shares regardless of whether those amounts had been paid up. Consequently, when drafting class rights it is normal to provide that where a share is only partly paid, any dividend paid is only paid in proportion to the extent to which the share is paid up – otherwise the partly paid shareholders would be receiving a high rate of return on capital employed relative to those whose shares were fully paid up. For example, such a provision is to be found in Table A Article 104.
2. Where some special provision is made in the terms of issue or the Articles of Association of the company, those express rights are presumed to be exhaustive on the matter to which they relate. In *Scottish Insurance Corporation v Wilsons & Clyde Coal Co.* [1949] AC 462 the Articles provided that, in the event of a winding up of the company, any preference stock should rank before the ordinary stock for the repayment of all amounts called up and paid thereupon. It was held that, since the Articles gave the preference shareholders a prior right to the return of their capital, this was exhaustive and accordingly the preference shareholders were not entitled

to share in any surplus assets or to receive more than the amount of their paid-up capital. Again, this was an example of poor drafting, and nowadays preference shareholders will nearly always insist on being able to share in any surplus assets.

3 It follows from this that where a preference share is given a preferential right to a fixed dividend (which is the usual case) the share carries no entitlement to a dividend beyond the fixed amount. However, in regard to other matters such as voting rights, the share would rank equally with any ordinary shares of the company in the absence of any contrary provision. As a matter of practice, it is common for preference shareholders to have voting rights only in limited circumstances, such as a resolution to wind up the company, but there is no reason why preference shareholders should not build in any types of voting right they wish provided those rights are clearly expressed in the Articles.

4 A preferential dividend is presumed to be cumulative. In *Webb v Earle* (1875) LR 20 it was held that if no preference dividend is declared in any one year, the arrears of dividend should be carried forward as a future entitlement of the shareholder and must be paid before any dividend is paid on the other shares in the company.

7.2 Variation of class rights

Sometimes a company which has issued different classes of shares may wish to vary the rights attaching to a particular class. How it should go about this depends upon where those class rights are set out. It is usual that the Articles of Association of a company contain some provision by which the rights attached to any class of shares can be altered with the consent of the holders of a specified proportion (usually three-quarters) of the issued shares of that class, usually by means of an extraordinary resolution. However, Articles are sometimes silent as to how alteration may take place. In any case it is necessary that any alteration is preceded by the consent of the holders of the class of shares concerned. The form which consent should take depends on whether the class rights are contained in the documentation such as the Articles of Association or the terms of issue.

These days, it is very rare for class rights to be found in the Memorandum of a company, but when they are it is almost invariably for the purpose of entrenching them (i.e. making them as unalterable as possible). If the rights are attached to a class of shares by the Memorandum, and the Memorandum and Articles do not contain any provision with respect to the variation of those rights, the rights may only be varied if all the members of the company agree to the variation (CA 1985 s. 125(5)).

By CA 1985 s. 125(2), if the rights are attached to a class of shares otherwise than by the company's Memorandum, and the company's Articles contain no provision with respect to the variation of those rights, the rights may only be varied if either the holders of three-quarters in nominal value of the issued shares of that class consent in writing to the variation or an extraordinary resolution passed at a general meeting of the holders of that class sanctioned the variation. Additionally, any requirement, howsoever imposed, in relation to the variation of those rights must also be complied with.

If the class rights are conferred by the Memorandum or otherwise and the Memorandum or Articles contain some provision for the variation of those rights, then, if the variation of those rights is connected with the giving, variation, revocation or renewal of an authority to the allotment of shares under s. 80 or with a reduction of the share capital of the company under s. 135, those rights may not be varied unless the written consent is obtained of the holders of three-quarters in nominal value of the issued shares of that class or if an extraordinary resolution to sanction the variation is passed at a separate general meeting of the holders of that class (CA 1985 s. 125(3)).

If the rights are attached to a class of shares, whether by the Memorandum or otherwise, and the variation of rights is not connected with the grant, variation, revocation and renewal of an authorisation for the directors to issue shares, those rights may be varied in accordance with provision of the Articles. With a reduction of capital, the class rights can be altered if the Articles contain a provision with respect to their variation. In this case, if the class rights are provided by the Memorandum, the Articles must have contained the provision regarding the alteration of the rights as at the time of the company's original incorporation. If the class rights are contained in the Articles, then it does not matter when the provision for variation was put into the Articles (CA 1985 s. 125(4)).

Such complicated arrangements are rare nowadays, partly because the legislation is difficult to understand and partly because it is rarely in investors' interests to have class rights that are difficult to change. As circumstances change, entrenched rights which seemed a good idea at the time of incorporation may not be useful later. It is therefore customary to provide that a class of shareholders may change their own rights by means of an extraordinary resolution of that class of shareholders, and to provide that one of their class rights should be the right to object to any other class of shareholders improving its rights at the expense of the first class of shareholders' rights.

In *Greenhalgh* v *Arderne Cinemas Ltd* (see Case Example 3.7) the original ordinary shares constituted a class of shares within an Article which allowed for the variation of class rights. Similarly, in *Lord St David's* v *Union-Castle Mail Steamship Company Ltd* (*The Times*, 24 November 1934) the Articles of the company gave its preference shareholders the right to vote if the preference dividend was in arrears. The dividend was in arrears and the preference shareholders proposed an alteration to the Articles that would allow them to vote on all resolutions. It was held that the right to vote was a class right enjoyed by the ordinary shareholders and that the proposed resolution constituted a variation of class rights. On the other hand, in *White* v *Bristol Aeroplane Co* [1953] it was held that the issue of further shares by company which had the effect of reducing the overall voting power of the existing shareholders did not amount to a variation of class rights.

7.3 Shareholders' rights to object to variation of class rights

By CA 1985 s. 127, whenever there is a variation of class rights, the holders of not less than 15 per cent of the issued shares of the class concerned may apply to the court to have the variation cancelled, provided that they did not consent to or vote in favour of the resolution for the variation. When such an application is made, the variation has no effect unless and until it is confirmed by the court. Any application to the court under this provision must be made within 21 days of the consent being given or the resolution being passed. At the hearing the court may disallow the variation if it is satisfied that, having regard to all the circumstances of the case, the variation would unfairly prejudice the shareholders of the class represented by the applicant. If it is not satisfied that unfair prejudice would ensue, the court must confirm the variation. Within 15 days of the making of an order under this provision, the company must forward a copy of the order to the Registrar of Companies.

THEORY INTO PRACTICE 5.3

Suppose you are the liquidator of a company. Having paid back all the creditors and having held back sufficient funds to cover your fees, you have £60,000 in hand. The company has 10,000 £1 ordinary shares and 10,000 6 per cent £1 preference shares. How would you pay out the money?

Answer

£3 on each share. All shares are presumed to rank equally.

Suppose the Articles were to state that the preference shareholders were entitled to their capital back in priority to the ordinary shareholders; would your answer then be different?

Answer

The preference shares would simply have £1 returned on each. Once a right is given it is presumed to be exhaustive. Therefore, the ordinary shares would then have £5 returned.

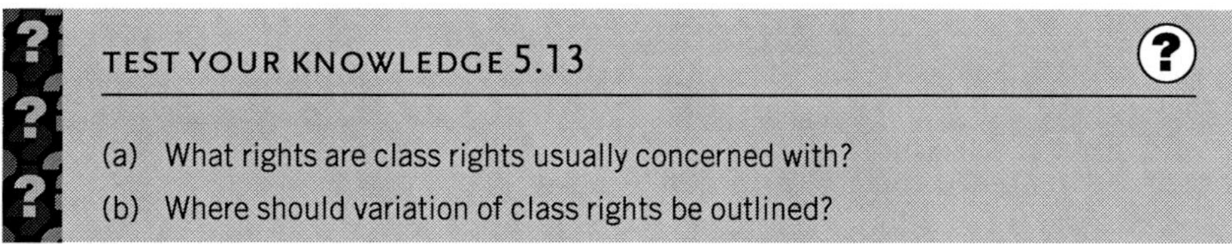

8 The register of members

Once a person becomes a member of a company, under s. 22 that fact must be recorded in the company's register of members which, by CA 1985 s. 352 it is obliged to maintain. The following information must be recorded in the register:

1. the addresses of the members;
2. details of how many shares they hold;
3. the distinguishing numbers of the shares (if there are any such numbers);
4. the date on which the person's name was entered on the register of members and the date on which the person ceased to be a member;
5. There must also be shown the amount credited as paid on each share.

The register is usually kept at the company's registered office. It may be kept elsewhere (at a transfer office) in which case notice must be given to the Registrar of Companies as to where it is being kept.

The register should be available for inspection by members of the company without charge, and by any other person on payment of a fee of £2.50 per hour taken. The company may close the register for up to 30 days each year after giving notice by advertisement in some newspaper circulating in the district in which the registered office is located.

By s. 360 no notice of any trust may be entered on the register (at least as far as England and Wales is concerned). Accordingly, it is only the legal owner of shares whose name is recorded on the register. The effect of this is that the company must treat the person whose name is in the register as the beneficial owner of the shares in question even where he is actually holding them on trust for a third party. The reason for this rule is that a company has no means of investigating the provisions of a trust attaching to any of its shares. A document which creates a trust is a private paper. In other words, it is not in the public domain like the Memorandum and Articles of a company. Therefore, the company is allowed to treat the person who is registered as the holder of shares as having absolute rights in the shares. A beneficiary may seek to protect his position by obtaining a stop notice. This is done by filing an affidavit expressing his interest in the shares in the Central Office of the Supreme Court or in a District Registry. An office copy (the stop notice) is served on the company. While such notice continues in force, the company must give notice of any transfer request it receives in respect of the shares to the person who served the notice. Within 14 days that person may apply to the court for an injunction restraining the transfer. If an injunction is not obtained, the company is free to go ahead with the transfer.

8.1 Rectification of the register

By CA 1985 s. 359, any interested person may apply to the court for an order of rectification of the register. Thus, if a person's name is wrongly removed or omitted from the register, he may apply to the court for an order restoring his name to the register.

9 Disclosure of interests in shares of public companies

A marked feature at general meetings of many public companies is the apathy of shareholders manifested by their absence from the meetings. The effect of this is that a person who arrives unexpectedly at a meeting with even 10 per cent of the shares of the company may be able negatively to affect the meeting by voting against the resolutions under consideration. (He could not make such an unexpected appearance to propose resolutions since notice has to be given to the company – see CA 1985 s. 376.)

So that companies may be protected against such risks, since 1967 substantial shareholders have had to give notice of their interest to the company (CA 1985 s. 198). This is so even where the interest is only beneficial and so not noted on the register of members. The duty to disclose arises when the shareholding reaches 3 per cent (s. 199). This protects companies from parties building stakes covertly (e.g. by 'warehousing' with associates or by using bank nominees) leading for example to a takeover under which not all shareholders would get the same price for their shares. By CA 1985 s. 203, the duty to disclose is extended to various family or company interests:

1 There must be disclosure of any substantial interest enjoyed by the spouse or the minor child or step-child of the disclosing shareholder (s. 203(1)).
2 There must also be disclosure of any substantial shareholding held by a body corporate in which that person is interested. A person is to be regarded as interested in a body corporate where he has control of one third of the voting power of the body corporate or where the body corporate or its directors are accustomed to act in accordance with his directions or instructions (s. 203(3)).

Having received such notification, the company must enter it upon a register of substantial share interests which must be kept at its registered office.

There is also a duty upon the person who has notified an interest under these provisions to notify the company further if there is any change in his holding which results in a change in the whole number of his holdings (s. 200(1)). Thus, a change from 3.9 per cent to 4.1 per cent would need to be notified while a change from 4.1 per cent to 4.9 per cent would not.

Since 1981 members of what are known as 'concert parties' have been under a similar obligation to disclose their interest to the company. These are agreements between two or more persons for the acquisition by one or more of the parties to the agreement of interests in the shares of the company concerned, known as the 'target company'. The parties to such agreements are regarded as being mutually interested in each others' shareholdings. As such, a duty is imposed upon them to report to the company (s. 204). This duty to disclose arises where two conditions are satisfied. First, the agreement must restrict the rights of anyone or more of the parties to the agreement with respect to their use, retention or disposal of interests in that company's shares acquired in pursuance of the agreement. These requirements mean that agreements not having as their object the acquisition of an interest in the target company are excluded from these provisions. However, the provisions are not limited to agreements which are legally binding. Non-legally binding agreements are also included in the restriction if they involve a mutuality in the undertakings, expectations or understandings of the parties thereto. Members of a concert party must keep each other informed of all matters relevant to the concert party provisions.

section 212 notice

A notice served by a public company on the registered holder of shares to enquire whether any other person has a beneficial interest in those shares.

Companies themselves require power to investigate shareholdings in them, and by CA 1985 **s. 212**, any public company may, by notice in writing, require any person whom the company believes to be interested in shares forming part of the voting capital to confirm whether in fact that is the situation or otherwise. If that person confirms it, he must give the company details of his interest in the shares. It should be noted here that the company can make its enquiries not only of registered members but of all persons whom it believes to be interested in the shares, even if the holding is below 3 per cent. Any information received by the company under this provision must be noted on the register of substantial share interests.

By CA 1935 s. 214, the holders of at least one-tenth of the paid-up voting capital of a company may require that the company investigate a shareholding in pursuance of its rights under s. 212 (above). The investigation must be speedily carried out. If it has not been completed within three months of the original requisition, the company must make an interim report of its progress to date. Further interim reports must then be made every three months. When the investigation is completed, the company must make its final report available for inspection at its registered office. The requisitionists must be notified that this report is available.

By CA 1985 s. 216, a company may apply to the court for an order that shares in which a person who fails to give the company any information required as stated above will be subject to restrictions on voting and receiving dividends. Thus, where such an order is obtained, the company has, in effect, the use of the shareholder's money without having to pay for that use. The court may order that the restrictions so imposed are lifted in due course. Most obviously this will be where the information required is supplied by the shareholder.

10 Dividends

dividend
That part of the profits made by a company that is paid to the members.

The income that shareholders receive from their shares is known as a **dividend**. Dividends are essentially payments from profits. This is part of the maintenance of capital theory. In just the same way that a company generally cannot make loans for the purchase of shares or buy back its own shares, so too it can only pay a dividend from profits. Put negatively, it cannot pay a dividend out of capital.

10.1 Distributable profits

realised profits test
A test to calculate the sums available to a company for the payment of a dividend.

The Companies Act refers to the payment of a dividend as a distribution. It is not the only method in which a distribution can occur since a distribution means every description of distribution of a company's assets to its members, whether in cash or otherwise. What sums are available to a company for the payment of a dividend depends, in the case of both public and private companies, upon a fairly straightforward test, the **realised profits test**. In the case of public companies, there has also to be applied a net asset test.

The realised profits test is provided in s. 263(3). 'A company's profits available for distribution are its accumulated realised profits, so far as not previously utilised by distribution or capitalisation, less its accumulated realised losses, so far as not previously written off in a reduction or re-organisation of capital duly made.' In essence, this means that dividends must be paid from the accumulated realised profits less the accumulated realised losses. This can be broken down into a number of straightforward principles:

1 A company must make profits before it can pay a dividend.
2 These profits must be realised. This means they cannot be 'paper profits'. For example, if a company owns the freehold of its warehouse and, on a re-valuation, the warehouse is found to have increased in value, it cannot use that increase for the purpose of paying a dividend.
3 Past profits from previous years trading can be brought forward and used for the purpose of payment of dividend.
4 Since references to 'accumulated' profits, this means that even if a loss is made on a current years trading, so long as there are past profits brought forward, these can be used for the payment of the dividend so long as they exceed the current deficit.
5 The fact that it is 'accumulated realised losses' which are required to be set against

profits means that there is no need to depreciate fixed assets before ascertaining the profits available for the payment of a dividend. (It will be seen in the following text that this requirement only applies to public companies.)

net assets test

The aggregate of a company's assets less the aggragate of its liabilities.

10.2 The net assets test for public companies

As this has been said above, there is a further restriction as to what a public company can use for the payment of dividends. By s. 264, 'a public company may only make a distribution . . . if the amount of its net assets is not less than the aggregate of its called up share capital and undistributable reserves and if, and to the extent that, the distribution does not reduce the amount of those assets to less than the aggregate'. In this context, net assets means the aggregate of a company's assets less the aggregate of its liabilities, including any provision for liabilities or charges in the accounts. In this regard, uncalled capital is not an asset. These net assets must be set against the called up share capital and undistributable reserves. Undistributable reserve are:

1. the share premium account;
2. the capital redemption reserve;
3. the amount by which the company's unrealised profits, so far as not previously utilised by capitalisation, exceed its accumulated unrealised profits (so far as not previously written off in a reduction or re-organisation of capital duly made); and
4. any other reserve which the company is prohibited from distributing by any statutory provision or by its Memorandum or Articles.

This looks rather complicated but, boiled down to its essentials, this rule means that whereas a private company can pay a dividend so long as it has sufficient realised profits, a public company may only do so if it has sufficient profits available after providing for any net unrealised losses. In short, public companies have to depreciate fixed assets against the profits which they make before paying a dividend.

10.3 Consequences of an unlawful dividend

By s. 277 where a distribution is made to one of its members in contravention of the above rules and, at the time of the distribution, that member knows or has reasonable grounds for believing that it is so made, then he is liable to repay it to the company. Note here that the obligation to repay only applies to a member who knowingly receives an unlawful dividend. Thus if a payment is made to a member acting in good faith and without knowledge, it cannot be recovered by the company.

In *Precision Dippings Ltd v Precision Dippings Marketing Ltd* [1985] 1 BCC 99,539 a company paid an unlawful dividend to its parent company and then immediately went into liquidation. It was held that the liquidator could recover this payment from the parent.

10.4 The mechanics of the payment of a dividend

The actual method of paying dividends is laid down by a company's Articles. For example, Table A, Article 102 provides that 'subject to the provisions of the Acts, the company may by ordinary resolution declare dividends in accordance with the respective rights of the members, but no dividends shall exceed the amount recommended by the directors'. This means that the level of dividend is initially recommended by the directors. The matter has then to go before the general meeting of the company and the meeting may either approve the directors' recommendation by ordinary resolution or may reduce the level of dividend recommended by the directors. It cannot, however, increase the level of the dividend payable.

interim dividend

A dividend paid by the directors of a company of their own initiative between annual general meetings.

Article 103 provides that the directors may pay **interim dividends** if they are satisfied that there are profits available for such a distribution. This means that the directors may, during the course of a company's business year, pay an interim dividend on their own initiative. In this case, there is no need for the calling of a general meeting to approve it.

CHAPTER SUMMARY

There are two forms of capital with which a company operates: share capital and loan capital. Share capital is provided by the company's members, who may be granted different classes of shares enabling them to exercise different rights. Loan capital is dealt with in Chapter 7

In relation to all companies, the law imposes certain limits on the allotment at shares. These restrictions are greater for public than for private companies. The purpose of these restrictions is to ensure that the financial standing of the company bears some relation to the nominal value of its share capital. Thus, although a company may issue shares at a premium, there is a general prohibition on issue at a discount. Furthermore, all companies have restrictions placed on their power to reduce their capital by, for example, buying or redeeming their own shares, or by providing money for another person to acquire the company's shares. There are limited circumstances in which such transactions are permitted but, if a company gives financial assistance in other than these permitted cases, it will be liable to a fine. The overall principle is known as the capital maintenance rule.

CHAPTER 6

Dealings in shares

CONTENTS

LEARNING OUTCOMES

This chapter covers the transfer and transmission of shares. After reading and understanding the contents of the chapter, you should be able to:

- Understand the way in which shares are transferred from one person to another.
- Appreciate the nature of estoppel in relation to share transfers.
- Understand the law relating to forged transfers.
- Distinguish between transfer and transmission of shares.
- Understand mortgages of shares.
- Understand share warrants.

transfer
The process whereby a share passes from one person to another either on sale or by way of a gift.

transmission
The process whereby a share passes from one person to another by operation of law; following death shares pass to the deceased's personal representative; following bankruptcy shares pass to the trustee in bankruptcy.

Introduction

Many people hold shares as an investment. When shares are held in this way, the holder may wish to realise his investment. Alternatively, he may wish to give his shares away. In either case, he will **transfer** his shares. This is the voluntary movement of shares from one person to another. There are two occasions when shares move from one person to another by operation of law. This is known as **transmission**.

personal representative
An executor or administrator who administers a deceased person's estate.

bankruptcy
The formal state in personal insolvency where a person's assets move by operation of law to his trustee in bankruptcy for the benefit of his creditors.

1 When a person dies his estate passes by operation of law to his **personal representative**, who then has the legal responsibility of dealing with his assets.
2 When a person is made bankrupt his estate passes by operation of law to his trustee in **bankruptcy**, who then has the responsibility of dealing with his estate for the benefit of his creditors.

In this chapter, we shall be looking at the movement of shares from one person to another.

1 Formalities following the acquisition of shares

allotment
The issue of shares by a company.

share certificate
The documentary evidence issued by a company and held by a shareholder to indicate the ownership of shares.

When a person acquires shares, whether by **allotment** from the company or by transfer and registration, the company must deliver to him a **share certificate** within two months. This is a formal statement by the company that the person named in the certificate is the holder of the number of shares specified.

By CA 1985 s. 186, a certificate under seal is prima facie evidence of the title or the person stated on it to be the shareholder. In other words, it is proof that the holder of the shares is legally entitled to them. However, because it is only prima facie evidence, it is not conclusive of this fact and so evidence may be brought to prove that the certificate is wrong in what it provides.

2 Estoppel

When a share certificate is issued, there arises an estoppel against the company. Estoppel is a rule of evidence. It arises in certain circumstances where a person makes a statement on which someone else relies. In certain circumstances the person who made the statement cannot, as against the person with whom he is dealing, deny the truth of that statement. Such an estoppel can arise against a company, which has issued a share certificate containing erroneous information. This principle will be illustrated later in the chapter. It is, however, first necessary to consider the transfer of shares in some detail.

3 The transfer of shares

In its simplest form, the transfer of shares may be illustrated by Figure 6.1.

John is a shareholder and is transferring his shares to Jill. The process is as follows:

stock transfer form
Instrument of transfer; the form completed by the transferor of shares to transfer title to the shares to the transferee.

1 The company will have issued John with a share certificate in his name.
2 John now sells the shares to Jill. He does this by handing over to Jill his share certificate together with a **stock transfer form** (also known as an instrument of transfer). This is the form which is used to provide the information to the company to allow it to remove John from the register and put Jill's name in his place. The form (shown below) states the names and addresses of both seller and buyer, the date of the transaction and the consideration being paid.
3 In return, Jill will make a payment to John for the shares.
4 Jill will then send to the company the share certificate and the stock transfer form.
5 In return, the company registers Jill's name in the register of members and removes John's.
6 It then issues to Jill a share certificate in her name.

Stamp duty has to be paid by the transferee of the shares (Jill) and the fact that payment has been made is recorded on the stock transfer form. The present rate of stamp duty is 0.5 per cent of the transfer price of the shares rounded up to the nearest £5. It is an offence under the Stamp Act 1891 for directors of a company to register a transfer unless it has been correctly stamped.

Under the Stamp Duty (Exempt Instruments) Regulations 1987, certain documents are exempt from stamp duty. These include:

1 transfers made within trusts;
2 transfers made in settlement of an estate;
3 transfers made on marriage or divorce.

Transfers made on a change of nominees are subject to a £5 fixed duty.

FIGURE 6.1 **Transfer of shares**

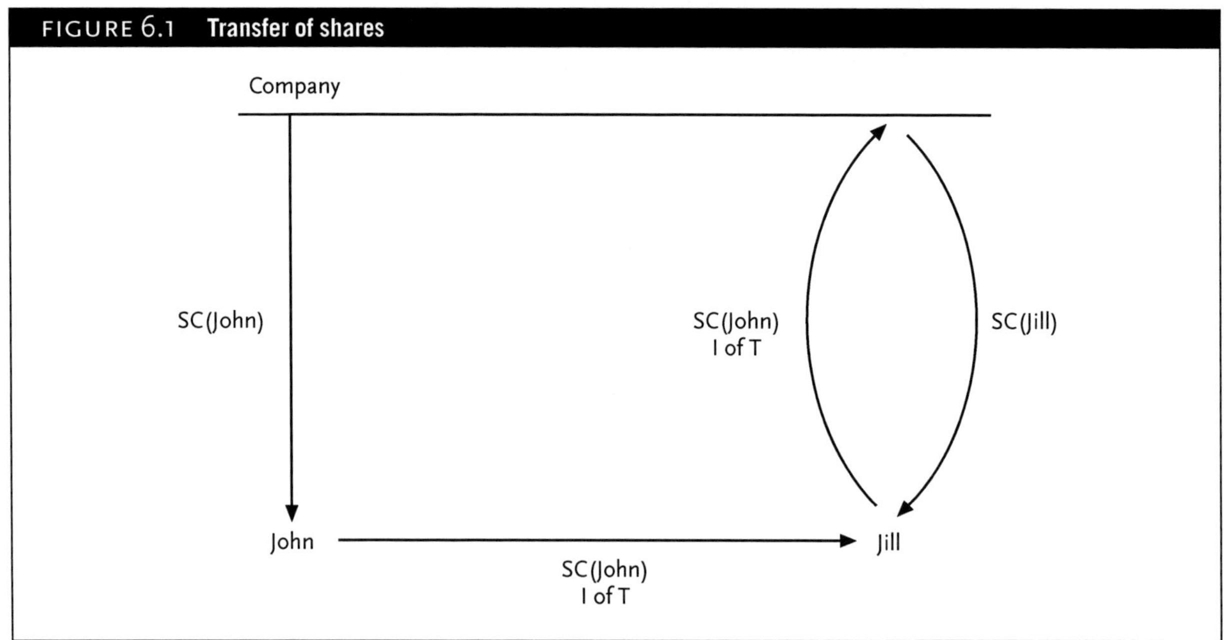

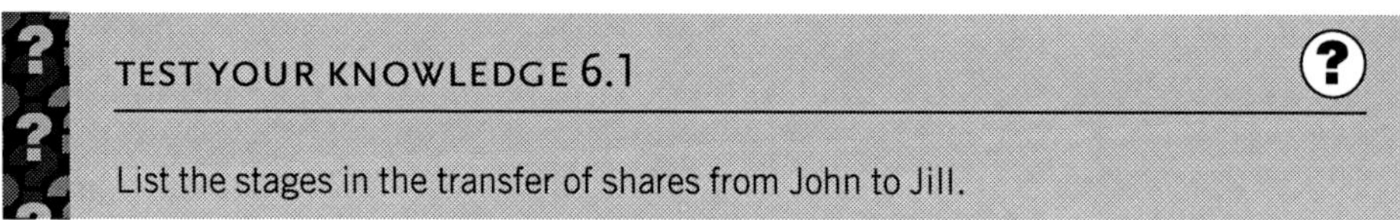

TEST YOUR KNOWLEDGE 6.1

List the stages in the transfer of shares from John to Jill.

4 The transferability of shares

There is a general principle in company law of free transferability of shares. As a general rule, directors may decline to register a transfer only if it has not been properly stamped or where the shares are partly paid and the directors are unhappy with the creditworthiness of the proposed transferee. However, there is, in the Articles of the most private companies, a further restriction upon transferability. For example, there may be a provision that the directors may refuse to register a transfer of shares to any person of whom they do not approve. This is a fiduciary power of directors and so must be exercised in good faith. This means that the directors must have acted in the best interests of the company and properly considered the matter at a board meeting. There is, however, a presumption that the directors have acted in good faith and, if they do not give their reasons for refusing to register a transfer, their refusal cannot generally be challenged. The reason for this rule is the general principle in litigation that 'he who asserts must prove'. A challenge may only arise if there is evidence that the directors have not acted in good faith, but it is almost impossible to obtain such evidence.

CASE EXAMPLE 6.1

***Re Smith and Fawcett Ltd* [1942] Ch 304**

The company's Articles gave the directors 'an absolute and uncontrolled discretion' to refuse to register the transfer of any shares in the company. The company had 8,002 ordinary shares of which each of the two directors held 4,001. A shareholder died and his son applied to have the shares registered in his name. The other director refused to allow registration of all the shares but offered to register 2,001 provided the remaining 2,000 were transferred by the deceased director's son to him, the remaining director. The son challenged this in court. He failed. It was held that there was nothing in the evidence which showed that the director's discretion had been exercised other than in good faith.

If the directors do give reasons for their refusal, then the court may enquire into those reasons and consider whether they were adequate to justify the refusal.

If a transfer is to be rejected, a positive resolution to that effect is necessary by the board. If there is deadlock the transfer must be registered. By s. 185 any refusal to register a transfer must be noted to the transferee within two months after the transfer request was lodged with the company. Failure on the part of the company to do this results in the company losing its right to refuse the transfer and the transferee can, if necessary, force the registration by applying to the court for rectification of the register under s. 359.

SHARE CERTIFICATE

ORDINARY SHARES

Certificate No. No. of Shares

.... p.l.c.
(*Incorporated under the Companies Act 1948*)
(Registered in England and Wales No. 1234567)

THIS IS TO CERTIFY that ....

....

is/are the Registered Holder(s) of .... fully paid Ordinary Shares of Ten Pence each in the above-named Company, subject to the Memorandum and Articles of Association of the Company.

Executed by .... p.l.c.

this .... day of .... 20 .... (*note)

(Signed) .... (Director)

.... (Secretary/Director)

T. No. .....**No Transfer of the Shares (or any portion thereof) comprised in this Certificate can be registered without the production of this Certificate.**
Exd. ....

STOCK TRANSFER FORM

[This form to be printed on white paper] STOCK TRANSFER FORM Consideration Money £			Certificate lodged with the Registrar (For completion by the Registrar/ Stock Exchange)
Name of Undertaking			
Description of Security			
Number or amount of Shares, Stock or other security and, in figures column only, number and denomination of units, if any.	Words	Figures (units of)	
Name(s) of registered holder(s) should be given in full: the address should be given where there is only one holder. If the transfer is not made by the registered holder(s) insert also the name(s) and capacity (e.g., Executor(s)), of the person(s) making the transfer.	in the name(s) of		

Delete word in italics except for stock exchange transactions	I/We hereby transfer the above security out of the name(s) aforesaid to the person(s) named below *or to the several persons named in Parts 2 of Broker Transfer Forms relating to the above security:* Signature of transferor(s)	Stamp of Selling Broker(s), for transactions which are not stock exchange transactions, of Agent(s), if any, acting for the Transferor(s).
1. .... 2.	3. .... 4.	
A body corporate should execute the transfer under its common seal or otherwise in accordance with applicable statutory requirements.		Date

Full name(s), full postal address(es) (including County or, if applicable, Postal District number) of the person(s) to whom the security is transferred. Please state title, if any, or whether Mr, Mrs or Miss. Please complete in type or in Block Capitals.	

I/We request that such entries be made in the register as are necessary to give effect to this transfer.

Stamp of Buying Broker(s) (if any).	Stamp or name and address of person lodging this form (if other than the Buying Broker(s))

(Endorsement for use only in stock exchange transactions)
The security represented by the transfer overleaf has been sold as follows:-

………………………………..*shares/stock* ………………………………..*shares/stock*
………………………………..*shares/stock* ………………………………..*shares/stock*

Balance (if any) due to Selling Broker(s)
Amount of certificate(s)

Brokers Transfer Forms for above amount certified

Stamp of certifying Stock Exchange *Stamp of Selling Broker(s)*

Form of certificate required for exemption from stamp duty

Instruments of transfer executed on or after 1st May 1987 are exempt from stamp duty when the transaction falls within one of the following categories and will not need to be seen in stamp offices, provided they are certified as below in accordance with the Stamp Duty (Exempt Instruments) Regulations 1987:

(a) The vesting of property subject to a trust in the trustees of the trust on the appointment of a new trustee, or in the continuing trustees on the retirement of a trustee.
(b) The conveyance or transfer of property the subject of a specific devise or legacy to the beneficiary named in the will (or his nominee).
(c) The conveyance or transfer of property which forms part of an intestate's estate to the person entitled on intestacy (or his nominee).
(d) The appropriation of property with in Section 84(4) of the Finance Act 1985 (death: appropriation in satisfaction of a general legacy of money) or Section 84(5) or (7) of that Act (death: appropriation in satisfaction of any interest of surviving spouse and in Scotland also of any interest of issue).
(e) The conveyance or transfer of property which forms part of the residuary estate of a testator to a beneficiary(or his no nominee) entitled solely by virtue of his entitlement under the will.
(f) The conveyance or transfer of property out of a settlement in or towards satisfaction of a beneficiary's interest, not being an interest acquired for money or money's worth, being a conveyance or transfer constituting a distribution of property in accordance with the provisions of the settlement.
(g) The conveyance or transfer of property on and in consideration only of marriage to a party to the marriage (or his nominee) or to trustees to be held on the terms of a settlement made in consideration only of the marriage.
(h) The conveyance or transfer of property within Section 83(1) of the Finance Act 1985 (transfers in connection with divorce, etc.)
(i) The conveyance or transfer by the liquidator of property which formed part of the assets of the company in liquidation to a shareholder of that company (or his nominee) in or towards satisfaction of the shareholder's rights on a winding-up.
(j) The grant in fee simple of an easement in or over land for no consideration in money or money's worth.
(k) The grant of a servitude for no consideration in money or money's worth.
(l) The conveyance or transfer of property operating as a voluntary disposition *inter vivos* for no consideration in money or money's worth nor any consideration referred to in Section 57 of the Stamp Act 1891 (conveyance in consideration of a debt, etc.).
(m) The conveyance or transfer of property by an instrument within Section 84(1) of the Finance Act 1985 (death: varying disposition).

Certificate

(1) Insert appropriate category

(2) Delete if the certificate is given by the transferor or his solicitor

I/We hereby certify that this instrument falls within category ………… (1) in the schedule to the Stamp Duty (Exempt Instruments) Regulations 1987.
I/We confirm that I/we have been duly authorised by the transferor to sign this certificate and that the facts of the transaction are within my/our knowledge.(2)

Signature(s) ……………………………………… *Description ('Transferor', 'Solicitor' etc)*
Name(s) …………………………………………… ……………………………………………
Address …………………………………………… ……………………………………………
…………………………………………………… ……………………………………………
Date ………………………………… 20 ….. ……………………………………………

Form of certificate required where transfer is not exempt but is not liable to *ad valorem* stamp duty (£5.00 fixed duty payable)

Some instruments of transfer are liable to a fixed duty of £5.00 when the transaction falls within one of the following categories for which the certificate below may be completed.

(1) Transfer by way of security for a loan or re-transfer to the original transferor on repayment of a loan.
(2) Transfer, not on sale and not arising under any contract of sale and where no beneficial interest in the property passes: (a) to a person who is a mere nominee of, and is nominated only by, the transferor; (b) from a mere nominee who has at all times held the property on behalf of the transferee; (c) from one nominee to another nominee of the same beneficial owner where the first nominee has at all times held the property on behalf of that beneficial owner. (NOTE – This category does not include a transfer made in any of the following circumstances: (i) by a holder of stock, etc., following the grant of an option to purchase the stock, to the person entitled to the option or his nominee; (ii) to a nominee in contemplation of a contract for the sale of stock, etc., then about to be entered into; (iii) from the nominee of a vendor, who has instructed the nominee orally or by some unstamped writing to hold stock, etc., in trust for a purchaser, to such purchaser).

(1) Insert '(1)' or '(2)'

(2) Here set out concisely the facts explaining the transaction in cases falling within (1) or (2) or in any other case where £5.00 fixed duty is offered.

I/We hereby certify that the transaction in respect of which this transfer is made is one which falls within the category ………… (1) above.
I/We confirm that I/we have been duly authorised by the transferor to sign this certificate and that the facts of the transaction are within my/our knowledge.

(2)……………………………………………………………………………………………
……………………………………………………………………………………………

Signature(s) *Description ('Transferor', 'Solicitor' etc)*
…………………………………………… ……………………………………………
…………………………………………… ……………………………………………
…………………………………………… ……………………………………………
Date ……………………………………… 20 …. ……………………………………………

5 Certification of a share transfer

The method of transferring shares described above is only safe from John's point of view if he is transferring his entire holding. Suppose he were transferring only part of his shareholding; for example, he has 1,000 shares and is transferring only 400 of them to Jill. He would have a share certificate for 1,000 shares and it would be obviously dangerous for him to hand this to Jill together with a stock transfer form for only 400 shares. All that Jill would have to do to obtain the full 1,000 shares would be to make a slight alteration to the stock transfer form. This is one of the instances where certification occurs. The other instance is where John is transferring his entire shareholding but to two (or more) transferees.

The procedure is shown in Figure 6.2.

FIGURE 6.2 **Certification (1)**

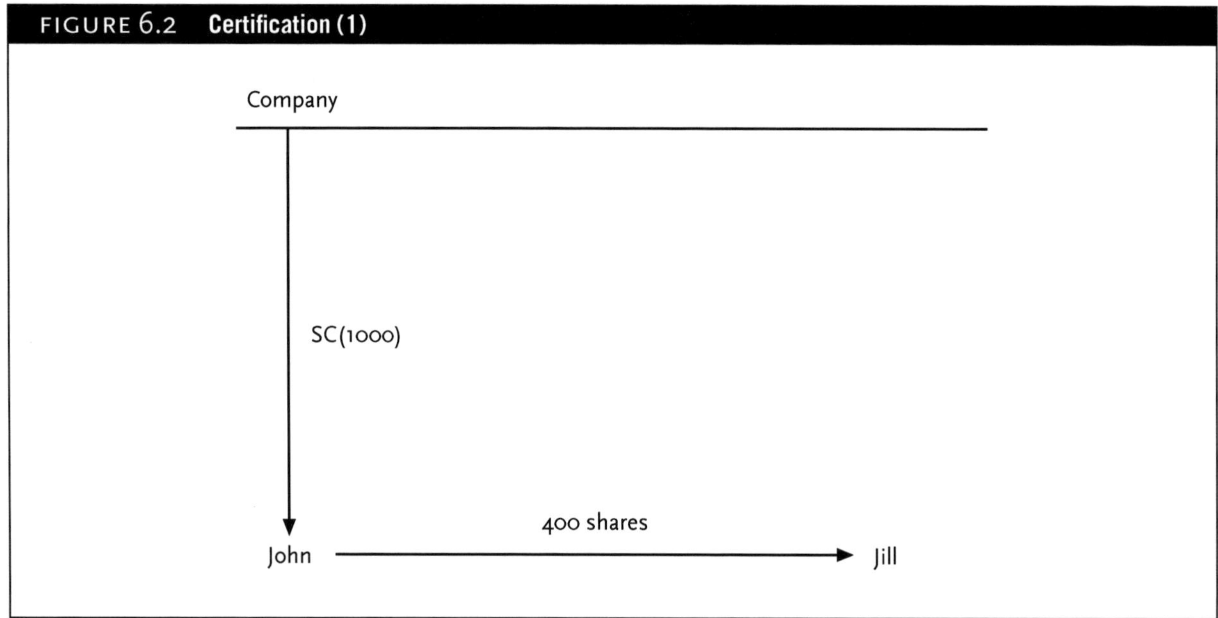

John owns 1,000 shares. He is transferring 400 to Jill. He fills in the stock transfer form and sends it to the company with his share certificate. The next stage is illustrated in Figure 6.3.

FIGURE 6.3 **Certification (2)**

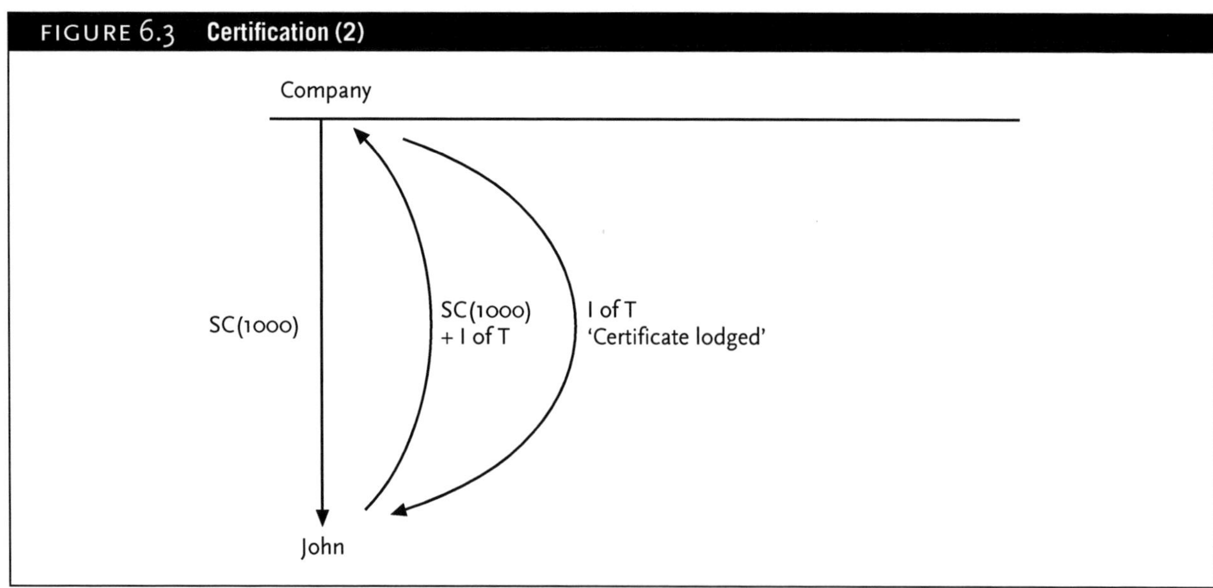

The company retains the share certificate and returns the stock transfer form to John. On this the company will have stamped words along the lines of 'certificate for 400 shares has been lodged at the company's registered office'. This certificate will be signed by the company secretary. John then hands this **certificated instrument of transfer** to Jill.

Then the picture is completed by Figure 6.4.

FIGURE 6.4 **Certification (3)**

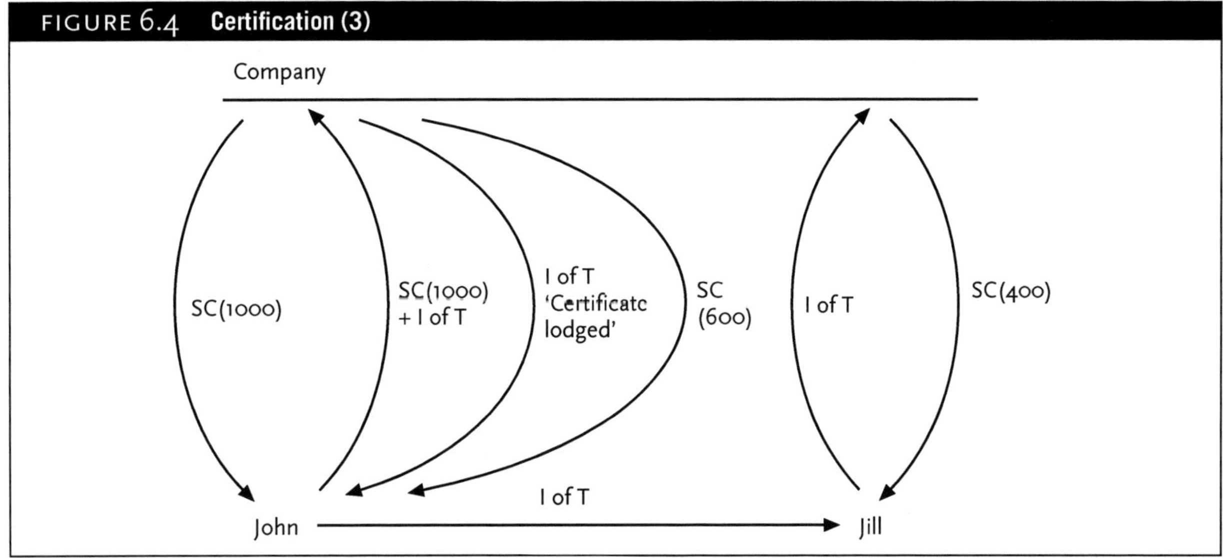

certificated instrument of transfer

An instrument of transfer of shares that that been marked by a company's secretary to indicate that the share certificate to which it relates has been deposited with the company.

Jill sends the certificated instrument of transfer back to the company. The company retains it. It cancels the share certificate for 1,000 shares. It then sends John a new certificate for 600 shares, the remainder of his holding, and Jill a certificate for 400 shares.

In a case where John is transferring his entire shareholding but to two different purchasers, he will return his share certificate to the company together with two stock transfer forms. These will be certificated by the company and returned to him. He will then hand these to the respective purchasers who will be registered as shareholders in the normal way.

Since CREST (electronic share dealing) was introduced for quoted companies, certification is very seldom encountered. It is almost never encountered in small private companies since a departing shareholder will almost always want to dispose of all of his shares.

6 Forged transfers

Forged transfers often cause a degree of difficulty for students. This difficulty can often be minimised by bearing in mind a few basic points. These are:

1 As has been said above, a share certificate issued by a company operates as an estoppel against anyone relying upon it. Thus, the company cannot deny to a third party seeking to rely upon a share certificate what is actually stated on the share certificate. For example, if a share certificate states that Peter is the holder of 100 fully paid shares of £1 each, it cannot deny to a third party that Peter is the owner of the shares, nor can it deny that the shares are fully paid.

2 In English law a forgery is a nullity. Anyone who tries to rely on a forged document may be held personally liable upon it even where he is completely innocent of the forgery. This is best illustrated by a person who quite innocently hands a forged £5 note over in a shop in return for goods. If the forgery is discovered, the shopkeeper may refuse to accept the forged note. In other words the customer must pay in genuine money for the goods or else not have them. This applies even where the customer is completely innocent of the forgery, for example where he came into the possession of the forged note without realising that it was defective.

3 By CA 1985 s. 359, any aggrieved person may take action against a company for rectification of its register of members if he feels that a name has been improperly placed on or improperly removed from the register of members.

Bearing these facts in mind, we can now look at two leading cases on this area of law.

CASE EXAMPLE 6.2

***Sheffield Corporation* v *Barclay* [1905] AC 74**

Stock in the Corporation was registered in the joint names of T and H. T signed his own name on an instrument of transfer and then forged H's signature. Using the forgery, he then sold the stock to B. B's name was registered as the stockholder. B then transferred the stock to a third party. (The transaction is illustrated in Figure 6.5.)

After some time H discovered the forgery. He caused the corporation to acquire for him an equivalent amount of stock and to reimburse him any dividends which he had missed. The corporation was, however, estopped from denying to the third parties that B was the stockholder. It was held that B, who had sent the forged instrument of transfer to the corporation, albeit innocently, so that he could be registered as a stockholder, was liable to indemnify the corporation on his implied undertaking that the instrument of transfer was good.

FIGURE 6.5 **Forged transfers**

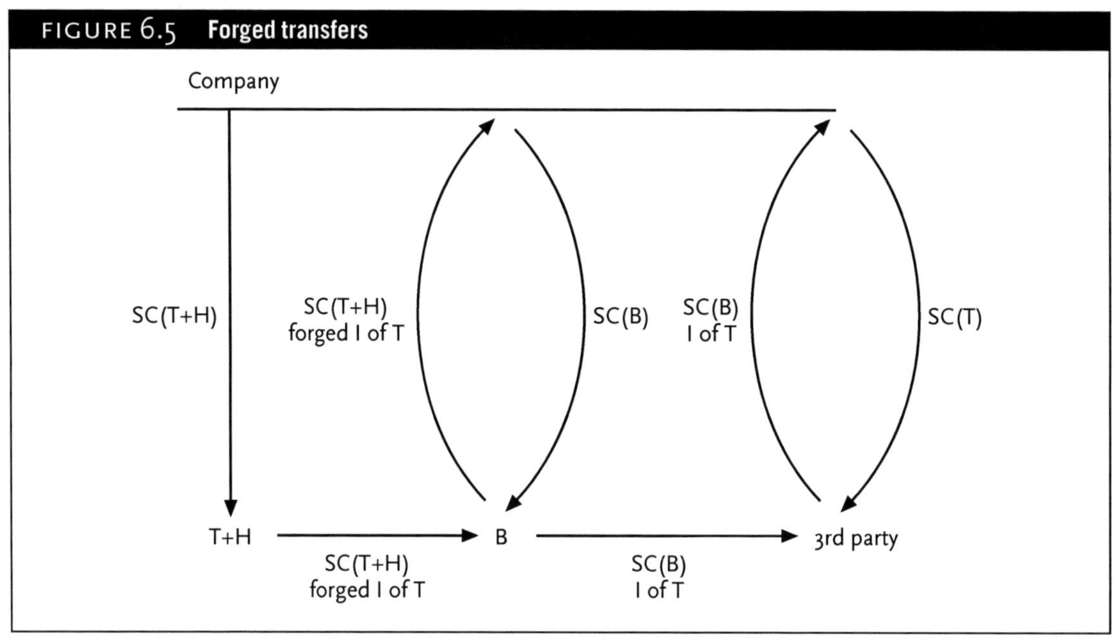

CASE EXAMPLE 6.3

***Re Bahia & San Francisco Railway Co.* (1868) LR 3 QB 584**

T was the registered holder of shares, the certificate for which she left with her broker. Her signature was forged on an instrument of transfer in favour of S. Notice of the transfer had been sent to her by the company but she had not responded to it. A new certificate was issued to S, who subsequently sold the shares to A. Lately the fraud was discovered and T's name was restored to the register. This can be illustrated by figure 6.6:

It was held that the company should indemnify A. The certificate issued by the company in favour of S constituted a statement by the company that S was entitled to the shares. The company was estopped from denying the truth of this statement. Thus, A was entitled to recover damages from the company (because her name had been removed from the register of members), the amount being the value of the shares as at the time the company removed her name from the register.

CASE EXAMPLE 6.3 CONTINUED

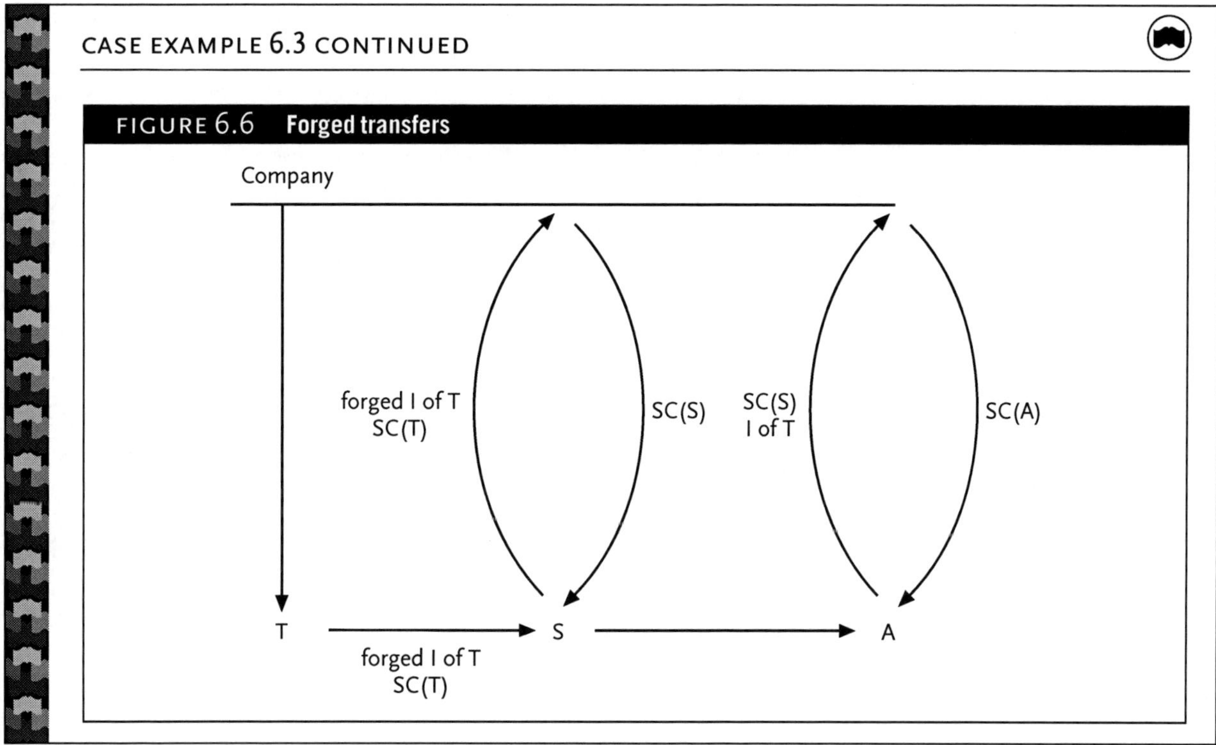

7 Transmission of shares

When a person dies, any shares that he holds move by transmission to his personal representative. Similarly, upon a person becoming bankrupt, any share he holds move by transmission to his trustee in bankruptcy. Transmission is different from transfer. Transmission occurs automatically by operation of law. A person acquiring shares by transmission may elect to have the shares registered in his own name, or to transfer them to a third party. When he wishes to take them in his own name, he sends to company a letter of request to this effect. When he wishes to transfer the shares, he does so using a stock transfer form. When the board receives a letter of request or a stock transfer form in this way it has the same right to reject the transfer as if the shares were being transferred by a living, or non-bankrupt owner.

mortgage
Security for a creditor traditionally created by the transfer of property to a lender on terms that upon repayment of the debt he will transfer the asset back to the borrower.

8 Mortgages of shares

To understand **mortgages** of shares, it is worth reviewing the basic principles of security. For obvious reasons, creditors prefer to take security for loans which they make. This is because if the debt is not paid, the creditor can sell the security to recover what is owing to him. Mortgages of shares are perhaps best understood by considering first the mortgage of domestic property. If a house owner wishes to raise some cash, he can do so by creating a mortgage over his house. In the early days of mortgages this actually involved transferring the title of the house to the lender. If the borrower defaulted on his payments, the lender could sell the house. Today with legal mortgages of land, the ownership of the land is not actually transferred to the lender.

Besides a legal mortgage, it is possible for a householder to create an equitable mortgage over his house. In this case he would give the title deeds of his house to the lender in return for the loan. If the borrower defaults, the lender can get an order of the court permitting him to sell the house. Thus, an equitable mortgage is created without many strict legal formalities, though today the borrower has to sign a document to the effect that he is depositing the deeds as security.

In much the same way, a shareholder can use his share certificate as security for a loan to create a mortgage of shares by depositing his share certificate with the lender together with an instrument of transfer which the borrower has signed but which has not otherwise been filled in. In the event of a default on the loan, the lender simply fills in the instrument of transfer and sells the shares without the need to go to court.

If the borrower were to create a legal mortgage, the shares would have to be transferred into the name of the lender. Since the lender's name would then be on the register of members as the holder of the shares, all dividends on the shares would be paid to him. This would make for some complicated accounting in dealing with the mortgage, with dividends paid having to be set off against interest payable.

The equitable mortgage of shares coupled with the use of the blank transfer form is a very simple way of using shares as security for a loan.

TEST YOUR KNOWLEDGE 6.2 

(a) How is a legal mortgage of shares created? How does this differ from an equitable mortgage?

(b) How is an equitable mortgage of shares usually created?

9 Share warrants

share warrant to bearer

The documentation issued to indicate the ownership of shares in a company where such shares are transferable merely by delivery, i.e. without the need for an instrument of transfer.

A **share warrant to bearer** is a document issued by a company stating that the bearer of the warrant is entitled to the shares specified therein. By CA 1985 s. 188, before a company may issue share warrants it must satisfy three criteria:

1 It must be limited by shares.
2 There must be authority in the Articles for the issue of warrants (there is no such authorisation in Table A).
3 The shares must be fully paid up.

When a warrant is issued, the company must remove the name of the holder from its register of members and enter on the register the fact that a warrant has been issued in respect of specified shares and its date.

Shares represented by warrants are freely transferable merely by delivery. The warrant is a negotiable instrument. If it is stolen and subsequently comes in to the possession of a purchaser in good faith and for value who does not have notice of the fraud, such purchaser can enforce against the company any rights represented by the warrant. It is for this reason that share warrants have never been popular in the United Kingdom. The company has no register of its warrant holders. Since they are transferable simply by delivery there is no obligation for the company to be informed of their transfer. This obviously is going to result in difficulties when it comes to the paying of dividends. This is overcome by attaching some coupons to the warrant. The fact that a dividend is payable is advertised in a specified newspaper. The warrant holder sends the appropriate coupon to the paying bank to send him the dividend. As well as the obvious dangers in the event of their being stolen, prior to 1979 they could not be issued without the consent of the Treasury and usually had also to be deposited with an 'authorised depository' such as a bank or solicitor. Although the restrictions no longer apply, warrants have not become popular.

TEST YOUR KNOWLEDGE 6.3 

State three reasons why, historically, share warrants are not popular in the United Kingdom.

CHAPTER SUMMARY

- Subject to any restrictions in a company's Articles, a shareholder may freely transfer his shares as he chooses.
- The company is informed of the transaction by the transferor completing a stock transfer form.
- On receipt of the document, the company will register the new holders name in the register and delete the transferor's entry.
- A share certificate in the transferee's name will then be issued to the new holder within two months of the transfer.
- If a shareholder is transferring part only of his shareholding, or is transferring to two or more different transferees, there is a need for certification.
- A company is estopped from denying the validity of the information contained in such a certificate.
- An equitable mortgage of shares is usually done by the shareholder depositing his share certificate with the lender together with a blank transfer form.
- Although certain companies have the power to issue share warrants, these are seldom encountered in practice.

CHAPTER 7

Debentures

CONTENTS

LEARNING OUTCOMES

This chapter covers borrowing by companies, including the creation of the loan and, where the loan is secured, the security documentation. It then covers what happens when the debtor company fails to make repayment and the lender seeks to enforce its security. After reading and understanding the contents of the chapter and studying the case examples you should be able to:

- Understand the nature of a debenture.
- Appreciate how companies can borrow and give security for loans.
- Understand the contents of security documentation.
- Understand the factors that can lead to the invalidation of a charge.
- Understand the different types of receivers and particularly the administrative receiver.
- Appreciate the effect of the appointment of a receiver.
- Understand what a receiver does and what are his duties.

debenture

The written evidence of a debt owing by a company; the document which creates or evidences a debt. Usually, though by no means always, a debenture is secured. This gives the creditor holding the debenture a priority over the unsecured creditors

fixed charge

Security created over a fixed asset such as a warehouse or an office block.

floating charge

A charge secured on a class of assets, present and future. The class is likely to change in the ordinary course of business from time to time. It is anticipated that the company will be free to deal with those assets subject to the charge until such time as the company ceases to carry on business in the usual way.

naked (unsecured) debenture

A debenture that is not supported by any security.

Introduction

The Companies Act makes no attempt to define the meaning of the word **debenture**. Section 744 merely states that debenture 'includes debenture stock, bonds and any other securities of a company, whether constituting a charge on the assets of the company or not'. The most widely used definition is that of Chitty J in *Levy v Abercorris Slate and Slab Co.* (1887) 37 Ch D 37 where he said:

> 'in my opinion a debenture means a document which either creates a debt or acknowledges it, and any document which fulfils either of these conditions is a debenture.'

Thus, a debenture is a written acknowledgement of a debt. It is important to note that the statutory statement of what a debenture includes uses the words 'whether constituting a charge on the assets of the company or not'. So a debenture need not necessarily be secured. Often it is secured either by a **fixed** or **floating charge** over assets of the company or by both a fixed and a floating charge. A fixed charge is a security created over a specific asset such as a warehouse or an office block. It is the same as the mortgage that an individual might have on his house. The essence of the charge is the stranglehold that the lender has over the secured property. The borrower cannot himself sell the property without the consent of the lender. A floating charge is far less specific and a great deal more flexible. Floating charges were the creation of Victorian lawyers to enable manufacturing companies to borrow on the security of those assets which, of their nature, the directors must be free to deal with. A floating charge would be over things such as raw materials, work in progress and finished products, which the directors need to be able to deal with so long as the company is viable and solvent. A debenture that does not have a security right attached to it (i.e. an unsecured debenture) is sometimes referred to as a **'naked' debenture**.

Later, we shall examine the remedies of debenture holders, but it is important, at this stage, to note that the significance between **secured debentures** and unsecured debentures lies in the remedies available to the debenture holder. A holder of an unsecured debenture has the same remedies open to him in the event of default by the company that are enjoyed by an unsecured creditor. Thus, he can sue for the money (and, having obtained judgment, enforce that judgment in the usual way) and, if he is owed more than £750, petition as a creditor for the winding up of the company. These remedies are also open to the secured debenture holder but his real power lies in the fact that he can either appoint a receiver under the terms of the debenture itself or apply to the court for the appointment of a receiver.

CASE EXAMPLE 7.1

Suppose a secured loan has been made to a landlord so that he can buy a block of flats. In the ordinary course of things, the rent from the tenants would be used by the landlord to pay the mortgage. Suppose the landlord were to default in his mortgage repayments. A receiver might be appointed on terms that the tenants should pay their rent to him, and he, from this rent, would discharge the landlord's obligations to the mortgage lender.

THEORY INTO PRACTICE 7.1

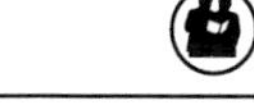

It should be noted at this stage that a receiver is very different from a liquidator. When a company is wound up a liquidator is appointed whose role is to get in the assets of the company and to pay as many of the company's debts as possible. The receiver, on the other hand, is appointed by a secured lender and once he has paid back the secured lender he must vacate office. In other words, it does not follow that just because a receiver is appointed that the end of the company is inevitable.

secured debenture

A debenture in which the lender enjoys security over some asset or assets of the company whether by way of a fixed or floating charge.

These remedies will be discussed in much more detail in this chapter, but it is of paramount importance to fix firmly in our minds at this stage that if a debenture is secured, the lender has the power to appoint a receiver. As has been said, debentures may be either unsecured or secured. In the case of the holder of an unsecured debenture, his remedies are limited. First, he may sue for the principal owing to him together with interest (if any). Having obtained judgment in this way he may levy execution on the company and seize assets which he can sell in order to pay his debts. Second, he may petition for the winding up of the company on the ground that it is unable to pay its debts. The holder of the secured debenture has both of these remedies, but in addition he can either appoint a receiver under the terms of the debenture or apply to the court for such an appointment to be made. The power to appoint or have appointed a receiver is one of the factors which gives a secured creditor particular power as compared with an unsecured creditor.

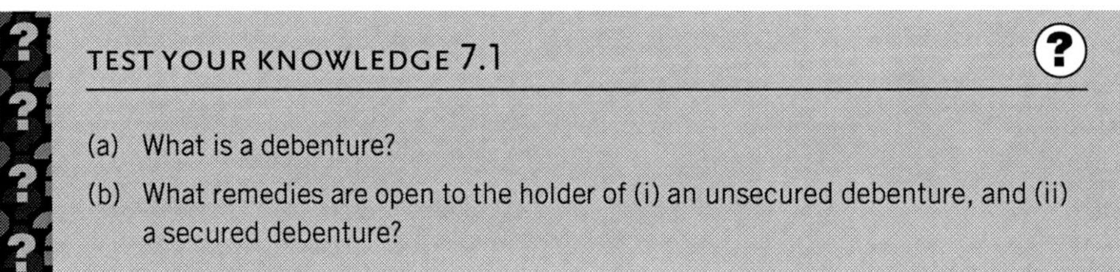

TEST YOUR KNOWLEDGE 7.1

(a) What is a debenture?

(b) What remedies are open to the holder of (i) an unsecured debenture, and (ii) a secured debenture?

1 Power to borrow

The Memorandum of Association of almost all companies contains an express power to borrow money. Since a debenture involves a loan to the company, to be able to enter into a debenture, the company must first have power to borrow. Even if no specific power is expressed in its objects, a trading company has an implied power to borrow for the purpose of carrying on its business and also to give security for the loan by way of creating a charge over its property. If the company is not formed for the purpose of trade, it must have a specific power to borrow in its objects clause. It will be recalled that, since the considerable inroads made into the *ultra vires* doctrine by the legislative changes of 1989, a third party can usually enforce a loan against a company, notwithstanding that it was entered into beyond the company's express or implied powers (CA 1985 s. 35(1)).

Sometimes the Articles of the company contain some restriction as to the amount which the directors can borrow of their own volition and without the consent of the company in general meeting. For example, the 1948 Table A stated in Article 79 that the directors could not without the previous sanction of the company in general meeting borrow a sum greater than the nominal amount of share capital of the company issued at the time of the loan. There is no such restriction in the 1985 Table A and borrowing limits are commonly found in the Articles of listed/quoted companies. Even where there is a restriction a third party is nevertheless able to enforce the loan against the company. It will be recalled that the amended s. 35 provides that a third party can treat the directors' powers to bind the company as being without limit.

2 The issue of debentures

The rules described above governing the public offer of shares apply equally to the public offer of debentures. However, as with the issue of shares, it is an extremely small proportion of companies that do actually offer them to the public. Most debentures are simply issued privately by the company to its bank or to some other lender.

Debentures are issued in accordance with the company' s Articles. Since Table A Article 70 provides that the day-to-day business of the company is conducted by the directors, the issue of debentures is usually made following a resolution of the board of directors. In other words, the members are not involved.

By CA 1985 s. 185, debenture certificates must be issued by the company within two months after the allotment of any debenture or debenture stock or within two months of the transfer of any debenture or debenture stock. The rules governing the transfer of shares (see Chapter 6) apply equally to the transfer of debentures. A contract to take up and pay for debentures may be enforced by means of an action brought by the company for an order for a specific performance. This is expressly provided by CA s. 195 and is an exception to the general rule of law that specific performance will never be granted in respect of a contract for the lending of money because damages are an adequate remedy.

TEST YOUR KNOWLEDGE 7.2 

How soon after the allotment or transfer of a debenture must a company issue a debenture certificate?

3 Security

The exact nature of the security which can be given by a company is discussed below. However it is important to understand in outline the type of security which can be created. As has been said, the security can take the form of a fixed or floating charge. The word 'charge' is generally used to describe a security created by a company.

3.1 Fixed charge

A fixed charge created by a company has exactly the same features as a mortgage created by an individual over his own house. Thus, the holder of a fixed charge has an immediate security over specific property and the company cannot dispose of the asset subject to the fixed charge without the consent of the charge holder. In the same way, a person lending money to a company on the security of say a warehouse or an office block is in the same position as a building society lending money to an individual on the security of his house. So long as the specific property which is subject to the charge does not fall in value, the loan is extremely safe, and the lender's loan is well protected. In return, the lender may charge a lower rate of interest for his loan.

3.2 Floating charge

The floating charge is very different from a fixed charge. A company whose line of business is manufacturing will have assets such as raw materials, work in progress, finished products and debts owing to the company which of their nature are constantly changing. Such a company can use these assets as the subject of a charge. However, a floating charge must leave the directors free to deal with these assets in the normal course of business. The directors must be able to call the raw materials into use, sell off the finished products, and generally carry on business in a normal way without having to seek the consent of the charge holder. This is the primary feature of the floating charge. A floating charge is particularly useful for a company that does not have any assets which could be the subject of a fixed charge. At least by granting a floating charge, the company can grant some form of security, which in turn may reduce the interest rate charged by the lender to the borrower for the loan, and may reduce the need for the company's directors to grant personal guarantees. However, as will be seen shortly, one major disadvantage of the floating charge is that when the time comes to realise the assets secured by the floating charge, the receiver will have to account to the company's preferential creditors before repaying the lender his loan; and the sums due to the preferential creditors frequently eat into the funds that might otherwise have been available to the lender. Preferential creditors include employees for arrears of wages and currently, the Inland Revenue and the Customs and Excise. However, Crown preference for tax liabilities is due to be abolished in the Enterprise Bill, which also provides for a proportion of assets covered by a floating charge to be available for unsecured creditors.

TEST YOUR KNOWLEDGE 7.3 

(a) What is the difference between a fixed and floating charge?

(b) What are the advantages to a lender in having (i) a fixed charge and (ii) a floating charge?

(c) What are the advantages to a borrower in having (i) a fixed charge and (ii) a floating charge?

4 Register of debenture holders

There is no statutory obligation on a company to keep a register of debenture holders. However, when there is a flotation of debenture stock the company usually undertakes, by a provision in the debenture itself, that it will keep a register, and if there is such a register it must be kept at the company's registered office or at any office of the company at which the work of making it up is done (CA 1985 s. 190). It must be available for inspection on the same terms as the register of members (CA 1985 s. 191).

5 Types of debenture

As has been said, a debenture is a written Memorandum of a loan and as such is a formal legal document. There are two main types of debenture:

1 A single debenture where the company borrows from a particular lender, for example from a bank.
2 Debenture stock subscribed by a large number of lenders. This is the method whereby a public company raises loan capital from the public generally. Here the lender is referred to as holding debenture stock.

A registered debenture (i.e. a debenture noted in the company's own register of debenture holders) is transferable, as has been said, in the same way as shares. A registered debenture is a **chose in action**. In other words, it is a right to sue for the recovery of a debt. It is, however, not a negotiable instrument and so a transferee will, in the absence of an express provision in the debenture itself to the contrary, take subject to equities, i.e. subject to any claims which the company may have against prior holders of the debenture as at the date of the transfer (see Case Example 7.2).

d

chose in action
A right to sue for the recovery of a debt.

CASE EXAMPLE 7.2 

***Re Rhodesia Gold Fields Limited* [1910] 1 Ch 239**

A holder of debenture stock transferred the stock to another person who was duly registered by the company. The transferor was a director of the company and owed money to the company. If the transferor had still been in possession of the debenture stock, the company would have been entitled to set off the amount which he owed to the company against the money owed by the company under the debenture. In other words, when repaying the amount of the debenture the company could deduct such sum as the transferor owed to the company. It was held that the transferee was in exactly the same position as the transferor would have been in. He took subject to equities and so, when the company came to repay the debenture, it could deduct from the sum payable the amount owed to it by the transferor.

In order to avoid this situation there is now usually an express provision in the debenture itself to state that the principal and interest shall be paid to a registered holder without regard to any equities. In effect this is a contract that the company will not rely on equities. This, of course, makes the debentures far more marketable.

CASE EXAMPLE 7.3

***Re Goy & Co. Ltd* [1900] 2 Ch 149**

A director of a company transferred debentures which he held in the company to a transferee as security for a loan. There was an express provision in the debentures that any transferee took free from equities. The company went into liquidation and the liquidator took proceedings for misfeasance against the director. The court found against the director and ordered him to pay compensation to the liquidator. It was held that the liquidator had no entitlement to set off the amount owed by the transferor director against any monies due under the debentures to the transferee.

TEST YOUR KNOWLEDGE 7.4

What are the two kinds of debenture?

6 Perpetual debentures

By CA 1985 s. 193, a condition in a debenture is not invalid by reason only that the debentures are made irredeemable or only redeemable on the happening of a contingency or on the expiration of a specified period of time. This is said to be notwithstanding any rule of equity to the contrary. This means that a company can issue a debenture which it undertakes not to repay until the occurrence of a specified event (for example, the company going into liquidation) or until the expiration of a long period of time (e.g. ten years). At first sight it might appear rather odd that the Act should take the trouble to make this statement. However, it is necessary that it should be made as this is in sharp contradiction to an ordinary mortgage that an individual may have over his house. In this situation, the individual can discharge the mortgage at any time despite the undertaking to repay over a period of years (the most common house mortgage is for 25 years).

The rule of equity referred to in s. 193 is that there can be no 'clogs on the equity of redemption'. A clog means a bar and the equity of redemption is the right to pay off a mortgage. Therefore, the rule of equity is that there can be no provision in a mortgage which bars the mortgagor from paying off the mortgage prematurely. This is necessary with a domestic mortgage because the mortgagor may need to move house and must be free to pay off his mortgage early. However, a company may bind itself only to borrow over a long period of time and in this situation it would be unfair to the lender for the company to be able to pay off the loan prematurely, for example if interest rates were to fall. An example of the operation of the rule occurred in *Knightsbridge Estates Trust Limited* v *Byrne*.

friendly society

A type of insurance company; amongst other things, a friendly society will often lend money to borrowers on the security of a mortgage.

CASE EXAMPLE 7.4

***Knightsbridge Estates Trust Limited* v *Byrne* [1940] AC 613**

A company mortgaged freehold property to a **friendly society** to secure a loan of £310,000, which it agreed to pay by instalments of principal and interest over a period of 40 years. Interest rates fell before the expiration of the 40-year period and the company sought to redeem the mortgage and borrow the money elsewhere at a cheaper rate. It was held that the mortgage was in fact a debenture and that it was not redeemable. Under what is now s. 193, the loan could only be redeemed at the time provided in the debenture.

7 Re-issue of redeemed debentures

A company may issue debentures on terms that they are redeemable at the option of the company. This is as distinct from their being irredeemable. By s. 194, when debentures have been redeemed the company may re-issue them or issue other debentures in their place. This is a rule of general application to which there are a number of exceptions. The company may not re-issue debentures if:

1 There is provision to the contrary in the company's Articles.
2 There is provision to the contrary in any contract entered into by the company.
3 The company has passed a resolution in general meeting or carried out some other act which manifests its intention that the debentures should be cancelled.

TEST YOUR KNOWLEDGE 7.5 

Normally a company may re-issue redeemed debentures, but under certain circumstances this is forbidden. What are these circumstances?

8 Convertible debentures

Sometimes a company issues convertible debentures. These are debentures which the holder may convert into shares at a stated time. To understand why a company may wish to do this it is necessary to remember the difference between shares and debentures.

THEORY INTO PRACTICE 7.2 

What is the difference between shares and debentures?

Answer

A company may only pay an income on shares (i.e. dividends) in the event of the company's making profits. Assuming that a person who buys shares in a company does so for the purpose of obtaining an income, he is unlikely to want to buy shares in a long-term venture which may not make a profit for some time. On the other hand, a company must pay interest on a debenture otherwise, in the event of its being secured, it will find a receiver being appointed by the secured lender.

A debenture on which interest must be paid is obviously more attractive to an investor in a situation where it may be some years before the company is making any profits. On the other hand, the threat of a receiver and indeed the obligation to pay interest is something such a company may well wish to avoid.

Moreover, in the event of the company making profits, capital growth is likely to occur in the market value of the shares as the dividend income per share rises with the profits whereas, since the interest on debentures is fixed, the market value of the debenture is likely to remain fairly static.

Because of these factors, a company embarking on a long-term project – for example, the acquisition of a site on which a factory is going to be built and which will not be in profit for a number of years – may well seek to raise the capital initially by way of debentures and then allow the debenture holders to convert the debentures into shares at a specified time in the future (usually the date when the directors estimate the company will be into profit). There is, of course, a general prohibition under s. 100 against a company issuing shares at a discount. There is, however, no such prohibition in respect of debentures. Thus, a company may issue a £100 debenture for £80 redeemable at par value in five years time. Thus, the debenture holder pays only £80 for the debenture, but receives income as though he had paid the full

£100 and also obtains a £20 capital growth over the five-year period. The problem of convertible debentures issued at a discount was considered in the case of *Mosely* v *Koffyfontein Mines Ltd* [1904] 2 Ch 108.

CASE EXAMPLE 7.5 

***Mosely* v *Koffyfontein Mines Ltd* [1904] 2 Ch 108**

A debenture was issued at a discount on terms that it could immediately be converted into fully paid shares equal to par. It was held that since the debentures were immediately convertible this was, in fact, an issue of shares at a discount and therefore unlawful. Cozens-Hardy LJ reserved judgment on the question whether an option to convert was valid if it were stated not to be exercisable until some time after the date of issue of the debenture. Some writers have suggested that the issue at a discount of a convertible debenture which is convertible only on or after a specified date in the future will not result in the shares being issued at a discount. Others, however, have suggested otherwise. Until the courts specifically rule on this matter it must remain undecided.

TEST YOUR KNOWLEDGE 7.6 

What do you understand by a convertible debenture?

9 The form of the debenture

As was stated above, the debenture is usually a formal legal document and may fall into one of two broad types:

1 *A single debenture*. A typical example of this is where a company obtains a loan or overdraft from a bank. In this case, the debenture will be on the bank's own standard form which will create security for the bank by way of a fixed charge over the company's fixed assets and floating charge over the remainder of the undertaking.
2 *Debenture stock*. This is where a public company raises loan capital from the public generally. The borrowing by the company is treated as a single loan but each lender has a specified amount of debenture stock. The terms on which the debenture stock is issued are to be found in a debenture **trust deed**.

trust deed

A deed issued where there is a public flotation of debenture stock and which appoints trustees in whom the underlying security can be vested and who represent the interests of the individual debenture holders.

A trust deed is necessary for two main reasons:

1 In English law a legal estate in land (such as the freehold of the land) can never be vested in more than four persons. This prohibition is to be found in the Law of Property Act 1925, the principal Act in English Law concerned with **real property**. Thus if land is owned by six persons, the actual estate must be stated to vest in four or fewer of them and they will then hold the land on trust for the six. A legal mortgage is a legal estate and so the mortgage cannot be vested in more than four persons. In the case of a public company raising money from a large number of individuals it is obviously necessary for trustees to be appointed (in whom the fixed charge or mortgage can be vested as security for the loan as a whole) and this is done in the trust deed.
2 There is also a practical reason that an individual lender may not have a sufficient financial interest to justify him in enforcing his loan. For example, if a person invests £1,000 in 8 per cent debenture stock then, assuming that interest is paid twice yearly, he will receive the sum of £40 (less tax) twice each year. In the event of this interest not being paid he may find it uneconomical to enforce his right to interest against the company. Obviously, however, where the entitlements of all the individual lenders are consolidated in trustees, the trustees are under an obligation to enforce these entitlements.

real property

Land.

The main terms of a debenture trust deed are:

1 the appointment of trustees (often a merchant bank or an insurance company),
2 provision for the remuneration of the trustees,
3 provision for an indemnity for the trustees,
4 creation of a legal mortgage on the company's fixed assets,
5 creation of a floating charge on the undertaking of the company generally,
6 an undertaking by the company to pay interest on the loan and to repay the principal moneys at specified times,
7 a statement of the circumstances in which these securities may be enforced (e.g. default in payment of principal or interest),
8 provision for the trustee to take possession of the charged property when the security becomes enforceable,
9 undertaking by the company to maintain a register of debenture holders,
10 undertaking by the company to keep in repair and insure any property charged,
11 provision for meetings of debenture holders,
12 provision for the trustees to appoint an administrative receiver in the event of the security becoming enforceable.

The advantages of a trust deed include:

1 The creation of a legal mortgage over the fixed assets of the company means that no person who subsequently lends money to the company may obtain priority over the debenture holders.
2 The trustees can act quickly in order to protect the debenture holders in the event of a default occurring.
3 The powers enjoyed by the trustees mean that they are in a position to see that the company performs all its obligations under the debenture trust deed.
4 The power of the trustees to appoint an administrative receiver in the event of default by the company avoids the need to apply to the court for the appointment.
5 So long as the floating charge has not crystallised (i.e. attaches to specific assets), the company may use the property subject to the floating charge in the normal course of business.

Finally, it should be noted that, by s. 192, any provision in a trust deed or in any contract with the holders of debentures secured by a trust deed, which purports to exempt a trustee of the deed or indemnify him against liability for breach of trust where he fails to show the degree of care and diligence required of him as trustee, is void. This does not, however, apply in the case of:

1 A release given after the liability has arisen.
2 Any provision which permits such a release to be given by a majority of not less than three-fourths in value of the debenture holders present and voting in person or by proxy at a meeting specifically summoned for that purpose. The release may be either in respect of specific acts or omissions or upon the trustee dying or ceasing to act.
3 Any provision which was in force on 1 July 1948 so long as there remains at least one trustee who was appointed prior to that date. Whilst such a trustee is in post, the protection given by such a provision can be extended to all trustees of the deed by resolution passed, again, by a majority of not less than three-fourths in value of the debenture holders present or voting by proxy at a meeting specifically summoned for that purpose.

TEST YOUR KNOWLEDGE 7.7 

(a) What are the two main types of debenture in English law?
(b) When and why is a debenture trust deed necessary?
(c) What are the main provisions of a debenture trust deed?

10 Secure debentures

crystallisation

The process whereby a floating charge becomes fixed.

preferential creditors

Creditors entitled to receive payment on a liquidation in advance of the floating charge holders and unsecured creditors: amongst the preferential creditors are £800 arrears of pay for employees, the last 12 months PAYE and NI due from the company and also the last six months' VAT.

As has been stated above, the real significance of a secured debenture is that the debenture holder may appoint a receiver in the event of specified occurrences and also apply to the court for the appointment of a receiver. Thus, in practice the majority of debentures are secured. It is necessary now to look at the two methods of securing debentures, namely fixed and floating charges.

10.1 Fixed charge

A fixed charge is straightforward. It can be created by either a legal or an equitable mortgage on specific property. A fixed charge has all the features of a normal domestic mortgage. It is created by following the procedure appropriate to mortgage property of the type in question. The obvious advantage of a fixed charge is that it attaches to specific property at the time that it is created and therefore gives the holder an immediate security over that property in priority to any subsequent claimant. Thus, the company cannot dispose of the property without the consent of the charge holder. This is the key feature of a fixed charge – the control over the secured property exercisable by the creditor or chargee.

10.2 Floating charge

A floating charge is an equitable charge on some or all of the company's undertaking, in other words, its property both present and future. The classic definition of a floating charge is contained in the judgment of Romer LJ:

CASE EXAMPLE 7.6

***Re Yorkshire Woolcombers Association Ltd* [1903] 2 Ch 284**

Romer LJ said that a floating charge had three characteristics:

1 It is a charge on all the assets of the company present and future.
2 The class is one which, in the ordinary course of the company's business, is changing from time to time.
3 It is contemplated by the charge that, until some future step is taken by or on behalf of those interested in the charge, the company may carry on its business in the ordinary way, so far as concerns the particular class of assets.

invoice discounting

The process whereby following the supply of goods or services to a customer a company sends a copy of the relevant invoice to a banking institution which then immediately pays a substantial proportion of the amount invoiced to the company.

book debts

Cash sums owing to a company, for example after the supply of goods or services to a customer.

Notwithstanding this, the security becomes enforceable when the charge crystallises. Usually the debenture will state that an administrative receiver may be appointed over the property charged when certain occurrences arise, e.g. where there is default in the payment of interest or principal. **Crystallisation** is discussed more fully in the next chapter. It is only necessary at this stage to appreciate that when crystallisation does occur, the right of the directors to deal with the assets subject to the charge ceases. It follows, therefore, that the exact value of the security will not be known until crystallisation and as such it is not as good a protection for the lender as a fixed charge.

Because of the disadvantage of floating charges in that they rank after the **preferential creditors** and the advent of **invoice discounting**, lenders have over recent decades sought to develop a form of fixed charge over **book debts** owing to a company. However, the practice has been dealt a substantial blow in *Re Brumark Investments Ltd* [2001] BCC 259, also reported as *Agnew* v *CIR* [2001] BCLC 188) (generally known by the former title since technically these are the first words in the case reference).

CASE EXAMPLE 7.7

Re Brumark Investments Ltd **[2001] BCC 259 (also reported as *Agnew* v *CIR* [2001] BCLC 188)**

A company had attempted to create a fixed charge over book debts owing to it. The Privy Council explained that the essence of a fixed charge was the complete control that the lender had over the secured asset. (Think of a mortgage over one's own home. The consent of the mortgage lender is required before the borrower can sell the property.) The distinguishing feature of a floating charge is the fact that the company can carry on business in the ordinary way with the asset concerned. In the absence of absolute control by the lender then, regardless of how the parties themselves described the security, it could be no more than a floating charge.

TEST YOUR KNOWLEDGE 7.8

(a) What is the difference between a fixed and a floating charge?

(b) Define a floating charge.

(c) Can a charge described by the parties as a fixed charge ever be found by the courts to be no more than a floating charge?

11 The avoidance of charges

A charge is void and the holder ranks merely as an unsecured creditor in three circumstances:

1 Where the charge is not registered within 21 days of creation (CA s. 395).
2 Where it was given as a preference within six months of the commencement of a winding up of the company. This period is extended to two years where the preference is given to a connected person (IA 1986 s. 239).
3 In the case of a floating charge, where it was created within 12 months of the commencement of a winding up, with certain exceptions (again the period is extended to two years where the charge is in favour of a connected person) (IA s. 245).

11.1 Non-registration

By CA s. 395, every charge must be registered with the Registrar of Companies within 21 days of its creation. Failure to register the charge within this period renders the charge void and any moneys secured by the charge for which the loan was given become immediately repayable. Late registration is only possible with the leave of the court and then only if it can be established that the failure to register was due to accident, inadvertence or other sufficient cause.

11.2 Preferences

By IA 1986 s. 239, a company gives a preference to a person if it does something or suffers anything to be done which has the effect of putting that person in a position which, in the event of the company going into insolvent liquidation, will be better than the position he would have been in if the thing had not been done. The person preferred must be one of the company's creditors or a surety or guarantor for any of the company's debts or other liabilities.

An obvious example of a preference in this situation would occur where a manufacturing company is heavily insolvent. The directors intend winding up and starting up another company in the same line of business. They wish to ensure that the supply of certain raw materials to the new company from a particular creditor of the old company is assured. They do not have sufficient money in the old company to pay off the creditor, but they do have some freehold land on which there is no existing charge. Thus, they give that creditor a fixed charge over the land and then put the company into liquidation. The intention is clearly that the creditor will be paid in advance of all other creditors of the company. In a case such as this the liquidator may make an application to the court which has power to make such order as it thinks fit for restoring the position to what it would have been had the company not given the preference. It cannot make an order unless it is satisfied that the company in giving the preference was influenced by a desire to produce, in relation to the person to whom the preference was given, the preferential position described above. Exactly what is meant by the expression 'influenced ... by such a desire' has yet to be pronounced upon by the courts, but there is no doubt that there would be a preference in the situation just described. On the other hand, had the creditor been threatening to put the company into liquidation if he were not given the charge, then there might not be a preference since the overwhelming intention of the directors was not so much to prefer the creditor as to prevent winding up proceedings.

For there to be a preference, the charge must have been created in the period of six months prior to the commencement of the winding up. In the case of a compulsory liquidation, this means the date of presentation of the petition (IA 1986 s. 129). In the case of a voluntary winding up, it means the date of the passing of the resolution to wind up by the members (IA 1986 s. 86). Where the company is wound up immediately following the discharge of an administration order, it commences at the date of presentation of the petition pursuant to which the administration order was made (IA 1986 s. 240).

In the case of the charge being created in favour of a person connected with the company, then this period of time in which it can be invalidated is extended to two years prior to the commencement of the winding up. By IA 1986 s. 249, a person is connected with the company if he is a director or shadow director of the company or an associate of a director or shadow director or of the company itself. An associate of an individual means that individual's spouse or a relative of the individual or the spouse. In this context, relative means mother, father, brother, sister, son, daughter, uncle, aunt, nephew and niece and a company is an associate of a person having control of it.

11.3 Invalidation of floating charges

By IA 1986 s. 245, any floating charge created by the company in the 12-month period prior to the commencement of the winding up (as defined above) is void except to the extent that money was paid for goods or services supplied to the company or a debt of the company was reduced or discharged in consideration of and at the same time as or immediately after the creation of the charge. The charge is not invalidated if the company can show that it was solvent immediately after the creation of the charge.

The clear policy behind s. 245 is to prevent the directors of an insolvent company from creating a floating charge so as to allow creditors to get into a position of priority over other creditors of the company during the 12 months prior to the commencement of the winding up. As has been said, this does not apply where the charge is created in return for value given to the company. Moreover, as has been said, the charge is not invalidated if the company can show that it was solvent immediately after the creation of the charge.

TEST YOUR KNOWLEDGE 7.9

(a) Review the following sequence:

1 Debt incurred.
2 Company completely solvent.
3 Floating charge created to secure the debt.
4 Company goes into insolvent liquidation within one year.

Is the charge valid or invalid, and why?

(b) Review the following sequence:

1 Company insolvent.
2 Company incurs debt.
3 Company creates floating charge to secure debt.
4 Company goes into insolvent liquidation within one year.

Is the charge valid or invalid, and why?

(c) Review this sequence:

1 Company insolvent.
2 Company asks bank for an overdraft facility – floating charge created to secure overdraft.
3 Company borrows on the security of the overdraft.
4 Company goes into insolvent liquidation within one year of the creation of the charge.

Is the charge valid or invalid, and why?

The situation is slightly different where the floating charge is created in favour of a connected person (as described above). In such a case, the period of time in which the charge can be invalidated can be extended to two years prior to the commencement of the winding up. Moreover, the fact that the company was able to pay its debts immediately after the creation of the charge does not validate the charge.

It should be noted that when a company has an overdraft and creates a floating charge to secure that overdraft, as soon as sufficient sums have been paid into the account equal to the amount of the overdraft all further borrowing constitutes fresh money. This is illustrated in Case Example 7.8.

CASE EXAMPLE 7.8

***Re Yeovil Glove Co. Ltd* [1965] Ch 148**

The company had a current account overdraft of £65,000. It created a floating charge to secure this amount and subsequently in the course of normal trading it paid in cheques to the value of £110,000, and also withdrew £110,000. Within a year of the creation of the floating charge the company went into liquidation. The overdraft stood at £64,000. It was held that the sums trading to the account after the creation of the charge discharged the earlier indebtedness and thus the whole of the £65,000 owing at the time of creation of the charge had been repaid. Thus the £64,000 overdraft, as at the date when the company went into liquidation, was new money and therefore fully secured.

The exception that the charge is valid in so far as any sums are paid to the company at or after the time of and in consideration of the creation of the charge only applies where the charge is created for the benefit of the company. This is illustrated by Case Example 7.9.

CASE EXAMPLE 7.9

***Re Destone Fabrics Ltd* [1941] Ch 219**

The company was heavily insolvent. It owed £350 to each of two directors, and there was also a third party, D, who had guaranteed the company's overdraft of £200. In the event of the company's going into liquidation and the third party's being called upon to pay out on the guarantee then he would, of course, become a creditor of the company. D paid £900 to his nominee who then advanced the £900 to the company in return for a floating charge in the nominee's favour. As soon as the company had the £900 it paid the £350 owing to each of the directors and £200 to D. Shortly afterwards the company went into liquidation. It was held that the floating charge was invalid. Even though money had been received by the company in return for the charge, that money had been of no benefit to the company since it had immediately been paid out to the directors and to D.

register of charges
The statutory register that has to be maintained by every company to contain details of all charges over the company or its property.

12 Registration in the company's register of charges

By s. 407, every limited company must keep at its registered office a **register of charges**. This is mandatory, unlike the register of debenture holders referred to above. On the register of charges the company must enter all charges affecting the property of the company and all floating charges on the company's undertaking or any of its property. Each entry must give a short description of the property charged, the amount of the charge and the names of any persons entitled to it. Under s. 406, the company must also keep at its registered office a copy of every instrument creating the charge which has to be registered with the Registrar of Companies under s. 395. The register of charges and copies of the charges themselves must be available for inspection by members of the company, creditors or any other person. Failure to maintain the register of charges or to allow inspection is a criminal offence for which officers of the company can be prosecuted. It should be noted that this requirement for the company to maintain its own register of charges is over and above the need for charges to be registered with the Registrar of Companies. Unlike the case of registration with the Registrar, failure to register on the company's own register has no effect on the validity or otherwise of the charge. Failure to satisfy the statutory requirement does, however, result in a criminal offence being committed by any officer of the company responsible.

13 Priority of charges

judgment creditor
A creditor who has sued the company owing him money and obtained judgment from the court in his favour.

distress
The process whereby a landlord goes onto the premises of his tenant to seize goods that he can sell to reimburse himself for outstanding rent.

When a company creates successive charges on the same property, the basic rule is that they rank in the order of creation. Thus, a first legal mortgage ranks in priority to a second legal mortgage over the same land. Likewise, equitable mortgages over the same property rank in the order in which they were created. As a general rule a fixed charge, whether it is legal or equitable, over specific assets takes priority over a floating charge even where that floating charge was created prior to the creation of the fixed charge. There is an exception to this described below.

There are certain creditors who take priority over a floating charge. These include:

1 A **judgment creditor** who completes execution prior to crystallisation. This means a creditor who has sued the company for the money and obtained judgment and who then, not having been paid, asks the court to order that the sheriff should go to the company' s property and seize goods which he can sell in order to pay the judgment debt. Execution is complete once the goods have been sold by the sheriff and he has paid over the proceeds of sale to the creditor.
2 Landlords who have levied **distress** for rent prior to crystallisation. If a landlord is owed money for rent then in certain circumstances he can go onto the premises of

the company and seize assets which he can then sell in order to recover the rent owing to him.

3 The statutory preferential creditors who, although unsecured, rank before the floating charge holders.

retention of title clause

A clause sometimes inserted into a contract for the sale of goods providing that the ownership in the goods is not to pass to the buyer until such time as the goods have been paid for.

4 The owner of goods which are in the possession of the company under a hire-purchase agreement or on a hire contract, or which are subject to a retention of title clause. A **retention of title clause** is sometimes known as a Romalpa clause after the case *Aluminium Industrie Vaassen BV* v *Romalpa Aluminium Ltd* [1976] 2 All ER 552 in which the efficacy of such a clause was recognised. Whenever a person is selling goods he has a right to insert in the contract of sale a provision that the ownership of the goods shall not pass until the goods are paid for. For example, if one person sells his car to another he may put a provision in the contract of sale that until the cheque he received in payment for the car has been cleared, the ownership in the car will not pass to the purchaser. This has the effect that in the event of the cheque not being honoured and the purchaser going bankrupt the seller can recover the car rather than simply suing for the money and probably receiving a dividend of rather less than 100p in the pound. In exactly the same way, in a more commercial contract, a brick manufacturer may supply bricks to a builder subject to retention of title clause. Then in the event of a builder going into liquidation the brick manufacturer can recover the bricks rather than simply suing for the money.

5 A creditor in whose favour a floating charge has been created may try to protect himself against the loss of his priority by inserting a term in the floating charge prohibiting the company from creating a subsequent fixed charge over the same property. Although, as has been said above, if the company creates a fixed charge in contravention of this prohibition, the creditor taking the fixed charge nevertheless generally takes priority over the floating charge holder. This is not the case where the person taking the fixed charge actually knew of the prohibition in the floating charge. These points are illustrated by the facts of Case Example 7.10.

CASE EXAMPLE 7.10

***Wilson* v *Kelland* [1910] 2 Ch. 306**

A company created a floating charge particulars of which were duly filed with the Registrar of Companies. Amongst the particulars filed was a prohibition in the floating charge against the creation or subsequent fixed charges ranking in priority. Some time later a fixed charge was created in favour of a creditor who had not searched the company's file. It was held that since the fixed charge creditor was unaware of the prohibition in the floating charge, he enjoyed priority over the floating charge.

Had the creditor made the search at Companies House and thus learnt of the prohibition, and were the holder of the floating charge able to show that the creditor knew of the prohibition against subsequent fixed charges ranking in priority, he would have been in a completely different position. The floating charge would then have ranked in priority.

It is important to note here that for the floating charge to gain priority it must be shown that the person taking the fixed charge actually knew of the prohibition. Even where the priority is noted on the documentation used to register the charge with the Registrar, there is no constructive knowledge of this fact. The reason for this is because constructive knowledge can only relate to those things that have by law to be registered. There is no statutory requirement that a priority agreement should be registered. Therefore there is no constructive notice.

It should perhaps be added that it is most unusual for a creditor taking a charge not to carry out a company's search, and it would be difficult in practice for a creditor to argue that he was unaware of the priority agreement since they are so very common. A creditor could reasonably be expected to be aware of the likelihood of such an agreement – and of the need to look out for one. Nevertheless, a creditor taking a later fixed charge in theory only loses priority to an earlier floating charge if it can be shown that he actually knew of the prohibition.

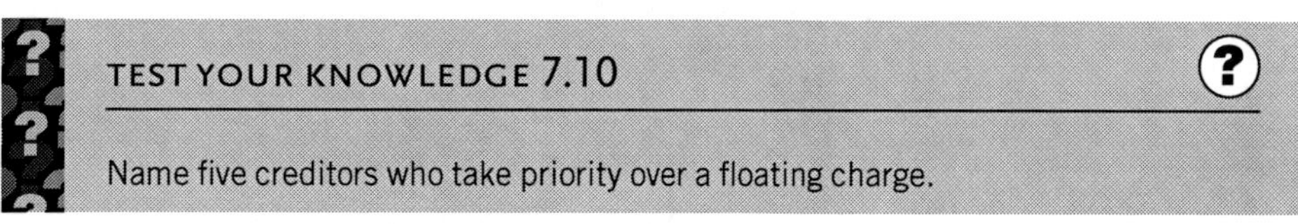
TEST YOUR KNOWLEDGE 7.10

Name five creditors who take priority over a floating charge.

14 Remedies on default: insolvency practitioners

Before we move on to look at the remedies available to the holders of secured debentures, it is necessary to consider how insolvency law has developed over recent decades. In the mid-1970s, a committee was set up under Sir Kenneth Cork to look in to the law on insolvency. The committee made certain recommendations, some of which found their way in to the Insolvency Act 1985 which has now been consolidated into the Insolvency Act 1986. Before the 1986 Act came into force there was widespread abuse by liquidators, frequently completely unqualified, who would act in a most unscrupulous manner in relation to the affairs of the company to which they had been appointed. The Cork Committee made a number of recommendations with a view to bringing this abuse to an end, one of which was the introduction of the requirement that all insolvency practitioners should have a formal qualification. By IA 1986 s. 389, it is a criminal offence for anyone to act as an insolvency practitioner unless qualified so to do. The expression 'act as an insolvency practitioner' means acting as a liquidator, administrator, administrative receiver or supervisor of a voluntary arrangement. However, it is important to note the two requirements of an insolvency practitioner:

1 he must be qualified under the rules of a recognised public body to act as an insolvency practitioner or be authorised so to act by the Secretary of State; and
2 he must have proper insurance bonding.

15 Types of receiver

The Insolvency Act 1986 draws a clear distinction between types of receiver. A receiver appointed under a floating charge is usually an administrative receiver and, as such, must be an insolvency practitioner. Other receivers need not be insolvency practitioners.

There are three main types of receivers:

1 *'Ordinary' receivers* 'Ordinary' receivers are appointed to receive income from a fixed charge, for example, to receive income from premises.
2 *Receivers and managers* A receiver and manager can be appointed under a floating charge and need not be an administrative receiver. Frequently, building companies acquire sites for development by borrowing on the security of a floating charge secured over the particular site in question. Land is, after all, stock in trade to a builder and not something to be retained indefinitely. If such a site does not constitute the whole or substantially the whole of the undertaking of the company then a receiver appointed over it will need to be appointed as receiver and manager.
3 *Administrative receivers* An administrative receiver is defined under IA 1986 s. 29 as a receiver appointed under a floating charge to manage 'the whole or substantially the whole of the company's property'. Most floating charges are, in practice, over the whole or substantially the whole of the company's property and so, as has been said, almost all receivers appointed under floating charges are administrative receivers. An administrative receiver must be an insolvency practitioner. It is a criminal offence for anyone other than a qualified insolvency practitioner to act as an administrative receiver.

TEST YOUR KNOWLEDGE 7.11 

What are the three main types of receiver?

receiver

A person appointed either to receive income or to preserve property.

15.1 Appointment of a receiver

As has been said, a **receiver** used to be appointed by the court. Now it is more usual for the appointment to be made out of court under some provision in the debenture creating the security. Indeed, it is impossible for an administrative receiver to be appointed other than out of court. It is generally preferable for a receiver to be appointed out of court because of the savings in costs and the consequent increase in funds available for the creditors.

15.2 Receiver appointed out of court

The appointment of a person as a receiver or manager of a company's property under powers contained in a debenture takes effect when the document of appointment is delivered to him, so long as he accepts the appointment by the end of the next business day. If the appointment of a person as a receiver or manager of a company's property is discovered to be invalid, for example because the charge was never registered or because of some defect in the appointment, the court may order the person making the appointment to indemnify the receiver against any liability which arises solely by reason of the invalidity (IA 1986 s. 34). This, however, does not protect a receiver from liability arising in any other way, for example through his negligence.

15.3 Appointment by the court

The court may appoint a receiver in three situations:

1 *Where the principal or interest is in arrear.* In practice it is never necessary to make an application to the court on such a ground because obviously this is provided for in the debenture itself.
2 *When the company is being wound up.* This highlights the essential difference between a receiver and a liquidator. Both may hold office simultaneously in respect of the same company. The receiver's obligations are very much narrower than the liquidator's. The receiver is concerned primarily with looking after the interests of the debenture holder who appointed him. The liquidator has a far wider brief, being concerned with the interests of the creditors generally.
3 *Where the security is in jeopardy.* Jeopardy arises when the security is at risk of being taken from the company and used for the payment of creditors ranking behind the debenture holder.

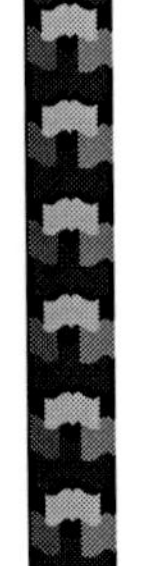

CASE EXAMPLE 7.11 

***Re London Pressed Hinge Co. Ltd* [1905] 1 Ch 576**

A company had created a debenture. There was no default either in payment of the principal or interest. An unsecured creditor had obtained judgment against the company and, because the judgment was unsatisfied, was about to levy execution.

It was held that the security was in jeopardy (i.e. it could be seized by the bailiff in enforcing the judgment in favour of the unsecured creditor) and so a receiver should be appointed.

Similarly in *McMahon v North Kent Iron Works*:

CASE EXAMPLE 7.12 

McMahon* v *North Kent Iron Works **[1891] 2 Ch 148**

The premises of a company had been closed and creditors were threatening to take action against the company. It was held that a receiver should be appointed to look after the interests of a debenture holder since his security was in jeopardy.

On the other hand, there is no jeopardy merely because the security is falling in value:

CASE EXAMPLE 7.13 

Re New York Taxicab Co. **[1913] 1 Ch 1**

The company's assets had fallen in value but there was no apparent risk of their being seized by creditors of the company. Indeed, there was no evidence of any pressure being put on the company by the creditors. It was held that there was no ground for the appointment of a receiver. The security was not in jeopardy.

TEST YOUR KNOWLEDGE 7.12 

When may a receiver be appointed by the court?

15.4 The effect of appointment

The following occurs when a receiver is appointed.

1 *Crystallisation*

Floating charges crystallise and become fixed. The receiver's powers in respect of those assets on which the charge crystallises displace the normal managerial powers of the directors in respect of that property, and the company cannot deal with those assets unless the receiver expressly consents. The crystallisation and fixing of the floating charge does not, however, mean that the chargee should be repaid before the preferential creditors. In this regard he remains in the same place in the pecking order for the creditors as he occupied before the crystallisation, i.e. after the preferential creditors.

TEST YOUR KNOWLEDGE 7.13 

In what order are creditors paid?

2 *The directors*

The directors are not dismissed by the appointment of a receiver, though their powers to deal with the assets subject to the floating charge come to an end. When the appointment of the receiver is over the undertaking of the company, the directors' powers in relation to the company are suspended. Nevertheless, since the directors continue in office they may take any action on behalf of the company so long as such conduct does not threaten the interests of the debenture holders.

CASE EXAMPLE 7.14

***Newhart Developments* v *Co-operative Commercial Bank* [1978] QB 814**

A receiver was appointed under a charge which, *inter alia,* entitled the receiver to bring legal proceedings in the name of the company. The directors felt that the bank which had appointed the receiver had been in breach of contract in connection with the loan agreement between it and the company. The receiver refused to take proceedings against the bank in this regard. It was held, however, that there was nothing to prevent the directors from enforcing a claim of the company. However, if damages were recovered, they would fall under the control of the receiver rather than the directors.

3 *Employees*

When the receiver is appointed by the court, all the company's employees are dismissed. When he is appointed by the debenture holders there is no automatic dismissal. Sometimes this latter point is somewhat difficult to understand. Doubtless when a company goes into receivership its employees will not view their long-term job prospects as being very rosy. However, unlike with an insolvent liquidation, there is not an automatic dismissal of employees. It might be that the receiver will be able to rescue the company, pay back the debts owing to the appointing bank and then hand the controls back to the directors. For this reason, there is no automatic dismissal of employees. The receiver, whether he is an administrative receiver or merely a receiver and manager (i.e. where his appointment does not result in his taking control of the whole or substantially the whole of the undertaking of the company) clearly requires some time to determine whether to continue contracts of employment or not. This will often depend on whether he intends to continue the business in whole or in part. For this reason, both administrative receivers and receivers and managers are given time to consider whether or not they will be able to continue the business of the company. By IA 1986 s. 44 an administrative receiver is not taken to have adopted the contract of employment by reason of anything done or omitted to be done within 14 days after his appointment. IA s. 37 gives a similar dispensation to a receiver and manager. However, it was held in *Re Paramount Airways Ltd* [1992] 3 All ER 1 that he does take on liability if he allows contracts of employment to continue beyond the 14-day cut-off point.

A receiver is personally liable upon any contract entered into by him in the performance of his functions or adopted by him in the performance of those functions unless he disclaims such liability in the contract. Thus, if he orders ten tons of widgets to finish off some work in progress he runs the risk of personal liability. However, in practice, he will always disclaim liability. He will state in the contract that he is ordering the goods on behalf of the company and as the agent of the company and that he accepts no personal liability on the contract.

4 *Publication*

By CA 1985 s. 405, if a person obtains an order for the appointment of a receiver or manager of a company's property or appoints such a receiver or manager under a debenture, he must within seven days of the order, or the appointment, give notice to the Registrar of Companies. The Registrar must enter this on to the register of charges. When a person ceases to act as receiver or manager he must give notice of that fact to the Registrar who again must note it on his register of charges. By IA 1986 s. 39, every invoice, order for goods or business letter issued by, or on behalf of, the company must state that a receiver or manager has been appointed.

TEST YOUR KNOWLEDGE 7.14

What is the effect of the appointment of a receiver other than by the court?

administrative receiver

A receiver and manager appointed by the holders of a floating charge, which appointment results in his taking control of the whole or substantially the whole of the undertaking of the company.

administrator

A person who administers the estate of a deceased person in the absence of an executor. Alternatively, it can mean a person appointed by the court to try to achieve some sort of rescue strategy for a company that is in difficulties.

15.5 The position and powers of the administrative receiver

The **administrative receiver** is deemed to be the agent of the company unless and until the company goes into liquidation (IA 1986 s. 44). He is personally liable on any contract entered into by him in the carrying out of his functions (except insofar as the contract otherwise provides), and on any contract, including any contract of employment, adopted by him in the carrying out of those functions. (It should be remembered, however, that a receiver is not taken to have adopted a contract of employment merely because of anything done in the first 14 days following his appointment.) Having said this, he is entitled in respect of any such liability to an indemnity out of the assets of the company.

An administrative receiver is given very wide powers under Schedule 1 to the Insolvency Act (they are, incidentally, exactly the same as the powers given to an **administrator**). These powers are as follows:

1 Power to take possession of, collect and get in the property of the company and, for that purpose, to take such proceedings as may seem to him expedient.
2 Power to sell or otherwise dispose of the property of the company by public auction or private auction or private contract.
3 Power to raise or borrow money and grant security therefore over the property of the company. (Usually the company will at this stage have little property which can be used as security for the raising of money.)
4 Power to appoint a solicitor or accountant or other professionally qualified person to assist him in the performance of his functions.
5 Power to bring or defend any action or other legal proceedings in the name and on behalf of the company. (This will often be needed to recover assets on behalf of the company.)
6 Power to refer to arbitration any question affecting the company.
7 Power to effect and maintain insurances in respect of the business and property of the company.
8 Power to use the company's seal.
9 Power to do all acts and execute in the name and on behalf of the company, any deed, receipt or other document.
10 Power to draw, accept, make and endorse any bill of exchange or promissory note in the name or on behalf of the company.
11 Power to appoint any agent to do any business which he is unable to do himself or which can be more conveniently done by an agent, and power to employ and dismiss employees.
12 Power to do all such things (including the carrying out of works) as may be necessary for the realisation of the property of the company. (This allows the receiver, for example in the case of a building company, to continue the company's building programme so that finished houses may be sold.)
13 Power to make any payment which is necessary or incidental to the performance of his functions.
14 Power to carry on the business of the company.
15 Power to establish subsidiaries of the company.
16 Power to transfer to subsidiaries of the company the whole or any part of the business or property of the company. (This allows the receiver to establish a subsidiary company for the purpose of transferring the viable part of the undertaking of the business to that subsidiary so that the subsidiary can be sold off as a going concern. This is known as hiving down.)
17 Power to grant or accept a surrender of a lease or tenancy or any of the property of the company and to take a lease or tenancy of any property required or convenient for the business of the company.
18 Power to make any arrangement or compromise on behalf of the company.
19 Power to call up any uncalled capital of the company.
20 Power to rank and claim in bankruptcy, insolvency, sequestration or liquidation

of any person indebted to the company and to receive dividends, and to accede to trust deeds for the creditors of any such person.

21 Power to present or defend a petition for the winding up of the company. (Once a receiver has repaid the debt owing to the debenture holder, he will usually return the company as a going concern to its directors. However, this power entitles him to petition for the company to be wound up, for example, if he feels that the business can never be viable.)

22 Power to change the situation of the company's registered office.

23 Power to do all other things incidental to the exercise of the foregoing powers.

By IA 1986 s. 42, a person dealing with an administrative receiver in good faith and for value is not concerned to enquire whether the receiver is acting within his powers. By s. 43, an administrative receiver may, with the approval of the court, dispose of any assets of the company subject to a security if the court is satisfied that such a sale would be likely to promote a more advantageous realisation of the company's assets than would otherwise be affected.

TEST YOUR KNOWLEDGE 7.15

State as many of the powers statutorily given to an administrative receiver as you can.

15.6 The position of other receivers

A receiver appointed by the court is an officer of the court. As such he may only sue or be sued with the leave of the court. If he is appointed under the debenture out of court, he is usually provided by that debenture to be the agent of the company. In the case of an administrative receiver this agency is expressly stated in the Insolvency Act. As a result of this, neither the debenture holder nor any trustees is liable for his acts.

A receiver or manager appointed under a debenture is in the same position in respect of contracts as an administrative receiver. By IA 1986 s. 37, he is personally liable on any contract entered into by him in the performance of his functions and on any contract of employment adopted by him in the performance of those functions. He is nevertheless entitled in respect of that liability to an indemnity out of the assets of the company. He is not taken to have adopted a contract of employment by reason of anything done or omitted to be done within 14 days after his appointment.

15.7 Duty to preferential creditors

By CA 1985 s. 196, where a receiver is appointed under a floating charge, he is under an obligation to see that the company's preferential debts are paid in full before he accounts to the debenture holder in respect of his claim. Thus, the receiver has a clear duty to pay the preferential debts first. This follows logically from the order in which debts are paid – costs, fixed charges, preferential creditors, floating charges, unsecured creditors and members. Clearly a receiver must ensure that one class of creditors is properly paid before starting to make any payments to the next in the pecking order.

15.8 Remuneration of the receiver

When a receiver is appointed by the court, his remuneration is fixed by the court. When he is appointed under a power in a debenture, the remuneration is in practice fixed by agreement with the debenture holder. If, subsequently, the company goes into liquidation, the liquidator may, under IA 1986 s. 36, apply to the court for an order to fix the amounts to be paid by way of remuneration to the receiver. Usually this power will be exercised when the receiver has been paid more than the liquidator thinks is proper and the court has power, *inter alia*, to order the repayment of excessive remuneration.

15.9 The duties of an administrative receiver

An administrative receiver has particular duties to undertake. By IA 1986 s. 46, he must within 28 days of his appointment send notice of his appointment to all creditors of the company. By s. 47, he is required to be supplied with a statement of affairs in respect of the company within 21 days. In practice, the primary duty for the submission of this statement lies upon persons who are, or have been, officers of the company. However, other persons such as promoters or employees of the company may also be required to assist in its preparation. The statement of affairs sets out the assets and liabilities of the company, detailing debtors and creditors and all securities owed or enjoyed by them.

By IA s. 48, the administrative receiver must, within three months (or such longer period as the court may allow) send to the Registrar of Companies, to any trustees or secured creditors of the company and to all creditors, a report detailing the events leading up to his appointment, any disposal or proposed disposal by him of any property of the company, and carrying on, or proposed carrying on, of any business of the company, the amounts or principal and interest payable to the debenture holders by whom or on whose behalf he was appointed as well as the amounts payable to preferential creditors, and the amount (if any) which the administrative receiver thinks will be available for the payment of other creditors. A copy of this report must also go to the court. In the event of the company going into liquidation, a copy of the report must be sent to the liquidator within seven days.

15.10 Vacation of office

An administrative receiver can only be removed from office by court order. He may, however, resign on giving notice. Should he cease to be a qualified insolvency practitioner, he must vacate office forthwith. When he ceases holding office, for whatever reason, he must give notice to the Registrar of Companies within 14 days.

CHAPTER SUMMARY

- A company's power to borrow is either expressly stated in the Memorandum or implied by the law as necessary for the company to carry on its business.
- The document which either creates the debt, or acknowledges it, is called a debenture.
- The majority of debentures are secured on either a fixed or floating charge.
- The advantage of such security is that it gives the debenture holder the right to appoint a receiver on the occurrence of certain specified events.
- For a secured debenture to have the desired effect, however, it must not have been given as a preference within six months of the company's winding up nor, if the charge is floating, must it be created within 12 months of the winding up commencing. If the charge comes within one of these categories it is void and the creditor is treated as unsecured.
- Although a company is not required to keep a register of debenture holders, it must keep a register of the charges it has granted. This register has to be maintained at the company's registered office.
- The holder of a secured debenture has several remedies in the event of non-payment of the debt. There is the right to sue for principal and interest, to petition for the company's winding up, and to appoint a receiver.
- If a debenture is secured by a floating charge, the debenture holder will normally appoint an administrative receiver under powers in the debenture.
- Alternatively, in certain circumstances, a receiver may be appointed by the court.
- Once such a receiver is appointed, the floating charge crystallises and the directors' powers to deal with the assets which are subject to the charge are suspended.
- The administrative receiver is deemed to be the agent of the company and is given very wide powers to deal with the company's property and to act on the company's behalf.
- Although the receiver is personally liable on any contract he makes in the course of carrying out his duties, he has a right to be indemnified out of the company's assets.

part **three**

Company Officers and Shareholder Relations

LIST OF CHAPTERS

Overview

All UK companies must appoint certain key officers to oversee the management of the company and protect its interests on behalf of the shareholders or members. These officers are: the director or directors, a company secretary and (unless a company is exempted) an auditor. Chapter 8 looks in details at the roles these officers play and how their appointments are made and terminated. It also looks at the relationship between a company's directors and its shareholders, and how shareholders can influence how a company is managed.

All directors owe a number of legally defined duties to their companies, and these are dealt with in more detail by Chapter 9. This chapter also looks at the (increasingly few) instances where directors are released from liability, the rules governing loans to directors and the criminal offence of insider dealing.

The relationship between a company's directors and its shareholders is introduced in Chapter 8. Chapter 10 looks at other remedies available to shareholders – especially minority shareholders – where they consider that the company is being badly or unfairly managed. The chapter also covers the regulatory role of the Department of Trade and Industry and its right to inspect companies it believes to be acting illegally.

CHAPTER **8**

Directors and other officers

CONTENTS

LEARNING OUTCOMES

This chapter covers the directors and other officers of a company, including the different types of director, how they are appointed and how they cease to hold office, and the two other principal officers within most companies: the company secretary and the auditor. After reading and understanding the contents of the chapter and studying the case examples, you should be able to:

- Understand what a director is.
- Appreciate how the members can control the powers of directors.
- Understand how directors are appointed and how they cease to hold office.
- Understand what information is publicly available regarding directors.
- Distinguish between payments of damages and compensation when they are removed from office.
- Appreciate the significance and duties of the company secretary.
- Appreciate the significance and function of the auditor.

Introduction

Under company law, every company must have a director or directors. By CA 1985 s. 282:

- public companies must have at least two directors; and
- private companies must have at least one director.

It is possible for a company's Articles to provide that it shall have more directors than the statutory minimum. For example, Table A provides that all companies subject to it must have at least two directors. By CA 1985 s. 741, a director is said to include: 'any person occupying the position of director, by whatever name called'.

This chapter, and Chapter 9, look at powers, duties and responsibilities which directors have and must exercise. For example, a director must ensure that his signed consent to act is filed with the Registrar of Companies and that his name is entered on the company's register of directors. However, it is important at this point to note that these things do not make him a director. He is a director by virtue of occupying the position of director. Because he occupies that position there follow a number of statutory formalities with which he must comply.

1 Types of director

Case law in this area suggests that there are different types of directors, differentiated by the method of their appointment and the role they play in the running of a company. In the course of its judgment in the case *Re Hydrodan (Corby) Ltd* [1994] BCC 161, the court suggested that there are three types of director:

de jure director

A person who acts as a director and who has not only been properly appointed but who has satisfied the legal formalities that have to be observed by directors.

de facto director

A person who acts as a director in spite of the fact that he has never been appointed as such.

shadow director

Any person in accordance with whose directions or instructions the directors are accustomed to act.

1 **De jure directors**: Directors who have been properly appointed and who have satisfied the legal formalities regarding their appointment (see below).
2 **De facto directors**: Employees and other persons who are within the company and who fulfil the role of director even though never (formally) appointed as such.
3 **Shadow directors**: By s. 741, a shadow director is a person who does not operate within a company, but in accordance with whose directions or instructions the directors of the company are accustomed to act. This would include, for example, a member with a large shareholding whose name is not entered on the register of directors but who makes a practice of telling the directors what to do.

It could be argued that the judiciary is introducing an unnecessary degree of complexity into the law, but the distinction between these three types of directors seems to be likely to persist. In *Re H Laing Demolition Building Contractors Limited* [1998] BCC 561 there was an application for the disqualification of an employee of the company as a director. The application by the Secretary of State was worded so as to describe the employee as having being either a shadow or a de facto director. The judge said that this application had to be corrected. Shadow and de facto directors are mutually exclusive. A de facto director is someone inside the company such as an employee. A shadow director is someone outside the company who is telling the directors what to do.

THEORY INTO PRACTICE 8.1

Could a professional adviser – such as an auditor – be considered to be acting as a shadow director of a company merely by providing professional advice?

Answer

Section 741 provides that a person does not become a shadow director merely because he gives advice in a professional capacity and the directors act upon it. Thus, an auditor whose instructions are always followed by the directors of a client company does not become a shadow director merely because of his client's compliance. However, in *Secretary of State* v *Deverell* [2000] BCC 1057 the Court of Appeal stated the protection afforded to professional advisers had to be narrowly interpreted. The purpose of the legislation was to identify – and to make liable – those, other than professional advisers, with real influence in the corporate affairs of the company.

1.1 Other classifications

There are other classifications used to identify the type and role played by a company's directors.

alternate director

A person appointed by a director to represent him as a director, particularly at board meetings that the appointor is unable to attend.

Alternate directors

Table A refers to **alternate directors**, who can be nominated by an existing director to act at board meetings in place of them, for example, because the appointing director is going to be unable to be present for a series of board meetings. Alternate directors are covered in more detail in section 3.3 below.

Executive/non-executive directors

Another common distinction is between executive and non-executive directors. Executive directors are working directors who have executive responsibilities and are thus employees of the company. Non-executive directors are not employees, have no executive responsibilities and bring an independent view to board meetings where the company's business is discussed. Because they are not involved in the day-to-day management of the company, the assumption is that they will raise issues that the other directors might overlook or not wish to have discussed.

Non-executive directors fulfil an important function under the Combined Code and other corporate governance guidelines. Their role and significance in the effective running of company boards is covered in more detail in the Corporate Governance and Corporate Secretaryship modules and study texts.

Whatever classifications are used to identify different types of director, it is important to understand that the legal duties and responsibilities– and liabilities – of anyone considered to be acting as a director are the same.

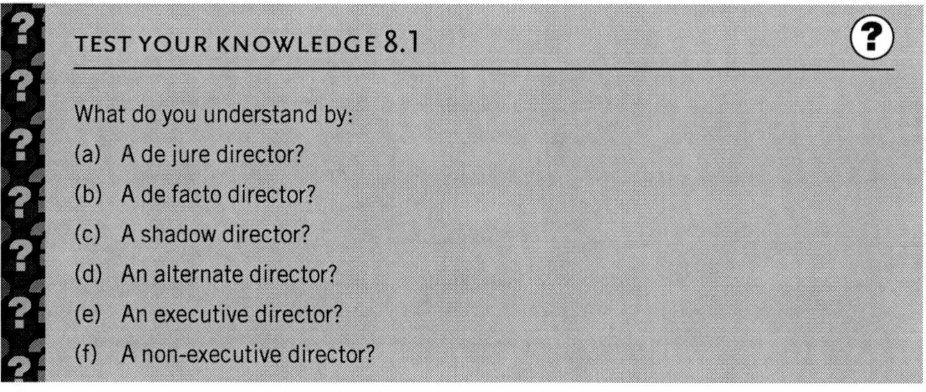

TEST YOUR KNOWLEDGE 8.1

What do you understand by:

(a) A de jure director?

(b) A de facto director?

(c) A shadow director?

(d) An alternate director?

(e) An executive director?

(f) A non-executive director?

2 Directors and shareholders

2.1 The division of power within companies

All companies, whether large or small, and whether the shares are held exclusively by the directors or not, are subject to the Companies Act 1985. This Act is based on the principle that certain things are done by the members in general meeting while others are done by the directors. For example, a decision to alter the objects of the company under the Companies Act 1985 s. 4 can only be made by members in general meeting, whereas the day-to-day running of the business is in the hands of the directors. The procedure on the issue of shares (outlined in more detail in Chapter 5) clearly illustrates this division: it is the members in general meeting who pass ordinary resolutions under s. 121 to ensure that the authorised share capital in the Memorandum of the company is adequate to permit the issue and under s. 80 to ensure that the directors had the appropriate authority to issue the shares. However, it is the directors who actually issue the shares.

For the great majority of companies, where the people who own the business (as shareholders) also run the business (as directors), this distinction may seem rather artificial. However, the distinction is critical where the majority of shares in a company are held by people other than the directors. The most obvious example is a public limited company whose shares are dealt on a Recognised Investment Exchange like the London Stock Exchange. Here, the distinction is quite clear: shares are held by ordinary individuals and institutional investors and the management is carried on by the board of directors.

Generally, the only time that the members hear from the directors is when they receive their notice of the annual general meeting. Recent debates about company performance have led to calls for shareholders to take a more active role in the companies in which they invest, especially through the vehicle of general meetings. It has certainly been said that within a company there are two main power organs – the members in general meeting and the directors. However, the real power within a company undoubtedly lies with the board of directors. The reason for this is twofold:

1 Regulation 70 of Table A provides that, subject to the provisions of the Act, the Memorandum and the Articles, and subject to any directions given by special resolution, the business of the company shall be managed by the directors who may exercise all the powers of the company. No alteration of the Memorandum or Articles and no direction given by special resolution can invalidate any prior act of the directors which would have been valid if that alteration had not been made or that direction had not been given. The powers given by this regulation cannot be limited by any special power given to the directors by the Articles, and a meeting of directors at which a quorum is present may exercise all the powers exercisable by the directors.
   Thus, the directors are responsible for the day-to-day running of the company. They may do anything in connection with the affairs of the company unless the Companies Act, the Memorandum or the Articles provide otherwise. For example, taking again the procedure for the issue of shares, the Act states that the increase of capital and the authorisation of the directors to allot shares must be given by the members in a general meeting. There is, however, no provision in the Act for the actual allotment of shares and this is entirely within the discretion of the board of directors. For private companies, the passing of an elective resolution even disposes of the need to obtain such consent from the general meeting in the first place.

2 The second and more practical reason is that the directors are in regular contact with each other and therefore are in a far stronger position than is generally enjoyed by the body of shareholders.

While any person may inspect the register of members (CA 1985 s. 356), this is rarely done and it is unlikely that a shareholder in a large company will be in close contact with many of the other shareholders. This situation clearly reduces the effectiveness of the members in general meeting as a significant influence in managing a company, even though they have the ultimate power to dismiss directors or to give them direction by special resolution (see below).

2.2 Board delegation

In many small companies there are only one or at most two directors. In this case there is no practical difference between the directors acting as individual directors or acting as a board of directors. In larger companies, however, there may be several directors and it is likely that certain functions will be delegated to specific members of the board. While the underlying principle of the Companies Act and Table A is that the board of directors acts as a whole and accepts collegiate responsibility for what it does, it is nevertheless recognised by Regulation 72 that there may be delegation. Regulation 72 provides that:

> 'the directors may delegate any of their powers to any committee consisting of any one or more directors. They may also delegate to any managing director or any director holding any other executive office such of their powers as they consider desirable to be exercised by him. Any such delegation may be made subject to any conditions the directors may impose, and either collaterally with or to the exclusion of their own powers and may be revoked or altered. Subject to any such conditions, the proceedings of a committee with two or more members shall be governed by the Articles regulating the proceedings of directors so far as they are capable of applying.'

However, if the board has made no such delegation, then a director cannot enforce any rights to which he might claim to be entitled in consequence of such improper action.

A company may frequently have a managing director, personnel director, sales director, finance director, and so on. When this happens, there may be three or more power organs within the company. The degree of power to be exercised by the individual director concerned or the committee of directors depends, as Article 72 states, on the terms of the delegation as decided upon by the board of directors. If the delegation has been properly authorised, it is lawful and the powers delegated can be exercised. If, on the other hand, there has been no such delegation, as shown by *Guinness plc* v *Saunders*, no rights can be acquired.

CASE EXAMPLE 8.1

***Guinness plc* v *Saunders* [1990] 2 AC 663**

A director had successfully negotiated a takeover bid. An improperly constituted committee of the board of directors, having no authority to do so, approved a substantial bonus for the director concerned. It was held that he was not entitled to claim the bonus.

2.3 Directors' meetings

Companies are run through meetings either of the directors (known as board meetings) or of the members (general meetings).

A company's Articles generally provide, as does Table A, that the directors may regulate their meetings as they think fit. A director (or a secretary acting under instruction) may summon a board meeting at any time. Reasonable notice is all that is required, and Table A provides that notice need not be given to a director who is absent from the United Kingdom. What is reasonable depends on the circumstances of the case and the practice of the company. If all the directors are present in one place and with no other engagements, a few moments would be regarded as reasonable notice. On the other hand, many major listed companies have Articles which require one week's notice to be given, except in a major emergency.

The Articles usually fix the quorum at the meeting. Table A requires a minimum of two directors to be present, although most listed companies set the quorum for board meetings rather higher than this. Voting is by way of a simple majority, with no account being taken of the size of a director's shareholding in the company.

TEST YOUR KNOWLEDGE 8.2 

Why in practice does control of a company lie with the directors?

2.4 Shareholder duties

As a general principle those shareholders who control the majority of the voting rights in a company may use their votes in general meeting as they wish so long as they comply with the provisions of the law generally and the Companies Act in particular. While the directors of the company owe a fiduciary duty to the company (see below) shareholders do not. Accordingly, the shareholders may have regard to their own interests whereas the directors must have regard to the interests of the company. For example, a shareholder may enter into a contractual undertaking to vote in a particular way. He may put his shares into trust for a third party and vote on his shares as directed by the third party. This is illustrated in Case Example 8.2.

CASE EXAMPLE 8.2 

***Greenwell* v *Potter* [1902] 1 Ch 530**

Some executors under a will held shares in that capacity. They agreed to sell some to Greenwell who, as a condition of buying the shares, stipulated that he should nominate a third party to be a director of the company. The executors agreed that when the third party came to retire by rotation, they would vote in support of his re-election. It was held that this agreement was binding upon the executors and thus could be enforced against them.

In spite of the fact that majority shareholders do not owe a fiduciary duty in the same way as a director does, they must nevertheless exercise their power in such a way as not to be unfair to a minority shareholder. This is sometimes expressed by saying that the power must be exercised subject to equitable considerations, as illustrated by Case Example 8.3 and confirmed in Case Example 8.4.

CASE EXAMPLE 8.3 

***Clemens* v *Clemens Bros Ltd* [1976] 2 All ER 268**

The plaintiff held 45 per cent and her aunt 55 per cent of the issued share capital of a very successful family company. The aunt was one of five directors, but the plaintiff was not. The directors proposed to increase the company's share capital in such a way as to provide shares for the other directors and to establish a trust for the benefit of long-service employees of the company. The effect of this increase in capital would be that the plaintiff's shareholding would fall to below 25 per cent and thus she would be unable to block the passing of any special resolution. A general meeting of the company was held and the resolution to increase the share capital was duly passed as a result of the aunt's exercising her majority voting rights. The plaintiff then brought proceedings against both the company and the aunt seeking a declaration that the increase in share capital was oppressive to her (the niece) and that it should be set aside. The aunt on the other hand argued that she, as a majority shareholder, was entitled to vote as she wished. It was held that the aunt's right to exercise her majority vote was subject to equitable considerations. Such considerations might make it unjust to exercise it in a particular way.

Although the desire to set up a trust for long-service employees was worthy, there was a very clear inference that the increase in share capital had been carried out in such a way as to put the complete control of the company into the hands of the aunt and the other directors and thus to deprive the plaintiff of such rights she had as a shareholder with more than 25 per cent of the votes in the company Such consideration was sufficient in equity to prevent the aunt from using her votes as she had. Thus, the increase in share capital should be set aside.

CASE EXAMPLE 8.4

***Estmanco (Kilner House) Ltd* v *Greater London Council* [1982] 1 All ER 437**

A majority shareholder in a company proposed a resolution in general meeting which had the effect of preventing the company from taking proceedings under a contract. The majority shareholder then used its shares in order to vote and pass the resolution. A minority shareholder tried to bring proceedings on behalf of the company in respect of this breach of contract and the majority shareholder claimed in defence that it had exercised its voting rights in its own interest as it was entitled to do. It was held that the minority shareholder was entitled to bring proceedings in this way. Sir Robert Megarry VC stated:

> ‘plainly there must be some limit on the power of the majority to pass resolutions which they believe to be in the best interests of the company and yet remain immune from interference by the courts. It may be in the best interests of the company to deprive the minority of some of their rights or some of their property, yet I do not think that this gives the majority an unrestricted right to do this, however unjust it may be, and however much it may harm shareholders whose rights as a class differ from those of the majority . . . No right of a shareholder to vote in his own selfish interests or to ignore the interests of the company entitles him with impunity to injure his voteless fellow shareholders by depriving the company of a course of action and stultifying the purpose for which the company was formed.’

2.5 Shareholders in general meeting

Chapter 10 looks in more detail at the rights afforded to company shareholders to take action to prevent wrongdoing against or on behalf of the company - notably the exceptions to the rule in *Foss* v *Harbottle* (1843) 2 Ha 461 and remedies under CA 1985 s. 459. Additional, and potentially restrictive, controls over the board of directors can also be exercised by members of a company in general meeting.

There are four ways in which members may use a general meeting in this way:

1 By s. 303 a director may, by ordinary resolution passed by the company in a general meeting, be removed from holding office before the expiration of his period of office. This procedure represents the most effective direct control which the members of most companies can exercise over directors.

2 A company's Articles can provide for the directors to present themselves periodically for re-election by the members in general meeting, a procedure known as 'retirement by rotation'. Article 73 of Table A provides that, 'at the first annual general meeting all the directors shall retire from office and at every subsequent annual general meeting one third of the directors who are subject to retirement by rotation or, if there number is not three or a multiple of three, the number nearest to one third shall retire from office; but, if there is only one director who is subject to retirement by rotation, he shall retire'.

   This is a far less active method of control than (1) above. It involves waiting until the director is due to present himself for re-election and then not voting for his re-appointment. In practice, too, the requirement for retirement by rotation under Article 73 is generally omitted from the Articles of private companies

3 By CA 1985 s. 9, the Articles of a company may be amended by special resolution. It is possible, though in practice uncommon, that the general meeting of the company may amend its Articles to reduce the power exercised by the directors.

4 Table A Regulation 70, which sets out the role of the directors in the management of the business, commences with the words: 'subject to . . . any directions given by special resolution, the business of the company shall be managed by the directors'. This implies that the members in general meeting may pass a special resolution directing a course of action which the directors should follow. These words did not appear in any previous Table A.

Before an item may be put on the agenda at a general meeting, it must be supported by the holders of:

(a) not less than 5 per cent of the total voting rights of all the members; or
(b) not less than 100 members holding shares in the company on which there has been paid up an average sum per member of not less than £100 (CA 1985 s. 376).

The purpose of this provision is to ensure that before any item can be put on the agenda, there must be this prima facie support, so that there is no question of a member with only a small shareholding getting such a resolution put before the meeting without support from other members – unless he himself holds 5 per cent of the total voting rights in the company.

Under s.379A, a private company can pass an elective resolution to dispense with the requirement to hold an annual general meeting (AGM). Such a resolution has to be passed with the unanimous consent of every member. Even if an elective resolution has been passed, however, any member can, under s 366A, require that an annual general meeting be held so long as he gives notice to the company not later than three months before the end of the year to which the annual general meeting would relate. This is an important right for members. They are always entitled to have an annual general meeting held at which they can question the directors in relation to their stewardship of the company.

TEST YOUR KNOWLEDGE 8.3 

(a) What is the significance of the decision of the court in Clemens v Clemens Bros Ltd?
(b) How can members in general meeting control the actions of directors?

3 Appointment of directors

As outlined in Chapter 2, when a company is incorporated, the relevant statutory forms must be sent to the Registrar of Companies. One of these, Form 10, is a statement of the person or persons who are to be the first director or directors of the company. By CA 1985 s. 13(5), the person/s named in that statement are deemed to have been appointed as the company's first directors. The subsequent appointment of directors is governed by the Articles.

No formal qualifications are required to become a director, but certain categories of individuals are excluded from acting as a director either by law and/or a company's Articles (see below). The specific provisions for exclusion under the Company Directors' Disqualification Act 1986 are detailed in section 6 below. Under CA 1989, s. 27 the auditor of a company cannot also be director or company secretary and under s. 283, the same person cannot be both the sole director and the company secretary.

retirement by rotation
The process whereby one third of the directors of a company retire and present themselves for re-election.

Retirement by rotation

Table A Article 73 provides that all the directors of the company must retire and apply for re-election at the first annual general meeting after incorporation. Assuming that they are re-elected at this meeting, then, also by Article 73, one third of the board must retire and apply for re-election at each subsequent annual general meeting. Thus each director must stand for re-election at least once in every three years that he is in office. However, by Table A Article 84, a managing director, and any other director holding executive office, is not subject to retirement by rotation. The requirement to retire by rotation is also frequently omitted from the Articles of private companies.

Appointment and public companies

By CA 1985 s. 282, when a director is seeking appointment to office in a public company he should stand for election individually. By CA s. 292, two or more persons may not be appointed as directors of a public company by a single resolution of the members in general meeting unless there has first been a separate resolution, passed without a single vote against, that this block voting should be permitted. A resolution in contravention of this rule is void and any appointment ineffective.

Casual and additional vacancies

A casual vacancy occurs when a board vacancy occurs between annual general meetings. For example, it might happen if a director dies or resigns during his term of office. When this happens, the vacancy should strictly be filled by an appointment made by the members in general meeting. In practice, however, because of the inconvenience of having to call a general meeting for this purpose, the company's Articles will usually contain some provision allowing the directors themselves to make an appointment which will be valid until the next annual general meeting of the company (Table A Article 79).

For example, if a sales director dies and the other directors appoint someone else to fill the vacancy, the appointee is a perfectly properly appointed director, but he must retire at the next annual general meeting of the company and give the members an opportunity to vote against him if they wish.

The same procedure applies to the appointment of an additional director.

Directors' service contracts

Directors holding executive office within the company are employees of the company as well as directors, and will usually have an appropriate service contract with the company. These are discussed in more detail below.

3.1 Qualification shares

A company will sometimes require that a person must hold a minimum number of shares in it before he can hold office as a director. The 1948 Table A stated that the shareholding qualifications for directors may be fixed by the company in general meeting and, unless and until so fixed, no qualification was required. There was no equivalent provision in the 1985 Table A so qualification shares are only required in companies subject to the 1985 Table A if there is a special Article to that effect.

If qualification shares are required by the company's Articles, every director must, by CA 1985 s. 291, obtain his qualification shares within two months of his appointment or such shorter time as may be fixed by the Articles. If he fails to obtain his qualification shares within the appropriate period or if he subsequently ceases to hold the qualification shares, he must vacate office as a director and is liable to a fine for such period as he acts as a director while unqualified.

3.2 Assignment of office

By CA 1985 s. 308, a company's Articles may empower a director to assign his office as director to another person. Such an assignment is of no effect unless and until it is approved by a special resolution of the company. Since directors can be appointed and removed by ordinary resolution, the power for the assignment of office is very seldom encountered in practice since it requires authorisation by means of a special resolution.

3.3 Alternate directors

The 1985 Table A (Articles 65–69) envisages the appointment of alternate directors. Any director may appoint another director, or some other person, to act as his alternate. If he appoints a fellow director to be alternate there is no consent needed other than that of the appointee. If the person appointed is someone who is not a director, the board itself must approve the appointment. Except as may otherwise be provided by a company's Articles, an alternate director is for all purposes a director of the company and is responsible for his own acts and defaults and is not deemed to be the agent of the director appointing him.

3.4 Invalidity in appointment

By CA 1985 s. 285, the acts of a director are valid notwithstanding any defect which may afterwards be discovered in his appointment. The effect of this provision is to validate the acts of a director who has not been properly appointed merely because of some technical error in his appointment. In other words, a third party dealing with the company may assume that the director, who appears to be properly qualified and appointed, is indeed so qualified and appointed.

For example, in the past many small private companies have gone in breach of the law and failed to hold annual general meetings. Thus directors who should have retired and presented themselves for re-election have failed to do so. For this reason they were not properly appointed. Nevertheless, s. 285 has the effect of rendering their acts valid and binding on the company and on persons dealing with the company. Section 285 does not apply where an appointment was never properly made. It only remedies the situation where there has been no dishonesty. There must have been an honestly made appointment but one in which there is some defect. Compare Case Examples 8.5 and 8.6.

CASE EXAMPLE 8.5

***Morris* v *Kanssen* [1946] AC 459**

The original directors and shareholders of the company were Kanssen and Cromie. Between 1940 and 1942, Cromie and another person, Strelitz, held 'meetings' without Kanssen's being present. They falsified alleged minutes to show that Kanssen had been replaced as a director by Strelitz. Later, Cromie and Strelitz held another meeting at which they appointed Morris as another director and then the three of them, Cromie, Strelitz and Morris, allotted all the unissued shares in the company to themselves. In fact, unknown to these three, each of them had ceased to hold office at the end of 1941 as they had not come before a general meeting before this time as required by the Articles. Therefore, since this date there had been no directors properly appointed. Cromie, Strelitz and Morris argued that, by virtue of what is now s. 285, the defective appointment of a director was cured. The House of Lords, however, held that this was not so. Section 285 could not validate the acts of persons who had not been appointed at all.

CASE EXAMPLE 8.6

***Dawson* v *African Consolidated Land Company Ltd* [1898] 1 Ch 6**

A company had three directors. One of them had ceased to hold his qualification shares. The three directors made a call on the shares of the company. It was claimed that because of the irregularity in the appointment of the one director, the call was invalid. It was held, however, that the irregularity in the appointment did not invalidate what the director had done.

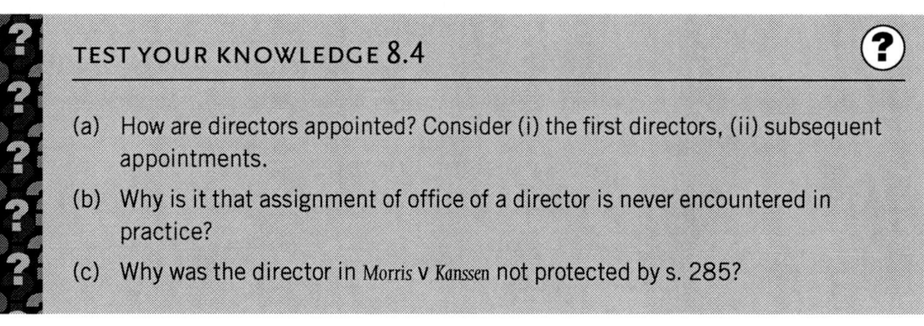

TEST YOUR KNOWLEDGE 8.4

(a) How are directors appointed? Consider (i) the first directors, (ii) subsequent appointments.

(b) Why is it that assignment of office of a director is never encountered in practice?

(c) Why was the director in *Morris v Kanssen* not protected by s. 285?

4 Directors and disclosure

4.1 Register of directors and secretaries

By CA 1985 s. 283, every company must keep a register of its directors and secretaries at its registered office. This must be available for inspection during business hours, subject to any reasonable restrictions that the company may, by its Articles or general meeting, impose. At least two hours in each day must be allowed for inspection. Any member of the company may inspect without charge. Other persons may be charged a small fee for inspection.

4.2 Register of directors' shareholdings

By CA 1985 s. 324, any person who becomes a director of a company and holds shares in or debentures of the company or its subsidiary holding or other subsidiary company must, within five days, give written notice to the company of his interests and of the number of shares and the amount of debentures which he has. Likewise, a person who is a director must give notice to the company if he becomes or ceases to hold shares in or debentures of the company. Contravention is a criminal offence. For all these purposes an interest of the spouse of a director or of an infant child of a director is treated as if it were the interest of the director himself.

Information notified by a director under these provisions must be kept in a register of directors' interests maintained by the company. It is subject to the same rules regarding inspection as the register of directors.

4.3 Disclosure of interest in contracts

By CA 1985 s. 317 it is the duty of every director who is in any way, whether directly or indirectly, interested in a contract or proposed contract with the company to declare the nature of his interest at a meeting of the directors of the company. In any case where the director becomes interested in a contract only after it is made, the declaration must be made at the first meeting of the directors held after he had become interested. In the case of a proposed contract the declaration must be made at the meeting of directors at which the question of entering into the contract is first taken in to consideration or, if the director was not at the date of that meeting interested in the proposed contract, at the next meeting of the directors after he became interested. The duty to disclose applies to any transaction or arrangement whether or not it constitutes a contract and also to any loan concerning a director (see also Chapter 9).

4.4 Other disclosure

Publication of names

A company must not state in any form (other than as signatory) the name of any of its directors on any business letter on which the company's name appears unless it states the name of every director of the company (CA 1985 s. 305).

Particulars of salaries, pensions, etc.

By Schedule 6 of the Companies Act 1985 (as amended) aggregate amounts of a directors' emoluments must be shown in accounts.

Copies of service contracts

By CA 1985 s. 318, directors' service contracts (or particulars thereof if not in writing) must be kept at the registered office of the company or its principal place of business and be available for inspection by members of the company without charge.

Particulars of loans

Generally all loans made to directors must be disclosed in accounts. This topic is covered in more detail in Chapter 9.

5 Termination of office

A person may cease to be a director by:

1 retirement;
2 resignation;
3 removal;
4 death;
5 disqualification (see section 6).

5.1 Retirement

A director may cease to hold office by retirement. This usually occurs by virtue of some provision in the Articles which requires him to retire, as in the case of the Table A provision for retirement by rotation.

CA 1985 s. 293 requires all directors over the age of 70 to retire at the end of the first annual general meeting after they reach the age of 70. However, this does not apply where:

1 the company is a private company which is not the subsidiary of a public company;
2 the Articles otherwise provide; or
3 the director in question was appointed or approved by the company in a general meeting by a resolution of which special (i.e. 28 days') notice, stating his age, had been given

Any person who is appointed or proposed to be appointed as a director of a company to which s. 293 applies must give notice of his age to the company. Failure to do so is a criminal offence.

5.2 Resignation

A director may resign his office in the manner provided by the company's Articles. If there is no such provision in the Articles, the resignation should be on reasonable notice or as provided by his service contract. A director who has given proper notice of resignation cannot withdraw that notice.

5.3 Removal

By CA 1985 s. 303 a company may, by ordinary resolution, remove a director before the expiration of his period of office, regardless of anything to the contrary in the Articles or any contract with the director.

As with the appointment of over-age directors, the removal must follow special notice. As soon as the 28 days' special notice of the proposed resolution is given to the company, the company must also send a copy to the director concerned. He is then entitled to make a statement about the resolution at the general meeting where it is proposed to remove him from office. He is also entitled to make written representations before the meeting and ask that these be notified to shareholders.

Before the Companies Act 1948, it was not unusual for private companies to provide in their Articles that a particular director should be irremovable or removable only by special or extraordinary resolution. Section 303 was introduced to abolish this. The section does not apply to directors appointed for life to private companies prior to 18 July 1948, although, in more ways than one, such directors are very much a dying breed.

However, it is possible in a small company for a director to entrench his appointment by using a method recognised as valid by the House of Lords in the case of Case Example 8.7.

CASE EXAMPLE 8.7

***Bushell* v *Faith* [1970] AC 1099**

The company had an issued share capital of 300 fully paid shares of £1 each. They were held equally by two sisters and a brother. The sisters, Mrs Bushell and Dr Bain, held 100 shares each. The brother, Mr Faith, also held 100 shares. All three were directors of the company. The company's Articles provided that in the event of a resolution being proposed at any general meeting of the company for the removal from office of any director, any shares held by that director should carry the right to three votes. Problems arose between the sisters and the brother, and the sisters sought to remove the brother from office. When a vote was taken on a poll at the general meeting of the company, the brother exercised the weighted voting rights attaching to his shares and defeated the sisters' resolution by 300 votes to 200. Mrs Bushell then sought an order that the Article giving the director three votes for every share he held was unlawful as being contrary to what is now s. 303. The House of Lords held that the Article was valid. The practical effect was therefore to prevent the removal of Mr Faith from office.

THEORY INTO PRACTICE 8.2

Is there anything the sisters in Case Example 8.7 might have done to remove the brother from office, for example, the deletion of the Article?

Answer

The sisters were powerless to alter the offending Article to take away the weighted voting rights since they had only two-thirds of the shares in the company between them and a three-quarters majority is needed to alter the Articles under CA 1985 s. 9. Had Mr Faith had three sisters, each of whom held 25 per cent of the shares, the story would have been very different.

When a director is removed from office without good cause he is entitled to receive damages for breach of contract. In the case of a small company he may also have an entitlement to complain of having been treated unfairly prejudicially under s.459 (see Chapter 10) or seek a winding up of the company on the just and equitable ground (see Chapter 12).

5.4 **Death**

A director obviously vacates office upon his death, which also terminates the contract of employment. As such, the director is only entitled to be paid salary up to the moment of death.

TEST YOUR KNOWLEDGE 8.5

(a) In what ways may a person may cease to be a director?

(b) What are the three exceptions to the rule that a director must retire?

6 Disqualification

A director may be forced to vacate his office under the Articles of the company or disqualification by the court.

Table A provides, in Article 81, that the office of a director should be vacated if:

1 He ceases to be a director by virtue of any provision of the Act or he becomes prohibited by law from becoming a director.
2 He becomes bankrupt or makes any arrangement or composition with his creditors generally.
3 He is, or may be, suffering from mental disorder and either:
   (a) he is admitted to hospital in pursuance of an application for admission for treatment under the Mental Health Act 1983; or
   (b) an order is made by a court having jurisdiction in matters concerning mental disorder for his detention or for the appointment of a receiver in respect of his property or affairs.
4 He resigns his office by notice to the company.
5 He has been absent for more than six consecutive months without permission of the directors from board meetings held during that period and the board pass a resolution to that effect.

Some of these provisions are simply indicative of the general law. For example, bankruptcy of itself disqualifies a person from holding office as a company director unless he has the express consent of the court to do so. Other provisions, such as the one relating to six months absence from board meetings, can be removed or varied by the company's own special Articles.

The provision relating to mental disorder requires a court order regarding the mental state of the director for disqualification to follow from the illness. Also, it refers only to mental and not physical disability. Many companies have a special Article providing for vacation of office if, in the opinion of the other board members, a director is no longer mentally or physically up to the task.

The six-month absence Article can be circumvented by board approval. This might be required if a director is to have a major operation followed by a long period of recuperation. Moreover, even where a six-month absence is taken without leave, the board must resolve that the director should cease to hold office.

6.1 Company Directors' Disqualification Act 1986

As well as the provisions in the Articles which result in a director vacating his office, a disqualification order may be made by the court under the Company Directors' Disqualification Act 1986 (CDDA).

CDDA 1986 s.1 states that any person against whom a disqualification order has been made may not, without leave of the court, be a director of the company, or be a liquidator or administrator of the company, or be a receiver or manager of the company's property, or be in any way, whether directly or indirectly, concerned or take part in the promotion, formation or management of the company. This applies throughout the entire period of the disqualification order.

The words 'without the leave of the court' clearly imply that even disqualified directors may be permitted by the court to be a director of one or more stated companies, and indeed this is the case. Where such consent is given, the court will usually impose some condition upon the director such as that the company must hold monthly board meetings that are attended by the company's auditor or that a named qualified accountant should also serve as a part-time executive finance director of the company.

Breach of a disqualification order or undertaking, or where a bankrupt acts as a director, renders the offender liable to criminal proceedings, which may result in up to two years' imprisonment (CDDA 1986 s.13). He may also be personal liability for the debts of the company, which does not necessarily have to be insolvent for this provision to be activated (CDDA 1986 s.15). As such, this provision may be looked upon as a kind of forward-looking lifting of the veil of incorporation. Just as a person may be made liable for the debts of his company where the court finds that there has been fraudulent or wrongful trading, in the case of disqualification, the law considers that where a person has shown himself not fit to be a director, the veil of any company with which he associates during the disqualification will be lifted and he is at risk of being made personally liable for its debts.

6.2 **Grounds for disqualification**

The grounds for disqualification under CDDA 19086 are as follows:

Conviction of an indictable offence (s. 2)

The court may make a disqualification order against a person where he is convicted of an indictable offence, such as fraud, in connection with the promotion, formation, management or liquidation of a company, or the receivership or management of a company's property.

Although the provision states that the offence must be one that is indictable (i.e. capable of being tried before the Crown Court) it is not necessary that the conviction should have been obtained on indictment. Thus, a disqualification order may follow even where the conviction was merely before magistrates.

Persistent breaches of company's legislation (s. 3)

The court may make a disqualification order against a person where it appears that he has been persistently in default in relation to the provisions of company legislation requiring any return, account or document to be filed with the Registrar of Companies. There is a presumption that a person has been persistently in default if he has been convicted of a default three times in the preceding five years.

Disqualification for fraud, fraudulent trading or breach of duty revealed in a winding up (s. 4)

A court may make a disqualification order against a person if, in the course of the winding up, it appears that he has been guilty of an offence for which he is liable (whether he has been convicted or not), of fraudulent trading or otherwise has been guilty, while an officer or liquidator of the company or receiver or manager of its property, of any fraud in relation to the company or of any breach of his duty as such officer, liquidator, receiver or manager.

Disqualification on summary conviction (s. 5)

A disqualification order may be made against a person who has been guilty of failing to make returns to the Registrar of Companies on at least three occasions within the period of five years. This is very similar to the ground of persistent breaches of the company's legislation referred to in paragraph (2) above. The main difference between the two is that, with the persistent breach, a separate application has to be made to a court of civil jurisdiction for the disqualification order. Under s. 5, the disqualification order may be made by the magistrates court. This usually coincides with the third conviction of the offender.

Disqualification for unfitness (s. 6)

This is the most recent ground which was introduced initially by the Insolvency Act 1985, and is now to be found in CDDA 1986 s. 6. Whenever a company becomes insolvent, any person holding office in connection with the administration of the insolvency, such as the official receiver, the liquidator, the administrator or the administrative receiver, must make a return to the Secretary of State about the conduct of any of the company's directors whom he considers to be unfit to be a company director.

If the Secretary of State feels that a disqualification order should be made, he must apply to the court for such an order against the director concerned. Schedule 1 to the Act indicates a number of criteria to be borne in mind by the court in determining the unfitness of directors to hold office.

These criteria, generally colloquially referred to as 'the badges of unfitness' include:

(a) any misfeasance or breach of any fiduciary or other duty by the director in relation to the company;
(b) any misapplication or retention by the director of any money or other property of the company;
(c) the director's responsibility for the company entering into transactions liable to be set aside by a liquidator;
(d) the director's responsibility for any failure by the company to keep proper records;
(e) the director's responsibility for any failure by the company to prepare and file annual accounts;
(f) the director's responsibility for the company becoming insolvent;
(g) the director's responsibility for any failure by the company to supply goods or services which have already been paid for;
(h) the director's responsibility for failing to call a creditors' meeting in a creditors' voluntary winding up;
(i) any failure by the director to produce a statement of affairs as required in any insolvency proceedings concerning the company.

A disqualification order can only be made under this ground of unfitness if the company has become insolvent. In this context the company becomes insolvent if:

(a) it goes into liquidation at a time when its assets are insufficient for the payment of its debts or other liabilities and the expenses of the winding up;
(b) an administration order is made in relation to the company; or
(c) an administrative receiver of the company is appointed.

Wrongful and fraudulent trading

Whenever a civil order is made against a director for fraudulent or wrongful trading under IA 1986 s. 213 or s. 214, a disqualification order may be made against the director concerned.

Disqualification after investigation of a company (s. 8)

If there has been an investigation by the DTI of the affairs of a company and from the report of the inspectors it appears to the Secretary of State that a disqualification order should be made in the public interest, he may apply for such an order to be made.

6.3 **Period of disqualification**

As a general rule, the maximum period for disqualification is 15 years.

Where 'unfitness' is proved, there is also a minimum disqualification period of two years. In *Re Sevenoaks Stationers (Retail) Ltd* [1992] Ch 164 the Court of Appeal said that the length of disqualification should fall within one of three bands, i.e. 2–5 years, 6–10 years and 11–15 years, obviously reflecting the degree of misconduct by the director. In *Re Carecraft Construction Ltd* [1993] 4 All ER 499 it was stated that a director could accept liability and suggest the band within which his case fell. Then, if the Secretary of State and the court were of the opinion that any alleged misconduct that had been denied by the director concerned would not, if it were to be proved, lift the director into a higher band of disqualification, the court could proceed with making a summary disqualification order.

In the case of disqualification for persistent breaches of company legislation (s. 3) and disqualification on summary conviction (s.5), the maximum period of disqualification is five years.

6.4 Insolvency Act 2000

As well as automatic disqualification for bankruptcy, and the grounds stated above under CDDA 1986, the Insolvency Act 2000 also introduced the system of voluntary undertaking not to act as a director. This means that a director may give an undertaking to the Department of Trade and Industry that he will not act as a company director for a specified period, usually between 2 and 15 years.

Since its introduction in 2001, this option has proved to be popular. The number of disqualification applications has dropped considerably over the last two years and many more undertakings are being seen.

6.5 Enterprise Act

Under the Enterprise Act, there are many new provisions concerning breaches of competition law. Offences can be committed by companies and their directors when they breach the provisions that have been enacted to ensure that dominant companies do not abuse their positions. Directors whose companies infringe these provisions can have disqualification proceedings brought against them by the Office of Fair Trading. As with disqualification for unfitness under the Company Directors Disqualification Act, the order can run for between 2 and 15 years.

TEST YOUR KNOWLEDGE 8.6

(a) On what grounds can a person be disqualified as a director under Table A?
(b) On what grounds can the court make a disqualification order?
(c) What are the so-called 'badges of unfitness' when the Secretary of State is seeking a disqualification order?

7 Compensation and damages on ceasing to hold office

When a director ceases to hold office he may wish to be paid some sort of compensation or damages. The Companies Act draws a clear distinction between compensation and damages:

Compensation is non-contractual: By s. 312, it is unlawful for a company to make any payment to a director by way of compensation for loss of office, or as consideration for, or in connection with, his retirement from office unless particulars of the proposed payment are disclosed to the members of the company and the proposal is approved by the company.

Damages are contractual: By s. 303, when a director is removed from office this cannot deprive him of his entitlement to damages in respect of the termination of his appointment as director. A contract of service enjoyed by a director is in essence the same as a contract of service of any other employee. The normal remedy for breach of contract is damages. In the case of a contract of service being prematurely terminated, the breach basically means that the plaintiff loses what he would have earned during the contracted period of notice.

7.1 Directors' service contracts and long notice periods

Since the directors are responsible for the day-to-day running of the company, it is the board of directors that makes the contract with each individual director. Sometimes, boards give their members rather longer notice entitlements than they do other employees. For example, the contract might provide for one, or two or even ten years notice. Obviously, there is a potential for abuse here if a director can take a long notice entitlement and receive a substantial payment of damages upon premature termination of the contract. Accordingly, CA 1985 s. 319 is specifically designed to prevent directors from creating long-term service agreements for themselves where such an agreement is primarily designed to provide them with large sums of money in the event of their being dismissed.

This does not mean that directors may not have long-term service contracts. The section provides that any term in the contract of service which allows for more than five years' notice, or which provides that the contract cannot be terminated at all, or which provides that the contract may only be terminated in specified circumstances, such as the incapacity of the director, is void unless the employing company has approved the term in general meeting. Thus, if a company, acting through its board of directors rather than the general meeting, enters into a service agreement with its managing director, under which the agreement may only be terminated within ten years in the event of the director becoming so ill as to be unable to fulfil the obligations of his office, such a term would be void.

Where a term is found to be void in this way, there will be implied in its place a term entitling the company to terminate it at any time by giving reasonable notice. What is meant by reasonable notice has yet to be determined by the courts, but 12–18 months is a likely period of reasonable notice.

7.2 Common law mitigation

At common law a person claiming damages for breach of contract must take steps to mitigate his loss. This means that he must do all that he can to keep the level of damages as low as possible. Thus, a director claiming damages for wrongful dismissal must look for alternative work and must also reduce his claim to take account of accelerated payment because the salary will be paid 'up front' rather than monthly in arrears. There is also a rather more lenient tax regime for a payment on termination of employment.

THEORY INTO PRACTICE 8.3

A director is employed under a service contract entitling him to 4 years, 11 months and 3 weeks' notice. His annual salary is £1,000,000. What is his entitlement to damages if he is dismissed without notice?

Answer

The opening claim would be five years' salary, i.e. £5,000,000.

However, from this must be made deductions for what might reasonably be expected to be earned in an alternative job, for accelerated payment and for the rather more lenient taxation imposed upon payments on termination of employment. In the event the director concerned received £2,000,000.

8 The company secretary

Every company must have a secretary, and, although a director may be the secretary, a sole director may not be. Thus, there must always be at least two persons concerned in the management of a company, either two directors one of whom is the secretary, or a director and a secretary. Even in a single-member company with a single-member board there must be at least two persons involved, the single member and the secretary. Table A, Article 99 provides that the directors should appoint the secretary, on such terms as they may think fit. It is also the directors who may remove a secretary.

8.1 The contractual authority of the secretary

At one time it was believed that the company secretary had no contractual authority and so could not bind the company contractually. This is not now the case. He has the ostensible authority to bind the company in any contract of an administrative nature. This was decided by the Court of Appeal in Case Example 8.8.

CASE EXAMPLE 8.8

***Panorama Developments (Guildford) Ltd* v *Fidelis Furnishing Fabrics Ltd* [1971] 2 QB 711**

The secretary of the defendant company hired cars in the name of the company. The ostensible reason for the hirings was to meet customers of the company but in reality he was using the cars for his own purposes. It was held that the secretary had the ostensible authority to enter into such contracts on behalf of his company, and so the company was liable to pay the hire charges.

The decision in this case is confirmed by CA s. 35A which provides that a third party dealing with a company in good faith can assume that there is no limitation under the company's constitution on the power of the board of directors to bind the company or to authorise others to do so. Therefore a third party can assume that the secretary has the power that the board appears to be holding him out as having.

8.2 The qualification of a public company secretary

The increased recognition of the significance of the company secretary is reflected in the provisions for the qualification of a public company secretary. By CA 1985 s. 286, the directors of a public company must ensure that any secretary whom they appoint satisfies two criteria:

1 They must be satisfied that he appears to them to have the requisite knowledge and experience to discharge the functions of secretary of the company. And,
2 The company secretary must have one of the following qualifications:
   (a) he must have been in a post as a secretary of the company, or been a deputy or assistant to the secretary, on 22 December 1980;
   (b) for at least three of the five years immediately preceding his appointment, he has held the office of secretary of some other public company;
   (c) he is a member of any of the following professional bodies: Chartered Accountants, Certified Accountants, Chartered Secretaries, Chartered Management Accountants, Chartered Institute of Public Finance and Accountancy;
   (d) he is a barrister or solicitor; or
   (e) he is a person who, by virtue of his holding or having held any other position or his being a member of any other body, appears to the directors to be capable of discharging the functions of secretary of the company.

STOP AND THINK 8.1

The current DTI-led Company Law Review proposes the abolition of the need for private companies to appoint a company secretary. What are the arguments for and against this proposal?

TEST YOUR KNOWLEDGE 8.7

(a) What qualifications does a plc secretary need?

(b) What authority is a company secretary normally expected to have in matters relating to his company?

9 The auditor

Unless exempted, every company must appoint an auditor to review and approve their annual accounts (CA 1985 s. 384(1)). No person maybe appointed as auditor of a company unless he is qualified for appointment (CA 1989 Part II). The auditor must be a registered auditor. At the present time this means that he must be a chartered or certified accountant, with a few minor exceptions. However, the Companies Act 1989 envisages the possibility of the holders of other qualifications for appointment. What is essential is that the auditor must satisfy the criteria of qualification and independence laid down by the Act and regulations made under it.

9.1 Appointment

The directors may make the first appointment of an auditor at any time before the first annual general meeting of the company (CA 1985 s. 385(3)). They may also make an appointment to fill a casual vacancy under s. 388. In each case the auditor so appointed holds office until the end of the next general meeting at which accounts are laid (s. 385). The appointment and the auditor's remuneration should then be approved by the meeting.

If no auditor is appointed, the company must notify the Secretary of State of this within one week, and the Secretary of State may then appoint an auditor to fill the vacancy (s. 387).

9.2 Removal and resignation

An auditor may be removed from office by the shareholders. By CA 1985 s. 391, an ordinary resolution is all that is required to effect this following special notice of the resolution being given to the company. When such a move is made, the auditor has a right to make written representations to the company and to have them circulated by the company to all members to whom notice of the meeting at which the resolution is to be proposed has been given. He also has the right to attend and speak at the meeting at which the resolution to remove him will be moved (CA 1985 Sch. 15A para. 1). It is not permissible to remove an auditor by means of a written resolution because of this right.

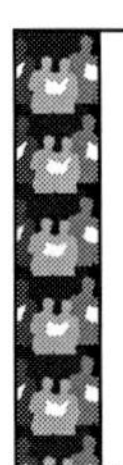

THEORY INTO PRACTICE 8.4 

What is the procedure for the removal of an auditor from office?

Answer

It is the same as for the removal of a director under CA s. 303.

An auditor may also resign from office by depositing a notice in writing to that effect at the company's registered office (s. 392). In this case, the notice is ineffective unless it:

(a) either contains a statement that there are no circumstances connected with the resignation which should be brought to the attention of the members or creditors of the company; or
(b) contains a statement of such circumstances (ss. 392(1) and 394).

If such a statement is contained in the notice of resignation, the company must within 14 days send a copy of the notice to every member of the company, to every debenture-holder, and to every person entitled to receive notices of the general meetings of the company. A copy of the notice of resignation must be filed with the Registrar of Companies. Any statement of the circumstances connected with the resignation should also be filed and sent to members.

Auditor-convened EGM

In these circumstances, the auditor may also deposit with his notice of resignation a requisition calling upon the directors to convene an extraordinary general meeting of the company for the purpose of receiving and considering his explanation of the reasons for his resignation. Although seldom used, the threat of resignation is an important weapon in the auditor's armoury.

This power is given to the resigning auditor because, since it is he who certifies that the accounts give a true and fair view of the financial position of the company, he must have a complementary power to explain to the members if he feels he is not getting the appropriate cooperation from the directors.

9.3 **Audit exemption**

Under s. 388A, private companies with a turnover of £1 million or less are exempt from the requirement for an annual audit, provided that the company has not during the year been:

(a) registered as a plc;
(b) a parent company or a subsidiary;
(c) subject to the regulatory regimes specified in s.249B such as banking and insurance companies, trade unions or employers' associations.

9.4 **The auditor's duties**

The duties of the auditor fall under three main headings:

1 to report to the members of the company;
2 to be aware of their duties both under the Companies Acts and under the Articles of the company; and
3 to exercise reasonable care and skill.

Reporting to the members

The first of these duties requires the auditors to report to the members regarding the accounts. Put in general terms, the auditor has to state that in his opinion the accounts give a true and fair view of the company's position.This goes beyond merely reflecting what the books show; it requires the auditor to ascertain that the books reflect the company's actual financial position.

Knowledge of the law

The auditor is a professional person and, as such, is expected to know the relevant law that applies to the company. For example, notes to the accounts must show any loans made by a company to its directors. It therefore follows that an auditor should be fully conversant with the law regarding loans to directors.

Care and skill

The duty of showing reasonable care and skill is of prime importance. It is well expressed in two dicta from cases on an auditor's duties.

In *Re Kingston Cotton Mill* [1896] 2 Ch 279, Lopes LJ said:

> 'An auditor is not bound to be a detective, or . . . to approach his work . . . with a foregone conclusion that there is something wrong. He is a watchdog, but not a bloodhound. He is justified in believing tried servants of the company . . . He is entitled to assume that they are honest.'

Lindley LJ said in *Re London and General Bank* [1895] 2 Ch 673:

> 'It is the duty of an auditor to bring to bear on the work he has to perform that skill, care and caution which a reasonably competent, careful and cautious auditor would use . . . An auditor . . . is not bound to do more than exercise reasonable care

and skill in making enquiries . . . He is not an insurer; he does not guarantee that the books do correctly show the true position of the company's affairs.'

In considering the duty of the auditor, it is important to look at to whom the duty is owed. The reason for this is so that we can say who can sue an auditor who is in breach of duty. (Look upon these points as two sides of the same coin. On the one side is the question: 'to whom is the duty of care owed?' On the other side is the question: 'who can sue for damages when there is a breach of the duty of care?')

To establish a valid claim in negligence (as breach of duty of care and skill is more generally called in other areas of liability) there must be shown four separate factors:

1 an existence of a duty of care and skill;
2 which was owed to the plaintiff;
3 breach of that duty;
4 resulting in loss to the plaintiff.

It would seem that the duty of an auditor is owed only to the company and to the shareholders as a body. It is not owed to individual shareholders either as shareholders or as potential investors in the company. Nor is the duty of care owed to creditors of the company. This aspect of the law was clarified in Case Example 8.9.

CASE EXAMPLE 8.9

***Caparo Industries plc* v *Dickman and others* [1990] 1 All ER 568**

The auditors of a company negligently audited its accounts, with the result that the accounts showed a £1.2m profit rather than a real loss of £400,000. In reliance on these accounts, the respondents made a takeover bid for the company, which bid was ultimately successful. Subsequently, the respondents brought proceedings against the auditors for breach of duty of care and skill.

It was held by the House of Lords that there was no liability since the auditor owed no duty of care to a member of the public who relied on the accounts to buy shares in the company. To hold otherwise would give rise to unlimited liability on the part of the auditor. The auditor's duty is owed simply to the company and to its shareholders as a body.

The role and independence of auditors has been called into question by recent Corporate Governance scandals in the US.

TEST YOUR KNOWLEDGE 8.8

(a) What are the weapons at the disposal of an auditor who feels there is misconduct within the company that leaves him with no alternative but to resign?
(b) What duty of care is owed by an auditor and to whom is it owed?

CHAPTER SUMMARY

- All private companies are required by law to appoint at least one director, and public companies at least two.
- The definition of a 'director' includes not only people appointed as such but also any person occupying the position of director. In other words, a person is a director because he occupies the position of director, regardless of what he is called by the company
- There are two bases of power in a company: the members and the directors, but the day-to-day running of the business is in the hands of the directors.
- The directors' power to act in relation to the company is limited only by the Companies Act and the company's Memorandum and Articles and by the directors' duty to have regard to the company's interests.
- There is also a limited control exercised by the company's members who may, for example, remove a director from office or refuse to re-elect a director who has retired by rotation.
- Unlike directors, shareholders owe no fiduciary duty to the company. The majority can vote in whichever way best suits their own interests. In passing resolutions, however, shareholders must have regard to the interests of minority shareholders.
- There are no formal qualifications to become a director, but certain categories are excluded from acting as a direct, either by a company's Articles, or under CDDA 1986.
- Every company must keep a register of its directors and secretaries, and a register of director's shareholdings.
- A person may cease to be a director by retirement, resignation, removal or death. Directors may also be disqualified under regulations provided in a company's' Articles or by court order under CDDA 1986. Under IA 2000, directors may also voluntarily undertake not to act as a director for a specified period.
- Every UK company must also appoint a company secretary. Public companies must appoint a professionally qualified secretary who has the requisite knowledge to carry out his duties.
- Unless exempted, companies must also appoint an auditor to undertake an annual audit of their accounts.

CHAPTER 9

Directors' duties

CONTENTS

LEARNING OUTCOMES

This chapter covers the duties owed by directors to their companies. After reading and understanding the contents of the chapter you should be able to:

- Understand to whom directors owe their duties and who can enforce them.
- Appreciate the fiduciary duties of directors.
- Appreciate the duty of skill and care of directors.
- Appreciate the statutory duties of directors.
- Describe the rules relating to loans and quasi-loans to directors
- Understand the nature of, and the general defences against, the crime of insider dealing.

Introduction

The business of a company is conducted by the directors. The precise relationship between directors and the company is difficult to define. They are managers rather than servants and, on occasions, have been said to occupy the position of trustees and agents. The general nature of their duties was described by Lord Cranworth LC in *Aberdeen Railway Co v Blaikie Bros* (1854) 1 Macq 461:

> 'The directors are a body to whom is delegated the duty of managing the general affairs of the company. A corporate body can only act by agents, and it is of course

the duty of those agents so to act as best to promote the interests of the corporation whose affairs they are conducting. Such agents have duties to discharge of a fiduciary nature towards their principal. And it is a rule of universal application, that no one having such duties to discharge, shall be allowed to enter into engagements in which he has, or can have, a personal interest conflicting, or which possibly may conflict, with the interests of those whom he is bound to protect.'

In some regards the directors may indeed be described as trustees. The property of the company is under their control, just as if they were trustees, and they must use it for the benefit of the company. As such, they occupy a fiduciary relationship and may be called upon to account to the company if they abuse such trust. However, the property of the company is not actually owned by the directors but by the company. In this respect they are not true trustees, and their role is necessarily different.

Directors' duties are of three kinds:

1 fiduciary duties;
2 duty of care and skill;
3 statutory duties.

1 To whom is a duty owed?

Whenever the question as to whom a duty is owed is raised, the other side of the same coin has to be the question: 'who can enforce those duties?' Directors' duties are owed to the company and not to its shareholders, its employees or its creditors. Thus, it is the company (i.e. the members suing as a body or through the board of directors) who may seek a remedy from the directors. This is illustrated in Case Example 9.1.

CASE EXAMPLE 9.1 

***Percival* v *Wright* [1902] 2 Ch 421**

The directors of the company bought some shares in the company from another member. At the time of the acquisition there were negotiations taking place in respect of a takeover of the company by a third party, but the directors did not tell the member from whom they bought shares about this. Had the takeover have gone through, the directors would have made a profit on the shares. The member sued to have the sale of the shares to the directors set aside. It was held that he was not entitled to do so. The sale was binding. The directors had no duty to inform him about the negotiations for the takeover.

From time to time, the courts have suggested that there may be occasions when an individual shareholder may sue a director who has been in breach of duty. However, the general correctness of *Percival* v *Wright* was confirmed by the court.

CASE EXAMPLE 9.2 

***Peskin* v *Anderson* [2000] BCC 1110**

The motoring services business owned by the Royal Automobile Club was sold in 1998. The sale resulting in a windfall to members of £34,000 each. The claimants were former members of the Club who had ceased to be members just before the sale, and so who did not receive such a payment. They claimed that the committee members (i.e. the directors) should have informed them of the possibility of the sale and consequent windfall. It was held that as a matter of principle and in the light of the authorities the principle in *Percival* v *Wright* was good law. A director's main fiduciary duty was to the company. While there might be restricted circumstances where a director could find himself owing a fiduciary duty to a shareholder, it would place an unfair, unrealistic and uncertain burden on directors to hold that there generally was such a duty.

TEST YOUR KNOWLEDGE 9.1 

(a) To whom does a director owe his duties?

(b) Who can sue a director when he goes in breach of duty?

fiduciary duty

The duty owed by a director to his company that requires him to act in good faith and not to allow any conflict to arise between his interest in himself and his duty to his company.

2 Fiduciary duties

The **fiduciary duties** of directors fall under two headings:

1 They must exercise their powers *bona fide* for the benefit of the company.
2 They must not allow a conflict to arise between their personal interests (i.e. the interest they have in themselves) and the company's (i.e. the duty that they owe to their company).

As we saw earlier, when considering the issue of shares, the actual issue is done by the directors as part of their day-to-day management of the company. However, if an issue is made purely out of self interest then it may be a breach of fiduciary duty, as illustrated in Case Example 9.3.

CASE EXAMPLE 9.3 

***Hogg* v *Cramphorn Ltd* [1967] Ch 254**

Directors of a company were anxious to fight off a takeover bid. They issued shares to trustees to be held for the benefit of employees. The trustees were helped to pay for the shares by means of an interest-free loan from the company. It was held that the directors had broken their fiduciary duty in making these arrangements.

The court accepted that the members, by a simple majority in general meeting, could ratify (i.e. approve) the directors' acts. If the directors were to seek this ratification, the shares issued to the trustees could not be used to vote for the ratification.

It has been said that the only reason why directors may issue shares is to raise capital. If they do so for any other motive they will be in breach of their fiduciary duty. This was the view of the Privy Council in *Howard Smith Ltd* v *Ampol Petroleum Ltd*.

CASE EXAMPLE 9.4 

***Howard Smith Ltd* v *Ampol Petroleum Ltd* [1974] AC 821**

Two shareholders held between them 55 per cent of the shares in the company. They made it known that they would reject any takeover attempt. The board of directors issued new shares in the company to a company which had indicated its intention to make a takeover bid. The motive behind this was to destroy the blocking power of the 55 per cent shareholders. It was not to raise cash.

It was held by the Privy Council that the board had acted improperly, even though there was no doubt that they had acted honestly and within the powers given them by the company's constitution. Accordingly, the issue of shares should be set aside.

2.1 Secret profits

The duty of the director not to put himself in a position of conflict between his own interests and those of his company is sometimes expressed as a duty not to make a secret profit. In company law, the word 'secret' has its own specific meaning. A profit made by a director ceases to be secret when it is both disclosed by him and approved by the company in general meeting. Thus, it is not the disclosure alone which prevents it being secret; it is both the disclosure and the approval. Approval may be by either the board of directors or by the members in general passing an ordinary resolution to that effect. A secret profit obviously arises if a director takes a bribe.

CASE EXAMPLE 9.5

***Boston Deep Sea Fishing Co.* v *Ansell* (1888) 39 Ch D 339**

Ansell was a director of Boston Deep Sea Fishing. On behalf of the company he placed a contract for the building of some boats. He was paid commission on the contract by the shipbuilders. He was also a shareholder in an ice company which paid bonuses to shareholders who owned fishing boats and to whom it supplied ice. Ansell bought ice on behalf of his company from the ice company and so received a bonus on his shares. It was held that he must account to his company for both the commission and the bonus.

A director is also liable to account for a secret profit even if he could not have made the profit itself.

CASE EXAMPLE 9.6

***Regal (Hastings) Ltd* v *Gulliver* [1967] 2 AC 134**

Regal (Hastings) Ltd owned a cinema. Through their involvement in the cinema trade, the directors learnt that the other two cinemas in the town were for sale. Obviously, anyone owning all three cinemas in a town had something of greater value than simply the three constituent parts. They wanted somehow to acquire the two other cinemas with a view to selling all three. Regal (Hastings) Ltd had insufficient capital to acquire the further two cinemas itself and so it formed a subsidiary company in which it held some of the shares. The other shares were bought by directors of Regal (Hastings) Ltd. The cinemas were duly acquired and then the shares in both Regal (Hastings) Ltd and the subsidiary were sold.

It was held that the directors of Regal (Hastings) Ltd who had acquired and then sold shares in the subsidiary must account to Regal (Hastings) Ltd for the profit that they had made. Had they not have been directors of the company that owned the first cinema, they would not have had either the knowledge or the opportunity to make the profit on the shares. Had the directors disclosed this profit to the members in general meeting, and had the members approved it, the directors would have been able to retain it.

A similar decision was reached in *Industrial Development Consultants* v *Cooley*.

CASE EXAMPLE 9.7

***Industrial Development Consultants* v *Cooley* [1972] 1 All ER 443**

Cooley was the managing director of a design company. He tried to obtain for the company a contract to do some design work for a gas board. His attempt failed but he was later approached by the gas board with an offer that he should do the work in his private capacity. The gas board stated that it would not give the order for the design to the company. Cooley pretended that his health was deteriorating and obtained a premature release from his service contract. He immediately started up his own company and took on the gas board design contract. It was held that he must account to his former company for the profit he made as a result of the contract.

A similar breach of duty occurs if directors, having negotiated a contract on behalf of the company, then divert it to themselves. This occurred in *Cook* v *Deeks*.

CASE EXAMPLE 9.8

***Cook* v *Deeks* (1916)**

Directors of a construction company negotiated for a construction contract and then took the contract in their own name. The directors held 75 per cent of the shares in the company and a meeting was called of its members at which a resolution was passed stating that the company had no interest in the contract. It was held that the directors had to account to the company for the profit on the contract: The attempt at ratification was a fraud on the minority and thus of no effect.

TEST YOUR KNOWLEDGE 9.2

(a) What is a secret profit?

(b) What should a director ensure is done so that a profit that he is making is not secret?

3 Duty of skill and care

The leading case on which any discussion on duty of skill and care is outlined in Case Example 9.9.

CASE EXAMPLE 9.9

***Re City Equitable Fire Insurance Co. Ltd* [1925] Ch 407**

The directors of an insurance company delegated virtually all aspects of management to its managing director. The director stole large amounts of cash from the company, largely because of inadequate supervision by the other directors. It was held that the directors had been in breach of their duty of skill and care.

The importance of the case lies in the judgment of Romer J in which he laid down the directors' duties of skill and care towards the company. They were expressed in three propositions.

1 A director need not show a greater degree of skill than may be reasonably expected of a person of his knowledge and experience.
2 A director need not give continuous attention to the affairs of the company.
3 A director may delegate duties to some other official in the company and trust him to perform them properly so long as the director has no reason to mistrust or doubt the official.

The requirement that a director should show the skill of a person of his knowledge and experience means that different directors owe different standards of skill to their companies. Whereas an accountant on the board of a company might be expected to show a high degree of skill in respect of financial matters, an inexperienced newcomer on the board for some other purpose would not. This standard of care and skill arises in the duty owing to the company by a director. It is interesting to note that a different standard is expected when the company goes into liquidation, which contracts with potential liability for wrongful trading, where the standard expected of a director is the higher of that which he actually possesses and that which the director in his position should possess.

More recently, the very subjective standard expressed in *Re City Equitable Fire Insurance Co. Ltd* has been supplanted by a more realistic objective standard in the majority of instances, as illustrated by Case Example 9.10.

CASE EXAMPLE 9.10

***Re D'Jan of London Ltd* [1994] BCLC 561**

A liquidator brought proceedings in negligence against a director. Hoffmann LJ stated that the standard expected of a director today was as stated in s. 214 of the Insolvency Act 1986 (where the provisions regarding wrongful trading are to be found), namely that a director must show the higher of either the skill actually possessed by him or that which would objectively be expected of such a director of such a company.

In other words, it can be said with reasonable certainty that the relatively low standard stated to be required of directors in *Re City Equitable Fire Insurance Co. Ltd* has long since passed its sell-by date. Directors have now to be up to the task.

The current Company Law Review envisages that the next Companies Act will contain a schedule setting out the duties of directors more explicitly. In relation to his duty of care and skill this more realistic objective standard is what will usually be required. In other words he will have to show the higher of that standard of skill which he actually posses and that which a director in his position could reasonably be expected to possess.

3.1 Negligence and fraud

Generally a director cannot be held personally liable in tort to a third party when he has been negligent in some aspect of his work. In *Williams* v *Natural Life Health Foods Limited* [1998] BCC 428 the managing director of a small company was responsible for the making of negligent mis-statements to a customer. It was held that he fell under no personal liability. Liability lay exclusively with the company which he made vicariously liable for his wrongs. The House of Lords, however, did suggest that perhaps if he had dealt face to face with the customer and the customer had placed a personal reliance upon what he was saying then the director may have faced a personal liability.

However, a director can never hide from personal liability behind his company if he commits a fraud. In *Standard Chartered Bank* v *Pakistan National Shipping Corp* (No. 2) [2003] 1 AllER 173 a director fraudulently altered a document so as to make a third party liable upon it. It was held that he was personally liable for this fraudulent alteration.

4 Release of directors from liability

CA 1985, s. 310

In *Re City Equitable Fire Insurance Co. Ltd*, the Articles of the company protected the directors from liability in cases other than where there had been wilful neglect or default, and the directors avoided liability. There was much criticism of this and such a provision was made void by CA 1985 s. 310. This means that the company cannot engage a person as a director and provide in his service contract that he will not, in any circumstances, be liable for any harm which he does to the company. Any provision in the Articles to this effect is void.

The effects of s. 310 are lessened by the provision which permits a company to indemnify the director against any liability in defending either civil or criminal proceedings in which judgment has been given in his favour or in respect of which he has been acquitted. If proceedings are taken against the director and the court finds him under no liability, the company may, by an ordinary resolution in a general meeting, indemnify him against any costs he has incurred.

Section 310 applies whether the indemnity against liability is contained in a company's Articles or in any contract with the company or otherwise. The words 'in any contract with the company or otherwise' were taken to include insurance contracts taken out by a company to protect their directors against possible claims. However, CA 1989 s. 137 amended CA 1985 s. 310 so that companies may purchase and maintain insurance against liability for any officer in respect of any negligence, default, breach of duty or breach of trust of which he may be guilty in relation to the company. It is no longer a requirement that if a company takes out insurance on behalf of its officers, that fact must be disclosed in the directors' report.

CA 1985, s. 727

CA 1985 s. 727 provides that in any proceedings for negligence, default, breach of duty or breach of trust against an officer of the company, the officer concerned may seek relief from the court on the grounds that he acted honestly and reasonably and, having regard to all the circumstances of the case, he ought fairly to be excused. The court may grant relief, either wholly or partly, on such terms as it thinks fit. To get such relief, the director must show that he acted both honestly and reasonably, as shown in Case Example 9.11.

CASE EXAMPLE 9.11

***Re Duomatic Ltd* [1969] 2 Ch 365**

A director was party to the payment of compensation for loss of office to another director in circumstances where the payment had not been disclosed to and approved by the members of the company in a general meeting as is required by CA 1985 s. 312. The director concerned had not taken legal advice on the matter when taking the decision to pay the compensation and for that reason the court refused to grant relief. Buckley J said: '*a director of the company dealing with a matter of this kind who does not seek any legal advice at all but elects to deal with the matter himself without a proper exploration of the considerations which contribute, or ought to contribute, to a decision as to what should be done on the company's behalf, cannot be said to act reasonably*'.

Unless a director can show that he acted with absolute honesty and integrity the defence in s. 727 will not be available to him. The limitation of the protection offered by s.727 is shown by Case Example 9.12.

CASE EXAMPLE 9.12

***Bairstow* v *Queens Moat Houses* [2002] BCC 91**

In this case, some directors of a public company caused a dividend to be paid based on accounts that did not give a true and fair view of the company's financial position. The directors were dismissed by the company and brought proceedings for wrongful dismissal. The company defended the action on the basis that the dismissal was justified and counter-claimed for the repayment of the dividends that had been wrongfully paid. The directors defended this counterclaim by the use of s. 727. It was held that the defence was not available unless the directors could show that they had acted with complete honesty and reasonableness. As the dividends were paid out of accounts which the directors knew did not give a fair and true view of the financial position of the company, the payments constituted a breach of trust and fiduciary duty as they did not act in the best interest of their company. In this case, the concepts of honesty and reasonableness were held to be are absolute. If complete integrity could not be shown then the defence was not available.

Since *Re City Equitable Fire Insurance Co. Ltd*, the aim of the law has been to prevent any blanket indemnity for directors when they are appointed but to permit an indemnity to be given either:

(a) by the members in general meeting in the limited circumstances of s. 310; or
(b) by the court under s. 727 in any proceedings against the directors

Any relief can only be given after liability has arisen.

TEST YOUR KNOWLEDGE 9.3

(a) What standard of skill should a director show in his stewardship of a company's affairs?

(b) A director has been negligent in the carrying out of his duties. An Article states that the company will indemnify him against any loss incurred by him in the carrying out of his duties. The company is about to commence proceedings against the director for negligence. If the action is successful will the director be able to claim an indemnity from the company for any damages or costs that he is ordered to pay? Is there any other way in which a director can be exonerated from his liability?

5 Statutory duties

The general duties of directors contained in common law are augmented by a range of duties imposed by statute. These can be divided into several categories:

1 administrative and compliance duties;
2 a duty to employees;
3 a duty to other stakeholders such as customers and creditors under consumer protection, trades descriptions and consumer protection legislation;
4 a duty to avoid pollution and protect the environment;
5 a duty to provide a safe working environment under Health & Safety legislation.

5.1 Administrative and compliance duties

The duties which fall into this category are duties for which the company as a whole is responsible but, by virtue of their position and authority, directors are intimately responsible for ensuring compliance. Even where directors delegate responsibility to the company secretary, as is common practice, the directors remain ultimately responsible and in many cases will be liable with the company for contravention of statutory requirements. For example, a director may be disqualified for persistent breaches of company legislation or on summary conviction (CDDA 1986, ss. 3 and 5, outlined in more detail in Chapter 8).

Administrative and compliance duties include the directors' responsibility for:

- appointing and removing officers (see Chapter 8);
- maintaining statutory records, such as the register of members or the register of directors' interests (CA 1985);
- statutory filing requirements (CA 1985);
- retaining documents;
- displaying company details (CA 1985 ss. 348–51);
- paying dividends (CA 1985 and specific provisions in a company's Articles);
- political donations (Political Parties, Elections and Referendums 2000, CA 1985 s.347);
- managing bank accounts and paying tax;
- arranging insurance.

5.2 Duty to employees

By CA 1985 s. 309, directors are obliged to have regard to the interests of the company's employees in general as well as to the interests of its members. This is stated to be a duty owed by the directors to the company (and the company alone) and is enforceable in the same way as any other fiduciary duty owed to a company by its directors. So while there appears to be a duty owed to the employees, they seem to have no way of enforcing it.

So to give the provision some meaning, it is necessary to look at it another way.The Act refers to the provision as conferring on the directors a 'duty to employees'. However, think instead of it as though it were entitled 'defence to directors when they act decently towards employees'. If the company has to make some employees redundant and the directors decide to pay them rather more by way of a redundancy payment than that to which they are entitled by law, some shareholders might complain.The directors can, in these circumstances, use s. 309 as a defence.Amongst their duties is a requirement to have regard to the interests of employees.They owe this duty to the company. In looking after the interests of the employees they were doing no more than discharging that duty. What right, therefore, have the shareholders to complain?

6 Restricted and prohibited transactions

6.1 Substantial property transactions involving directors

By CA 1985 s. 320, a contract may not be made where a company transfers to a director, or a director transfers to the company, a non-cash asset, if its value exceeds £100,000 or 10 per cent of the value of the company's net assets subject to a minimum value of £2,000, unless approved by the members in a general meeting.

In this context the term 'director' includes:

(a) shadow directors, i.e., persons in accordance with whose directions or instructions the directors are accustomed to act; and
(b) connected persons, i.e. a director's spouse, his minor children or step-children, his business partners and companies in which he or an associate has a 20 per cent shareholding.

An arrangement entered into in contravention of this may be set aside by the company except in three situations:

1 Where restitution of any money, or other asset, associated with the transaction is no longer possible or the company has been indemnified by any other person for the loss or damage suffered by it.
2 Where any rights acquired bona fide for value and without notice of the contravention by any person who was not a party to the transaction would be affected by its avoidance.
3 Where the arrangement is, within a reasonable period, confirmed by the company in a general meeting or, if it is an arrangement for the transfer of an asset to, or by, a director of its holding company or a person who is connected to such a director, is confirmed with the approval of the holding company given by a resolution in a general meeting.

A example of the sort of risk that can be incurred when this statutory requirement is ignored can be found in the case of Case Example 9.13.

CASE EXAMPLE 9.13

British Racing Drivers Club Ltd v Hextall Erskine & Co. **[1996] 3 All ER 667**

The company was entering into a joint venture with a limited company which happened to be a connected person. The solicitors advising the company on the transaction failed to recognise the need for members' approval pursuant to s. 320. The joint venture went ahead, and substantial losses were incurred. It was held that the solicitors were liable for the losses; their failure to advise as to the need to comply with s. 320 coupled with the consequent loss to the company was negligence such as to cause the solicitors to be liable for the loss.

6.2 **Loans to directors**

Prohibitions

By CA 1985 s. 330 a company may not make a loan to a director, a shadow director or a person connected with such a director. The law regarding loans to directors is complex, but is based largely on the following principles:

1 Companies should not make loans to directors. A company is a separate legal entity. A director owes a fiduciary duty to his company. He should allow no conflict to arise between his duty to his company and his interest in himself. Taking a loan is likely to compromise this duty.
2 Directors of small private companies often view the company's bank account as an extension of their own. Secretaries or accountants can tell directors about the separate legal entity of the company for all they are worth, but the directors who are the controlling shareholders of the company nevertheless regard the company as indistinct from themselves.
3 This means that the only prohibition likely to be workable in practicable terms is one concerning public companies, where outside money is likely to be involved.
4 However, if the law were simply to bar public companies from making loans, such a prohibition could easily be evaded by the company's lending through a private subsidiary.

It is for this last reason that, in regard to loans to directors, the law does not draw the usual distinction between public and private companies, but rather between relevant and non-relevant companies.

A relevant company means any public company or any company which is in a group which includes a public company.

All other companies are non-relevant.

As has been said, the basic rule regarding loans is contained in s. 330. No company, public or private, relevant or otherwise, may make a loan to a director of the company, nor to a director of its holding company. Nor may a company enter into any guarantee nor provide any security in connection with such a loan.

Other forbidden transactions

Besides these prohibitions, there are five other transactions which a relevant company is forbidden to make.

1 It may not make a quasi-loan to a director of the company or its holding company (CA 1985 s. 331(3)). A quasi-loan arises where a company gives a director a credit card and the director uses the card to pay for goods for himself. He then has to reimburse the company. Although the giving of the credit card to the director does not of itself create a loan, the position could arise where the director owes the company money. Thus the possession of the credit card is a quasi-loan.
2 The company may not make a loan or a quasi-loan to a person connected with a director (CA 1985 s. 346).

3 A relevant company may not enter into any guarantee or provide any security in connection with a loan or quasi-loan made by a third party for such a director or connected person (CA 1985 s. 330(3)).
4 A relevant company may not enter into a credit transaction as a creditor for a director or a connected person. In this context a credit transaction means a situation where a person supplies goods or sells land under a hire purchase or conditional sale agreement, or where a person leases or hires land or goods in return for periodical payments, or where a person otherwise disposes of land or supplies goods or services on the understanding that payment is to be deferred in some way (CA 1985 s. 330(4)(a)).
5 A relevant company may not enter into any guarantee or provide any security in connection with a credit transaction made by a third party for such a director or connected person (CA 1985 s. 330(4)(b)). These restrictions are strengthened by prohibitions on backdoor methods of getting around them.

For example, a company may not arrange for an assignment to it, or the assumption by it, of any rights, obligations or liabilities under the transaction which, had it been entered into by the company itself, would have been unlawful. So, a director is prohibited from taking a loan from a third party, and then arranging that the third party's rights be assigned to his company.

Again, the company may not take part in any arrangement under which another person enters into a loan transaction with a director when that other person, in pursuance of the arrangement, obtains or is set to obtain any benefit from the company. This outlaws the back-to-back type of arrangement under which a company makes a loan to a third party in return for that third party making a counter loan to the directors of the first company.

Lawful loans

Some loans to directors are lawful. Sections 332–38 of CA 1985 detail a list of permitted exceptions:

1 By s. 332 a relevant company may, in spite of the prohibition described above, make a small quasi-loan to one of its directors. This means a quasi-loan which requires the director, or someone on his behalf, to reimburse the creditor his expenditure within two months of the quasi-loan being incurred. The amount involved must not exceed £5,000.
2 By s. 333, where a director of a relevant company or its holding company is associated with a subsidiary of either of those companies, the relevant company may make a loan or quasi-loan or guarantee a loan or quasi-loan by a third party to that subsidiary.
3 By s. 334 any company may make a loan to a director for any purpose of up to £5,000. For example, a director of a small private company taking his family on holiday might write a cheque on the company's bank account to cover his expenses, leaving it to the company's accountant to sort this out by way of a director's loan account. Without this small loan exemption, all such loans would be unlawful.
4 By s. 335, a relevant company may enter into a credit transaction with a director so long as the value of the proposed transaction does not exceed £10,000.
5 Alternatively, such a credit transaction is permissible if the company enters into it in the ordinary course of business and the overall terms of the transaction are no more favourable than the company would offer in like circumstances to a third party unconnected with the company. Thus, a company may enter into a transaction for the value in excess of £10,000 for a director if it is in the business of providing finance and it would provide such finance, all other factors being equal, on the same terms for a third party unconnected with the business.
6 By s. 337 a company can assist a director in the performance of his duties. Such assistance may be approved by the company in general meeting before the expen-

diture is incurred. In this case, the purpose of the expenditure, the amount involved, and the extent of the company's liability should be disclosed. Alternatively, the assistance can be approved at the next annual general meeting of the company. If such approval is not given by the members, the loan must be repaid or the liability discharged within six months.

Under this exception, the company may do anything to provide any of its directors with funds to meet expenditure incurred or to be incurred by them for the purposes of the company or for the purpose of enabling them properly to perform their duties as officers of the company.

If the company concerned is a relevant company, there is an upper limit on the amount which may be advanced of £20,000. If the company is non-relevant, there is no upper limit.

7 By s. 338, a money-lending company may make a loan or quasi-loan to a director or enter into a guarantee of such a loan or quasi-loan so long as it is done in the ordinary course of business. There is again a proviso that the overall terms of the transaction may be no more favourable than the company would offer in like circumstances to a third party unconnected with the company. There is an upper limit for such loans if made by relevant companies other than recognised banks. A recognised bank is a company which is an authorised institution for the purposes of the Banking Act 1987. A relevant company which is not a banking company may not enter into any transaction if the amount exceeds £100,000.

8 If the loan is to do with house purchase, and if the money-lending company is one which normally makes loans for house purchase, it may make a loan on favourable terms to a director. The loan may be for house purchase or house improvement. There are four conditions which have to be satisfied for beneficial house purchase loans:
   - The company must normally make loans for such purposes.
   - The house must be the director's only or main residence.
   - The amount involved must not exceed £100,000.
   - Loans of this description must be available to employees of the company on no less favourable terms.

By s. 339, in considering how much can be advanced to a director under a particular exception, there has to be aggregated the value of any other existing transaction made in favour of a director or connected person under that specific head. If the amount of the sums aggregated exceeds the maximum amount permitted under the head in question, then the company may not enter into that further transaction.

Contravention

If the provisions of s. 330 are contravened, both civil and criminal consequences may follow. By s. 341 such a transaction is voidable. It may be set aside by the company, though not by the other party. A voidance is not permitted in three instances:

- If restitution is impossible.
- Where the company has been indemnified against any loss incurred.
- Where a third party has acquired rights, in good faith, without notice of the contravention, and having given value for those rights, and to avoid the transaction would adversely affect the third party.

Where there is a contravention of s. 330, the director involved, together with any other director who authorised the transaction, will incur personal liability. So, too, does any connected person involved. They must account to the company for any personal gain made, whether directly or indirectly. They are also jointly and severally liable to indemnify the company against any loss it has sustained.

In addition, by s. 342, a director of a relevant company who authorises or permits the company to enter into a transaction or arrangement in contravention of these rules commits a criminal offence if he knew or had reasonable cause to believe the company was contravening s. 330. The company itself is also committing a criminal offence, as is any other person who knowingly procures a relevant company to commit a breach of s. 330.

Disclosure

Whenever a company enters into any transaction covered by s. 330, the transaction must be disclosed in notes to its accounts, even if the transaction is a permitted one. So too must any agreement to enter into any such transaction or arrangement with the company in which the director, whether directly or indirectly, has a material interest (see Chapter 8). Disclosure must be made of the principal terms of the transaction. This obviously includes details of the parties involved and particulars of the terms and purpose of the arrangement.

However, there are certain transactions which are exempt from disclosure requirements:

1 any transaction between one company and another in which a director of the first company is only interested by virtue of being a director of the other;
2 a contract of service between that company and one of its directors;
3 a transaction which was not entered into during the period to which the accounts relate or which did not subsist during that period;
4 a transaction which was made before the section was brought into force and did not subsist after that time.

There are also some specific exclusions:

1 There need not be disclosed credit transactions, guarantees or similar arrangements made under s. 330 so long as the net balance outstanding did not at any time during the accounting period to which the accounts relate exceed £10,000.
2 There need not be disclosed transactions which do not fall within s. 330 in which the interest of the director in question was worth less than £10,000 or 1 per cent of the company's net assets whichever is less. Transactions below £2,000 aggregate value are to be ignored.

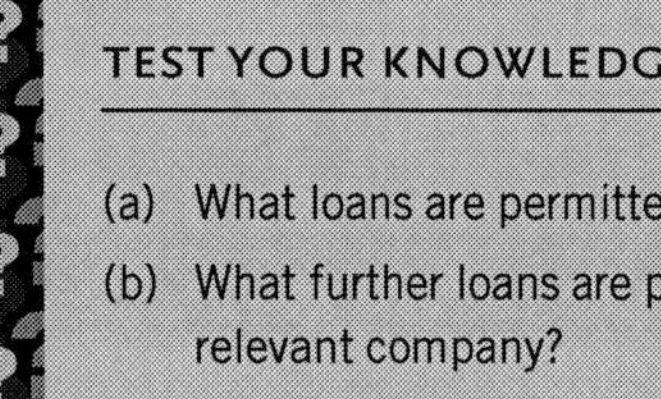

TEST YOUR KNOWLEDGE 9.4

(a) What loans are permitted in the case of a director of a relevant company?

(b) What further loans are permitted in the case of a company that is not a relevant company?

7 Insider dealing

The directors of companies whose shares are listed on the markets are in a privileged position as regards information concerning the company. They will know before the market of losses or profits being made by the company. The term insider dealing is used to describe any dealing in shares by an individual who uses such prior knowledge of undisclosed market information to their own personal advantage.

7.1 Definitions

The rules on insider dealing are contained in Part V of the Criminal Justice Act 1993. Insiders are defined in s. 57 to include anyone who obtains inside information as a result of their employment or position or from an insider. There does not need to be a connections between the alleged insider and the company in whose securities he deals.

A person is an insider if he has, and knows that he has, unpublished price-sensitive information as a result of his being, or obtaining the information from, a director, employee or shareholder of an issuer of securities. The company need not necessarily be the issuer of the securities involved in the insider dealing, although, in a prosecution, the court may imply this requirement.

The securities which may be the subject of insider dealing include public and government authorities, debt securities, as well as companies' share and debt securities (CJA 1993 s. 54 and Sch. 2). The market on which the insider dealing takes place must be one prescribed by the Treasury (and thus not exclusively the London Stock Exchange) (CJA 1993 s. 60(1)). For example, the AIM is a prescribed market. Alternatively, the alleged insider must deal through a professional intermediary.

7.2 **Offences**

There are three separate offences created by s. 52 each of which may only be committed by an individual and within the UK. These are:

1 dealing in securities to which the inside information relates (the dealing offence);
2 encouraging another person to deal in such securities, knowing or having reasonable cause to believe that the other person will do so (the encouraging offence);
3 disclosing inside information to another person other than in the proper performance of his employment, office or profession (the disclosure offence).

A person who is convicted of any of these offences faces up to 7 years' imprisonment together with an unlimited fine. However, a prosecution may not be bought except with the consent of either the Secretary of State for Trade and Industry or the Director of Public Prosecutions.

The insider dealing legislation gives no new remedy in the civil courts to the victims of insider dealing. Indeed it is provided by s. 63 (2) that no contract is void or unenforceable by reason only of s. 52. There was a similar provision in the earlier legislation. However, this did not prevent the court in *Chase Manhattan Equities Limited* v *Goodman* [1999] BCC 308 holding that a contract that infringed the statutory provisions was unenforceable because of its being tainted by illegality.

7.3 **What constitutes inside information?**

Under s. 56 inside information is information relating to securities which not been made public or published in any of the following ways:

- under the rules of a regulated market to inform investors or their professional advisers;
- contained in records which by statute are open to inspection by the public;
- such that it can be readily acquired by persons likely to deal in the securities to which the information relates; or
- such that it can be derived from information which has been made public.

However, under s. 58(3) information may not be regarded as having been made public even though:

- it can be acquired only by exercising diligence or expertise;
- it has been communicated to a section of the public at large;
- it can be acquired only by observation (such as by comparing different entries in continuous records where the individual entries are not themselves price-sensitive information);
- it is communicated only on payment of a fee;
- it is published only outside the UK.

There are no specific exceptions for dealings by liquidators, receivers, trustees in bankruptcy, trustees or personal representatives.

7.4 **Defences**

Under s. 53 defences to insider dealing include:

1 That at the time the accused did not expect the dealing to result in a profit or the

avoidance of a loss attributable to the information possessed by him being price-sensitive information relating to the securities concerned.

2 That at the time of dealing the accused believed on reasonable grounds that the price-sensitive information had been disclosed sufficiently widely to ensure that none of the persons taking part in the dealing would be prejudiced by not having the information.

3 That the accused would have dealt in the securities even if he had not had the price-sensitive information.

4 That the accused would have encouraged the other person to deal in the securities even if he had not had the price-sensitive information.

5 That the accused in good faith dealt in price-sensitive securities, or encouraged another person to do so in course of his business or employment as a market maker.

6 That the accused dealt in securities or encouraged another person to do so in order to establish the dealing price of newly issued or marketed securities and that he acted in accordance with the rules made under the Financial Services Act 1986 governing price-stabilisation operations.

Insider dealing is very difficult to prove and there are very few prosecutions. Abuses by directors might be better dealt with by the Financial Services Authority's own rules on market abuse introduced by the Financial Services and Markets Act 2000. Market abuse is a civil, rather than a criminal, offence, carrying a lesser burden of proof than insider dealing. It also applies generally, not just to company directors.

TEST YOUR KNOWLEDGE 9.5

(a) What are the three insider dealing offences?

(b) Why is insider dealing so difficult to prove?

CHAPTER SUMMARY

- Directors owe a number of duties to the company. These duties are owed to the company itself and not to its shareholders, employees or creditors.
- Directors, therefore, must exercise their powers in good faith for the company's benefit and must not allow there to be any conflict between their interests and the company's.
- They owe the company a duty of care and, in exercising their powers, must have regard to the interests of the company's employees and other statutory requirements.
- Because directors are in a powerful position their personal dealings with the company are restricted by the law. So, they cannot enter into substantial property transactions with the company and, if the directors have any interest in dealings which involve the company, they must make full disclosure of this.
- Subject to certain exceptions, the company is not permitted to make loans or quasi-loans to its directors.
- Directors of public companies must not indulge in insider dealing, and need to be aware of the civil offence of market abuse.

CHAPTER 10

Shareholder remedies

CONTENTS

LEARNING OUTCOMES

This chapter covers the principle of majority rule and the remedies available to minority shareholders. After reading and understanding the contents of the chapter and studying the case examples, you should be able to:

- Understand the nature of majority rule.
- Explain the exceptions to the rule in *Foss* v *Harbottle*.
- Appreciate the s. 459 remedy.
- Understand the role of the Department of Trade and Industry.

Introduction

In this chapter we examine the ways in which shareholders who are dissatisfied with the way in which their company is being run can obtain a remedy. The redress of shareholders' grievances can be achieved in two principal ways, either by way of an action permitted by the courts or by proceedings taken under CA 1985 s. 459. However, before considering this, remind yourself of something which was considered at the beginning of Chapter 8.

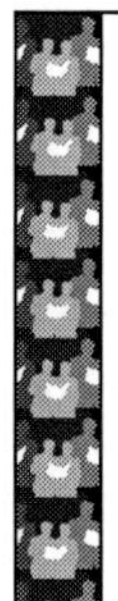

THEORY INTO PRACTICE 10.1

Where does power lie within a company? Is it with the members or the directors and why?

Answer

Power very definitely lies with the directors. By Article 70 of Table A they are given the day-to-day management of the company. Moreover, they know each other and meet regularly together whereas the membership of many companies is far more disparate and it is difficult for them to present a cohesive front against the board.

1 The principle of majority rule

It is necessary first to look at the principle of majority rule and then at those instances at common law where an individual shareholder can obtain a remedy.

1.1 The rule in *Foss* v *Harbottle*

Once a company has been formed, it is a separate legal person in its own right. This was the reasoning behind the judgment in *Salomon v Salomon & Co. Ltd* [1897] AC 22. As a separate legal entity in its own right, a company can make contracts, own property and participate in legal proceedings. Within companies there is a general principle of majority rule. In other words, if the majority shareholders decide to follow a particular course of action there is generally nothing that minority shareholders can do to challenge this. This is particularly important where there is a company in which the directors own the majority of the shares but where there are minority shareholders.

CASE EXAMPLE 10.1

***Foss* v *Harbottle* (1843) 2 Ha 461**

Two minority shareholders in a company brought an action against the company's directors alleging that certain assets of the company had been misapplied by the directors and that the directors had improperly created mortgages over some of the company's property. It was held that the shareholders were not competent to act as plaintiffs in these proceedings. When a wrong is done to a company, the proper plaintiff in any action to remedy that wrong is the company itself.

Reasons for this rule

Three reasons are usually given for the rule in *Foss* v *Harbottle*:

1. It asserts the separate legal personality of the company. When a wrong is done to the company, the proper person to sue to remedy the situation is the company itself. For example, since directors' duties are owed to the company, the proper plaintiff in any action to enforce those duties is the company itself.
2. It prevents a multiplicity of actions in the name of the company. It would be absurd if every member of a company to which a harm had been done could sue in the name of the company to recover compensation for that harm.
3. It prevents futile litigation.

In *MacDougall* v *Gardiner* (1875) 1 Ch D 13, Mellish LJ said:

> 'If the thing complained of is a thing which in substance the majority of the company are entitled to do, or if something has been done irregularly which the majority of the company are entitled to do regularly, or if something has been done illegally which the majority of the company are entitled to do legally, there can be no use in having litigation about it, the ultimate end of which is only that a meeting has to be called, and then ultimately the majority gets its wishes.'

A good example of this is to be found in the facts of the case itself:

CASE EXAMPLE 10.2

***MacDougall* v *Gardiner* (1875)**

Gardiner was the chairman of a company. He adjourned a general meeting of the company in circumstances where, in accordance with the Articles, certain shareholders wanted a poll to be taken to determine whether there should be an adjournment or not. Subsequently, a shareholder brought an action against the directors and the company for a declaration that the chairman's action was improper.

It was held by the Court of Appeal that the court had no right to interfere in what was essentially an internal matter of the company. If the chairman had been wrong in the way in which he acted, the only person who would have the right to sue was the company itself.

The rule has recently been reiterated by the House of Lords in the case of *Johnson* v *Gore Wood & Co (a firm)* [2001] BCC 820.

CASE EXAMPLE 10.3

***Johnson* v *Gore Wood & Co (a firm)* [2001] BCC 820**

Johnson had owned almost all the shares in his company, W Ltd. The company suffered a substantial loss as a result of alleged negligence by its solicitors. The company's claim against the solicitors was compromised. Johnson then made a personal claim. Lord Bingham made the following points:

- Where a company suffers loss because of a breach of duty owed to it, only the company may sue in respect of that loss. A claim may not be brought by a shareholder to make good a loss in the value of his shares where that loss merely reflects the loss suffered by the company.
- Where a company suffers loss but has no cause of action to sue to recover that loss, the shareholder in the company may sue in respect of it (assuming that he has a cause of action), even though the loss is a diminution in the value of the shareholding.
- A shareholder can also sue in his own name notwithstanding that his company has suffered loss as a result of a breach of duty owed to it if he can show that a breach has occurred of a separate and distinct duty independently owed to him.

Thus the general rule remains: where a company has suffered a loss as a result of a breach of duty to it, only the company can sue for redress. A shareholder cannot claim for the diminution in his shareholding. This is so even where the company is the shareholder's alter ego.

1.2 Exceptions to the rule in *Foss* v *Harbottle*

The rule which provides that the company is the proper complainant in any action concerning a wrong done to itself is essentially a procedural rule. It will be appreciated that in *Foss* v *Harbottle* itself the decision was rather unfair on the minority shareholders in the company. For this reason a number of exceptions have been developed over the years. The courts have said that a mere procedural rule must not be allowed to result in injustice and so there are a number of exceptions to it. These exceptions are as follows:

1 Where the act complained of is illegal or *ultra vires*. An example of this arose in *Parke* v *Daily News*.

CASE EXAMPLE 10.4 

***Parke* v *Daily News* [1962] Ch 927**

A shareholder obtained a declaration from the court that *ex gratia* redundancy payments being made by the company were *ultra vires* and so the directors should be restrained from paying them.

2 Where the act complained of constitutes a fraud by the majority of the members on minority shareholders. An example of fraud is where directors of a company divert profitable contracts from the company and take the benefit themselves.

CASE EXAMPLE 10.5 

***Cook* v *Deeks* [1916] AC 554**

Directors who were controlling shareholders of the company negotiated a contract in the name of the company. They then took the contract in their own names. A minority shareholder was permitted to sue the directors on behalf of the company to compel them to account to the company for their profits. An action brought in such circumstances is known as a derivative action. In other words, the right to bring proceedings derives from that of the company.

It is important to distinguish between where the directors are fraudulent and where they are merely negligent. As a general rule a minority shareholders' action cannot be brought if the directors are simply negligent (e.g. Case Example 10.6).

CASE EXAMPLE 10.6 

***Pavlides* v *Jensen* [1956] Ch 565**

Directors who were in control of a company negligently sold an asbestos mine at a very considerable undervalue. A minority shareholder sought to bring an action on behalf of the company against the negligent directors. It was held that his action must fail. An individual plaintiff cannot sue if the claim is based only on negligence.

This is not the case where the negligence results in a benefit to the directors. Then it may amount to a fraud on the minority.

CASE EXAMPLE 10.7 

***Daniels* v *Daniels* [1978] Ch 406**

The controlling shareholders of the company were a Mr and Mrs Daniels who were the company's two directors. The company bought some land from the estate of a deceased shareholder for its probate value of £4,250. Subsequently, the company resold the land to Mrs Daniels for the same price. She then resold it a few years later for £120,000. Minority shareholders then tried to sue the directors to recover the loss caused to the company by their negligence. The plaintiffs did not allege fraud. The directors sought to defend the case by saying that since only negligence was alleged a minority shareholder's action could not be brought (as was decided in *Pavlides* v *Jensen*).

It was held, however, that fraud had a wider meaning than this. Templeman J, the judge in the case, stated: 'If minority shareholders can sue if there is fraud, I see no reason why they cannot sue where the action of the majority and the directors, though without fraud, confers some benefit on those directors and majority shareholders themselves.'

He went on to explain the distinction between the facts in *Daniels* v *Daniels* and those in *Pavlides* v *Jensen*. Danckwerts J in *Pavlides* v *Jensen* accepted that the forbearance of shareholders extends to directors who are 'an amiable set of lunatics'. '*Examples, ancient and modern, abound. To put up with foolish directors is one thing, to put up with directors who are so foolish that they make a profit of £115,000 odd at the expense of the company is something entirely different . . . a minority shareholder who has no other remedy may sue where directors use their powers, intentionally or unintentionally, fraudulently or negligently, in a manner which benefits themselves at the expense of the company.*'

A similar decision was reached in *Estmanco (Kilner House) Ltd v GLC*.

CASE EXAMPLE 10.8

***Estmanco (Kilner House) Ltd* v *GLC* [1982] 1 All ER 437**

The GLC began to sell individual flats in a block to tenants in occupation of those flats. A management company was formed in which initially the GLC held all the shares. As a flat was sold, one share in the management company was transferred to the tenant purchasing the flat. It was intended that ultimately the individual owners of the flats would use their shares in the management company to give them a right to vote at meetings of the company and so determine the management policy of the block of flats. However, the individual shares were not to obtain the right to vote until all the flats, and consequently all the shares, had been transferred from the GLC. After some of the flats had been sold, there was a local council election and a different political party was elected to control of the GLC. This party adopted a different policy on the sale of council properties to tenants and decided not to complete the planned sale of the remainder of the flats. An individual tenant sought leave to bring proceedings on behalf of the company against the majority shareholder (i.e. the GLC) since its change of policy prevented the existing private shareholders in the company from exercising their voting rights.

It was held that the action should succeed since the GLC's conduct amounted to a fraud on the minority. It stultified the purposes for which the company had been formed and so deprived the minority shareholders of their entitlement to vote.

3 Where the Articles of a company require a particular procedure to be followed. This is illustrated by Case Example 10.9.

CASE EXAMPLE 10.9

***Baillie* v *Oriental Telephone Co Ltd* [1915] 1 Ch 503**

The directors of the company called a meeting at which a special resolution was to be passed. They failed to give proper notice of the resolution. It was held that a shareholder could obtain an injunction restraining the company from acting on the resolution.

(Note: This case is difficult to reconcile with the decision in *MacDougall* v *Gardiner* discussed above. It may well be that the *MacDougall* decision is wrong and would not be followed were the facts to arise again today.)

4 Any other case where justice demands. An instance of this arose in the case of *Pender* v *Lushington*.

CASE EXAMPLE 10.10

***Pender* v *Lushington* [1877] 6 Ch D 70**

A shareholder was held to be entitled to enforce an Article giving him a right to vote at the general meetings of the company and to compel the directors to record his vote.

1.3 The nature of the action brought by a shareholder

An action brought by a shareholder may take one of two forms. It may be a derivative action or it may be a representative action. The former is a procedural device allowing the aggrieved shareholder to sue in the name of the company. In other words, his right to sue derives from the company. Before the court will allow such an action to be brought, it must be satisfied that the plaintiff is a proper person to bring the action. If, for example, a shareholder's conduct is in some way tainted, then he may not bring an action.

CASE EXAMPLE 10.11 

***Nurcombe* v *Nurcombe* [1985] 1 WLR 370**

A husband and wife were respectively the majority and minority shareholders in a small business. The husband had taken money from the company for his own use. There had been difficulties in the marriage, and the wife had brought matrimonial proceedings in which she had been awarded a sum representing that money taken by the husband. It was held that she was not a proper person to bring a derivative action on behalf of the company since she had already dealt with the matter by means of a matrimonial action. It would be unfair for her to have, as it were, a double claim.

A representative action is brought by a member to enforce a right enjoyed by him in his individual capacity. For example, the action in *Pender* v *Lushington* discussed above was a representative one.

TEST YOUR KNOWLEDGE 10.1 

(a) What is the rule in Foss v Harbottle? What are the reasons for the rule?
(b) What are the exceptions to the rule?
(c) What is the difference between a derivative and a representative action?

2 The statutory remedy

Until 1948 the principal remedies available to a shareholder who was dissatisfied with the way in which the company was being run were either to sell his shares (if there were an available market) or to petition for the company to be wound up.

It was thought, and properly so, that there should be some other remedy available which would have the effect of allowing the court to make whatever order it thought fit in order to grant relief in respect of the matters complained of. This remedy is now to be found in s. 459 of the Companies Act 1985. It is frequently referred to as 'the alternative remedy', and in this context the word 'alternative' means that the remedy in s. 459 is an alternative to a formal winding up of the company.

2.1 The ground for an s. 459 petition

Any member of a company may apply to the court for an order under s. 459 on the grounds that the company's affairs are being or have been conducted in a manner which is unfairly prejudicial to the interests of some part of, or all the members of, the company, including himself, would be similarly beneficial.

When this remedy was first introduced into the law back in the 1940s, the petitioner had to prove that the conduct against him had been oppressive. Now it is sufficient for him to show that the manner in which the company has been or will be run is unfairly prejudicial to him. Obviously, it is very much easier to show the existence of prejudice than actual oppression.

2.2 Orders available to the court

If the court finds that the grounds alleged in the petition are proved, it may make such an order as it thinks fit for granting relief in respect of the matters complained of. This is extremely wide and gives the court power to make any order which it thinks proper having regard to the specific circumstances of the case.

However, without prejudice to this extremely wide power, s. 461 refers specifically to four particular orders the court may make:

1 It may regulate the company's affairs in the future.

CASE EXAMPLE 10.12

***Re H R Harmer Ltd* [1958] 3 All ER 689**

A father was the controlling shareholder in a family business. His two sons also had shares in the company. The father ran the business in a particularly autocratic manner. He ran the business of the company as if it were his own, ignoring any resolutions of the board and the wishes of his fellow directors. Eventually, the sons lost patience with him and sought the alternative remedy. The court made an order that the father should not interfere in the affairs of the company other than pursuant to a valid decision of the board of directors. The father was to be the president of the company for life but this office did not give him any rights or powers.

2 It may require the company to refrain from doing, or continuing to do, the act complained of by the petitioner or to do an act which the petitioner has complained that the company has omitted to do. For example, if a minority shareholder complains that the company has not paid him a dividend in circumstances where there are profits available for such a purpose, the court could order that a dividend should be paid.
3 It can authorise civil proceedings to be brought in the name and on behalf of the company by such persons and on such terms as the court may direct.
4 It will be appreciated that this power is an alternative for a member seeking a remedy under one of the *Foss* v *Harbottle* exceptions.
5 It can provide for the purchase of the shares by any member of the company, by all or some of the other members, or by the company itself and, in the case of a purchase by the company itself, the reduction of the company's capital accordingly. This occurred in *Scottish CWS Ltd* v *Meyer*:

CASE EXAMPLE 10.13

***Scottish CWS Ltd* v *Meyer* [1958] AC 324**

The Scottish CWS Ltd was the holding company of a private manufacturing subsidiary in which Meyer was a minority shareholder. Scottish CWS decided to close down this subsidiary and by their conduct caused it to cease trading. Shares in the subsidiary, which at one time had been worth £3.75 each, fell in value to below £1 each. The holding company was ordered to purchase the shares of the minority members at the value at which they had stood before the prejudicial conduct commenced.

It should be noted that an order that the majority shareholder should buy the shares of the unhappy petitioner is by far the most common remedy of the court, and for obvious reasons. In the majority of cases an s. 459 action stems from an exclusion from management of the petitioner. Thus his relationship with the other members will have broken down. For this reason there will be no question of his going back into the company. What he will want, therefore, is his money out.

2.3 Valuing the shares

A very real practical problem with a s. 459 action is how the court should value the shares that it orders to be bought by the other shareholders. Generally, when shares are being valued, for example, for probate purposes (in order to ascertain the value of an estate for the assessment of inheritance tax) a discount will be applied to take account of the lack of control enjoyed by a minority shareholder. In such a case a shareholding of 20 per cent might be valued at 5 per cent of the net worth of the company since the shareholder does not even have the power to prevent the passing of a special resolution. It is more likely, however, in a s. 459 case that the court will order a pro rata valuation.

CASE EXAMPLE 10.14

***Re Bird Precision Bellows* [1985] 3 All ER 523**

Minority shareholders had been excluded from the management of a private company. The trial judge valued the shares pro rata according to the value of the company's shares as a whole. He refused to apply a discount to reflect the fact that the petitioners' shares constituted a minority holding. The Court of Appeal upheld this approach.

It was made clear that the court had an unfettered discretion to put whatever value it wished on the petitioner's shareholding. It might, in an appropriate case, order a discount to be applied to reflect apathy on the part of the petitioner. However, in *Re Ghyll Beck Driving Range* [1993] BCLC 1126 it ordered a premium to be paid on the shares to reflect the petitioner's loss of business opportunity. It has to be said, however, that usually the court applies a straight pro rata valuation with no discount.

TEST YOUR KNOWLEDGE 10.2

(a) What does a petitioner have to establish in order to obtain an s. 459 remedy?
(b) What are the remedies that the court can award?
(c) Which of these is the most common?
(d) If an order is made for the majority to buy the shares of the minority, how are those shares valued?

2.4 Limitations on the s. 459 remedy

There are a number of limitations on the availability of a s. 459 remedy:

1 It is only available to a member complaining of conduct prejudicial to him in his capacity as a member. For example:

CASE EXAMPLE 10.15

***Elder* v *Elder & Watson Ltd* [1952] 152 SC 49**

The applicants claimed they had wrongfully been removed from office as directors and from employment as secretary and manager of the company. It was held that the alternative remedy was not available to them since no wrong had been done to them in their capacity as members.

2 The petitioner must not have been the cause of his own problems.

CASE EXAMPLE 10.16

***Re R A Noble (Clothing) Ltd* [1983] BCLC 273**

The petitioner provided the capital for a company but left the management in the hands of the other director on the understanding that the other director would speak with him about any important matters which arose in connection with the company's business. The other director did not do so, but the petitioner took no interest in the business of the company whatever. Subsequently, the relationship between the two deteriorated and the petitioner sought the alternative remedy. It was held that he must fail since his exclusion from managerial decisions in the company was essentially the result of his own lack of interest.

However, a member probably does not lose his right to petition merely because he had not himself acted completely honourably. For example, in Case Example 10.17.

CASE EXAMPLE 10.17

***Re London School of Electronics Ltd* [1986] Ch 211**

A company provided courses of study in electronics in conjunction with CTC Ltd, the majority shareholder. A minority shareholder complained that the two individuals who owned the shares in CTC Ltd had decided to transfer all London School of Electronics students to CTC Ltd. The petitioning minority shareholder then set up a rival school and took a number of students from London School of Electronics himself. He then claimed relief on the ground that CTC Ltd had acted oppressively towards him. It was held that he did not lose his right to relief merely because he had not himself acted with 'clean hands'.

2.5 The remedy today

From 1980, when the requirement for the petitioner to show unfair prejudice rather than oppression became the basis of this remedy, until 1987, when the Law Commission published a consultation paper 'Shareholder Remedies', s. 459 was a panacea for almost all wrongs and injustices suffered by shareholders. However, the Law Commission's paper might be said to have been something of a turning point in the history of unfair prejudice. It made two particular points:

1 Unfair prejudice proceedings are potentially very expensive. The litigation will almost certainly be in two stages:
   (a) an initial freeing injunction to stop the loss of funds and assets from the company at the hands of those remaining in control
   (b) then the subsequent substantive proceedings to enable the aggrieved shareholder to obtain the desired remedy.
2 In consequence of this, perhaps it would be better for a company's Articles to contain an 'escape route' so that an unhappy shareholder could request the others to buy his shares from him at an appropriate valuation.

This has been followed over recent years by a series of cases where the higher courts have been very willing to throw out unfair prejudice applications. This happened, for instance, in *O'Neill v. Phillips*.

CASE EXAMPLE 10.18

***O'Neill* v *Phillips* [1999] BCC 600**

This was the first case on this section to be considered by the House of Lords. The case concerned a small company in which one director held 75 per cent of the shares and the other 25 per cent. The 75 per cent shareholder was the founder of the company, but increasingly he was allowing the 25 per cent shareholder to run the business. Then the company went through a difficult period and the 75 per cent shareholder resumed control. He did not, however, remove the other director from office, he had, instead, allowed him to remain as a director and to continue to earn his salary. Therefore, there had been no unfair prejudice. The court accordingly dismissed the action. The minority shareholder was getting that to which his shareholding entitled him, namely the junior directorship and 25 per cent of any dividend declared. What was needed was that the two should sit down together and negotiate a price at which the major shareholder should buy out the minor.

A case giving rise to a similar result was *Re Legal Costs Negotiators Ltd*.

CASE EXAMPLE 10.19

***Re Legal Costs Negotiators Ltd* [1999] BCC 547**

Four people had formed a company in which all were directors and equal shareholders. One was effectively removed as a director and the others wanted to buy his shares from him. He, however, refused to sell out. The other three claimed this was unfairly prejudicial to them. It was held that there was no unfair prejudice. If a member who was not a director wanted to retain his shares that was entirely his own decision and could not be unfairly prejudicial to the other members. Moreover, since the others had 75 per cent of the shares in the company, they could, if they wished, pass a special resolution to place the company in liquidation. This would have the effect of bringing to an end any perceived prejudicial state of the affairs of the company

Again the Court of Appeal struck out proceedings in *Arrow Nominees Inc.* v *Blackedge*.

CASE EXAMPLE 10.20

***Arrow Nominees Inc.* v *Blackedge* [2001] BCC 591**

In this case the petitioner forged certain documents on which he sought to rely in his s. 459 petition. A litigant who had demonstrated that he was determined to pursue proceedings with the object of preventing a fair trial had forfeited the right to take part in a trial.

There has also been a similar willingness to throw cases out in the lower courts.

CASE EXAMPLE 10.21

***Re Alchemea Ltd* [1998] BCC 964**

This concerned a company limited by guarantee with no share capital. It was to be run as a cooperative for the running of a college for the teaching of audiovisual and visual engineering and production. There was no entitlement to dividends in the company. There was a written contract between the incorporators setting out the rules of the cooperative. The petitioner was removed in accordance with these rules. It was held that this was not unfair prejudice. The removal had in no way affected the petitioner as a member.

Similarly in Case Example 10.22.

CASE EXAMPLE 10.22

***Re Powerhouse Promotions Ltd* (2000 unreported)**

An unfair prejudice application was thrown out since the petitioner's shares were valueless.

Again the remedy cannot be allowed to provide an escape route whenever a person wishes to leave his company.

CASE EXAMPLE 10.23

***Phoenix Office Supplies Limited* v *Larvin* [2002] EWCA Civ 1740**

The company had three members each with an equal shareholding and each of whom was a director.

Its Articles were based upon Table A with the usual extension to Article 24 that the directors had an absolute discretion to decline to register any transfer of shares.

One of the members, following a change of domestic partner, decided to withdraw from the company and move to another town. He notified the other two of his intention to cease being an employee of the company and asked them to buy his shares from him at full value. It is not clear whether at this stage he indicated that he wished no longer to be a director of the company. However, he certainly had no intention of taking any further part in its management. The other two members were unwilling to buy the shares of the one who was departing and so he commenced s. 459 proceedings.

The Court of Appeal held that the unfair prejudice provisions are not intended to provide an escape route whenever a member wishes to leave a company. Lord Hoffmann in *O'Neill* v *Phillips* said that the provision had two roles:

- It protects shareholders against the breach of terms on which they have agreed the affairs of the company should be conducted through the Articles of Association or through some collateral agreement.
- It protects them against some inequity that makes it unfair for those conducting the company's affairs to rely upon their strict legal powers e.g. a resolution by majority shareholders to remove a minority shareholder from office as a director.

Auld LJ said that s. 459 was not intended to enable a member to negotiate a satisfactory sale of his shareholding simply because he has no further interest in the affairs of the company. It was for this reason that the appeal should be permitted. However, if the departing shareholder had enjoyed some equitable entitlement, for example under a shareholder agreement, to require the other members to acquire his shares at their full undiscounted value when he chose to leave the company then he would be able to look to s. 459 for protection.

Jonathan Parker J summed the matter up like this: '*the issue which lies at the heart of this appeal, as I see it, is whether s. 459 extends to affording a member of a quasi-partnership company who wishes, for entirely his own reasons, to sever his connection with the company – and who de facto has done so – an opportunity to "put" his shareholding onto the other members at its full, undiscounted, value when he has no contractual right to do so. I can for my part see no basis for concluding that s. 459 can have such a Draconian effect*'.

Thus it can be seen that there appears to have been something of a change of heart by the judiciary as to how willingly it will allow successful s. 459 proceedings, and it must be the case at the present time that lawyers are much more reticent in advising clients to bring such actions than they were a few years ago.

TEST YOUR KNOWLEDGE 10.3

State what has happened over recent years to discourage petitioners from using the s. 459 remedy?

As an alternative to bringing s. 459 proceedings a petitioner could apply instead for an order of the court to wind up the company on the ground that it is just and equitable to do so. This remedy is described more fully in Chapter 12.

DTI

Department of Trade and Industry – the department of the British government responsible for the supervision of commerce and industry in the UK.

3 The Role of the DTI

The governmental body that oversees business in the UK is the **Department of Trade and Industry** (DTI). This exercises regulatory control over business in this country. The main way in which it does this is by way of investigations. It is also responsible for prosecuting offences of insider dealing.

By s. 341 the Secretary of State can appoint inspectors to investigate the affairs of a company. By s. 432 he must make such an appointment if ordered to do so by the court. By s. 431 he may appoint following the application of either not less than one tenth of its issued share capital or of 200 members of the company. He may also of his own volition appoint if it appears to him that there are circumstances suggesting:

1 That the company's affairs are being, or have been, conducted with an intent to defraud its creditors or creditors of any other person or otherwise for some fraudulent purpose or in a manner which is unfairly prejudicial to some part of its members.
2 That any actual or proposed act or omission of the company is, or would be, so prejudicial, or that the company was formed for any fraudulent or unlawful purpose.
3 That the persons concerned with the company's formation or the management of its affairs have in connection therewith been guilty of fraud, misfeasance or other misconduct towards it or towards its members. Or,
4 That the company's members have not been given all the information with respect to its affairs which they might reasonably expect.

Once inspectors have been appointed, all officers and agents of the company are under an obligation to produce any documents of, or relating to, the company, to attend before the inspectors when required to do so and otherwise to give the inspectors all assistance in connection with the investigation which they are reasonably able to give. By s. 442 the DTI has a similar power to appoint inspectors to investigate the ownership of a company. A more informal inquiry can be made by way of an order under s. 437 that documents relating to the company should be produced. Failure to comply with such a request is a criminal offence.

TEST YOUR KNOWLEDGE 10.4 

What is the role of the DTI in the regulation of companies and in what circumstances can inspectors be appointed?

It is thought that the use of DTI investigations might well decline over the coming years. Under s. 434 inspectors can examine any person on oath for the purposes of an investigation. However, it has been held in *Saunders* v *UK* [1998] 1 BCLC 362 that evidence acquired under such compulsion cannot be used in a subsequent prosecution since to do so is contrary to the European Convention for the Protection of Human Rights and Fundamental Freedoms. Accordingly inspectors have now to balance the need to obtain evidence and the desire to use that evidence in a subsequent prosecution.

CHAPTER SUMMARY

- Shareholders who are dissatisfied with the way their company is being run may obtain a remedy from the court or bring proceedings under CA 1985, s. 459.
- The difficulty faced by shareholders is that, by the rule in *Foss* v *Harbottle,* the proper plaintiff in any action alleging wrongdoing on the part of the company's management is the company itself.
- This rule, however, is procedural and there are a number of exceptions to it. These can be invoked, *inter alia,* where the use of the rule would result in injustice. If a shareholder is permitted to bring an action, it may be either a derivative or a representative action.
- Instead of bringing an action under one of the exceptions to *Foss* v *Harbottle,* a shareholder may apply to the court for an order under s. 459 on the grounds that the company has been, or will be, run in a way which is prejudicial to his interests and that he was not the cause of his own problems.
- If the court decides that the allegation is true it may make whatever order it thinks fit for granting relief in respect of the matters complained of.
- Having said this, the courts have recently been somewhat less willing than they were a few years ago to allow s. 459 proceedings to go ahead.
- The DTI has regulatory powers over companies registered in the UK.

part **four**

Companies in Difficulty

LIST OF CHAPTERS

Overview

At the end of its life, a company is usually wound up. However, when a company gets into difficulties there are other routes that can be taken short of a full winding up procedure that will achieve the rescue of some companies. This Part looks at looks in details at these procedures, reconstructions, arrangements and administrations before moving on to the process of winding up.

Winding up results in the ending of the life of a company. The other procedures fall short of this, and are of increasing significance as more and more concentration is placed by government on the rescue rather than the destruction of companies. They can be summarised as follows:

1 Arrangements involve some sort of compromise between a company and its creditors. They usually allow the company to remain in existence and perhaps seek to pay some or even all of its debts over a period of time.

2 Administrations are primarily designed to ensure the survival of the company in whole or in part or, failing this, a better realisation of the assets that would be expected on a formal winding up.

3. Reconstructions are most frequently used when two companies are merging. The companies themselves are put into liquidation. A new company is formed to take over the two businesses. The undertakings are then transferred to the new company.
4. In takeovers both the bidder company and minority shareholders in the target company are given rights under the Companies Act and it is these rights at which we shall be looking.

The final chapter looks at the different types of winding up in English law.

CHAPTER 11

Arrangements, administrations, reconstructions and takeovers

CONTENTS

LEARNING OUTCOMES

This chapter covers arrangements, administrations, takeovers and reconstructions. After reading and understanding the contents of the chapter and studying the case examples you should be able to:

- Understand how a scheme of arrangement can be entered into under CA s. 425.
- Understand how a company in financial difficulties can enter into a corporate voluntary arrangement.
- Appreciate the procedure for and purpose of administrations.
- Comprehend the procedure for a reconstruction.
- Understand the Companies Act provisions on takeovers.

d

scheme of arrangement
A compromise arrived at between a company and its creditors or between a company and its members pursuant to s.425 of the Companies Act 1985.

Introduction

This chapter examines a variety of means whereby a company in difficulties can reach some sort of arrangement with its creditors or otherwise enter into a reconstruction. The first of these is a **scheme of arrangement** under CA 1985 s. 425. This is a rather cumbersome procedure and its repeal was recommended by the Cork Committee on whose recommendations the Insolvency Act 1986 was largely based.

In spite of this, a repeal was never effected and the procedure remains on the Statute Book. It is, however, supplemented by voluntary arrangements under Part 1 of the Insolvency Act 1986 which are far easier to bring about.

As well as these procedures, the chapter also looks at:

- the more formal administration order;
- the process of reconstructions when a company is winding up under IA 1986 s. 110;
- the rules of CA 1985, s. 428 which assist takeovers.

1 Schemes of arrangement

When a company is in difficulties, the directors might suggest some sort of arrangement with its creditors as an alternative to bringing the company to an end by means of a formal winding up. The types of arrangement which can be entered into are practically limitless. Examples include a scheme where the debts of the company are exchanged by the creditors for shares in the company ('**a debt–equity swap**') or one where a person other than the company, for example a director, makes a payment out of his own pocket to the creditors if they will forego their claims against the company.

debt-equity swap

A corporate arrangement under which the creditors of a company exchange the debts that they are owed for shares in the company.

There are three ways in which such a scheme can be brought about:

1 *Unanimous creditor agreement* If all of the creditors agree to the arrangement, there is no need for any more formal procedure. For example, a director of a company that is in difficulties might call together the company's creditors and say to them that if the company were to be wound up they, the creditors, would receive nothing because of the likely level of the liquidator's fees. Therefore he proposes selling some of his private assets and will personally pay the company's creditors 30p in the £ of what they are owed by the company. If they are prepared to accept this in full and final settlement of what the company owes to them, and every creditor agrees to this, then it becomes binding upon all of them. It is only where unanimity cannot be obtained betwee the creditors that a more formal statutory arrangement needs to be sought.
2 A more formal voluntary arranagement brought about following the procedures laid down by *Companies Act* ss. 425–426 (see section 2 below).
3 *Corporate voluntary arrangement* under Part 1 of IA (see section 3 below).

For (2) and (3), an arrangement binding upon all creditors can be achieved by a vote of the appropriate majority of them.

2 Companies Act ss. 425–426

The key stages in a s. 425 arrangement are:

1 arrangement drawn up;
2 application to court;
3 meetings of classes concerned (agree by simple majority in number representing three-quarters in value);
4 sanction of court;
5 registration.

2.1 Meetings of creditors

For an arrangement under s. 425 to be brought it must be approved at a meeting or meetings or creditors and/or members. The company, or any of its creditors or members, can apply to the courts to order a meeting of creditors or members, depending on the type of scheme being proposed. It is for the court to order what meetings should be held. The wording of the Act appears rather unclear; it states that the meeting(s) might be of 'the creditors or class of creditors, or of the members of the company or class of members'.

What this effectively means can be illustrated by two examples:

(a) If a director were to propose that he, personally, should pay 50p in the £1 on all the company's debts and that this sum should be accepted by the creditors in full and final settlement of those debts, then there would be a single meeting of the creditors.
(b) If a debt–equity swap were proposed, there would then be two meetings, one of the creditors and one of the members, since the members would obviously be affected by the increase in their number following completion of the swap.

By s. 425(2) if a simple majority in number, representing three-quarters in value of the creditors or class of creditors or members or class of members, present and voting either in person or by proxy at the meeting, agree to any arrangement, it is binding on all the creditors or class of creditors or members or class of members and on the company so long as it is sanctioned by the court. Thus, the majority at each meeting needs to be a composite one: there has to be the agreement of a simple majority in number in those voting, and there has to be a three-quarters majority in value. Both majorities need to be achieved for the arrangement to come into place.

Information to be circulated with notice of meeting

By s. 426(2), when a company sends out a notice of a meeting under s. 425 it must send with it a statement which explains the effect of the arrangement, stating in particular any material interests of the directors of the company and the effect which the scheme will have upon them.

2.2 **Sanction of the court**

Once agreed at the meeting or meetings, the scheme must be sanctioned by the court. The court will obviously be concerned that the meetings have been properly convened and held. In the words of Maugham J in *Re Dorman Long & Co Ltd* [1934] Ch 635, it must also be satisfied that '*the proposal is such that an intelligent and honest man, a member of the class concerned and acting in respect of his interests might normally approve*'.

2.3 **Registration**

Once the sanction has been given, the court order has no effect until a copy has been delivered to the Registrar of Companies for registration. A copy of every order must also be attached to every copy of the company's Memorandum which is issued after the date of the order being made.

2.4 **Other uses to which this procedure can be put**

Varying class rights

A scheme of arrangement can be used to vary rights attaching to a class of shares in circumstances where those rights have been entrenched in the company's Memorandum of Association. It is seldom used for this purpose today because of the rather easier procedure under CA 1985 s. 125 (described in Chapter 5).

Transfer of undertakings and mergers

It is also possible that the scheme could be used for the purpose of transferring the whole or part of the company's undertaking or property to another company as part of a scheme of reconstruction of that company or as part of a reconstruction or amalgamation of any two or more companies. When the scheme is designed to achieve this purpose, the court's order may make provision for:

1 the transfer to the transferee company of the whole or any part of the undertaking and of the property or liabilities of any transferor company;
2 the allotting or appropriation by the transferee company of any shares, debentures, policies or similar interests in that company which under the compromise or arrangement are to be allotted or appropriated by that company to or for any person;
3 the continuation by or against the transferee company, of any legal proceedings pending by or against any transferor company;
4 the dissolution, without winding up, of any transferor company;
5 the provision to be made for any persons who, within such time and in such manner as the court directs, dissent from the compromise or arrangement; and
6 any incidental matters as are necessary to secure that the reconstruction or amalgamation is fully and effectively carried out.

If s. 425 is used to bring about a merger involving a public company, then the additional requirements of s. 427A and Schedule 15B must be observed. In essence these requirements are:

1 The boards concerned must at least a month before the holding of the meetings draw up a draft of the proposed scheme and deliver a copy to the Registrar of Companies who must then advertise its receipt in the *Gazette*.
2 There should be a written report on the scheme sent to the members of each company. The reports should be prepared by an independent expert appointed by each respective company. Alternatively, with the approval of the court, a single independent expert may be appointed by the merging companies to produce a joint report.
   The recent merger of Halifax plc and Bank of Scotland plc was achieved by the use of this procedure.

TEST YOUR KNOWLEDGE 11.1 

A company has got into financial difficulties and 90 per cent in value of the creditors are prepared to agree to a debt–equity swap. Outline the procedure to achieve this under s. 425, noting particularly the meeting(s) that need to be held and the majorities required for the arrangement to become binding upon all.

3 Company voluntary arrangements (CVA)

As was noted above, the Cork Committee felt it desirable that a simpler and less formal procedure than CA 1985 s. 425 should be introduced for a company to try reach an arrangement to get over its debt problems. The result is the system of company voluntary arrangements or CVA.

Because of the comparative informality of a CVA scheme it was felt that safeguards were necessary to protect the interests of creditors and members. The main safeguard is that the person to whom the proposal is made and who ultimately will implement the scheme must generally be an insolvency practitioner. This last requirement was relaxed by the Insolvency Act 2000, but has not yet come into force.

Figure 11.1 illustrates the key stages of the procedure for a CVA. These are outlined in more detail below.

FIGURE 11.1 **Procedure for a CVA**

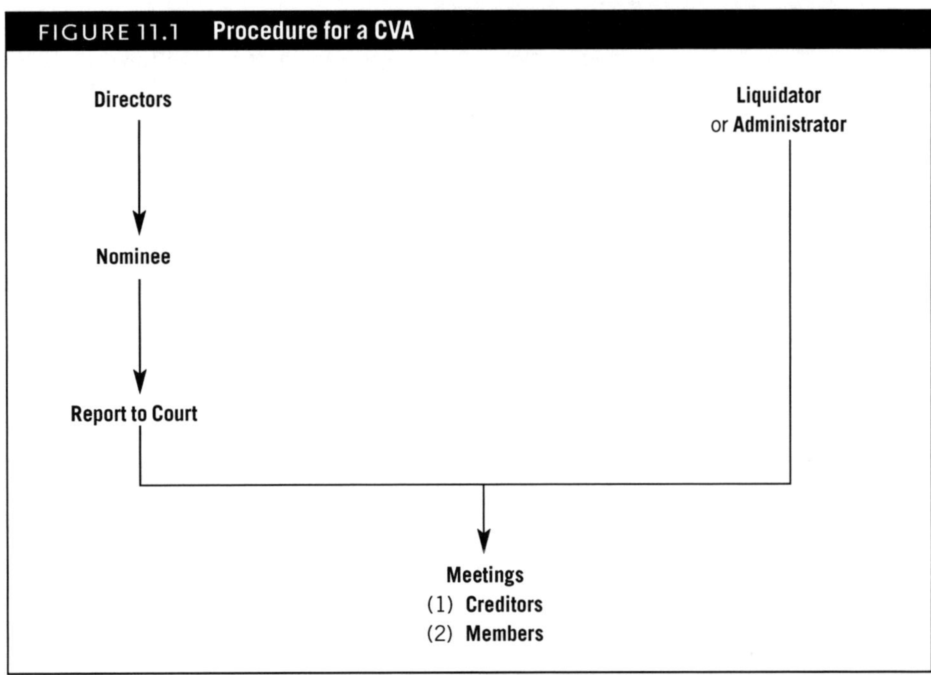

3.1 The proposal

By IA s. 1, the proposal for the scheme may come from either:

1 the directors of the company, so long as it is not in **liquidation** or **administration**, or
2 its liquidator or administrator if one is in post

liquidation
The winding up of a company; the process whereby the existence of a company is brought to an end.

composition
A sum of money agreed to be accepted by creditors in satisfaction of debts owed to them by a company.

For (1), the proposal is made to an insolvency practitioner, known at this stage as the nominee, who it is intended shall be responsible for the implementation of the scheme. It is open to the directors of any company to make a proposal to the company and its creditors for a **composition** in satisfaction of its debts, or a scheme of arrangement of its affairs. Such an approach to a nominee will normally be made by the directors of a company which is in financial difficulties, probably on the suggestion of the company's auditor or solicitor. The proposal to the nominee must state the outline of the arrangement in broad terms and why the directors feel the creditors are likely to agree to it.

Alternatively, the scheme proposed may be instigated by the liquidator or administrator of the company if one is in post (2, above). In this case, he will be the nominee and may summon meetings of the company and of its creditors to consider proposals for such a time, date and place which he thinks fit.

3.2 The report to court

By IA s. 2 if the nominee is not the administrator or liquidator, he must, within 28 days of receiving the proposal (or such longer time as the court may allow), submit a report on the proposed arrangement to the court stating:

1 whether in his opinion, meetings of the company and its creditors should be summoned to consider the proposal; and
2 if so, the proposed date, time and place for the meetings to be held.

If a nominee fails to submit a report, the court may, on an application from the directors who made the proposal, direct that the nominee should be replaced as such by another person who again must be qualified to act as an insolvency practitioner in relation to the company.

The purpose of reporting to the court is essentially a matter of record and, although the court has the right to veto the holding of the meetings, it will seldom do so. In the absence of any contrary order by the court, the nominee must call the meetings in accordance with his report. It is essential that the nominee calls to the creditors' meeting every creditor of whose name and address he is aware. This is because the scheme, once implemented, is binding upon all creditors who have the right to attend and vote at the meeting.

3.3 The meetings

Whether the proposal comes from the directors or from the liquidator or administrator, the purpose of the meetings is to decide whether to approve the proposal. Such approval may be with or without modifications though no modification may be so radical as to result in the arrangement going beyond the definition of a voluntary arrangement in s. 1 of the Act (i.e. a composition in satisfaction of its debts or a scheme of arrangement of its affairs). The rights of any secured or preferential creditors cannot be altered by the arrangement unless they expressly agree to such alteration.

The creditors' meeting is the first to be held and it must approve the arrangement by a three-quarters majority in value of all creditors attending and voting or voting in proxy. On the same day a members' meeting is held and here approval is given by a simple majority. Once this second approval is obtained the arrangement is in force and the date of its commencement is backdated is to the passing of the creditors' resolution. The chairmen of the meetings must report the result to the court and also to all persons affected by the scheme.

3.4 The effect of approval

By IA s. 5 once approved, the arrangement binds every person who in accordance with the rules had notice of, and was entitled to vote at, the meetings as though he were a party to the voluntary arrangement. This is so whether or not he was present or represented at the meeting.

3.5 Implementation of the proposal

Once the voluntary arrangement has been approved, the nominee becomes known as the supervisor of the voluntary arrangement. It is then for him to implement the arrangement. He has a general power to apply to the court for directions in relation to any particular matter arising under the arrangement and is included among the persons who may apply to the court for the winding up of the company or for an administration order to be made in relation to it.

If any of the company's creditors or any other person is dissatisfied by any act, omission or decision of the supervisor, he may apply to the court and, when this happens, the court may:

1 confirm, reverse or modify any act or decision of the supervisor;
2 give him directions; or
3 make such other order as it thinks fit.

3.6 Moratorium under Insolvency Act 2000

Until recently, the general rights of self-help available to creditors have, in practice, prevented the implementation of corporate voluntary arrangements. For example, a creditor who has obtained judgement against a company can levy execution on that judgement by seizing and selling assets of the company. Similarly, a landlord can levy **distress** for unpaid rent by seizing assets held by the company. Such seizure of assets could obviously seriously affect the implementation of an arrangement.

distress

The process whereby a landlord goes onto the premises of his tenant to seize goods that he can sell to reimburse himself for outstanding rent.

Under IA 2000, it is now possible for the nominee in a company voluntary arrangement to bring about a moratorium during which the possibility of an arrangement can be further explored. If he wishes to do this he must be satisfied of the following:

- that the proposed arrangement has reasonable chance of being approved and implemented; and
- that the company has sufficient funds available to enable it to carry on its business during the proposed moratorium.

The effect of the moratorium is that no creditor action can be proceeded with while the moratorium is in place. As such a moratorium is potentially detrimental to creditors, a company may not go down this route more than once in any 12-month period. The moratorium will initially be for a period of 28 days. The meetings of creditors and members must be called for during this 28-day period. The meetings may resolve that they be adjourned and the moratorium extended though not for more than two months after the date on which the last of the meetings is held. During the moratorium the company continues to be run by the directors but with the nominee overseeing what they are doing.

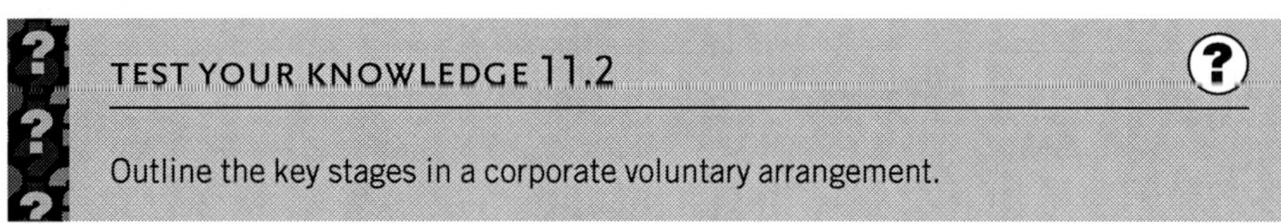
TEST YOUR KNOWLEDGE 11.2

Outline the key stages in a corporate voluntary arrangement.

4 Administration orders

administration order
An order directing that, during the period for which the order is in force, the affairs, business and property of the company shall be managed by an administrator appointed by the court.

administrator
A person who administers the estate of a deceased person in the absence of an executor. Alternatively, it can mean a person appointed by the court to try to achieve some sort of rescue strategy for a company that is in difficulties.

These are another rescue strategy for companies which are insolvent. They are less formal than the traditional schemes under CA 1985 s. 425 but are slightly more formal than the voluntary arrangements outlined in section 3. An **administration order** is defined by IA s. 8 as:

> 'an order directing that, during the period for which the order is in force, the affairs, business and property of the company shall be managed by a person to be known as the **administrator** appointed for the purpose by the court.'

4.1 Grounds for an order

By IA s. 8, before an administration order can be made the court must be satisfied of two matters:

1 That the company is or is likely to become unable to pay its debts. This has the same meaning as in s. 123 for the purposes of commencing a compulsory liquidation namely that either:
   (a) the company has failed to pay or offer security in respect of a debt of at least £750 within three weeks of receiving a statutory demand;
   (b) execution on a judgment against the company is unsatisfied in whole or in part; or
   (c) it is proved to the satisfaction of the court that the company is unable to pay its debts as they fall due.

2 That the making of the order will be likely to achieve one or more of the following purposes:
   (a) the survival of the company in whole or in part as a going concern;
   (b) the approval of a voluntary arrangement;
   (c) the sanctioning of an s. 245 scheme of arrangement;
   (d) a more advantageous realisation of the company's assets than would be effected on a formal winding up.

Both the petition and the order must specify the precise purpose of the winding up. An order is not available to banking or insurance companies nor in cases where the company has already gone into liquidation.

4.2 The application

By IA s. 9 the application for an administration order is by petition to the court. The petition must be supported by an affidavit and a statement showing the financial position of the company. It may be made by the company itself, the directors or any creditor or creditors. It is interesting to note that an individual member does not have the right to present a petition. This is in sharp contradiction to the right of an individual member to petition for a winding up of the company under the just and equitable ground under s. 122 or to petition on the ground of unfair prejudice under CA 1985 s. 459.

There is no requirement that the petition should be advertised or Gazetted but notice must be given to any debenture holder who is entitled to appoint an administrative receiver. It will be recalled that an administrative receiver is one appointed under a floating charge who takes control over the whole or substantially the whole of the undertaking of the company. In practice, this usually means the bank from which the company is doing its borrowing. Upon receiving such notice, the bank will often make the appointment of an administrative receiver.

4.3 The effect of the petition

Once a petition has been presented there is a moratorium giving immediate protection to the company's assets. No order can be made, or resolution passed, for the winding up of the company. Moreover, the consent of the court must be obtained before any creditors' rights can be enforced over any security of the company (other than the appointment of an administrative receiver). Thus the consent of the court is required for any creditor to be allowed to repossess goods in the possession of the company, for example under any hire-purchase, chattel leasing, retention of title or conditional sale agreement, and also before any other legal proceedings against the goods of the company may be taken such as execution or other legal process, including the levying of distress by a landlord. In the event of the court giving permission for the enforcement of a creditor right, it can do so on such terms as it thinks fit.

Although there is this general moratorium brought about by the presentation of the petition there are two creditor rights which can be exercised:

1 The appointment of an administrative receiver, as described above.
2 The presentation of a winding-up petition.

administrative receiver
A receiver and manager appointed by the holders of a floating charge, which appointment results in his taking control of the whole or substantially the whole of the undertaking of the company.

The effect of the appointment of an administrative receiver

By IA s. 9 if, by the time the petition comes to court, an **administrative receiver** has already been appointed, the court must dismiss the petition unless either the debenture holder who made the appointment agrees to the making of the administration order, or the court is satisfied that any security by virtue of which the receiver was appointed would be liable to be released, discharged or avoided under the provisions relating to transactions at an undervalue, preferences and the avoidance of certain floating charges.

4.4 The effect of an administration order

By s. 11, the effect of the making of an administration order is that:

1 any petition for the winding up of the company must be dismissed;
2 any administrative receiver has to vacate office (though, of course, as has been said above an administrator will only be appointed following the appointment of an administrative receiver if the receiver withdraws or is withdrawn from office);
3 any receiver on part of the company's property must vacate office on being required so to do by the administrator.

For so long as the order is in force:

1 No resolution can be passed or order made for the winding up of the company.
2 No administrative receiver may be appointed.
3 No other steps may be taken to enforce any security over the company's property or to repossess goods in the company's possession under any hire-purchase agreement other than with the consent of the administrator or by leave of the court. And,
4 No other proceedings and no other execution or other legal process may be commenced or continued and no distress may be levied against the company or its property except with the consent of the administrator or by leave of the court.
5 The fact that there is an administration and the name of the administrator must appear on all company documents. This is an exact parallel to the position which occurs when a company is in liquidation or in administrative receivership. Once again the name of the office holder must appear on all company documents.

4.5 The powers of the administrator

The administrator has similar powers to those of a receiver and manager appointed under a floating charge. Thus, he can carry on the business of the company, deal with and dispose of assets of the company and borrow in the name of the company. He has the general power to do all things necessary for the management of the affairs, business and property of the company. This general power, conferred upon the administrator by s. 14, is supplemented by 23 specific powers which are listed in the first schedule to the Act. These are the same powers as are enjoyed by an administrative receiver. They include:

1 the power to borrow money and grant security over the property of the company;
2 the power to participate in any legal proceedings for and on behalf of the company;
3 the power to employ agents;
4 the power to carry on the business of the company;
5 the power to establish subsidiaries of the company and transfer the whole or any part of the business to such subsidiaries;
6 the power to make any arrangement or compromise on behalf of the company;
7 the power to present or defend a petition for the winding up of the company.

Over and above this s. 14 gives him the following two specific powers:

1 to remove any director of the company and to appoint any person to be a director of it, whether to fill a vacancy or otherwise; and
2 to call any meeting of the members or creditors of the company.

He may apply to the court for directions in relation to any particular matter arising in connection with the carrying out of his functions. The administrator is deemed to be the agent of the company and any person dealing with him in good faith and for value is under no obligation to check whether the administrator is acting within his powers.

Power of the administrator to deal with charged property

charge
In corporate law the word 'charge' is usually used to mean a mortgage, i.e. a secured loan.

The administrator may dispose of property belonging to the company notwithstanding that it is subject to security rights. In the event of the security being a floating **charge**, the administrator can deal with the property on his own initiative and without consulting the debenture holder. Disposal of any other charged property or of any property or goods in the possession of the company under a hire-purchase, rental or similar agreement can only be made by order of the court. Where property subject to a floating charge is disposed of, the holder of the security has the same priority in respect of any property of the company which directly or indirectly represents the property so disposed of as he would have had in respect of the property subject to the security.

When there is a disposal of any other security by order of the court, the order must contain provision that the net proceeds of sale, and, where those net proceeds are less than the amount which the court reckons would be realised on a sale of the property or goods in the open market, such sums as may be required to make good the deficiency must be applied towards discharging the sum secured by the security or payable under the finance agreement.

4.6 The duties of the administrator

The duties of the administrator are set out in very much more general terms. He must take into his control all the property of the company and he must manage the company's business in accordance with the court's directions and in due course, in accordance with his proposals for the implementation of the order.

Statement of affairs

The administrator must require the preparation and submission to him of a statement of affairs. This must be verified by affidavit and give details of the company's assets, debts and liabilities together with particulars of all securities held over the company's property. The statement can be required to be prepared by all persons who are or have been officers of the company, or who have taken part in the formation of the company within the year prior to the making of the administration order, or those persons who have been employed by the company within that year and are in the administrator's opinion capable of giving the information required or all persons who have been officers of the company within that year. The statement of affairs must be submitted to the administrator within 21 days of his requesting it.

The administrator's proposals

Within three months of the making of the administration order, the administrator must send to the Registrar of Companies and to all creditors a statement of his proposals for achieving the purposes stated in the order. A copy must also be sent to all members of the company. A meeting of the creditors must be summoned and, unless this meeting approves the proposals, they cannot be implemented.

Controls over the administrator

If the creditors wish to have some form of ongoing control over the administrator, they may set up a committee known as the creditors' committee, which may compel the administrator to appear before it and to disclose such information as the committee may reasonably require.

There are further controls over the administration which may be exercised by the court. In particular, a disgruntled creditor or member may petition the court at any time on the grounds that the company's affairs are being managed by the administrator in a manner unfairly prejudicial to the interests of creditors or members or that any actual or proposed act or omission of the administrator is or would be so prejudicial. The court may, on such application make such order as it thinks fit to deal with the complaint.

The administrator may at any time be removed from office by the court. He must also vacate office if he ceases to be qualified as an insolvency practitioner or if the administration order is discharged.

Variation of the order

The administrator may at any time apply to the court for the order to be discharged or to be varied so as to specify an additional purpose. He must make such application if it appears to him that the purpose for which he was appointed either has been achieved or is incapable of achievement. He may also make the application if he is required to do so by a meeting of the company's creditors.

Release from duties

A person who has ceased to be the administrator of a company may apply to the court for his release. Such release, if given, discharges the administrator from all liability both in respect of acts or omissions of his in the administration and otherwise in relation to his conduct as administrator.

An excellent example of the purpose and operation of an administration order is illustrated by Case Example 11.1.

CASE EXAMPLE 11.1

Re Consumer & Industrial Press **(1988) 4 BCC 68**

The company was a small printing and publishing house. It had only one asset of any significant worth, a magazine title. It will be appreciated that the moment a magazine ceases to publish, any goodwill attaching to its title dissipates. An application was made for the appointment of an administrator so that he could exercise his power to borrow in order to continue publishing the magazine so that it could be sold as a going concern. It was held that the order should be granted.

THEORY INTO PRACTICE 11.1

Why is it that administrations are very rarely encountered?

Answer

Because the company's bank will invariably hold a floating charge over the undertaking of the company. This will allow the bank, upon being given notice of the application for an administration, to appoint an administrative receiver. This has the effect of causing the administration application to fail. Thus, by the pre-emptive appointment of an administrative receiver the bank will almost always prevent the appointment of an administrator.

TEST YOUR KNOWLEDGE 11.3

(a) What has to be proved in order to obtain an administration order?

(b) Who can make the application?

(c) Which class of creditor can effectively block an administration application?

(d) What is the effect of an administration order?

(e) State eight specific powers that are enjoyed by an administrator.

5 Powers of the court when a company is in liquidation or administration

If the company is being wound up or is subject to an administration order (see below), the court may do one or both of the following:

1 It may stay all proceedings in the winding up or discharge the administration order.
2 It may also give such directions with respect to the conduct of the winding up or the administration as it thinks fit for facilitating the implementation of an approved voluntary arrangement.

An order cannot be made to stay winding-up proceedings or discharge an administration order under (1) above until 28 days from the chairman reporting the result of the meeting to the court. Nor can it be made where an application is made to the court challenging the scheme.

By s. 6 there are a number of persons who may raise such an objection. These are any person entitled to vote either at the members' or creditors' meeting, the nominee himself and any administrator or liquidator in post at the company. The challenge should be on one or both of the following grounds:

1 that the arrangement unfairly prejudices the interests of any creditor, member or contributory of the company; or
2 that there has been some material irregularity in, at or in relation to either of the meetings.

Any such objection must be raised within the 28-day period following the chairman's reporting to the court. If the court is satisfied that there is substance in the objection it may do one or both of the following:

1 It may revoke or suspend the approval given by the meetings. Or,
2 It may give a direction to any person for the summoning of further meetings to consider any revised proposal the person who made the original proposal may make or, in the event of the objection arising because of some material irregularity in or in relation to either of the meetings, the court may direct that a further company or creditors' meeting should be held to reconsider the original proposal.

6 Enterprise Act 2002

The Enterprise Act 2002, which the DTI has said will come into force in June 2003, makes radical changes to the administration procedure. When this part of the Act comes into force, the law regarding administrations will be as follows:

There will be three ways in which an administrator may be appointed:

1 by order of the Court.
2 by the holder of a floating charge.
3 by the company or its directors.

The purpose of an administration will be that the administrator must seek to rescue the company as a going concern and, if this is not reasonably practicable, or it is not in the interest that the creditors of the company as a whole for the company to be rehabilitated as a going concern, then he must seek to achieve a better result for the creditors as a whole than would occur if the company were to be wound up in the conventional way. If neither of these targets is reasonably practicable then he must seek to realise property so as to make a distribution to one or more secured or preferential creditors. He must perform his functions in the interests of the company as a whole and must act as quickly and as efficiently as reasonably possible.

Appointment by a floating charge holder

When a floating charge holder wants to make an appointment of an administrator he must give at least two clear days' written notice for the holder of any floating charge ranking in priority to him. Subject to this, the floating charge holder may appoint an administrator pursuant to the security held by him. Although the old administrative receiver provisions continue to apply to securities which are already in force when this part of the Enterprise Act comes into force, as far as new securities are concerned the administration will be the method of enforcement. For such an appointment by the holder of the floating charge, the charge must result in the administrator taking control of the whole or substantial of the whole of the undertaking of the company. If the charge is not such as to result in this happening, the charge holder would have to apply to the court for the appointment just as would any other creditor. Once again the purpose of the appointment must be to achieve the survival in the whole or in part of the company or a better realisation of the assets than would be achieved on a formal winding up: the administrator so appointed must act in the interests of the company.

Appointment by a company or its director

A company or its directors may also make an extra judicial appointment of an administrator. This is not permissible if during the previous 12 months there has been another administration order or where there has been presented winding up petition or an existing administration application is outstanding or an administrative receiver is in office. When an administrator is being appointed in this way, five days' written notice must be given to any person entitled to appoint an administrator or administrative receiver to the company. If that person then makes an appointment of an administrator himself then the Director's appointment fails. In other words the holder of security can always trump the wishes of the Directors so far as an extra judicial appointment is concerned.

Period of administration

It is intended that an administration will come to an end one year from the date of its commencement. The Court may extend this for a specified period on the application of the administrator. Alternatively, the period may be extended by up to 6 months with the consent of all the secured creditors and more than 50 per cent of the company's unsecured creditors disregarding the debts of any creditor who cannot be bothered to respond to an invitation to give or withhold consent.

Where the administrator takes the view that the total amount of which each secured creditor is likely to receive has been paid to him or set aside for him and that a distribution would be made to the unsecured creditors of the company, he must file with the Registrar of Companies a notice that has the effect of terminating his appointment as administrator and putting the company into creditors' voluntary liquidation. In these circumstances the liquidator can be nominated by the creditors. Failing such a nomination, the administrator is the liquidator.

If an administrator takes a view that the company has no property to distribute, he must file a notice with the Registrar of Companies sending copies to the Court and to all creditors of whose claims and address's he is aware. The company is then deemed to be resolved after three months.

TEST YOUR KNOWLEDGE 11.4

Under the Enterprise Act 2002, what are the three ways in which an administrator may be appointed?

7 Reconstructions

reconstruction

A procedure entered into under s.110 of the Insolvency Act 1986.

voluntary winding up

The winding up of a company commenced by a resolution of its members.

members' voluntary winding up

The solvent winding up of a company pursuant to a resolution passed by its members.

creditors' voluntary winding up

The insolvent winding up of a company following a resolution of its members.

The term '**reconstruction**' is applied to the situation where a liquidator disposes of the assets of a company in return for shares in another company. The result is that the members of the company winding up then become members of the transferee company rather than receiving a return for their capital in the company winding up by way of a cash payment.

Section 110 of IA 1986 provides that where a company is in a **voluntary winding up**, the liquidator may be authorised to receive, in payment for the assets of the company, shares in the transferee company. If the company is in a **members' voluntary winding up**, the authority to the liquidator is given by special resolution of the members. If the company is in a **creditors' voluntary winding up**, the authority is that of either the court or the winding up committee.

By s. 111 if any member of the transferor company who did not vote in favour of the special resolution expresses his dissent from it in writing to the liquidator within seven days of the passing of the resolution he may require the liquidator either to abstain from carrying the resolution into effect or to purchase his interest at a price to be determined by agreement. Usually the liquidator will decide to purchase the shares of the dissenting shareholder and, in this case, the purchase money must be paid before the company is dissolved. It must be raised by the liquidator in such a way as is determined by special resolution. This procedure may look a little absurd.

1 A company is put into liquidation.
2 The liquidator is authorised to sell the undertaking to another company in return for shares.
3 He does so and shares in the transferee company then go to the members of the company in liquidation.
4 The transferee company then carries on the business and the liquidation of the transferor company is completed.

The typical situation where this might happen is where two companies are merging.

1 A new company is formed specifically to carry on the merged business.
2 The merging companies are both put into liquidation
3 The liquidators of each are authorised to sell the undertaking of the respective companies to the new company in return for shares therein.
4 Those shares then go to the shareholders in the merging companies. Any shareholders who do not agree with the merger will be paid out the value of their shares.

TEST YOUR KNOWLEDGE 11.5

Assume you have two companies that are merging. A new company will be formed to take over the undertakings of the merging companies. Draw up a checklist detailing the steps that will be gone through.

8 Takeovers

takeover

The process whereby one company acquires another company.

Section 429 of CA 1985 contains a procedure designed to facilitate takeover bids. A **takeover** offer is defined by s. 248 as an offer to acquire all the shares or all the shares of any class or classes in a company (other than shares which at the date of the offer are already held by the offeror), being an offer on terms which are the same in relation to all the shares to which the offer relates or where those shares include shares of different classes in relation to all the shares of each class.

Section 429 provides that if the offeror has received acceptances of the offer from not less than nine-tenths of the shares to which the offer relates he must give the holder of any shares not so acquired notice that he wishes to acquire them. In order to exercise this right the offeror must have acquired the nine-tenths prior to the end of four months from the date of the initial offer and the notice given to the minority shareholders must be given within two months after the offeror has acquired his nine-tenths shareholding. The offeror must send a copy of this notice to the company together with a statutory declaration by him stating that the conditions of the giving of the notice have been satisfied. If the offeror is itself a company, this declaration must be signed by a director.

The effect of the giving of such a notice is, in the terms of s. 430, that the offeror is both entitled and bound to acquire those shares on the terms of the offer. At the end of six weeks from the date of the notice the offeror must send a copy of the notice to the company and pay or transfer to the company the consideration for the shares to which the notice relates. He must accompany this notice by a transfer executed on behalf of the shareholder concerned by a person appointed by the offeror. The company may use this transfer to effect the registration of the offeror as the holder of the shares. Until such time as the consideration received by the company is handed over to the shareholder concerned it must be held on trust by the company.

Clearly, the purpose of the statutory provision is to facilitate takeovers in that the power compulsorily to acquire the shares of a small minority of shareholders in a target company means that they cannot by their intransigence prevent a takeover.

Section 430 also contains a protection for minority shareholders. If a takeover offer results in the offeror becoming the owner of not less than nine-tenths in value of all the shares in the company, the holder of any shares to which the offer relates who has not accepted the offer may by written communication addressed to the offeror require him to acquire those shares. The effect of this request is that the offeror is both entitled and required to acquire the shares on the terms of the offer or on such other terms as may be agreed.

CHAPTER SUMMARY

- A company in financial difficulties may attempt to deal with its problems in a number of ways.
- If a company is able to enter into a voluntary arrangement with its shareholders, then no other, more formal arrangement is necessary. Such an arrangement must be approved unanimously by all creditors.
- By CA 1985 s. 425, a company may enter into a court approved scheme of arrangement with its creditors.
- Company voluntary arrangements are more informal than those under CA ss. 425–426, but, to safeguard creditor interests, must involve an insolvency practitioner.
- Another rescue strategy for a company is to apply to the court for the appointment of an administrator to run the company's business.
- An administration order will be made only if the company is, or is likely to become, insolvent and the order is likely to achieve certain specific purposes. Once it is made, there is a moratorium on all claims against the company.
- An administrator has powers which are similar to those of an administrative receiver and manager appointed under a floating charge. In other words, he will take control of the company's property and manage the company's business in accordance with directions from the court and with his proposals for rescuing the company.
- The Enterprise Act 2002 introduces significant changes to the procedure for an administrative order.
- Reconstructions under IA s. 110 allow merging companies to achieve their end by forming a new company and transferring their undertakings to that company.
- A takeover can be completely achieved once the bidder has acquired 90 per cent of the shares of the target company.

CHAPTER 12

Winding up

CONTENTS

LEARNING OUTCOMES

This chapter covers the winding up of companies. After reading and understanding the contents of the chapter and studying the case examples, you should be able to:

- Understand the nature of winding up.
- Appreciate how winding up is commenced.
- Understand how a liquidator is appointed.
- Appreciate the ways in which a liquidator can maximise the assets of a company.
- Appreciate the potential liability of members during winding up.
- Understand how the liquidator deals with the company's creditors.
- Understand the dissolution of the company.

Introduction

We now come to examine the winding up of a company. Sometimes this is referred to as liquidation and the two words are interchangeable. A winding up goes through four distinct stages:

1. the commencement and the appointment of the liquidator,
2. the calling in of the assets,
3. the distribution of the assets, and
4. the dissolution of the company.

The winding up of a company should be distinguished from the dissolution of a company. Dissolution is the actual striking off of the company from the records of the Registrar of Companies. Winding up is the process that sometimes precedes this. On other occasions the directors will simply make an application to the Registrar of Companies under CA s. 652A, stating that the company has ceased to trade and that there are no outstanding debts, and asking for the dissolution of the company. The corporate status of the company continues throughout the process of winding up. So in a sense we are looking at a situation which is analogous to someone being told they are terminally ill. The diagnosis of the illness, like the beginning of the winding up, is not the end of life. This continues until the moment of death: in the case of a company, its dissolution.

In the last chapter we looked at insolvency procedures which fell short of the full termination of a company's existence – arrangements, administrations and receiverships. What we are now concerned with are the procedures that result in the ending of a company's life.

This chapter looks at the way that a company is wound up either by a resolution of its members or by an order of the court and how a liquidator is appointed in each method. A court order is, of course, a far more expensive way of starting a winding up than the voluntary winding up. The respondent in any case for a compulsory winding up order is always the company. In English law, the loser in a case has to bear the costs of both sides. Thus, if a company is put into compulsory liquidation, it is the company which is the loser and, therefore, since the company bears the costs there will be less money at the end of the day for creditors having a claim against it. Because of this it is generally preferable for a winding up to be commenced voluntarily.

In spite of this, a compulsory winding up can have advantages over a voluntary one. For example, by IA 1986 s. 129, a compulsory winding up is deemed to commence at the presentation of the petition. A voluntary winding up is deemed to commence, by IA 1986 s. 86, at the time of the passing of the resolution. For the purposes of setting aside preferences under IA 1986 s. 239 or floating charges under IA 1986 s. 245 (these will be discussed later), it is sometimes preferable for the winding up to be compulsory rather than voluntary because of the earlier commencement. Another advantage of the compulsory winding up in certain circumstances is that there are wider investigative powers available in the former which may be useful in the event of the directors having acted wrongfully.

The role of the liquidator is to call in all the assets of the company, usually to convert them into cash and then to settle all the liabilities of the company in the order of priority as laid down by the Act. Towards the end of this chapter we shall consider the powers which the liquidator enjoys to enter the company's property, together with a number of other matters which are common to all types of liquidation.

TEST YOUR KNOWLEDGE 12.1 

State the relative advantages and disadvantages of the voluntary and compulsory liquidations.

1 Types of winding up

winding up order
A court order to commence the liquidation of a company.

There are various types of **winding up** (see Figure 12.1). The broad division is between compulsory and voluntary.

FIGURE 12.1 Types of winding up

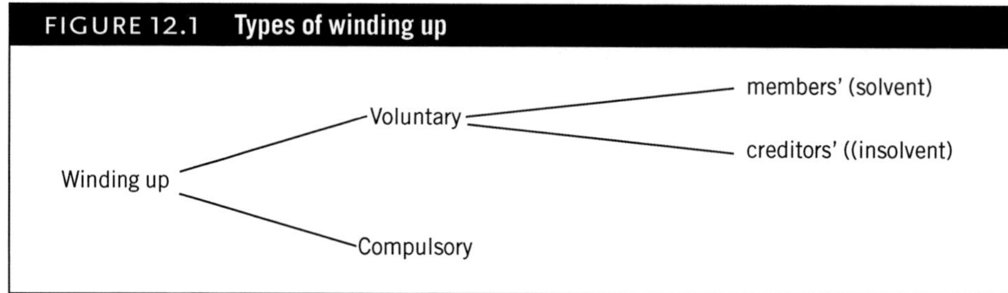

compulsory winding up
The winding up of a company by order of the court.

1 The **compulsory winding up** commences with a court order following the presentation of a petition for an order, usually by a creditor or a member of the company.
2 A voluntary winding up is commenced by a resolution of the members. The court has no involvement in the commencement of such a winding up. The division of voluntary winding up into members' voluntary and creditors' voluntary reflects the control of the winding up:
   (a) In a members' voluntary winding up, the liquidator is appointed by the members.
   (b) In a creditors' voluntary winding up, he is usually appointed by the creditors. In some cases the creditors are content to accept the liquidator appointed by the members of the company; in others they want to replace him with their own nominee.

Obviously, whoever makes the appointment has some degree of control over the liquidator.

The key to understanding winding up is to appreciate the four stages that every winding up goes through, which are listed at the beginning of this chapter.

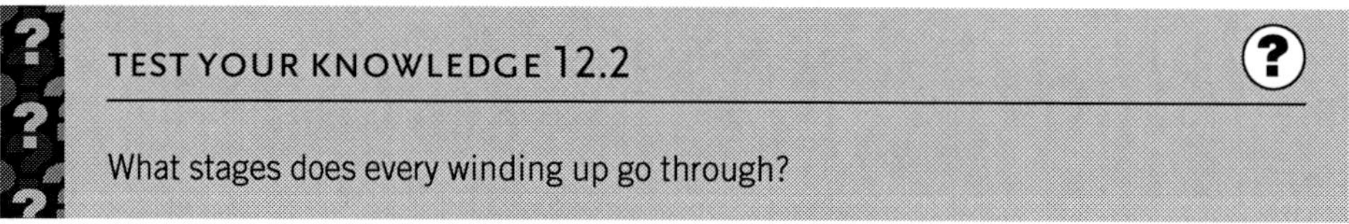

TEST YOUR KNOWLEDGE 12.2

What stages does every winding up go through?

2 Voluntary winding up

Section 84 of the Insolvency Act 1986 details three circumstances in which a company may be wound up voluntarily:

1 When the company has been formed for a fixed time or for a specific purpose, it may be wound up following an ordinary resolution passed by the members in a general meeting when that time has expired or the purpose has been achieved.
2 When the company resolves by special resolution that it should be wound up voluntarily.
3 When the company resolves by extraordinary resolution that it should be wound up because it cannot by reason of its liabilities continue its business.

Ground (1) is very seldom encountered in practice. Companies are rarely formed for a set period of time or for a single purpose. Because of the initial cost of setting up a company, they are almost always looked upon as continuing entities. The difference between the other two types of voluntary winding up is simply a matter of whether the company is solvent or not. It will be recalled that a special resolution requires 21 days' notice to the members and an extraordinary resolution requires 14 days' notice. The easy way to remember the difference is that if the company is solvent, there is no rush and the winding up can therefore be commenced by a special resolution. On the other hand, if the company is insolvent there is some urgency and so the resolution requiring the shorter notice is used.

TEST YOUR KNOWLEDGE 12.3 

In what three circumstances may a voluntary liquidation be commenced?

2.1 The consequences of passing a winding-up resolution

The passing of a resolution to wind up the company has the following effects:

1. The company must cease to carry on its business except insofar as may be required for its beneficial winding up (IA 1986 s. 87).
2. However, the corporate state and corporate powers of the company continue until the company is dissolved (IA 1986 s. 87).
3. Any transfer of shares made other than with the sanction of the liquidator is void (IA 1986 s. 88).
4. Upon the appointment of a liquidator, all the powers of the directors cease except insofar as, in the case of a members' voluntary winding up, the company in a general meeting or the liquidator sanctions their continuance, or, in the case of a creditors' voluntary winding up, the liquidation committee sanctions their continuance. If there is no liquidation committee, the creditors may sanction the continuance of the directors' powers.
5. Within 14 days of the passing of the resolution, the company must give notice of it in the Gazette (IA 1986 s. 85).
6. If the resolution is passed because of the insolvency of the company, employees are dismissed. This does not happen, however, if the company is solvent.

The entitlement of employees to claim damages for wrongful dismissal (because they have not been given notice) when they are automatically dismissed by virtue of the company's going into insolvent liquidation applies even though the employee may have been a member of the company who voted for the extraordinary resolution putting the company into liquidation.

CASE EXAMPLE 12.1 

***Fowler* v *Commercial Timber Co. Ltd* [1930] 2 KB 1**

Fowler had been appointed managing director of the company for a period of five years. Before the five years had expired, an extraordinary resolution was passed by the members putting the company into liquidation since it could not by reason of its liabilities continue business. Fowler, who was also a shareholder of the company, was one of the members who voted for the resolution. It was held that the voluntary winding up had the effect of wrongfully dismissing Fowler as an employee and that therefore he was entitled to claim damages for wrongful dismissal from the company.

2.2 Declaration of solvency

We have seen that the significant difference between a members' and a creditors' voluntary winding up is that in a members' voluntary winding up the company is solvent and in a creditors' voluntary winding up it is insolvent. In a members' voluntary winding up, the liquidator is appointed by the members. Thus, this mode of winding up is favoured by the directors since their conduct is likely to be less vigorously investigated by the liquidator than if he were the creditors' nominee.

declaration of solvency

The declaration made by the directors of a company prior to the commencement of a members' voluntary winding up.

So how does the regulation prevent the potential abuse of a members' voluntary winding up being commenced when the company is insolvent? The answer is that the directors are required to file a **declaration of solvency** if it is to be a members' voluntary winding up. The declaration must state that the members have made a full enquiry into the company's affairs and as a result have formed the opinion that the company will be able to pay its debts in full within a period not exceeding 12 months from the passing of the resolution. The resolution must be made within the five weeks immediately prior to the passing of the resolution and must contain a statement of the company's assets and liabilities as at the latest practicable date prior to the making of the declaration. A director making such a declaration without having reasonable grounds for the opinion of the company that it would be able to pay its debts as stated commits a criminal offence (IA 1986 s. 89).

By s. 90, a winding up following the making of a director's declaration of solvency is known as a members' voluntary winding up and a winding up where no such declaration has been made is known as a creditors' voluntary winding up.

2.3 Members' voluntary winding up procedures

By IA 1986 s. 91, in a members' voluntary winding up the liquidator is appointed by the members in general meeting. Thus, the procedure for a members' voluntary winding up is as follows:

1 The directors enquire into the affairs of the company.
2 The directors make a declaration of solvency.
3 (Within Five weeks) a general meeting of the company is held, at which the following resolutions are passed:
   (a) a special resolution putting the company into liquidation;
   (b) an ordinary resolution appointing a liquidator.
4 The powers of the directors cease and the liquidator proceeds with the winding up of the company.

In the event of a vacancy occurring in the office of liquidator, whether by death, resignation or otherwise, the company in a general meeting may appoint a replacement.

2.4 Creditors' voluntary winding up proceedures

If no declaration of solvency is made, the company must call a meeting of its creditors to be held not later than 14 days after the date on which the extraordinary resolution for a voluntary winding up was passed by the members in general meeting. Seven day's notice must be given to the creditors and the meeting must also be advertised once in the *Gazette* and at least once in two newspapers circulating in the locality of the company's principal place of business (IA 1986 s. 98). The notice of the meeting must state either:

1 the name and address of a person who is qualified to act as an insolvency practitioner in relation to the company who, during the period leading up to the meeting, will give to creditors, free of charge, such information concerning the affairs of the company as they may reasonably require; or
2 a place in the locality of the company's principal place of business in Great Britain where, on the two business days immediately before the holding of the meeting, a list of the names and addresses of the company's creditors will be available for inspection free of charge.

By IA 1986 s. 99 the directors must draw up a statement of the affairs of the company which they must lay before the creditors' meeting. They must appoint one of their number to be chairman of the meeting. The statement of affairs must give details of the company's assets, debts and liabilities, together with the names and addresses of creditors and particulars of any securities which they may hold, and has to be verified by affidavit (a sworn statement) by some or all of the directors.

Both the creditors and the company at their respective meetings have a right to nominate a person to be the liquidator. In the event of the meetings nominating different persons, the liquidator is the person nominated by the creditors. This is subject to a right of any director, member or creditor to appeal to the court within seven days of the creditors making their nomination for an order directing that someone else should be liquidator. In the event of the creditors not making a nomination then the members' nominee takes up post.

Thus, the procedure on a creditors' voluntary winding up is as follows:

1 There is no declaration of solvency.
2 A members' meeting at which the following resolutions are passed:
   (a) an extraordinary resolution putting the company into liquidation;
   (b) an ordinary resolution appointing a liquidator.
3 An insolvency practitioner is appointed to furnish creditors with information regarding the company's affairs or otherwise provides a list of names and addresses of company's creditors drawn up ready for inspection by creditors;
4 The directors prepare a statement of affairs to lay before a meeting of the creditors.
5 (Within 14 days) a meeting of creditors is held to pass a resolution appointing a liquidator. (If a different person is appointed from the nominee of the members' meeting, the creditors' nominee prevails.)

There is obviously a possibility that a members' liquidator could be in post for a period of time during the period between the members meeting appointing him and the subsequent creditors meeting appointing the creditors' nominee.

It was held in *Re Centrebind Ltd* [1967] 1 WLR 377 that the acts of the company's liquidator were not invalidated by a delay in the holding of the creditors' meeting. Certain disreputable liquidators used to take advantage of this and indulge in a practice known as 'centrebinding' whereby the assets of the company were put beyond the control of the creditors as a result of the members' liquidator selling them off. This practice has now been outlawed and, by IA 1986 s. 166, it is now a criminal offence for the liquidator to exercise any of his powers during the period prior to the holding of the creditors' meeting under s. 98, except with the sanction of the court. This does not apply in regard to the liquidator's power:

1 to take into his custody or control property to which the company is entitled;
2 to dispose of perishable goods and other goods the value of which is likely to diminish if they are not immediately disposed of; and
3 to do all such things as may be necessary for the protection of the company's assets.

The liquidation committee

In a creditors' voluntary winding up, the creditors may, at the s. 98 meeting, or at any subsequent meeting, appoint a liquidation committee of not more than five persons to act with the liquidator. If such a committee is appointed, the members may appoint up to five of their number to act as members of the committee, though the creditors may, if they think fit, resolve that these persons ought not to be members of the liquidation committee. If such a resolution is passed, the members cannot act on the committee unless the court otherwise directs (IA 1986 s. 101).

2.5 The effect of insolvency on a members' voluntary winding up

It is possible that sometimes the liquidator in a members' voluntary winding up discovers that the company is, in fact, going to be unable to pay its debts in full in spite of the statement to the contrary in the declaration of solvency which the directors made. By IA 1986 s. 95, when a members' liquidator forms the opinion that the company will be unable to pay its debts in full within the period stated in the directors' declaration of solvency, he must summon a meeting of creditors to be held within 28 days of his forming that opinion.The creditors must be given at least seven days' notice of the meeting and the meeting must be advertised once in the *Gazette* and once at least in two newspapers circulating in the locality of the company's principal place of business. During the period leading up to the holding of the creditors' meeting, the liquidator must furnish creditors free of charge with such information about the affairs of the company as they may reasonably require. He must also draw up a statement of affairs of the company detailing the company's assets, debts and liabilities, the names and addresses of creditors and any securities held by them. He must himself preside at the creditors' meeting and lay this statement before the meeting. By s. 96, as from the date on which the creditors' meeting is held, the winding up becomes a creditors' voluntary winding up.

2.6 Powers of the liquidator in a voluntary winding up

The Insolvency Act 1986 s. 165 and Sch. 4 provide that the liquidator in a voluntary winding up can exercise the following powers without sanction (either of the court or the creditors):

1 Bring or defend any action or any other legal proceedings on behalf of the company.
2 Carry on the business of the company so far as is necessary for its beneficial winding up.
3 Sell any of the company's property by public auction or private contract.
4 Carry out all acts and execute in the name and on behalf of the company all deeds, receipts and other documents and to use, where necessary, the company's seal.
5 Prove and claim in any insolvency proceedings taken on behalf of the company against any other insolvent estate.
6 Draw, accept, make and endorse any bill of exchange or promissory note in the name of and on behalf of the company.
7 Raise on the security of the assets of the company any money needed.
8 Take out in his official name letters of administration to the estate of any deceased contributory and to do in his official name any other act necessary for obtaining payment of any money due from a contributory (a contributory is any member who may be called upon to make a payment to the company in the course of the liquidation; the term is explained more fully below).
9 Appoint an agent to do any business which the liquidator cannot do himself.
10 Do all such things as may be necessary for winding up the company's affairs and distributing its assets.

In a members' voluntary winding up, with the sanction of an extraordinary resolution of the company, and in a creditors' voluntary winding up, with the sanction of the court or of the liquidation committee (or if there is no such committee, a meeting of the company's creditors), the liquidator may:

1 pay any class of creditors in full;
2 make any compromise or arrangement with creditors; and
3 compromise all calls and liabilities to calls and other debts and liabilities due to the company.

Sometimes, in the course of a winding up, a liquidator sells off the whole or part of the company's business or property to another company. When this happens he may, with the appropriate sanction, receive payment on behalf of the company by way of shares in the transferee company. The sanction required is, in the case of a members' voluntary winding up, that of a special resolution of the company in general meeting and, in the case of a creditors' voluntary' winding up, that of either the court or the liquidation committee.

By s. 112, the liquidator may apply to the court for a determination of any question arising in the course of the winding up of the company. This is an important power which gives the liquidator a right to apply to the court for guidance if ever he is unsure as to the correct way in which he should proceed.

2.7 Non-appointment of a liquidator

It sometimes happens in a voluntary winding up no liquidator is appointed. This may occur for a variety of reasons, probably the most important being that there are so few assets in the company that a liquidator does not wish to take up office and do work for which he will not get paid. By IA 1986 s. 114, if no liquidator has been appointed, the powers of the directors must not be exercised other than with the sanction of the court or, in the case of a creditors' voluntary winding up, so far as is necessary to call the creditors' meeting and prepare the statement of affairs. There is an exception, however, whereby the directors can dispose of perishable goods and any other goods the value of which are likely to diminish if they are not immediately disposed of and do all such other things as may be necessary for the protection of the company's assets.

2.8 Compulsory winding up following voluntary winding up

A voluntary winding up does not prevent any creditor or contributory applying to have it wound up by the court. Before the court will make an order in these circumstances it must be satisfied that there are sound reasons as to why a voluntary winding up is inappropriate in the circumstances. This might, for example, be the case where the liquidator is found to have some interest in the company other than by reason simply of his appointment. By IA 1986 s. 129 when a compulsory winding up follows a voluntary winding up, all proceedings taken in the voluntary winding up are treated as having been validly taken unless the court, on proof of fraud or mistake, directs otherwise.

TEST YOUR KNOWLEDGE 12.4 

(a) List the essential stages in (i) a members' voluntary winding up and (ii) a creditors' voluntary winding up.

(b) What must a members' voluntary liquidator to do if he discovers that the company will be unable to pay all of its debts in full?

3 Compulsory winding up

3.1 Grounds for a compulsory winding up

The grounds on which a petition may be presented are detailed in IA 1986 s. 122. They are as follows:

1 Where the company has by special resolution resolved that the company be wound up by the court. (This is very seldom encountered in practice because, as will be recalled, a company may by special or extraordinary resolution determine voluntarily that it should be wound up.)
2 Where the company is a public company which was registered as a public company on its original incorporation and has not been issued with a certificate under s. 117 of the Companies Act to permit it to commence trading and more than a year has expired since it was so registered. (The impact of the s. 117 certificate was discussed in Chapter 2.) Whereas a private company can commence trading upon incorporation, a public company formed as such must first obtain an s. 117 certificate. Without this certificate it cannot trade. Thus, it is only fair that a member can petition for a winding up of the company if the company does not obtain the certificate within one year of incorporation. This is, again, very seldom encountered in practice.
3 Where the company is an old public company within the meaning of the Companies Consolidation (Consequential Provisions) Act 1985. (The new definition of a public company was introduced by the Companies Act 1985. Old public companies had to re-register when that Act came into force. This ground allows a company that has not re-registered to be put into compulsory liquidation.) This ground is, again very seldom encountered in practice.

4 When the company does not commence its business within a year from its incorporation or suspends its business for a whole year. (This ground allows the shareholder who sees that his company is not trading to sue for a winding up so that he can get his money back from the company. It is discussed more fully below.)
5 Where the number of members of a public company falls to below two. (This enables a person who is the sole member of a company to avoid personal liability under s. 24 in the event of the company having only one member for more than six months. It is not a much used ground in practice since all that a sole member has to do to avoid personal liability in this situation is to transfer just one of his shares to a nominee. He need not even transfer beneficial interest in the share.)
6 Where the company is unable to pay its debts. (This, the most common ground, is described more fully below.)
7 Where the court is of the opinion that it is just and equitable that the company should be wound up. (This is also discussed more fully below.)

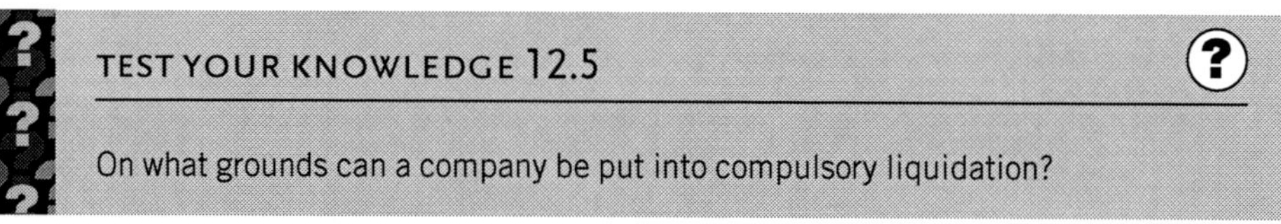
TEST YOUR KNOWLEDGE 12.5

On what grounds can a company be put into compulsory liquidation?

Inability to pay debts

The most common ground for a compulsory winding up order in practice is that a company cannot pay its debts. The meaning of inability to pay debts is set out in IA 1986 s. 123. It occurs:

1 If a creditor to whom the company is indebted in a sum exceeding £750 then due has served on the company, by leaving it at the company's registered office, a written demand requiring the company to pay the sum so due and the company has for three weeks thereafter neglected to pay the sum or to secure or compound for it to the reasonable satisfaction of the creditor.
2 If execution or other process issued on a judgment of any court in favour of any creditor of the company is returned unsatisfied in whole or in part.
3 If the court is of the opinion that the assets of the company, as realised, will be insufficient to meet the liabilities and the costs of the winding up. Or,
4 If it is proved to the satisfaction of the court that the company is unable to pay its debts as they fall due.

Some explanation of these is called for. Ground 1 lays down the procedure whereby an ordinary creditor of the company can petition for the company to be wound up. He must be owed at least £750, though two or more creditors can combine the debts which they claim the company owes so as to be able to present a petition so long as the aggregate sum owed exceeds £750. The figure is an arbitrary one intended to prevent these provisions being used as a mere debt-collecting process. The existence of the debt is not itself the basis of the petition. The creditor must serve a statutory demand upon the company requiring payment to be made within three weeks. As an alternative to making payment, the company can instead offer security, i.e. some form of charge over assets of the company.

Execution on a judgment occurs when a creditor, having sued the company and obtained judgment against it, and having still not been paid by the company, goes back to the court and asks for enforcement of the judgment. The court will then order that the sheriff or the sheriff's officer should go to the company's premises to seize assets which can be sold in order to discharge the debt outstanding. If the sheriff is unable to find any assets to sell then execution is unsatisfied. Obviously, where a company has no assets on which execution can be levied it is insolvent.

The fourth ground includes a situation where the court is satisfied that contingent and prospective liabilities (i.e. debts which are not yet due but which will have to be paid some time in the future) are such as to make the company unable to pay its debts. Thus, in *Re Taylor's Industrial Flooring* [1990] BCC 44, the court held that a company which persistently failed or neglected to pay its debts until forced to do so was, in fact, unable to pay its debts.

The just and equitable ground

This final ground on which a petition can be presented is independent of the previous six. It is a **residuary provision** and so new kinds of cases maybe brought under the head by judicial interpretation. Examples of instances which have arisen under this heading include:

1 Where the company's substratum has disappeared. The substratum is the purpose for which the company was formed to achieve, i.e. its main object. If the situation arises where the object is incapable of achievement, the substratum of the company has gone and it may be wound up. The leading case on this is *Re German Date Coffee Co.*

CASE EXAMPLE 12.2

***Re German Date Coffee Co.* (1882) 20 Ch D 169**

A company was formed with the main object of acquiring a German patent for the manufacture of a coffee substitute from dates. It had been formed at a time when the German patent had not actually been granted though the promoters of the company anticipated that it would be granted in the near future. In the event the patent was never granted though the company acquired a Swedish patent for the same purpose. Two shareholders petitioned for a winding up. It was held that the petition should be successful. The substratum had failed. The objects of the company could not be attained. It was therefore just and equitable that the company should be wound up.

2 Where the company has been formed for a fraudulent purpose as, for example, in Case Example 12.3.

CASE EXAMPLE 12.3

***Re Thomas Edward Brinsmead & Sons* (1897) 1 Ch 45**

A company was formed by three men named Brinsmead who were former employees of John Brinsmead & Sons, a well-known firm of piano makers. The new company had been formed also to make pianos which would be passed off as the product of the established and respected firm. It was held that a shareholder was entitled to a petition for the winding up of the company on the just and equitable ground.

3 Where there is a justifiable lack of confidence in the management of the company, as for example, in Case Example 12.4.

CASE EXAMPLE 12.4

***Loch* v *John Blackwood Ltd* [1924] AC 783**

John Blackwood had an engineering business. When he died a family company was formed to carry on the business and as a means whereby the profits could be divided amongst his family as provided by his will. The managing director, who enjoyed a preponderance of the voting power within the company, ran the company extremely profitably but in a way that was oppressive to the beneficiaries. He failed to hold general meetings, to submit accounts or to recommend dividends. It was thought by the beneficiaries that his purpose in acting in this way was so that he could acquire from the minority their shares at an undervalue. It was held that the lack of confidence in the management of the company's affairs was good cause for a winding up on the just and equitable ground.

4 If a company is in effect a partnership which has been incorporated then the court will order a winding up on those same grounds that would justify it to order the dissolution of a partnership. An example of this is shown in Case Example 12.5.

CASE EXAMPLE 12.5

***Re Yenidje Tobacco Co. Ltd* [1916] 2 Ch 426**

Two tobacco manufacturers formed the company so as to amalgamate their existing businesses. They were the only shareholders and the only directors. They had equal rights in the company. They fell out and communicated with each other only through the secretary. Although the company was at that time making large profits it was held that a winding-up order should be granted on the just and equitable ground.

winding-up order

A court order to commence the liquidation of a company

In similar circumstances, **a winding-up order** may be made on this ground even though the proprietors of the company have acted within their strict legal rights.

CASE EXAMPLE 12.6

***Ebrahimi* v *Westbourne Galleries Ltd* [1973] AC 360**

The company had three members, Ebrahimi, Nazar and Nazar's son. They were all director's of the company. Ebrahimi and Nazar each held 40 per cent of the shares and Nazar's son 20 per cent. After trading for some considerable time, a disagreement arose between the parties and the Nazar's passed an ordinary resolution, under what is now s. 303, removing Ebrahimi as a director. It was held that a winding-up order should be granted at Ebrahimi's petition for the winding up of the company.

Suspension of trading

This ground enables a shareholder to recover his money if the situation arises where the company ceases trading with the result that his money is, of course, not being used for the purpose for which he subscribed it. The order will not be granted unless it is proved to the satisfaction of the court that the company has no intention of recommencing business, as in Case Example 12.7.

CASE EXAMPLE 12.7

***Re Middlesborough Assembly Room Co.* (1880) 14 Ch D 104**

The company was formed with the main object of the building assembly rooms. There was a trade depression in consequence of which building was suspended for more than three years. The company fully intended, however, that it would recommence operations as soon as trade prospects improved. A shareholder sought a winding up on the ground that it had not carried on business for a year but this was opposed by the holders of more than 80 per cent of the shares of the company. It was held that the action should fail. The wishes of the majority could not be disregarded. Since there was every intention of recommencing business at the earliest opportunity the winding-up order should not be granted. It would have been difficult if the court had been satisfied that it would have been impossible to recommence business or that there was no intention of recommencing business.

TEST YOUR KNOWLEDGE 12.6

(a) How does a creditor of a company establish its inability to pay its debts when he is seeking to have the company wound up?

(b) What is meant by the just and equitable ground for winding up?

3.2 Who can petition?

Obviously, there must be someone who decides to take proceedings against a company for the case to come to court. The following are the persons who may petition:

1 *The company itself.* Before the application can be made, the company must have passed a special resolution (IA 1986 s. 122). This ground is, of course, rare in practice because members having three-quarters of the voting rights can pass a special or extraordinary resolution for a voluntary winding up which is much cheaper and quicker than a compulsory winding up.
2 *The directors of the company.*
3 *A creditor or creditors.* Although a secured creditor has the right to petition, he will usually rely on his security, so in practice, the petitioner will be an unsecured creditor.

contributory
The holder of a partly paid share who is required to pay up the unpaid element on his shares on a winding up.

4 *A* **contributory**. This term is somewhat misleading. It means every person liable to contribute to the assets of the company in the event of its being wound up. However, it includes all present members of the company and also some former members. The holders of fully paid shares are contributories even though they have contributed all that they have to by virtue of having paid the full amount due on their shares. A contributory may not petition unless:
   (a) the number of members is reduced below two; or
   (b) at least some of the shares held by him have been registered in his name for at least six months during the 18 months prior to the commencement of the winding up or have devolved on him through the death of a former holder.
5 *The Secretary of State.* A winding up petition may be presented by the Secretary of State under IA 1986 s. 122(1)(b) (failure to obtain s. 117 certificate), s. 122 (1)(c) (old public company failing to re-register) and CA 1985 s. 440 on the ground that it is expedient in the public interest following a report of Department of Trade and Industry inspectors.

official receiver
An officer of the Department of Trade and Industry who is attached to every court that enjoys an insolvency jurisdiction.

6 *The* **official receiver**. Where a company is being wound up voluntarily, a winding-up petition may be presented by the official receiver on the ground that the voluntary winding up cannot be continued with due regard to the interests of the creditors or contributories.

At the hearing, the court has a variety of orders which it can make. It may dismiss the petition on the ground that what is alleged has not been proved. It may adjourn the hearing for further evidence. It may make an interim order or any other order that it sees fit. Assuming, however, that a winding-up order is made, the winding up is deemed to commence at the presentation of the petition (IA 1986 s. 129). In other words, the winding up dates back to the date of the petition rather than commencing as from the date of the order. From the time of the order, the official receiver becomes the liquidator of the company and continues in office until some other person becomes liquidator (IA 1986 s. 136).

3.3 The winding-up order

When the petition is heard by the court, there are three possible orders which the court may make. The petition may be dismissed. The hearing may be adjourned for further evidence to be produced. The winding-up order may be granted. This chapter now proceeds on the assumption that it is the last of these orders which has been made.

The consequence of an order is that the company goes into liquidation and the commencement of this state of affairs dates back to the presentation of the petition. By IA 1986 s. 127 any disposition of the property of the company, and any transfer of shares or alteration in the status of the members, after the commencement of the winding up, is void unless the court orders to the contrary. The reason for this is that it prevents the disposal of assets during the period of time between the presentation of the petition and the making of the winding-up order.

CASE EXAMPLE 12.8

***Re Grey's Inn Construction Co Ltd* [1980] 1 WLR 711**

The company had carried on a building business. On 3 August 1972 a winding up petition had been presented. The company's bank learnt of this on 17 August when the petition was advertised. The bank, however, allowed the normal operation of the account until 9 October when a winding up order was made.

The liquidator sought an order to the effect that the dealings made on the bank account were void. It was held by the Court of Appeal that any payments made into an overdrawn bank account after the presentation of a winding up petition are dispositions of property since they discharged the company's liability to the bank.

Such payments could be validated by the court under what is now s.127. Having regard to the bank's failure to protect itself after learning of the petition, it was appropriate only to allow those sums paid into the account prior to the advertising of the petition to be validated. In *Bank of Ireland v Hollicourt (Contracts) Ltd* [2000] BCC 1210 the Court of Appeal held that the payment of cheques from a company's bank account after the presentation of a winding up petition was not invalidated by s. 127.

By IA 1986 s. 128 any distress or execution against the property of the company after the commencement of the winding up is void. By IA 1986 s. 130 no action may be proceeded with or commenced against the company except by leave of the court. Most of the powers of the directors cease upon the making of the order and are taken over by the liquidator.

By IA 1986 s. 136, the official receiver becomes the liquidator of the company. This is not necessarily a role he will occupy throughout the winding up as will be seen, but at least for the time being he assumes the powers of the directors. The official receiver is an officer of the DTI. There is one attached to every court having an insolvency jurisdiction. He takes an initial control of the affairs of a company after the making of a compulsory winding-up order.

The order results in the dismissal of the employees of the company. They may, of course, sue the company for damages for breach of contract since the dismissal will have occurred without notice being given.

TEST YOUR KNOWLEDGE 12.7

What is the effect of the making of a compulsory winding-up order?

Procedure following the making of the order

By IA 1986 s. 136, the official receiver becomes the first liquidator of the company, a post which he holds until another liquidator is appointed (if indeed there is another appointment made). Within 21 days of the order, the directors must supply to the official receiver a statement of affairs. It is then for the official receiver to decide whether he is going to continue to be the liquidator of the company or whether someone else should be appointed to that position. He must reach this decision within 12 weeks from the making of the winding-up order. If he wishes someone else to be appointed as liquidator he must summon meetings of the company's creditors and contributories for the purpose of their choosing a liquidator in his place.

Should he decide not to call these meetings, he must notify the court, the creditors and the contributories of his decision. When he does this, one quarter in value of the creditors may request that a meeting be held. The official receiver must then summon the meetings. The procedure of appointment by the meetings is very similar to that on a creditors' voluntary winding up. If the meetings respectively appoint different liquidators, it is the creditors' nominee who takes up office. If no liquidator is appointed by the meetings, the official receiver may apply to the Secretary of State for the appointment of a liquidator. In every compulsory liquidation, the official receiver is under a duty to carry out two investigations. He must examine the causes of the failure of the company, if indeed the company has failed. He must in all cases look into the promotion, formation, business dealings and affairs of the company. If he thinks fit he may report the findings of his investigations to the court.

3.4 Liquidation committee

Where the meetings of creditors and contributories appoint a liquidator, they may also appoint a liquidation committee. The role of the committee is to oversee the work of the liquidator, and he must report to the committee on all matters as appear to him to be, or as they have indicated to him as being, of concern to them with respect to the winding up.

4 Calling in of the assets

By IA 1986 s. 234 where any person has in his possession or control any property, books, papers or records to which the company appears to be entitled, the court may require that person to hand over the items to the liquidator. It sometimes happens, of course, that the liquidator seizes or disposes of property which is not actually the property of the company. For example, this might happen where there are goods on the premises of the company and which are subject to hire-purchase agreements but which the liquidator sells. The section contains a protection for the liquidator if he does so. He is under no liability for any loss or damage resulting from the seizure or disposal of such goods unless such loss or damage was caused by his own negligence. He also has a lien on the property or on the proceeds of its sale for such expenses as were incurred in connection with the seizure or disposal.

4.1 Duty to cooperate with the liquidator

By IA 1986 s. 235 it is the duty of persons who are or have been at any time officers of the company or have been in the employment of the company during the year prior to the winding up and certain other persons who have been involved with the company during that period to give to the liquidator (and in this context this includes the official receiver in a compulsory winding up) such information concerning the company and its dealings generally as the liquidator may at any time reasonably require. The liquidator may also require any such person to attend upon him at such times as he may reasonably require. It is a criminal offence for a person without reasonable excuse to fail to comply with an obligation imposed upon him by s. 235.

4.2 Enquiry into the company's dealings

By s. 236, on the application of the liquidator, the court may summon before it any officer of the company, any person known or suspected to have in his possession any property of the company or supposed to be indebted to the company, or any person whom the court thinks capable of giving information concerning the business and affairs of the company. The court may require any such person to submit an affidavit containing an account of his dealings with the company or to produce any documents of or relating to the company which are in his possession. The court enjoys wide enforcement powers in regard to this provision. It enjoys power to arrest persons and to keep them in custody and to seize any books, papers, records, money or goods in the possession of that person. If it appears to the court that any person has in his possession any property of the company the court may order him, on the application of the liquidator, to deliver the whole or any part of that property to the liquidator at such time, in such manner and on such terms as the court thinks fit. Likewise, if the court is of opinion that any person is indebted to the company, it may, on the application of the liquidator, order the debtor to pay to the liquidator all or part of the debt due. Further, it may order that any person who, in the jurisdiction of the court, would be liable to be summoned to appear before it under s. 236 or s. 237, shall be examined in any part of the UK where he may for the time being be, or in a place outside the UK. Such examination may take place on oath either orally or by interrogatories.

4.3 **Transactions at an undervalue**

By IA 1986 s. 238, if a company has entered into a transaction at an undervalue during the two years prior to the onset of insolvency the liquidator may apply to the court for an order for the setting aside of the transaction. The onset of insolvency in this context means either:

(a) the presentation of the petition which resulted in a compulsory winding up;
(b) the passing of the resolution resulting in a voluntary winding up;
(c) In the case of winding up which immediately follows the discharge of an administration order, the date of the presentation of the petition on which the administration order was made.

A company enters into a transaction with a person at an undervalue if the company makes a gift to that person or otherwise enters into a transaction with that person on terms such that the company is to receive no consideration. Alternatively, it may be at an undervalue if the consideration received by the company is significantly less in value than the consideration provided by the company. A transaction may be set aside only under this provision if at the time of the transaction being made the company was either unable to pay its debts as defined in IA 1986 s. 123 (see above) or the company became unable to pay its debts within the meaning of that section in consequence of the transaction. If the transaction is entered into by a company with a person who is connected with the company there is a presumption that the company was insolvent at the relevant time. Thus if, for example, one year before the commencement of an insolvent liquidation, the company gave one of its fleet of cars to a person unconnected with the company, the transaction could only be set aside if the liquidator could establish that the company had been insolvent at the time of the gift. However, if the gift had been made to the wife of a director, it would be for the wife to prove that the company had been solvent at the time of the gift if she wished to retain the car.

The court may not set aside a transaction at an undervalue if it is satisfied that the company which entered into the transaction did so in good faith and for the purpose of carrying on in business and that at the time it did so there were reasonable grounds for believing that the transaction would benefit the company. Thus, if a year before the commencement of an insolvent liquidation the company gave a modest gift to a prospective customer in the hope that this would encourage business there could be no possibility of the transaction being set aside.

In *Phillips v Brewin Dolphin Bell Lawrie Ltd* [2001] BCC 864 the House of Lords held that, when looking at an undervalue transaction, the court had to have regard to the total consideration being received by the insolveny company under the terms of the transaction.

4.4 **Preferences**

The court also has powers, at the instance of the liquidator, to set aside any preference made by the company. Once again the preference must have been made at a particular time prior to the onset of insolvency as defined above. In this context there are different time zones according to whom the alleged preference was in favour of. If it was in favour of a connected person, the relevant period is two years prior to the onset of insolvency. If it is in favour of any other person, the relevant period is six months. Once again at the time of the alleged preference the company must have been unable to pay its debts. A preference is given to a person if that person is one of the creditors of the company and the company does anything or allows anything to be done which has the effect of putting that person into a position which, in the event of the company going into insolvent liquidation, would be better than the position he would have been in if that thing had not been done. Thus, the state of mind of the directors of the company in making the alleged preference must always be investigated. A preference may be made by way of direct payment of money or by way of the giving of security; for example, the granting of a fixed charge over a freehold asset of the company. Such a preference might arise where the directors of a manufacturing company realise that it is hopelessly insolvent. They wish to put the company into liquidation and start up a new company in the same business. They wish to keep in with a particular supplier, hoping that he will supply the new company as he has the insolvent one. However, they do not have the cash available to settle the debts owing to him and so they grant him a fixed charge over the company's warehouse. Assuming that this occurs within the six months prior to the onset of insolvency, the transaction may be set aside as a preference. Having said that, the essence of a preference is the intention on the part of the person giving it to put the creditor into a better position. Thus, if the preference is given under threat, and such threat is its dominant motive, there can be no preference. Suppose the supplier were to have said to the directors that he would petition for a winding up if they did not give him the fixed charge over the company's warehouse; there would not in this situation be a preference. In *Re Ledingham-Smith* [1993] BCLC 635 it was held that the payment of fees outstanding to a firm of accountants was not a preference in circumstances where the firm refused to act further unless such payment were made.

A company which has given a preference to a person connected with the company (otherwise than simply by reason of being one of its employees) at the time the preference was given is presumed, unless the contrary is shown, to have been influenced in deciding to give it by such a desire to put the creditor in a better position. If the alleged preference is given to a person who is not connected with the company there is no such presumption.

4.5 Extortionate credit transactions

For many years an individual who has entered into an extortionate credit transaction (for example who has borrowed money at a very high rate of interest) has had the right to apply to the court for an order to vary the transaction, usually by way of mitigating his liability under it. By IA 1986 s. 244 this right is extended to companies which have gone into liquidation. If in the three years prior to the company going into liquidation it has entered into an extortionate credit transaction, the liquidator may apply to the court for an order to mitigate its liability under the transaction. A transaction is extortionate if, having regard to the risk accepted by the person providing the credit, the terms of it are grossly exorbitant or it has otherwise grossly contravened the ordinary principles of fair dealing. There is a presumption that any transaction in respect of which an application is made was extortionate and thus it is always for the creditor to prove to the contrary. In reaching its decision, the court must have regard to matters such as the degree of financial pressure that the company was under at the time, the business experience of the directors of the company as opposed to that of the creditor, the amount of security which the company could offer and all other relevant matters. If the court finds that the credit transaction was extortionate it may make an order containing one or more of the following provisions:

1. a provision setting aside the whole or part of any obligation created by the transaction;
2. a provision otherwise varying the terms of the transaction or varying the terms on which any security for the purpose of the transaction is held;
3. a provision requiring any person who is or was a party to the transaction to pay to

the liquidator any sums paid to that person by virtue of the transaction by the company;

4 a provision requiring any person to surrender to the liquidator any property held by him as security for the purposes of the transaction; and

a provision directing accounts to be taken between any persons.

Avoidance of certain floating charges

It will be recalled that floating charges created by the company within the 12 months prior to the onset of insolvency (two years if in favour of a connected person) are invalid except insofar as value was given in the company after the creation of the charge or unless it can be shown that at the time of creation of the charge the company was solvent.

Disclaimer of onerous property

Whenever a company is in liquidation, the liquidator has the right to disclaim what is known as onerous property. By IA 1986 s. 178 this means any unprofitable contract and any other property of the company which is either unsaleable or not readily saleable or is such that it may give rise to a liability to pay money or to perform any other onerous act. Examples of such property would be leasehold land or premises where the rent which has to be paid is more than the profit generated by its use, freehold land burdened by restrictive covenants which cost more to conform with than the land is worth and any other contracts which can only be carried out at a loss. A liquidator may disclaim such onerous property by giving notice to the other person interested in the transaction. The liquidator may give notice even though he himself has taken possession of the property, tried to sell it or otherwise exercised any other rights of ownership in relation to it. Any person who suffers loss or damage as a result of a disclaimer is deemed to be a creditor of the company to the extent of such loss or damage and so may prove as a creditor in the winding up. This means, for example, that when a liquidator disclaims a lease, the landlord can claim compensation against the company. As such he will be able to prove for the amount of the compensation as an unsecured creditor in the liquidation.

Suppliers of public utilities

Under the old law the suppliers of the public utilities such as gas, electricity, water and telephone were in a particularly advantageous position. When a liquidator took up post with a company he would obviously require a continuation of these services, if only for a short time. Sometimes, the utility in question would only continue the supply on condition that the liquidator settled the company's outstanding account. By means of such a threat an unsecured creditor was able to push itself forward into some sort of pre-preferential position. This position has been radically changed. Section 233 of IA 1986 provides that while the supplier of these utilities may require that the liquidator will personally guarantee any use which is made of the utility while he is in office he cannot make the discharge of outstanding indebtedness a condition of continued supply.

5 Fraudulent and wrongful trading

fraudulent trading

Carrying on business in the course of winding up with intent to defraud creditors.

5.1 Fraudulent trading

If in the course of liquidation it appears that the business of the company has been carried on with intent to defraud creditors or for any fraudulent purpose the liquidator may apply to the court for an order that any persons who are knowingly parties to the carrying on of the business in that way are to be liable to make such contributions to the assets of the company as the court thinks proper in the circumstances. Fraudulent trading is not defined by statute. IA s. 213 merely refers to it as carrying on the business with intent to defraud creditors. However, in *Re William C Leitch Bros Ltd* [1932] 2 Ch 71 it was said to occur when a company incurs debts either knowing it will not be able to pay them as and when they fall due or recklessly as to whether they will be able to pay them at that time. Further guidance is given in *Re Patrick & Lyon Ltd* [1933] Ch 786 where it was said that the conduct of the directors had to show real moral blame.

When fraudulent trading occurs it will probably be one or two of the creditors of the company who have been particularly defrauded. In spite of this, the remedy is essentially an action taken by the liquidator. Section 213 of IA 1986 provides that when fraudulent trading is established the court may declare that any persons who are knowingly parties to the carrying on of the business in this manner should be liable to make such contributions to the company's assets as the court thinks proper. Thus, the implication is that the payment is for the benefit of the creditors generally.

Fraudulent trading was never a very successful remedy because of the extreme difficulty in showing that the directors, in incurring the debts in question, knew that the company would be unable to pay them. Were the directors to say in the witness box that they honestly believed that, even though the company was insolvent at the time of incurring the debts, they nevertheless believed they would be able to pay them as and when they fell due, they would be highly likely to be found not liable.

Before leaving fraudulent trading, it should be noted that liability is not limited to the directors of the company. It extends to any person who was a party to the trading.

CASE EXAMPLE 12.9

***Re Gerald Cooper Chemicals Ltd* [1978] Ch 262**

Cooper was the director of Gerald Cooper Chemicals Ltd. The company took a loan from another company which it was due to repay within a few months. When the time for repayment arrived there was no prospect of the company making it. It negotiated to sell a consignment of indigo to a prospective customer. In fact it had in its possession no indigo, but the customer nevertheless made an advance payment. As soon as Gerald Cooper Chemicals Ltd received the advance payment it paid it over to the money-lending company and placed itself in liquidation. It was held that not only could Cooper himself be made liable for fraudulent trading but also the money-lending company and its directors could be made liable. It is clear from the case that the creditor in question had accepted the money knowing it had been obtained by the use of fraudulent trading and that itself was sufficient to implicate him in the fraudulent trading. As Templeman J said: '*a man who warms himself with the fire of fraud cannot complain if he is singed*'.

Because of the difficulty of establishing fraudulent trading, it was recommended by the Cork Committee that there should be a further liability of wrongful trading to cover those situations where the directors of a company had been careless rather than fraudulent in incurring debts.

wrongful trading

A liability recommended by the Cork Committee to cover situations where during winding up the director had been careless rather that fraudulent in incurring debts.

5.2 **Wrongful trading**

Once again, liability for wrongful trading is found as a result of an action by the liquidator. By IA s. 214 in order to establish liability the liquidator must show the following.

1 That the person against whom he is proceeding was at the time a director of the company.
2 That the company had gone into insolvent liquidation.
3 That at some time before the commencement of the winding up the person against whom he is proceeding knew or ought to have concluded that there was no reasonable prospect that the company would avoid going into insolvent liquidation.

These three criteria need further explanation.

Liability limited to directors of the company

The liability is limited to directors of the company. This includes shadow directors. A shadow director is any person in accordance with whose directions or instructions the directors are accustomed to act. It does not include a person who gives advice in a professional capacity. Thus, for example, an auditor whose advice is followed to the letter by the company would not be made liable. However, it has been held that a bank might be a shadow director. A bank manager giving advice to a customer does not do so in a professional capacity and indeed is not technically a professional person in the same way as an auditor. The prospect of banks being found to be shadow directors at first caused some trepidation amongst the banks when the provision was first introduced and their fears were confirmed when it was held by the court in *Re A Company* No. 005009 of 1987 (1988) 4 BCC 424 that a bank could be a shadow director. However, there has never been a case reported where a bank has actually been found to be shadow director. In *Secretary of State v Deverell* [2000] BCC 1057 it was said that the professional exemption had to be narrowly confined. The protection from liability could only be used by a professional person acting in a professional capacity.

The company must have gone into insolvent liquidation

In this context insolvent liquidation means the assets as realised in the liquidation are insufficient for the payment of the debts and other liabilities and expenses of the winding up. This is a particularly harsh definition of insolvency since the value of the assets is arrived at not on the basis of a going concern but on the basis of break-up value. Moreover, the liabilities are going to be those shown on the company's normal balance sheet together with all other liabilities arising in the liquidation such as damages for breaches of contract, for example to employees, and the costs of the winding up, which are frequently substantial.

Knowledge that that there was no reasonable prospect of avoiding insolvent liquidation

The liability is incurred only if the person in question knew or should have known that there was no reasonable prospect that the company would avoid going into insolvent liquidation. This involves a measure of judgment. What standard of skill is expected of the director? Section 214(4) of IA 1986 states that the judgment should be reached on the facts which a director of the company ought to know or ascertain, the conclusions which he ought to reach and the steps which he ought to take having regard to both the general knowledge, skill and experience that may reasonably be expected of a person carrying out the functions carried out by that director in relation to the company and the general knowledge, skill and experience which the director himself has. There is no doubt that the courts will apply whichever of these two criteria are the higher. Thus, if the director is a qualified accountant, a high degree of commercial skill would be expected of him. If, on the other hand, the director is newly appointed and inexperienced in commerce, the standard of skill which may reasonably be expected of such a director would be that applied.

The section contains a defence. No order may be made against a director if the court is satisfied that the person in question took every step with a view to minimising the potential loss to the company's creditors that he ought to have taken. Taken literally, once again, this defence is extremely harsh to the directors in question. When the House of Lords was considering the provision during the debate on the Bill it removed the word 'every' and replaced it with the expression 'all reasonable'. When the Bill was returned to the House of Commons, however, 'all reasonable' was removed and replaced by 'every'. It will be appreciated that 'every' is incapable of any degree. 'Every' means 'every'. Once again the term 'minimise' is absolute. The defence does not refer to reducing, lessening or keeping down the liability to creditors. It refers to 'minimising' the loss.

Wrongful trading was considered by the court in the case of *Re Produce Marketing Consortium Ltd* [1989] BCLC 520.

CASE EXAMPLE 12.10

***Re Produce Marketing Consortium Ltd* [1989] BCLC 520**

It was found that the directors in the case had continued to trade even when the accounts showed that the company was insolvent. When he had presented his claim the liquidator had claimed over £300,000, this being the deficiency shown on the statement of affairs. Subsequently, the claim was reduced to £108,000, this being based on the losses incurred by the directors after they should have been aware of the situation. In the end Knox J found that the directors were liable for wrongful trading. They had shown unjustified optimism in continuing to trade when the accounts had clearly shown the company to be insolvent. Seven months prior to ceasing trading the auditor had given them a warning regarding the risk of personal liability. The award made was of £75,000 together with interest at 15 per cent from the date of liquidation. This figure was arrived by the court deciding the date on which the directors should have realised that an insolvent liquidation was inevitable and then calculating the further deficit incurred by the company from that date until the date of the liquidation. The order further provided that the award should go initially to repay the bank where the company had its overdraft and thereby reduce a personal guarantee given by one of the directors. The effect of this was that, since one of the directors had already given a personal guarantee of £50,000 to the bank, only an award beyond this figure would actually increase the director's personal liability in the liquidation. Finally, the judge said that although both directors were culpable, one was more so than the other and as a result he ordered that two-thirds of the liability should be borne by one director and one third by the other.

There have been very few cases through the courts on wrongful trading even though, when taken literally, its implications for directors are very serious. Nevertheless, there is clear evidence that liquidators are using it as a threat against directors to persuade them to reach settlements out of court in liquidations. In other words, it is being used to persuade directors voluntarily to pay some of their own funds over to the liquidator for the benefit of creditors of the company.

Having said this, there have been a number of recent decisions of the courts that have made recovery for wrongful trading more difficult. In *Lewis v Commissioners for Inland Revenue* [2000] EWCA 74 it was held that the costs for wrongful trading proceedings should be borne by the unsecured creditors rather than as part of the costs of the winding up and so be borne by the preferential creditors. In *Re Cubelock Ltd* [2001] BCC 523 it was held that it is not automatically wrongful trading merely because the directors know that the company is insolvent. Wrongful trading occurs only when the directors knew or should have known that an insolvent liquidation was inevitable. In *Re Continental Assurance Ltd* (2001 unreported) it was held that it was not wrongful trading if the directors, knowing that their company was in difficulties, took proper outside advice and followed such advice

5.3 Transactions defrauding creditors

In addition to all the above provisions, the liquidator must also consider a general provision against debt avoidance, in IA 1986 s. 423. In any case, where the court is satisfied that a person has entered into a transaction specifically to put assets beyond the reach of a person who is making or at some time may make a claim against him or are otherwise prejudicing the interests of such a person in relation to the claim which he is making or may make, then it may order that the position is restored to what it would have been had the transaction not been entered into, and to protect the interests of persons who are victims of the transaction.

Section 423 envisages such a transaction being entered into by a company in two situations.

1. Where it makes a gift or otherwise enters into a transaction on terms which provide for it to receive no consideration.
2. Where it enters into a transaction for a consideration the value of which is significantly less than the consideration actually provided by the company.

The remedies available when such a transaction is found to have been entered into are, for all purposes, the same as those available under s. 238 and s. 239 discussed above. There is a very considerable degree of overlap between s. 423 now being discussed and s. 238, transactions at an undervalue. The only significant differences between the two remedies are that under s. 423 there is no time limit whereas under s. 238 there is a time limit of two years leading up to the onset of insolvency and that in s. 238 there is no need to show any intention whereas in s. 423 the intention to put assets beyond the reach of creditors needs to be shown. The overlap is somewhat anomalous and there are many situations where either remedy might be used by a liquidator.

5.4 Summary remedy against delinquent directors

By IA 1986 s. 212, if it appears in the course of the winding up that a person who is or has been an officer of the company, or has acted in connection with the company as its liquidator, administrator or administrative receiver or has otherwise been involved with the company in its promotion or management, has misapplied any money or other property of the company, then the liquidator or the official receiver may apply for the conduct of that person to be examined. Another word used to describe such conduct is misfeasance. An application in this regard may also be made by any creditor or contributory of the company. If the conduct is established, the court may order that person either:

1. to repay or account for the money or property or any part of it together with interest at such rate as the court thinks just; or
2. to contribute such a sum to the company's assets by way of compensation in respect of the breach of duty as the court thinks fit.

An example of this arose in the case of *Re D'Jan of London Ltd*:

CASE EXAMPLE 12.11

***Re D'Jan of London Ltd* [1994] BCLC 561**

The company had suffered a serious fire. Because there had been errors in answers given to the fire insurance proposal form by a director, the insurers refused to make any payment. Because of this the company went into insolvent liquidation. The liquidator bought misfeasance proceedings against the director concerned. It was held that he was liable, the end result being that he had to pay damages to the liquidator for the benefit of the creditors generally.

TEST YOUR KNOWLEDGE 12.8

Explain five ways in which a liquidator can increase the amount of funds that he has available to distribute to creditors.

6 Contributories

As was seen above in considering who may petition for the commencement of the winding up of a company, a 'contributory' is any person who is liable to contribute to the assets of the company in the event of its being wound up. Every present and past member is liable to contribute to the assets of the company to any amount sufficient to pay its debts and liabilities together with the expenses of the winding up. Section 74 contains some qualifications on liability. For example, a past member is not liable to contribute if he has ceased to be a member for one year or more prior to the commencement of the winding up, nor is he liable to contribute in respect of any debt or liability of the company incurred after he ceased to be a member. The primary obligation to pay rests with the present members, but a past member may also be called upon to contribute if it appears to the court that the existing members are unable to satisfy the contributions required to be made by them. No contribution is required from any member exceeding the amount unpaid on those shares in respect of which he is liable as a past or present member.

By IA 1986 s. 148, in a compulsory winding up the court must settle a list of contributories as soon as possible after the making of a winding-up order. A similar obligation falls upon the liquidator in a voluntary winding up. The list is in two parts:

1 The 'A' list consists of the present members of the company holding unpaid or partly paid shares.
2 The 'B' list comprises persons who held those shares in the year prior to the commencement of the winding up.

Calls on contributories may only be made with the leave of the court if the company is in compulsory liquidation or the sanction of the committee of inspection where it is in voluntary liquidation.

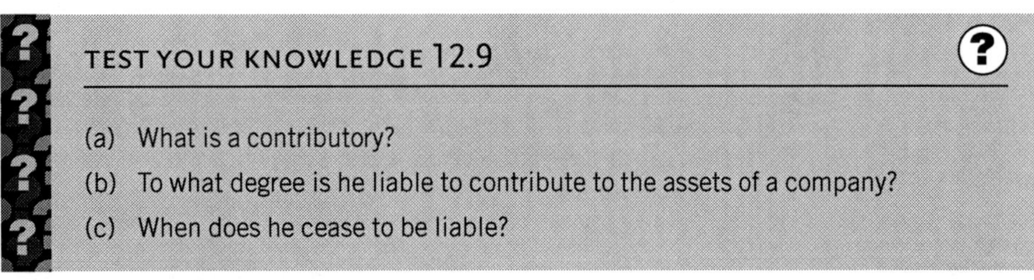
TEST YOUR KNOWLEDGE 12.9

(a) What is a contributory?
(b) To what degree is he liable to contribute to the assets of a company?
(c) When does he cease to be liable?

7 Distribution of assets

7.1 Secured creditors

secured creditor
A creditor who holds a secured debenture.

Generally a **secured creditor** will rely upon his security and not seek to prove in the winding up at all. If the security is of insufficient value to meet the liability of the company to the creditor, he has a number of options open to him. He may:

1 realise his security and prove as an unsecured creditor for any balance due to him;
2 value his security and prove as an unsecured creditor for any balance due; or
3 surrender his security and prove as an unsecured creditor for the entire debt.

7.2 Proof of debts

So long as the company is solvent, all debts may be proved by the respective creditors in the winding up. Thus, creditors may prove in respect of present or future debts, certain or contingent debts and liquidated or unliquidated debts. If the company is insolvent, debts which are present or future, certain or contingent may be proved except unliquidated damages arising other than by reason of breach of contract or breach of trust. Thus, the difference between the debts provable in a solvent and an insolvent winding up is mainly in respect of unliquidated damages in tort. In *Re Islington Metal & Plating Works Ltd* (1983) it was held that no tort claims may be proved in an insolvent winding up unless they are liquidated at the time. In other words, the person who claims to have been tortiously damaged by the company must have actually sued the company in tort and obtained judgement in his favour.

7.3 Order of application of assets

At the beginning of this text, when we were considering the case of *Salomon v Salomon & Co. Ltd* (see Chapter 1), we saw that on a winding up the debts of a company had to be paid in a certain order. In broad terms this is:

1 costs of the winding up;

2 fixed charges;
3 preferential debts;
4 floating charges; (see Chapter 7);
5 unsecured creditors;
6 return of surplus to members.

It is now necessary to look at this in a little more detail.

If the assets are insufficient to meet the liabilities of the company, the court may make an order for payment of the costs in such order of priority as it thinks just. Unless the court orders to the contrary, the order of priority is:

1 fees and expenses properly incurred in preserving, realising or getting in the assets;
2 the cost of the petition including the costs of those appearing on the petition whose costs are allowed by the court;
3 remuneration of any special manager;
4 the costs and expenses of any person who makes the company's statement of affairs;
5 the charges of a shorthand writer appointed to take an examination;
6 the disbursements of the liquidator;
7 the costs of any person properly employed by the liquidator;
8 the remuneration of the liquidator;
9 the expenses of the liquidation committee.

7.4 Secured creditors with a fixed charge

As has been said secured creditors with a fixed charge usually realise the security and discharge any debt owing to them out of the proceeds of sale. Any surplus they then hand over to the liquidator to be applied in the order of priority now being discussed. If the value of the fixed charge asset is insufficient to meet the secured debt, it is the costs of realisation which are met first. The secured creditor then takes the remainder of the realised monies in partial discharge of the debt owing to him. Any balance outstanding after this is claimed as an unsecured debt in the winding up.

7.5 Preferential debts

The next category of debts to be settled are the preferential debts. There are a number of preferential debts which will be discussed shortly in more detail. They include matters such as VAT, PAYE, National Insurance contributions and wages due to employees. The preferential debts are unsecured but rank well in advance of the other unsecured debts. If the assets are insufficient to meet the preferential debts in full then they abate in equal proportions. In other words the preferential creditors take a dividend of so many pence for each pound they are owed. The preferential debts include:

1 *PAYE owing by the company to the Inland Revenue:* These represent amounts deducted by the company from employees' emoluments paid during the period of 12 months preceding the relevant date. The term 'the relevant date' means the date of the appointment of a provisional liquidator or, if no such appointment has been made, the date of the winding-up order when the company is wound up. If the company is in voluntary liquidation, it refers to the date of the passing of the resolution. If the winding up follows immediately upon the discharge of an administration order, then it is the date of the making of the order.
2 *Debts due to Customs & Excise:* Any VAT which is referrable to the period of six months prior to the relevant date is a preferential debt. VAT falling outside this period is simply an unsecured debt. Certain other taxes owing to the Customs & Excise are also preferential. These are car tax which became due from the debtor within a period of 12 months prior to the relevant date, and also any general betting duty, bingo duty, pool betting duty or gaming licence due during that period.

3 *Social Security contributions*: All sums owing by the company in respect of Class I or Class II contributions under the Social Security Act 1975 are preferential. These are normal National Insurance deductions made by an employer from an employee's emoluments.
4 *Contributions to occupational pensions schemes*: Any sum which is owed by the company under Schedule 3 of the Social Security Pensions Act 1975 (Contributions to Occupational Pensions Schemes and State Scheme Pensions) are preferential.
5 *Remuneration of employees*: Any sum owing to an employee in respect of remuneration is preferential up to a limit of £800 or in respect of the four-month period preceding the relevant date, whichever is the greater. Added to this is the amount owed by way of accrued holiday remuneration in respect of any period of employment before the relevant date to a person whose employment by the company has been terminated whether before on or after that date.

7.6 Remuneration as a preferential debt

There are two particular points which should be noted in respect of remuneration as a preferential debt:

1 Directors as such are not employees. Thus directors' fees are not preferential. However, if a director is employed under a contract of service he is treated as an employee in respect of salary owing under the service agreement. In this regard he would be preferential up to the above limits. In other words, when considering emoluments being claimed by a director in a winding up it is important to distinguish carefully between fees owing to him as a director and salary owing to him as an employee.
2 Often when a company is in financial difficulties it seeks a bank loan in order to pay wages due to employees. Such a loan is itself treated as preferential up to the above limits (i.e. up to a maximum of £800 per employee). However, it must be paid from a separate bank account and be clearly distinguished from the normal borrowing of the company.

7.7 Floating charges

After the preferential creditors have been paid in full, the holders of any floating charge have a claim over assets on which the charge is secured. If there is more than one floating charge over the same assets, then they rank in the order of priority stated in Chapter 7.

7.8 Unsecured creditors

Any monies remaining at this stage are applied in paying the ordinary debts of the company. These also rank equally and abate in the same manner as the preferential debts.

7.9 Surplus

If when all of the above debts have been paid there are still monies over, the liquidator must ensure they are distributed among the contributories. By IA 1986 s. 154, a court order should be obtained to settle the rights of contributories.

In the case of a voluntary winding up, the liquidator will call a final meeting of the company or of its creditors for the purpose of obtaining his release. The effect of a release is to discharge him from any liability in respect of his acts or omissions while in office. In the case of a compulsory winding up, if the liquidator is a person other than the official receiver, he will call a final general meeting of the creditors for the purposes of obtaining his release. If the liquidator is the official receiver, his release is obtained by notifying the Secretary of State that for all practical purposes the winding up has been completed.

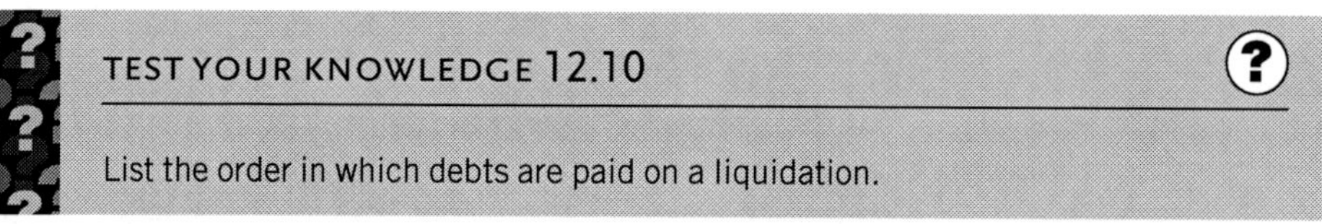

TEST YOUR KNOWLEDGE 12.10

List the order in which debts are paid on a liquidation.

8 Dissolution

8.1 Early dissolution of the company

If the company is in compulsory liquidation and the official receiver is in post as liquidator, it can happen that the assets of the company are insufficient to meet even the costs of the winding up. If this happens, then as long as the liquidator is satisfied that no further investigation of the company's affairs is necessary, he may apply to the Registrar of Companies for an early dissolution of the company. When he does this he must give 28 days' notice of his intention to seek an early dissolution to the creditors, contributories and any administrative receiver who may be in post.

8.2 Dissolution of the company

In a compulsory winding up, the liquidator gives notice to the Registrar of Companies that the final meeting of the creditors has been held and that he has vacated office. Alternatively, the official receiver gives notice that the winding up is complete. Once the notice has been given, there begins a period of three months at the end of which the dissolution of the company occurs automatically unless some interested party makes an application to the Secretary of State for the date to be deferred.

In the case of a voluntary winding up, the three-month period leading up to the dissolution of the company commences when the liquidator's final account and return is submitted to the Registrar of Companies. Once again an interested party can apply to the Secretary of State for the dissolution to be deferred.

8.3 Defunct companies

It sometimes occurs that the proprietors of a business simply stop trading without telling the Registrar of Companies. They may simply pay off the debts of the company out of available assets and not bother with a formal liquidation. If the Registrar of Companies has reasonable cause to believe that a company is not carrying on business or is not in operation he may initiate a procedure to strike the company off as defunct. The procedure is as follows:

1 The Registrar sends the company a letter by post inquiring whether the company is carrying on business or is in operation.
2 If he does not receive any answer to it within one month of sending the letter he will send within 14 days after the end of the month to the company by post a registered letter referring to the first letter and stating that no answer has been received and that if an answer is not received to the second letter within one month from its date, a notice will be published in the *Gazette* with a view to striking the company's name off the register.
3 If the Registrar receives an answer to the effect that the company is not carrying on business or does not within one month receive any answer he may publish in the *Gazette* and send to the company by post a notice that on the expiration of three months from the date of the notice the name of the company will be struck off the register and the company will be dissolved.
4 So long as the Registrar receives no notification that the company is trading during this period, he duly strikes the company off and publishes a notice in the *Gazette*. This has the effect of dissolving the company.

It should be noted that striking off in this way has no effect on any liability of any member of the company, and the company may still be wound up by an order of the court.

TEST YOUR KNOWLEDGE 12.11

What is the effect of the dissolution of a company?

CHAPTER SUMMARY

- A voluntary winding up is commenced by a resolution of the company's members. Once the resolution has been passed, the company must stop carrying on its business and, following the appointment of a liquidator, most of the directors' powers cease.
- If the company is solvent and is formally declared to be so by the directors, the winding up will be a members' voluntary; if the company is insolvent, it will be a creditors' voluntary.
- In a members' voluntary winding up, the liquidator will be appointed by the members in general meeting.
- In a creditor's winding up the appointment will be made by the creditors. The creditors may also appoint a liquidation committee to act with the liquidator.
- A liquidator in a voluntary winding up has wide powers to act for and in the name of the company without having to consult anyone. He may also exercise other powers, such as payment of any class of creditor in full, if he obtains the authority to do so from the court, or from the liquidation committee or from a meeting of the creditors.
- Compulsory winding up occurs when a company is put into liquidation by order of the court. There are a number of grounds for such an order, the most common of which is that the company is unable to pay its debts. Another ground is that the court considers that it would be just and equitable to wind the company up because, for example, the substratum of the company has disappeared or the company was formed for a fraudulent purpose.
- A petition for compulsory winding up may be presented by the company itself, or by its directors or a creditor, by a contributory, or by the Secretary of State, or by the official receiver. If the court grants the petition, the official receiver becomes the liquidator of the company until such time as another person may be appointed to the post. If no such appointment is made then the official receiver remains as the liquidator of the company.
- A liquidator's function is to call in the company's assets, realise them, and settle the company's liabilities in the prescribed order of priorities. The liquidator has the power to require any past or present officers of the company or certain other people to give such information about the company and its dealings as the liquidator requires.
- As well as collecting in the company's existing assets, the liquidator also has the power to apply to the court for an order to recover assets transferred under a transaction at an undervalue or by way of a preference or to vary the terms of an extortionate credit bargain into which the company has entered. He may also obtain an order requiring a party to any fraudulent trading to contribute to the assets of the company or for a contribution from a director who is liable for wrongful trading.

Companies Act 1985 Table A (as amended)

Regulations for management of a company limited by shares

INTERPRETATION

1. In these regulations:
   'the Act' means the Companies Act 1985 including any statutory modification or re-enactment thereof for the time being in force.
   'the articles' means the articles of the company.
   'clear days' in relation to the period of notice means that period excluding the day when the notice is given or deemed to be given and the day for which it is given or on which it is to take effect.
   'communication' means the same as in the Electronic Communications Act 2000.
   'electronic communication' means the same as in the Electronic Communications Act 2000.
   'executed' includes any mode of execution.
   'office' means the registered office of the company.
   'the holder' in relation to shares means the member whose name is entered in the register of members as the holder of the shares.
   'the seal' means the common seal of the company.
   'secretary' means the secretary of the company or any person appointed to perform the duties of the secretary of the company, including a joint, assistant or deputy secretary.
   'the United Kingdom' means Great Britain and Northern Ireland.

Unless the context otherwise requires, words or expressions contained in these regulations bear the same meaning as in the Act but excluding any statutory modification thereof not in force when these regulations become binding on the company.

SHARE CAPITAL

2. Subject to the provisions of the Act and without prejudice to the rights attached to any existing shares, any share may be issued with such rights or restrictions as the company may by ordinary resolution determine.

3. Subject to the provisions of the Act, shares may be issued which are to be redeemed or are to be held liable to be redeemed at the option of the company or the holder on such terms and in such manner as may be provided by the articles.

4. The company may exercise the powers of paying commissions conferred by the Act. Subject to the provisions of the Act, any such commissions may be satisfied by the payment of cash or by the allotment of fully or partly paid shares or partly in one way and partly in the other.

5. Except as required by law, no person shall be recognised by the company as holding a share upon any trust and (except as otherwise provided by the articles or by law) the company shall not be bound by or recognise any interest in any share except an absolute right to the entirety thereof in the holder.

SHARE CERTIFICATES

6. Every member, upon becoming the holder of any shares, shall be entitled without payment to one certificate for all the shares of each class held by him (and, upon transferring part of his holding of shares of any class, to a certificate for the balance of such holding) or several certificates each for one or more of his shares upon payment for every certificate after the first of such reasonable sum as the directors may determine. Every certificate shall be sealed with the seal and shall specify the number, class and respective amounts paid thereon. The company shall not be bound to issue more than one certificate for shares held jointly by several persons and delivery of a certificate to one joint holder shall be sufficient delivery to all of them.

7. If a share certificate is defaced, worn-out, lost or destroyed, it may be renewed on such terms (if any) as to evidence and indemnity and payment of the expenses reasonably incurred by the company in investigating evidence as the directors may determine but otherwise free of charge, and (in the case of defacement or wearing-out) on delivery up of the old certificate.

LIEN

8. The company shall have a first and paramount lien on every share (not being a fully paid share) for all moneys (whether presently payable or not) payable at a fixed time or called in respect of that share. The directors may at any time declare any share to be wholly or in part exempt from the provisions of this regulation. The company's lien on a share shall extend to any amount payable in respect of it.

9. The company may sell in such manner as the directors determine any shares on which the company has a lien if a sum in respect of which the lien exists is presently payable and is not paid within fourteen clear days after notice has been given to the holder of the share or to the person entitled to it in consequence of the death or bankruptcy of the holder, demanding payment and stating that if the notice is not complied with the shares may be sold.

10. To give effect to a sale the directors may authorise some person to execute an instrument of transfer of the shares sold to, or in accordance with the directions of, the purchaser. The title of the transferee to the shares shall not be affected by any irregularity in or invalidity of the proceedings in reference to the sale.

11. The net proceeds of the sale, after payment of the costs, shall be applied in payment of so much of the sum for which the lien exists as is presently payable, and any residue shall (upon surrender to the company for cancellation of the certificate for the shares sold and subject to a like lien for any moneys not pres-

ently payable as existed upon the shares before the sale) be paid to the person entitled to the shares at the date of the sale.

CALLS ON SHARES AND FORFEITURE

12. Subject to the terms of allotment, the directors may make calls upon the members in respect of any moneys unpaid on their shares (whether in respect of nominal value or premium) and each member shall (subject to receiving at least fourteen clear days' notice specifying when and where payment is to be made) pay to the company as required by the notice the amount called on his shares. A call may be required to be paid by instalments. A call may, before receipt by the company of any sum due thereunder, be revoked in whole or part and payment of a call may be postponed in whole or part. A person upon whom a call is made shall remain liable for calls made upon him notwithstanding the subsequent transfer of the shares in respect whereof the call was made.

13. A call shall be deemed to have been made at the time when the resolution of the directors authorising the call was passed.

14. The joint holders of a share shall be jointly and severally liable to pay all calls in respect thereof.

15. If a call remains unpaid after it has become due and payable the person from whom it is due and payable shall pay interest on the amount unpaid from the day it became due and payable until it is paid at the rate fixed by the terms of allotment of the share or in the notice of the call or, if no rate is fixed, at the appropriate rate (as defined by the Act) but the directors may waive payment of the interest wholly or in part.

16. An amount payable in respect of a share on allotment or at any fixed date, whether in respect of nominal value or premium or as an instalment of a call, shall be deemed to be a call and if it is not paid the provisions of the articles shall apply as if the amount had become due and payable by virtue of a call.

17. Subject to the terms of allotment, the directors may make arrangements on the issue of shares for a difference between the holders in the amounts and times of payment of calls on their shares.

18. If a call remains unpaid after it has become due and payable the directors may give to the person from whom it is due not less than fourteen clear days' notice requiring payment of the amount unpaid together with any interest which may have accrued. The notice shall name the place where payment is to be made and shall state that if the notice is not complied with the shares in respect of which the call was made will be liable to be forfeited.

19. If the notice is not complied with any share in respect of which it was given may, before the payment required by the notice has been made, be forfeited by a resolution of the directors and the forfeiture shall include all dividends or other moneys payable in respect of the forfeited shares and not paid before the forfeiture.

20. Subject to the provisions of the Act, a forfeited share may be sold, re-allotted or otherwise disposed of on such terms and in such manner as the directors determine either to the person who was before the forfeiture the holder or to any other person and at any time before sale, re-allotment or other disposition, the forfeiture may be cancelled on such terms as the directors think fit. Where for the purposes of its disposal a forfeited share is to be transferred to any person the directors may authorise some person to execute an instrument of transfer of the shares to that person.

21. A person any of whose shares have been forfeited shall cease to be a member in respect of them and shall surrender to the company for cancellation the certificate for the shares forfeited but shall remain liable to the company for all moneys which at the date of forfeiture were presently payable by him to the company in respect of those shares with interest at the rate at which interest was payable on those moneys before the forfeiture or, if no interest was so payable, at the appropriate rate (as defined by the Act) from the date of forfeiture until payment but the directors may waive payment wholly or in part or enforce payment without any allowance for the value of the shares at the time of forfeiture or for any consideration received on their disposal.

22. A statutory declaration by a director or the secretary that a share has been forfeited on a specified date shall be conclusive evidence of the facts stated in it as against all persons claiming to be entitled to the share and the declaration shall (subject to the execution of an instrument of transfer if necessary) constitute a good title to the share and the person to whom the share is disposed of shall not be bound to see to the application of the consideration, if any, nor shall his title to the share be affected by any irregularity in or invalidity of the proceedings in reference to the forfeiture or disposal of the share.

TRANSFER OF SHARES

23. The instrument of transfer of a share may be in any usual form or in any other form which the directors may approve and shall be executed by or on behalf of the transferor and, unless the share is fully paid, by or on behalf of the transferee.

24. The directors may refuse to register the transfer of a share which is not fully paid to a person of whom they do not approve and they may refuse to register the transfer of a share on which the company has a lien. They may also refuse to register a transfer unless:
(a) it is lodged at the office or at such other place as the directors may appoint and is accompanied by the certificate for the shares to which it relates and such other evidence as the directors may reasonably require to show the right of the transferor to make the transfer;
(b) it is in respect of only one class of shares; and
(c) it is in favour of not more than four transferees.

25. If the directors refuse to register a transfer of a share, they shall within two months after the date on which the transfer was lodged with the company send to the transferee notice of the refusal.

26. The registration of transfers of shares or of transfers of any class of shares may be suspended at such times and for such periods (not exceeding thirty days in any year) as the directors may determine.

27. No fee shall be charged for the registration of any instrument of transfer or other document relating to or affecting the title to any share.

28. The company shall be entitled to retain any instrument of transfer which is registered, but any instrument of transfer which the directors refuse to register shall be returned to the person lodging it when notice of the refusal is given.

TRANSMISSION OF SHARES

29. If a member dies the survivor or survivors where he was a joint holder, and his personal representatives where he was a sole holder or the only survivor of joint holders, shall be the persons recognised by the company as having any title to his interest; but nothing herein contained shall release the estate of a deceased member from any liability in respect of any share which had been jointly held by him.

30. A person becoming entitled to a share in consequence of the death or bankruptcy of a member may, upon such evidence being produced as the directors may properly require, elect either to become the holder of the share or to have some other person nominated by him registered as the transferee. If he elects to become the holder he shall give notice to the company to that effect. If he elects to have another person registered he shall execute an instrument of transfer of the share to that person. All the articles relating o the transfer of shares shall apply to the notice or instrument of transfer as if it were an instrument of transfer executed by the member and the death or bankruptcy of the member had not occurred.

31. A person becoming entitled to a share in consequence of the death or bankruptcy of a member shall have the rights to which he would be entitled if he were the holder of the share, except that he shall not, before being registered as the holder of the share, be entitled in respect of it to attend or vote at any meeting of the company or at any separate meeting of the holders of any class of shares in the company.

ALTERATION OF SHARE CAPITAL

32. The company may by ordinary resolution:

(a) increase its share capital by new shares of such amount as the resolution prescribes;

(b) consolidate and divide all or any of its share capital into shares of larger amount than its existing shares;

(c) subject to the provisions of the Act, sub-divide its shares, or any of them, into shares of smaller amount and the resolution may determine that, as between the shares resulting from the sub-division, any of them may have any preference or advantage as compared with the others; and

(d) cancel shares which, at the date of the passing of the resolution, have not been taken or agreed to be taken by any person and diminish the amount of its share capital by the amount of the shares so cancelled.

33. Whenever as a result of a consolidation of shares any members would become entitled to fractions of a share, the directors may, on behalf of those members, sell the shares representing the fractions for the best price reasonably obtainable to any person (including, subject to the provisions of the Act, the company) and distribute the net proceeds of sale in due proportion among those members, and the directors may authorise some person to execute an instrument of transfer of the shares to, or in accordance with the directions of, the purchaser. The transferee shall not be bound to see to the application of the purchase money nor shall his title to the shares be affected by any irregularity in or invalidity of the proceedings in reference to the sale.

34. Subject to the provisions of the Act, the company may by special resolution reduce its share capital, any capital redemption reserve and any share premium account in any way.

PURCHASE OF OWN SHARES

35. Subject to the provisions of the Act, the company may purchase its own shares (including any redeemable shares) and, if it is a private company, make a payment in respect of the redemption or purchase of its own shares otherwise than out of distributable profits of the company or the proceeds of a fresh issue of shares.

GENERAL MEETINGS

36. All general meetings other than annual general meetings shall be called extraordinary general meetings.

37. The directors may call general meetings and, on the requisition of members pursuant to the provisions of the Act, shall forthwith proceed to convene an extraordinary general meeting for a date not later than eight weeks after receipt of the requisition. If there are not within the United Kingdom sufficient directors to call a general meeting, any director or any member of the company may call a general meeting.

NOTICE OF GENERAL MEETINGS

38. An annual general meeting and an extraordinary general meeting called for the passing of a special resolution or a resolution appointing a person as a director shall be called by at least twenty-one clear days' notice. All other extraordinary general meetings shall be called by at least fourteen clear days' notice but a general meeting may be called by shorter notice if it is so agreed:

(a) in the case of an annual general meeting, by all the members entitled to attend and vote thereat; and

(b) in the case of any other meeting by a majority in number of the members having a right to attend and vote being a majority together holding not less than ninety-five per cent in the nominal value of the shares giving that right.
The notice shall specify the time and place of the meeting and the general nature of the business to be transacted and, in the case of an annual general meeting, shall specify the meeting as such.
Subject to the provisions of the articles and to any restriction imposed on any shares, the notice shall be given to all members, to all persons entitled to a share in consequence of the death or bankruptcy of a member and to the directors and auditors.

39. The accidental omission to give notice of a meeting to, or the non-receipt of notice of a meeting by, any person entitled to receive notice shall not invalidate the proceedings at that meeting.

PROCEEDINGS AT GENERAL MEETINGS

40. No business shall be transacted at any meeting unless a quorum is present. Two persons entitled to vote upon the business to be transacted, each being a member or a proxy for a member or a duly authorised representative of a corporation, shall be a quorum.

41. If such a quorum is not present within half an hour from the time appointed for the meeting, or if during a meeting such a quorum ceases to be present, the meeting shall stand adjourned to the same day in the next week at the same time and place or to such time and place as the directors may determine.

42. The chairman, if any, of the board of directors or in his absence some other director nominated by the directors shall preside as chairman of the meeting, but if neither the chairman nor any such other director (if any) be present within fifteen minutes after the time appointed for holding the meeting and willing to act, the directors present shall elect one of their number to be chairman and, if there is only one director present and willing to act, he shall be chairman.

43. If no director is willing to act as chairman, or if no director is present within fifteen minutes after the time appointed for holding the meeting, the members present and entitled to vote shall choose one of their number to be chairman.

44. A director shall, notwithstanding that he is not a member, be entitled to attend and speak at any general meeting and at any separate meeting of the holders of any class of shares in the company.

45. The chairman may, with the consent of a meeting at which a quorum is present (and shall if so directed by the meeting), adjourn the meeting from time to time and from place to place, but no business shall be transacted at an adjourned meeting other than that business which might properly have been transacted at the meeting had the adjournment not taken place. When a meeting is adjourned for fourteen days or more, at least seven days' notice shall be given specifying the time and place of the adjourned meeting and the general nature of the business to be transacted. Otherwise it shall not be necessary to give any such notice.

46. A resolution put to the vote of a meeting shall be decided on a show of hands unless before, or on the declaration of the result of, the show of hands a poll is duly demanded. Subject to the provisions of the Act, a poll may be demanded:

(a) by the chairman; or

(b) by at least two members having the right to vote at the meeting; or

(c) by a member or members representing not less than one-tenth of the total voting rights of all the members having the right to vote at the meeting; or

(d) by a member or members holding shares conferring a right to vote at the meeting being shares on which an aggregate sum has been paid up equal to not less than one-tenth of the total sum paid up on all the shares conferring that right;

and a demand by a person as proxy for a member shall be the same as a demand by the member.

47. Unless a poll is duly demanded a declaration by the chairman that a resolution has been carried unanimously, or by a particular majority, or lost, or not carried by a particular majority and an entry to that effect in the minutes of the meeting shall be conclusive evidence of the fact without proof of the number or proportion of the votes recorded in favour or against the resolution.

48. The demand for a poll may, before the poll is taken, be withdrawn but only with the consent of the chairman and a demand so withdrawn shall not be taken to have invalidated the result of a show of hands declared before the demand was made.

49. A poll shall be taken as the chairman directs and he may appoint scrutineers (who need not be members) and fix a time and place for declaring the result of the poll. The result of the poll shall be deemed to be the resolution of the meeting at which the poll was demanded.

50. In the case of an equality of votes, whether on a show of hands or on a poll, the chairman shall be entitled to a casting vote in addition to any other vote he may have.

51. A poll demanded on the election of a chairman or on a question of adjournment shall be taken forthwith. A poll demanded on any other question shall be taken either forthwith or at such time and place as the chairman directs not being more than thirty days after the poll is demanded. The demand for a poll shall not prevent the continuance of a meeting for the transaction of any business other than the question on which the poll was demanded. If a poll is demanded before the declaration of the result of a show of hands and the demand is duly withdrawn, the meeting shall continue as if the demand had not been made.

52. No notice need be given of a poll not taken forthwith if the time and place at which it is to be taken are announced at the meeting at which it is demanded. In any other case at least seven clear days' notice shall be given specifying the time and place at which the poll is to be taken.

53. A resolution in writing executed by or on behalf of each member who would have been entitled to vote upon it if it had been proposed at a general meeting at which he was present shall be as effectual as if it had been passed at a general meeting duly convened and held and may consist of several instruments in the like form executed by or on behalf of one or more members.

VOTES OF MEMBERS

54. Subject to any rights or restrictions attached to any shares, on a show of hands every member who (being an individual) is present in person or (being a corporation) present by a duly authorised representative, not being himself a member entitled to vote, shall have one vote and on a poll every member shall have one vote for every share of which he is the holder.

55. In the case of joint holders the vote of the senior who tenders a vote, whether in person or by proxy, shall be accepted to the exclusion of the votes of the other joint holders; and seniority shall be determined by the order in which the names of the holders stand in the register of members.

56. A member in respect of whom an order has been made by any court having jurisdiction (whether in the UK or elsewhere) in matters concerning mental disorder may vote, whether on a show of hands or on a poll, by his receiver, curator bonis or other person authorised in that behalf appointed by that court, and any such receiver, curator bonis or other person may, on a poll, vote by proxy. Evidence to the satisfaction of the directors of the authority of the person claiming to exercise the right to vote shall be deposited at the office, or at such other place as is specified in accordance with the articles for the deposit of instruments of proxy, not less than 48 hours before the time appointed for holding the meeting or adjourned meeting at which the right to vote is to be exercised and in default the right to vote shall not be exercisable.

57. No member shall vote at any general meeting or at any separate meeting of the holders of any class of shares in the company, either in person or by proxy, in respect of any share held by him unless all moneys presently payable by him in respect of that share have been paid.

58. No objection shall be raised to the qualification of any voter except at the meeting or adjourned meeting at which the vote objected to is tendered, and every vote not disallowed at the meeting shall be valid. Any objection made in due time shall be referred to the chairman whose decision shall be final and conclusive.

59. On a poll votes may be given either personally or by proxy. A member may appoint more than one proxy to attend on the same occasion.

60. The appointment of a proxy shall be executed by or on behalf of the appointor and shall be in the following form (or in a form as near thereto as circumstances allow or in any other form which is usual or which the directors may approve).

' PLC/Limited

I/We, , of , being a member/members of the above-named company, hereby appoint of , or failing him, of , as my/our proxy to vote in my/our name[s] and on my/our behalf at the annual/extraordinary general meeting of the company to be held on 19 , and at any adjournment thereof.

Signed on 19 .'

61. Where it is desired to afford members an opportunity of instructing the proxy how he shall act the appointment of a proxy shall be in the following form (or in a form as near thereto as circumstances allow or in any other form which is usual or which the directors may approve):

' PLC/Limited

I/We, , of , being a member/members of the above-named company, hereby appoint of , or failing him, of , as my/our proxy to vote in my/our name[s] and on my/our behalf at the annual/extraordinary general meeting of the company to be held on 19 , and at any adjournment thereof.

This form is to be used in respect of the resolutions mentioned below as follows:

Resolution No 1 *for *against

Resolution No 2 *for *against.

*Strike out whichever is not desired.

Unless otherwise instructed, the proxy may vote as he thinks fit or abstain from voting.

Signed this day of 19 .'][1]

62. The appointment of a proxy and any authority under which it is executed or a copy of such authority certified notarially or in some other way approved by the directors may:

(a) in the case of an instrument in writing, be deposited at the office or such other place within the United Kingdom as is specified in the notice convening the meeting or in any instrument of proxy sent out by the company in relation to the meeting not less than 48 hours before the time for holding the meeting or adjourned meeting at which the person named in the instrument proposes to vote; or

(aa) in the case of an appointment contained in an electronic communication, where an address has been specified for the purpose of receiving electronic communications:

(i) in the notice convening the meeting, or

(ii) in any instrument of proxy sent out by the company in relation to the meeting, or

(iii) in any invitation contained in an electronic communication to appoint a proxy issued by the company in relation to the meeting,

be received at such address not less than 48 hours before the time for holding the meeting or adjourned meeting at which the person named in the appointment proposes to vote;

(b) in the case of a poll taken more than 48 hours after it is demanded, be deposited or received as aforesaid after the poll has been demanded and not less than 24 hours before the time appointed for the taking of the poll; or

(c) where the poll is not taken forthwith but is taken not more than 48 hours after it was demanded, be delivered at the meeting at which the poll was demanded to the chairman or to the secretary or to any director;

and an appointment of proxy which is not deposited, delivered or received in a manner so permitted shall be invalid. In this regulation and the next, Aaddress@, in relation to electronic communications, includes any number or address used for the purposes of such communications.

63. A vote given or poll demanded by proxy or by the duly authorised representative of a corporation shall be valid notwithstanding the previous determination of the authority of the person voting or demanding a poll unless notice of the determination was received by the company at the office or at such other place at which the instrument of proxy was duly deposited or, where the appointment of the proxy was contained in an electronic communication, at the address at which the appointment was duly received before the commencement of the meeting or adjourned meeting at which the vote is given or the poll demanded or (in the case of a poll taken otherwise than on the same day as the meeting or adjourned meeting) the time appointed for taking the poll.

NUMBER OF DIRECTORS

64. Unless otherwise determined by ordinary resolution, the number of directors (other than alternate directors) shall not be subject to any maximum but shall be not less than two.

ALTERNATE DIRECTORS

65. Any director (other than an alternate director) may appoint any other director, or any other person approved by resolution of the directors and willing to act, to be an alternate director and may remove from office an alternate director so appointed by him.

66. An alternate director shall be entitled to receive notice of all meetings of directors and of all meetings of committees of directors of which his appointor is a member, to attend and vote at any such meeting at which the director appointing him is not personally present, and generally to perform all the functions of his appointor as a director in his absence but shall not be entitled to receive any remuneration from the company for his services as an alternate director. But it shall not be necessary to give notice of such a meeting to alternate director who is absent from the United Kingdom.

67. An alternate director shall cease to be an alternate director if his appointor ceases to be a director; but if a director retires by rotation or otherwise but is reappointed or deemed to have been reappointed at the meeting at which he retires, any appointment of an alternate director made by him which was in force immediately prior to his retirement shall continue after his reappointment.

68. Any appointment or removal of an alternate director shall be by notice to the company signed by the director making or revoking the appointment or in any other manner approved by the directors.

69. Save as otherwise provided in the articles, an alternate director shall be deemed for all purposes to be a director and shall alone be responsible for his own acts and defaults and he shall not be deemed to be the agent of the director appointing him.

POWERS OF DIRECTORS

70. Subject to the provisions of the Act, the Memorandum and the Articles and to any directions given by special resolution, the business of the company shall be managed by the directors who may exercise all the powers of the company. No alteration of the Memorandum or Articles and no such direction shall invalidate any prior act of the directors which would have been valid if that alteration had not been made or that direction had not been given. The powers given by this regulation shall not be limited by any special power given to the directors by the Articles and a meeting of directors at which a quorum is present may exercise all powers exercisable by the directors.

71. The directors may, by power of attorney or otherwise, appoint any person to be the agent of the company for such purposes and on such conditions as they determine, including authority for the agent to delegate all or any of his powers.

DELEGATION OF DIRECTORS' POWERS

72. The directors may delegate any of their powers to any committee consisting of one or more directors. They may also delegate to any managing director or any director holding any other executive office such of their powers as they consider desirable to be exercised by him. Any such delegation may be made subject to any conditions the directors may impose, and either collaterally with or to the exclusion of their own powers and may be revoked or altered. Subject to any such conditions, the proceedings of a committee with two or more members shall be governed by the articles regulating the proceedings of directors so far as they are capable of applying.

APPOINTMENT AND RETIREMENT OF DIRECTORS

73. At the first annual general meeting all the directors shall retire from office, and at every subsequent annual general meeting one-third of the directors who are subject to retirement by rotation or, if their number is not three or a multiple of three, the number nearest to one third shall retire from office; but, if there is only one director who is subject to retirement by rotation, he shall retire.

74. Subject to the provisions of the Act, the directors to retire by rotation shall be those who have served longest in office since their last appointment or reappointment, but as between persons who became or were last reappointed directors on the same day those to retire shall (unless they otherwise agree among themselves) be determined by lot.

75. If the company, at the meeting at which a director retires by rotation, does not fill the vacancy the retiring director shall, if willing to act, be deemed to have been reappointed unless at the meeting it is resolved not to fill the vacancy or unless a resolution for the reappointment of the director is put to the meeting and lost.

76. No person other than a director retiring by rotation shall be appointed or reappointed a director at any general meeting unless:

(a) he is recommended by the directors; or

(b) not less than fourteen nor more than thirty-five clear days before the date appointed for the meeting, notice executed by a member qualified to vote at the meeting has been given to the company of the intention to propose that person for appointment or reappointment stating the particulars which would, if he were so appointed or reappointed, be required to be included in the company's register of directors together with notice executed by that person of his willingness to be appointed or reappointed.

77. Not less than seven nor more than twenty-eight clear days before the date appointed for holding a general meeting notice shall be given to all who are entitled to receive notice of the meeting of any person (other than a director retiring by rotation at the meeting) who is recommended by the directors for appointment or reappointment as a director at the meeting or in respect of whom notice has been duly given to the company of the intention to propose him at the meeting for appointment or reappointment as a director. The notice shall give particulars of that person which would, if he were so appointed or reappointed, be required to be included in the company's register of directors.

78. Subject as aforesaid, the company may by ordinary resolution appoint a person who is willing to act to be a director either to fill a vacancy or as an additional director and may also determine the rotation in which any additional directors are to retire.

79. The directors may appoint a person who is willing to act to be director, either to fill a vacancy or as an additional director, provided that the appointment does not cause the number of directors to exceed the number fixed by or in accordance with the Articles as the maximum number of directors. A director so appointed shall hold office only until the next following annual general meeting and shall not be taken into account in determining the directors who are to retire by rotation at the meeting. If not reappointed at such annual general meeting, he shall vacate office at the conclusion thereof.

80. Subject as aforesaid, a director who retires at an annual general meeting may, if willing to act, be reappointed. If he is not reappointed, he shall retain office until the meeting appoints someone in his place, or if it does not do so, until the end of the meeting.

DISQUALIFICATION AND REMOVAL OF DIRECTORS

81. The office of director shall be vacated if:

(a) he ceases to be a director by virtue of any provision of the Act or becomes prohibited by law from being a director; or

(b) he becomes bankrupt or makes any arrangement or composition with his creditors generally; or

(c) he is, or may be, suffering from mental disorder and either:

(i) he is admitted to hospital in pursuance of an application for treatment under the Mental Health Act 1983 or, in Scotland, an application for admission under the Mental Health (Scotland) Act 1960, or

(ii) an order is made by a court having jurisdiction (whether in the United Kingdom or elsewhere) in matters concerning mental disorder for his detention or for the appointment of a receiver, curator bonis or other person to exercise powers with respect to his property or affairs; or

(d) he resigns his office by notice to the company; or

(e) he shall for more than six consecutive months have been absent without permission of the directors from meetings of the directors held during that period and the directors resolve that his office be vacated.

REMUNERATION OF DIRECTORS

82. The directors shall be entitled to such remuneration as the company may by ordinary resolution determine and, unless the resolution provides otherwise, the remuneration shall be deemed to accrue from day to day.

DIRECTORS' EXPENSES

83. The directors may be paid all travelling, hotel, and other expenses properly incurred by them in connection with their attendance at meetings of directors or committees of directors or general meetings or separate meetings of the holders of any class of shares or of debentures of the company or otherwise connection with the discharge of their duties.

DIRECTORS' APPOINTMENTS AND INTERESTS

84. Subject to the provisions of the Act, the directors may appoint one or more of their number to the office of managing director or to any other executive office under the company and may enter into an agreement or arrangement with any director for his employment by the company or for the provision by him of any services outside the scope of the ordinary duties of a director. Any such appointment, agreement or arrangement may be made on such terms as the directors determine and they may remunerate any such director for his services as they think fit. Any appointment of a director to an executive office shall terminate if he ceases to be a director but without prejudice to any claim for damages for breach of the contract of service between the director and the company. A managing director and a director holding any other executive office shall not be subject to retirement by rotation.

85. Subject to the provisions of the Act, and provided that he has disclosed to the directors the nature and extent of any material interest of his, a director notwithstanding his office:

(a) may be a party to, or otherwise interested in, any transaction or arrangement with the company or in which the company is otherwise interested;

(b) may be a director or other officer of, or employed by, or party to any transaction or arrangement with, or otherwise interested in, any body corporate promoted by the company or in which the company is otherwise interested; and

(c) shall not, by reason of his office, be accountable to the company for any benefit which he derives from any such office or employment or from any such transaction or arrangement or from any interest in any such body corporate and no such transaction or arrangement shall be liable to be avoided on the ground of any such interest or benefit.

86. For the purposes of regulation 85:

(a) a general notice given to the directors that a director is to be regarded as having an interest of the nature and extent specified in the notice in any transactions or arrangement in which a specified person or class of persons is interested shall be deemed to be a disclosure that the director has an interest in any such transaction of the nature and extent so specified; and

(b) an interest of which a director has no knowledge and of which it is unreasonable to expect him to have knowledge shall not be treated as an interest of his.

DIRECTOR'S GRATUITIES AND PENSIONS

87. The directors may provide benefits, whether by payment of gratuities or pensions or by insurance or otherwise, for any director who has held but no longer holds any executive office or employment with the company or with any body corporate which is or has been a subsidiary of the company or a predecessor in business of the company or of any such subsidiary, and for any member of his family (including a spouse and a former spouse) or any person who is or was dependent upon him, and may (as well before as after he ceases to hold such office or employment) contribute to any fund and pay premiums for the purchase of any such benefit.

PROCEEDINGS OF DIRECTORS

88. Subject to the provisions of the Articles, the directors may regulate their proceedings as they think fit. A director may, and the secretary at the request of a director shall, call a meeting of the directors. It shall not be necessary to give notice of a meeting to a director who is absent from the United Kingdom. Questions arising at a meeting shall be decided by a majority of votes. In the case of an equality of votes, the chairman shall have a second or casting vote. A director who is also an alternate director shall be entitled in the absence of his appointor to a separate vote on behalf of his appointor in addition to his own vote.

89. The quorum for the transaction of business of the directors may be fixed by the directors and unless so fixed at any other number shall be two. A person who holds office only as an alternate director shall, if his appointor is not present, be counted in the quorum.

90. The continuing directors or a sole continuing director may act notwithstanding any vacancies in their number, but, if the number of directors is less than the number fixed as the quorum, the continuing directors or director may act only for the purpose of filling vacancies or of calling a general meeting.

91. The directors may appoint one of their number to be the chairman of the board of directors and may at any time remove him from that office. Unless he is unwilling to do so, the director so appointed shall preside at every meeting of directors at which he is present. But if there is no director holding that office, or if the director holding it is unwilling to preside or is not present within five minutes after the time appointed for the meeting, the directors present may appoint one of their number to be chairman of the meeting.

92. All acts done by a meeting of directors, or of a committee of directors, or by a person acting as a director shall, notwithstanding that it be afterwards discovered that there was a defect in the appointment of any director or that any of them were disqualified from holding office, or had vacated office, or were not entitled to vote, be as valid as if every such person had been duly appointed and was qualified and had continued to be a director and had been entitled to vote.

93. A resolution signed in writing by all the directors entitled to receive notice of a meeting of directors or of a committee of directors shall be as valid and effectual as if it had been passed at a meeting of directors or (as the case may be) a committee of directors duly convened and held and may consist of several documents in the like form each signed by one or more directors; but a resolution signed by an alternate director need not also be signed by his appointor and, if it is signed by a director who has appointed an alternate director, it need not be signed by the alternate in that capacity.

94. Save as otherwise provided by the articles, a director shall not vote at a meeting of directors or a committee of directors on any resolution concerning a matter in which he has, directly or indirectly, an interest or duty which is material and which conflicts or may conflict with the interests of the company unless his interest or duty arises only because the case falls within one or more of the following paragraphs:

(a) the resolution relates to the giving to him of a guarantee, security, or indemnity in respect of money lent to, or an obligation incurred by him for the benefit of, the company or any of its subsidiaries;

(b) the resolution relates to the giving to a third party of a guarantee, security, or indemnity in respect of an obligation the company or any of its subsidiaries for which the director has assumed responsibility in whole or in part and whether alone or jointly with others under a guarantee or indemnity or by the giving of security;

(c) his interest arises by virtue of his subscribing or agreeing to subscribe for any shares, debentures or other securities of the company or any of its subsidiaries, or by virtue of his being, or intending to become, a participant in the underwriting or sub-underwriting of an offer of any such shares, debentures or other securities by the company or any of its subsidiaries for subscription, purchase or exchange;

(d) the resolution relates in any way to a retirement benefits scheme which has been approved, or is conditional upon approval, by the Board of Inland Revenue for taxation purposes.

For the purposes of this regulation, an interest of a person who is, for any purpose of the Act (excluding any statutory modification thereof not in force when this regulation becomes binding on the company), connected with a director shall be treated as an interest of the director and, in relation to an alternate director, an interest of his appointor shall be treated as an interest of the alternate director without prejudice to any interest which the alternate director has otherwise.

95. A director shall not be counted in the quorum present at a meeting in relation to a resolution on which he is not entitled to vote.

96. The company may by ordinary resolution suspend or relax to any extent, either generally or in respect of any particular matter, any provision of the articles prohibiting a director from voting at a meeting of directors or of a committee of directors.

97. Where proposals are under consideration concerning the appointment of two or more directors to offices or employments with the company or any body corporate in which the company is interested the proposals may be divided and considered in relation to each director separately and (provided he is not for another reason precluded from voting) each of the directors concerned shall be entitled to vote and be counted in the quorum in respect of each resolution except that concerning his own appointment.

98. If a question arises at a meeting of directors or of a committee of directors as to the right of a director to vote, the question may, before the conclusion of the meeting, be referred to the chairman of the meeting and his ruling in relation to any director other than himself shall be final and conclusive.

SECRETARY

99. Subject to the provisions of the Act, the secretary shall be appointed by the directors for such term, at such remuneration and upon such conditions as they may think fit; and any secretary so appointed may be removed by them.

MINUTES

100. The directors shall cause minutes to be made in books kept for the purpose:
(a) of all appointments of officers made by the directors; and
(b) of all proceedings at meetings of the company, of the holders of any class of shares in the company, and of the directors, and of committees of directors, including the names of the directors present at each such meeting.

THE SEAL

101. The seal shall only be used by the authority of the directors or of a committee of directors authorised by the directors. The directors may determine who shall sign any instrument to which the seal is affixed and unless otherwise so determined it shall be signed by a director and by the secretary or by a second director.

DIVIDENDS

102. Subject to the provisions of the Act, the company may by ordinary resolution declare dividends in accordance with the respective rights of members, but no dividend shall exceed the amount recommended by the directors.

103. Subject to the provisions of the Act, the directors may pay interim dividends if it appears to them that they are justified by the profits of the company available for distribution. If the share capital is divided into different classes, the directors may pay interim dividends on shares which confer deferred or non-preferred rights with regard to dividend as well as on shares which confer preferential rights with regard to dividend, but no interim dividend shall be paid on shares carrying deferred or non-preferred rights if, at the time of payment, any preferential dividend is in arrear. The directors may also pay at intervals settled by them any dividend payable at a fixed rate if it appears to them that the profits available for distribution justify the payment. Provided the directors act in good faith they shall not incur any liability to the holders of shares conferring preferred rights for any loss they may suffer by the lawful payment of an interim dividend on any shares having deferred or non-preferred rights.

104. Except as otherwise provided by the rights attached to shares, all dividends shall be declared and paid according to the amounts paid up on the shares on which the dividend is paid. All dividends shall be apportioned and paid proportionately to the amounts paid up on the shares during any portion or portions of the period in respect of which the dividend is paid; but, if any share is issued on terms providing that it shall rank for dividend from a particular date, that share shall rank for dividend accordingly.

105. A general meeting declaring a dividend may, upon the recommendation of the directors, direct that it shall be satisfied wholly or partly by the distribution of assets and, where any difficulty arises in regard to the distribution, the directors may settle the same and in particular may issue fractional certificates and fix the value for distribution of any assets and may determine that cash shall be paid to any member upon the footing of the value so fixed in order to adjust the rights of members and may vest assets in trustees.

106. Any dividend or other moneys payable in respect of a share may be paid by cheque sent by post to the registered address of the person entitled or, if two or more persons are the holders of the share or are jointly entitled to it by reason of the death or bankruptcy of the holder, to the registered address of that one of those persons who is first named on the register of members or to such person and to such address as the person or persons entitled may in writing direct. Every cheque shall be made payable to the order of the person or persons entitled or to such other person as the person or persons entitled may in writing direct and payment of the cheque shall be a good discharge to the company. Any joint holder or other person jointly entitled to a share as aforesaid may give receipts for any dividend or other moneys payable in respect of the share.

107. No dividend or other moneys payable in respect of a share shall bear interest against the company unless otherwise provided by the rights attached to the share.

108. Any dividend which has remained unclaimed for twelve years from the date when it became due for payment shall, if the directors so resolve, be forfeited and cease to remain owing by the company.

ACCOUNTS

109. No member shall (as such) have any right of inspecting any accounting records or other book or document of the company except as conferred by statute or authorised by the directors or by ordinary resolution of the company.

CAPITALISATION OF PROFITS

110. The directors may with the authority of an ordinary resolution of the company:

(a) subject as hereinafter provided, resolve to capitalise any undivided profits of the company not required for paying any preferential dividend (whether or not they are available for distribution) or any sum standing to the credit of the company's share premium account or capital redemption reserve;

(b) appropriate the sum resolved to be capitalised to the members who would have been entitled to it if it were distributed by way of dividend and in the same proportion and apply such sum on their behalf either in or towards paying up the amounts, if any, for the time being unpaid on any shares held by them respectively, or in paying up in full unissued shares or debentures of the company of a nominal amount equal to that sum, and allot the shares or debentures credited as fully paid to those members, or as they may direct, in those proportions, or partly in one way and partly in the other: but the share premium account, the capital redemption reserve, and any profits which are not available for distribution may, for the purposes of this regulation, only be applied in paying up unissued shares to be allotted members credited as fully paid;

(c) make such provision by the issue of fractional certificates or by payment in cash or otherwise as they determine in the case of shares or debentures becoming distributable under this regulation in fractions; and

(d) authorise any person to enter on behalf of all members concerned into an agreement with the company providing for the allotment to them respectively, credited as fully paid, of any shares or debentures to which they are entitled upon such capitalisation, any agreement made under such authority being binding on all such members.

NOTICES

111. Any notice to be given to or by any person pursuant to the articles (other than a notice calling a meeting of the directors) shall be in writing or shall be given using electronic communications to an address for the time being notified for that purpose to the person giving the notice.

In this regulation, 'address', in relation to electronic communications, includes any number or address used for the purposes of such communications.

112. The company may give any notice to a member either personally or by sending it by post in a prepaid envelope addressed to the member at his registered address or by leaving it at that address or by giving it using electronic communications to an address for the time being notified to the company by the member. In the case of joint holders of a share, all notices shall be given to the joint holder whose name stands first in the register of members in respect of the joint holding and notice so given shall be sufficient notice to all the joint holders. A member whose registered address is not within the United Kingdom and who gives to the company an address within the United Kingdom at which notices may be given to him, or an address to which notices may be sent by electronic communications, shall be entitled to have notices given to him at that address, but otherwise no such member shall be entitled to receive any notice from the company. In this regulation and the next, Aaddress@, in relation to electronic communications, includes any number or address used for the purposes of such communications.

113. A member present, either in person or by proxy, at any meeting of the company or of holders of any class of shares in the company shall be deemed to have received notice of the meeting and, where requisite, of the purposes for which it was called.

114. Every person who becomes entitled to a share shall be bound by any notice in respect of that share which, before his name is entered in the register of members, has been duly given to a person from whom he derives his title.

115. Proof that an envelope containing a notice was properly addressed, prepaid and posted shall be conclusive evidence that the notice was given. Proof that notice contained in an electronic communication was sent in accordance with guidance issued by the Institute of Chartered Secretaries and Administrators shall be conclusive evidence that the notice was given. A notice shall be deemed to be given at the expiration of 48 hours after the envelope containing it was posted or, in the case of a notice contained in an electronic communication, at the expiration of 48 hours after the time it was sent.

116. A notice may be given by the company to the persons entitled to a share in consequence of death or bankruptcy of a member by sending or delivering it, in any manner authorised by the articles for the giving of notice to a member, addressed to them by name, or by the title of representatives of the deceased, or trustee of the bankrupt or by any description at the address, if any, within the United Kingdom supplied for that purpose by the persons claiming to be so entitled. Until such an address has been supplied, a notice may be given in any manner in which it might have been given if the death or bankruptcy had not occurred.

WINDING UP

117. If the company is wound up, the liquidator may, with the sanction of an extraordinary resolution of the company and any other sanction required by the Act, divide among the members in specie the whole or any part of the assets of the company and may, for that purpose, value any assets and determine how the division shall be carried out as between members or different classes of members. The liquidator may, with the like sanction, vest the whole or any part of the assets in trustees upon such trusts for the benefit of the members as he with the like sanction determines, but no member shall be compelled to accept any assets upon which there is a liability.

INDEMNITY

118. Subject to the provisions of the Act, but without prejudice to any indemnity to which a director may otherwise be entitled, every director or other officer or auditor of the company shall be indemnified out of the assets of the company against any liability incurred by him in defending any proceedings, whether civil or criminal, in which judgment is given in his favour or in which he is acquitted or in connection with any application in which relief is granted to him by the court from liability for negligence, default, breach of duty or breach of trust in relation to the affairs of the company.

APPENDIX 2

Sample Memorandum

COMPANIES ACT 1985
as amended by
COMPANIES ACT 1989

PRIVATE COMPANY LIMITED BY SHARES

MEMORANDUM OF ASSOCIATION
of
**** LIMITED**

---

1 The name of the company is ** Limited.

2 The registered office of the company will be in England.

3 The object of the company is to carry on business as a general commercial company.

4 The liability of the members is limited.

5 The share capital of the company is £ ** divided into ** shares of ** each.

We, the subscribers to this memorandum of association, wish to be formed into a company pursuant to this memorandum and we agree to take the number of shares shown against our respective names.

Names and addresses of subscribers	Number of shares to be taken
1.. 2..	
Total shares taken	

Witness(es) to both (all) the above signatures:
Name:
Address:
Occupation:

Glossary

administration order An order directing that, during the period for which the order is in force, the affairs, business and property of the company shall be managed by an administrator appointed by the court.

administrative receiver A receiver and manager appointed by the holders of a floating charge, which appointment results in his taking control of the whole or substantially the whole of the undertaking of the company.

administrator A person who administers the estate of a deceased person in the absence of an executor. Alternatively, it can mean a person appointed by the court to try to achieve some sort of rescue strategy for a company that is in difficulties.

allotment The issue of shares by a company.

allottee A person to whom shares have been allotted by a company; a shareholder.

alternate director A person appointed by a director to represent him as a director, particularly at board meetings that the appointor is unable to attend.

Articles (of Association) The internal regulations of a company sent to the Registrar on incorporation.

asset value The underlying value of a share expressed in terms of the assets that it represents. It is calculated by taking the net value of all the assets of the company and dividing this figure by the number of shares that the company has issued.

authorised or nominal capital The face value of the shares of a company which the company is permitted to issue by its Memorandum of Association.

bankruptcy The formal state in personal insolvency where a person's assets move by operation of law to his trustee in bankruptcy for the benefit of his creditors.

book debts Cash sums owing to a company, for example after the supply of goods or services to a customer.

capital The money or money's worth through which a company finances its business.

capital redemption reserve A reserve fund into which profits are allocated for the purpose of redeeming or buying back shares in the company.

certificated instrument of transfer An instrument of transfer of shares that that been marked by a company's secretary to indicate that the share certificate to which it relates has been deposited with the company.

certificate of incorporation The document that brings a company into existence. The 'birth certificate' of a company.

charge In corporate law the word 'charge' is usually used to mean a mortgage, i.e. a secured loan.

charterparty A contract for the hire of a ship.

chose in action A right to sue for the recovery of a debt.

class right A right attaching to a class of share, usually in regard to a right to receive a dividend, the right to receive a return of capital on a winding up or the right to vote in general meeting.

common seal The seal of a company; a device used for making an impressed mark upon a document so as to authenticate it.

company voluntary arrangement An arrangement between a company and its members under the Insolvency Act 1986.

composition A sum of money agreed to be accepted by creditors in satisfaction of debts owed to them by a company.

compulsory winding up The winding up of a company by order of the court.

consideration The price for the promise; the value moving from one party to a contract to the other party.

constructive notice Deemed knowledge. A person dealing with a company traditionally is assumed to know of matters registered at Companies House. Thus, for example, a person taking security from a company is taken to be aware of any charges registered in the name of the company.

contributory The holder of a partly paid share who is required to pay up the unpaid element on his shares on a winding up.

creditors' voluntary winding up The insolvent winding up of a company following a resolution of its members.

Crown Court The criminal court that deals with the most serious cases.

crystallisation The process whereby a floating charge becomes fixed.

de facto In reality.

debenture The written evidence of a debt owing by a company; the document which creates or evidences a debt. Usually, though by no means always, a debenture is secured. This gives the creditor holding the debenture a priority over the unsecured creditors

debt–equity swap A corporate arrangement under which the creditors of a company exchange the debts that they are owed for shares in the company.

declaration of solvency The declaration made by the directors of a company prior to the commencement of a members' voluntary winding up.

de facto director A person who acts as a director in spite of the fact that he has never been appointed as such.

de jure director A person who acts as a director and who has not only been properly appointed but who has satisfied the legal formalities that have to be observed by directors.

DTI Department of Trade and Industry – the department of the British government responsible for the supervision of commerce and industry in the UK.

director Any person occupying the position of a director by whatever name he is called.

distress The process whereby a landlord goes onto the premises of his tenant to seize goods that he can sell to reimburse himself for outstanding rent.

distributable profits Profits within the company that may be used for the payment of a dividend.

dividend That part of the profits made by a company that is paid to the members.

domicile The place where a man or a company has his or its fixed or permanent home.

dormant company A company which, though registered, is not trading.

earnings per share The proportion of the income of a company that can attributed to a single share.

fiduciary duty The duty owed by a director to his company that requires him to act in good faith and not to allow any conflict to arise between his interest in himself and his duty to his company.

fixed charge Security created over a fixed asset such as a warehouse or an office block.

floating charge A charge secured on a class of assets, present and future. The class is likely to change in the ordinary course of business from time to time. It is anticipated that the company will be free to deal with those assets subject to the charge until such time as the company ceases to carry on business in the usual way.

flotation The offer of shares or debentures to the public.

fraudulent trading Carrying on business in the course of winding up with intent to defraud creditors.

friendly society A type of insurance company; amongst other things, a friendly society will often lend money to borrowers on the security of a mortgage.

Gazette An official publication of the Department of Trade and Industry which comes out every business day and in which formal announcements concerning companies are made, such as when a winding-up order is made or when a winding-up resolution is passed.

general meeting A meeting of the members of a company.

holding company A company having subsidiary companies.

indictable A serious criminal offence capable of trial before the Crown Court (as opposed to the less serious offences which are tried before magistrates).

injunction An order of the court preventing the doing of a specified thing.

insolvency jurisdiction The court having the power to make a winding-up order in respect of a company.

instrument of transfer Stock transfer form.

interim dividend A dividend paid by the directors of a company of their own initiative between annual general meetings.

invoice discounting The process whereby following the supply of goods or services to a customer a company sends a copy of the relevant invoice to a banking institution which then immediately pays a substantial proportion of the amount invoiced to the company.

judgment creditor A creditor who has sued the company owing him money and obtained judgment from the court in his favour.

limited company A company the liability of whose members is limited and formed either by Act of Parliament or by registration under the Companies Act.

limited liability partnership A body corporate the liability of whose members is limited and formed by registration under the Limited Partnerships Act 2000.

limited partnership A partnership having limited partners i.e. sleeping partners whose liability in the event of the partnership's insolvency is limited to the amount that such partner has agreed to contribute.

liquidation The winding up of a company; the process whereby the existence of a company is brought to an end.

liquidator The person who undertakes the liquidation of a company.

listed company A company the shares of which are listed on a recognised stock exchange.

maintenance of capital The principle whereby it is ensured that the capital of a company should at all times be a fund available for the payment of its creditors.

member A shareholder in a company limited by shares or a guarantor in a company limited by guarantee.

members' voluntary winding up The solvent winding up of a company pursuant to a resolution passed by its members.

Memorandum (of Association) The key constitutional document of a company setting out, amongst other things, its name, objects and capital.

misfeasance Misconduct or breach of duty. The remedy brought by a liquidator against directors and other officers of a company whom he thinks may have been in breach of their duty towards the company.

mortgage Security for a creditor traditionally created by the transfer of property to a lender on terms that upon repayment of the debt he will transfer the asset back to the borrower.

mortgage debenture A secured loan evidenced in writing and giving the lender a priority over other creditors of a company.

naked (unsecured) debenture A debenture that is not supported by any security.

Official Receiver An officer of the Department of Trade and Industry who is attached to every court that enjoys an insolvency jurisdiction.

Off market purchase The purchase back by a company of its shares when such shares are not dealt with on a market.

ordinary resolution A resolution passed by a simple majority of the members in a general meeting.

ordinary share A share entitling its owner to receive a dividend (if one is paid by the company) only after the payment of a set dividend to the holders of preference shares.

ostensible authority Apparent or seeming authority. The authority that one can assume a person purporting to act as an agent has.

paid-up capital That amount of a company's issued share capital that has been paid by its members.

partnership The relation which subsists between persons carrying on a business in common with a view of profit.

passing off A tort whereby a business wrongly adopts a name similar to that of a similar business in such a way as to cash in on its reputation and so expropriate its goodwill.

personal representative An executor or administrator who administers a deceased person's estate.

pre-emption or preferential right The right of an existing shareholder to acquire further shares in the company, the number of shares usually being in proportion to the number of shares at the time held by the shareholder.

preference share A share giving its holder preferential rights in respect of dividends and sometimes in respect of a return of capital on a winding up.

preferential creditors Creditors entitled to receive payment on a liquidation in advance of the floating charge holders and unsecured creditors: amongst the preferential creditors are £800 arrears of pay for employees, the last 12 months PAYE and NI due from the company and also the last six months' VAT.

premium The amount paid for a share by an allottee over and above the nominal value of that share.

prima facie On the face of it; at first sight.

private company Any company that is not a public company.

pro rata Rateably. In proportion.

promoter A person who undertakes to form a company and who takes the necessary steps to achieve that end.

public limited company A company the name of which ends with the letters plc (or the names represented by those letters in full), the Memorandum of which states that it is a public company, the share capital of which has a nominal value of at least £50,000 and which is registered as a public company.

real property Land.

realised profits test A test to calculate the sums available to a company for the payment of a dividend.

receiver A person appointed either to receive income or to preserve property.

receiver and manager A person appointed to realise the assets of a company on which a floating charge has crystallised but where he does not take control of the whole or substantially the whole of the undertaking of the company.

recognised investment exchange A place where shares in quoted companies may be dealt.

reconstruction A procedure entered into under s.110 of the Insolvency Act 1986.

redeemable shares Shares which may be redeemed or acquired back from their holders by a company.

registered office The address of the office of a company to which formal notices and legal documents should be addressed and sent.

register of charges The statutory register that has to be maintained by every company to contain details of all charges over the company or its property.

Registrar of Companies The person at Companies House to whom documents are sent to form a company and to whom the necessary returns are made during the lifetime of a company.

registration The process whereby a company comes into existence. Documents are sent to the Registrar of Companies and in return he sends out a certificate of incorporation.

register of members The record that a company must keep of its members.

reserve capital Unpaid capital of a company that can only be called up by a liquidator.

retention of title clause A clause sometimes inserted into a contract for the sale of goods providing that the ownership in the goods is not to pass to the buyer until such time as the goods have been paid for.

retirement by rotation The process whereby one third of the directors of a company retire and present themselves for re-election.

scheme of arrangement A compromise arrived at between a company and its creditors or between a company and its members pursuant to s.425 of the Companies Act 1985.

section 14 contract The statutory contract that states that the Memorandum and Articles, once registered, constitute a contract between the company and its members and between the members themselves.

section 117 trading certificate The certificate that has to be obtained by a public company before it can lawfully trade or borrow.

section 212 notice A notice served by a public company on the registered holder of shares to enquire whether any other person has a beneficial interest in those shares.

section 429 notice A notice that may be served either by a minority shareholder or a person taking over a company under s. 429 of the Companies Act 1985.

secured creditor A creditor who holds a secured debenture.

secured debenture A debenture in which the lender enjoys security over some asset or assets of the company whether by way of a fixed or floating charge.

shadow director Any person in accordance with whose directions or instructions the directors are accustomed to act.

share certificate The documentary evidence issued by a company and held by a shareholder to indicate the ownership of shares.

share premium *See* premium.

share premium account An account into which all payments made for shares over and above their nominal value are credited.

share warrant to bearer The documentation issued to indicate the ownership of shares in a company where such shares are transferable merely by delivery, i.e. without the need for an instrument of transfer.

sole trader An individual who is in business on his own account i.e. he is not in partnership on his nor does he trade through a corporate body.

special resolution A resolution passed by a three-quarters vote of those members present and voting or voting by proxy.

stock transfer form Instrument of transfer; the form completed by the transferor of shares to transfer title to the shares to the transferee.

stock watering The issue of shares by a company in return for the transfer to the company of assets worth significantly less than the value placed upon them in the contract.

subscription clause The clause at the end of the Memorandum which is signed by the subscribers and will result in their becoming the first members of the company.

subsidiary company A company which is controlled by another company, known as its parent or subsidiary company, which usually holds the majority of its voting shares.

takeover The process whereby one company acquires another company.

tort A civil wrong such as negligence, defamation, trespass or passing off.

transfer The process whereby a share passes from one person to another either on sale or by way of a gift.

transmission The process whereby a share passes from one person to another by operation of law; following death shares pass to the deceased's personal representative; following bankruptcy shares pass to the trustee in bankruptcy.

trust deed A deed issued where there is a public flotation of debenture stock and which appoints trustees in whom the underlying security can be vested and who represent the interests of the individual debenture holders.

ultra vires Literally 'beyond its powers'. The expression is usually used to refer to a transaction entered into by a company that is beyond its powers. Sometimes it is also used to refer to a transaction beyond the powers of the directors.

uncalled capital The amount of a company's issued share capital that remains to be paid by its members.

underwriter A person who agrees to take up a flotation if they are not applied for by the public.

unsecured (naked) debenture A debenture that is not supported by any security.

voluntary winding up The winding up of a company commenced by a resolution of its members.

winding up The liquidation of a company

winding up order A court order to commence the liquidation of a company.

wrongful trading A liability recommended by the Cork Committee to cover situations where during winding up the director had been careless rather that fraudulent in incurring debts.

Directory

Further reading

Books

Davies, P.L. and Prentice, D. (1997) *Gower's Principles of Modern Company Law*, Sweet & Maxwell: London

Farrar, J.F. (1998) *Farrar's Company Law*, Butterworths Law: London

Mayson, S., French, D. and Ryan, C. (2002) *Mason, French & Ryan on Company Law*, Oxford University Press: Oxford

Morse, G., Marshall, E., Morris, R. and Crabb, L. (eds.) (1999) *Charlesworth and Morse: Company Law*, Sweet & Maxwell: London

Pennington R.R. (2001) *Pennington's Company Law*, Butterworths Law: London

Source books

Sourcebooks are an essential tool for the company lawyer. A collected edition of the company and insolvency legislation is essential.

CCH collection of *British Companies Legislation*, Sweet & Maxwell: London

Hahlo, H.R. (1970) *Casebook on Company Law*, Sweet & Maxwell: London

Rajak, H. (1995) *A Sourcebook of Company Law*, Jordans: Bristol

Walmsley, K. (2001) *Butterworth's Company Law Handbook*, Butterworths Law: London

Loose-leaf manuals

Birds, J. and Leighton, H.G.M. (1984) *Secretarial Administration*, Jordans: Bristol

Loose P., Impey, D. and Griffiths, M. (2000) *The Company Director*, Jordans: Bristol

Walmsley, K. and Hamer, A. (2002) *Company Secretarial Practice*, ICSA Publishing: London

Croner CCH Company Law series are also useful for reference

Professional bodies and useful organisations

The Registrar of Companies (England and Wales)
Companies House
Crown Way
Cardiff CF14 3UZ
Tel: 0870 3333636
www.companieshouse.gov.uk

Department of Trade and Industry
1 Victoria Street
London SW1H 0ET
Tel: 020 7215 5000
www.dti.gov.uk

DTI Publications order line: 0870 1502 500

Financial Services Authority
25 The North Colonnade
Canary Wharf
London E14 5HS
Tel: 020 7676 1000
www.fsa.gov.uk

Her Majesty's Stationery Office
www.hmso.gov.uk

Law Society
The Law Society's Hall
113 Chancery Lane
London WC2A 1PL
Tel: 020 7242 1222
www.lawsoc.org.uk

London Stock Exchange
Old Broad Street
London EC2N 1HP
Tel: 020 7797 1600
www.londonstockexchange.com

Panel on Takeovers and Mergers
PO Box 226
The Stock Exchange Building
London EC2P 2JX
Tel: 020 7382 9026
www.thetakeoverpanel.org.uk

Index